Joining Complexity Science and Social Simulation for Innovation Policy

Joining Complexity Science and Social Simulation for Innovation Policy:

Agent-based Modelling using the SKIN Platform

Edited by

Petra Ahrweiler, Nigel Gilbert and Andreas Pyka

Cambridge Scholars Publishing

Joining Complexity Science and Social Simulation for Innovation Policy: Agent-based Modelling using the SKIN Platform

Edited by Petra Ahrweiler, Nigel Gilbert and Andreas Pyka

This book first published 2016

Cambridge Scholars Publishing

Lady Stephenson Library, Newcastle upon Tyne, NE6 2PA, UK

British Library Cataloguing in Publication Data
A catalogue record for this book is available from the British Library

ISBN (10): 1-4438-8460-X
ISBN (13): 978-1-4438-8460-0

TABLE OF CONTENTS

ACKNOWLEDGEMENTS

This book follows the international conference "SKIN 3 – Joining Complexity Science and Social Simulation for Policy" (May 22nd -23rd, 2014) at Eötvös Loránd University, Budapest, where some of the authors of this volume met to discuss the state of the art in this research area. The Conference was jointly sponsored by EA European Academy of Technology and Innovation Assessment in Germany, by the seventh Framework Programme EU project EGovPoliNet (The Policy Community), EU COST Action KnowEscape, and the Coordination and Support Action NESS. The editors gratefully acknowledge this financial support for the Conference without which this book would not have been possible. Furthermore, the Irish case study presented in the second part of the book stems from the PRTLI-funded project IPSE; this funding enabled a whole collection of chapters of this book. We would like to thank all authors of this book for their great contributions; IPSE administrator Kathryn Byrne-Schilperoord supported by IPSE research assistant Lvcheng Li for their part in developing the manuscript; and finally EA administrator Sarah Goetten for her meticulous proof-reading.

INTRODUCTION

PETRA AHRWEILER, NIGEL GILBERT
AND ANDREAS PYKA

In innovation policy, investments in measures such as fostering higher education institutions or science-industry networks are expected to produce high commercial returns although they very often fail to materialise promptly. These situations show the limits of conventional steering, control and policy functions associated with innovation support.

Socio-economic systems are complex systems, and have been studied in sociology and complexity science (cf. Castellani and Hafferty 2009). Complexity features such as uncertainty, non-linearity, emergence, path-dependency, contingency, multi-level and de-centralised organisation etc. particularly apply when it comes to the development of new knowledge, its diffusion, and its commercial application in innovation. Analytical approaches trying to offer guidance and support have to acknowledge that any forecasts and predictions of policy success or failure are difficult if not impossible.

For policy planning in innovation it is a fundamental problem that there is no linear relationship between a policy measure and its desired effect. This means high implementation risks for any new policies. Real-world implementations can be quite expensive if they turn out to be failures. Not only do they have the usual production and roll-out costs similar to their successful counter-parts; if they prove to be harmful, they might even lead to some unintended, not easy-to-remedy, and very costly side-effects. Finally, the time and effort wasted on the failure might have been better used for a potentially more appropriate policy change.

Social simulation can shed light into the darkness of the future: it can help to cope with the challenges of complexity by modelling the dynamics of the social systems under investigation, and by identifying potential access points for successful intervention. With simulation models, we can ask what-if questions for ex-ante evaluation of real-world policy implementations – an option that is normally not easily available in the policy-making world. Stakeholders such as innovation policy makers can use scenario modelling as a worksite for their 'reality constructions': simulation experiments can be used to give an indication of the likely effect of a wide variety of policy measures. Empirical 'un-observables' in this policy domain, such as knowledge flows in innovation or the learning of agents, can be observed, measured and assessed.

The agent-based **S**imulating **K**nowledge Dynamics in **I**nnovation **N**etworks (SKIN) model has been designed to simulate knowledge generation and diffusion in inter-organisational research and innovation networks. Since its first prototype in 2001 (http://jasss.soc.surrey.ac.uk/4/3/8.html), it has been developed into a platform with many modules and applications and has been adopted for a number of policy modelling studies. The largest policy testing application of the SKIN model to date focuses on impact assessment and ex-ante evaluation of European funding policies in the Information and Communication Technologies (ICT) research domain. The corresponding version of the model, referred to as INFSO-SKIN, was developed for the Directorate General Information Society and Media of the European Commission (DG INFSO) in 2011. It was intended to help to understand and manage the relationship between research funding and the goals of EU innovation policy. Changing parameters within the model is analogous to applying different policy options in the real world. The model could thus be used to examine the likely real-world effects of different policy options before they are implemented. Altering elements of the model that equate with policy interventions—such as the amount of funding, the size of consortia, or encouraging specific sections of the research community—made it possible to use INFSO-SKIN as a tool for modelling and evaluating the results of the policy interactions typically occurring between policy interventions, funding strategies and agents. The SKIN model applications use empirical data and claim to be realistic simulations insofar as the aim is to derive conclusions by so-called inductive theorising. This means that the quality of the SKIN simulations derives from an interaction between the theory underlying the simulation and the empirical data used for calibration and validation.

Joining complexity science and social simulation enables the modelling of innovation policy initiatives to take into account more parameters than previously possible and to perform simulations to forecast potential impacts of proposed innovation policy measures. In contrast to conventional methods of social research, this approach is capable of dealing with the fact that research and innovation do not follow a linear path and are highly complex.

To foster this approach requires outlining the benefits to stakeholders and showcasing example projects and their findings. However, at the same time, it is necessary to explain the limitations of the methodology, which can only offer a "weak prediction" in terms of likely scenarios and trends, as opposed to exact forecasts. For innovation policy projects using the combination of complexity science and social simulation, the interaction with stakeholders is key: this type of policy modelling is an area *par excellence* for participatory co-design. Finally, validation issues are crucially important: systematic checks of simulated policies against empirically implemented policies should be realised for all projects, which would require that stakeholders allow modellers to see how policies are actually formulated, implemented, and executed with or without relation to their model.

The general objective of this book is to explore how complexity science and social simulation can be used to improve and inform policy making in research and innovation. First, the challenges of research and innovation policy are outlined. This is followed by a conceptual overview of European policy agendas in this area and by a chapter on policy practice issues. The methodological discussions of the book begin with two studies applying traditional quantitative methods in innovation research. Both are exemplary of this body of literature in two ways: they are carefully crafted methodological applications with data providing interesting findings, but they are also very clear in stating their limitations concerning missing causality, small parameter sets and feedback learning of simultaneous processes. Like many such studies they end by asking for future research addressing these limitations and highlighting the areas where they have to remain speculative. This is exactly the space where complexity science and computational modelling techniques such as social simulation step in to meet the requirements of research and innovation policy.

The editors' bridging chapter then opens the main part of the book dedicated to the conceptual claims about what and how complexity science and social simulation can contribute to policy making in research and innovation. Policy modelling means to identify areas that need intervention, to specify the desired state of the target system, to find the regulating mechanisms, policy formation and implementation, and to control and evaluate the robustness of interventions. The difficulty is that policymaking in complex social systems is not a clear-cut cause and effect process, but is characterised by contingency and uncertainty. To take into account technological, social, economic, political, cultural, ecological and other relevant parameters, policy modelling has to be enhanced and supported by new ICT-oriented research initiatives. The need for policy intelligence dealing with complexity becomes more and more obvious. The two following chapters of the book provide modelling examples concerning the effects and impacts of decision making and policy changes on the structure, composition and outputs of research and innovation networks.

After having introduced some components of the approach this way, a fully-fledged example of a case study working with it is presented: a research initiative funded by the Irish Government on innovation policy simulation for economic recovery. The project consists of empirical research on Irish research and innovation networks, and simulations of technology transfer issues and the commercialisation of research in high-potential areas for innovation and economic growth.

The book finishes with two chapters featuring areas for future research on complexity and related modelling activities. The concluding essay reflects on the maturity and utility of the approach combining complexity science and social simulation for research and innovation policy.

The chapters of the book are now introduced in more detail:

Benjamin Schrempf outlines the challenges of research and innovation policy in his chapter, "European and National Innovation Agendas", with a conceptual overview of European policy agendas in this area. Research and innovation are regarded as essential factors for economic prosperity. The policy agendas fostering them, often referred to as 'Strategy for (Science,) Technology and Innovation' S(S)TI, contain measures to stimulate the generation of new ideas and knowledge, the transfer of knowledge between actors, the commercialisation of knowledge in marketable products and the protection of knowledge. The chapter provides information on five European countries based on the economic and political situations, the outlook and the main challenges for each country; the country sample includes Ireland as an introduction to the case study section of the book.

A policy practitioner perspective in addressing the challenges of research and innovation policy is presented by **Frigyes Hausz, Virág Zsár, and Bela Kardon** in Chapter 2, "Smart specialisation and universities – challenges and opportunities in the 2014-2020 programming period". From a governmental perspective, the authors discuss the Smart Specialisation Strategies (S3) of the European Commission, which require that higher education development policy and science policy are fine-tuned to the larger context of regional development. They use a case study of Hungary (lessons learnt in science policy during the 2014-2020 Programming Period) to formulate a set of recommendations concerning higher education R&D development, discussing issues such as technology transfer between universities and the entrepreneurial sphere, obstacles to successful technology transfer, and general misperceptions about funding higher education research.

The first of the two chapters of the methodological discussion about applying traditional quantitative methods in innovation research concerns "The Interplay between environmental and quality/lean practices in supply chains". **George Onofrei, Eamonn Ambrose, Frank Wiengarten and Brian Fynes** examine potential synergetic effects between investments in environmental and quality/lean practices within the supply chain using ordinary least square regression (OLS) analysis. The study does not confirm a linear relationship between investing in environmental practices and improved firm performance, but shows that environmental practices are important and are crucial support mechanisms for more traditional and existing practices, such as lean and quality practices, which again have an effect on firm performance. To investigate these non-linearities would require a complex systems perspective. Furthermore, from the data it is difficult to evaluate genuine causality, which "leaves room for speculation as to whether some portion of the interaction effect is based on some sort of learning effects due to implementing various programs simultaneously" (see the chapter). The concluding section can be read as a clear call for complexity science perspectives and methods.

The second example applying conventional methods to innovation research is Chapter 4 of **Peter McNamara, Cathal Ryan, Darran Jones, and Camilla Noonan** called "Appropriation Regimes and Firm Performance in Incumbent Services Firms". The authors study the mechanisms that are most effective in protecting profit streams using a survey design, which obtained responses from 188 CEOs or senior management of Irish service firms with more than 50 employees. They reject a linear relationship, showing that focusing on legal or non-legal regimes does not result in above average firm performance. Instead, mixed appropriation regimes containing legal and non-legal mechanisms were found to be the most effective at protecting process innovations. However, the exact composition of this mixture is unknown - again due to missing causality, small parameter sets and feedback learning of simultaneous processes. The authors discuss options for future research addressing these limitations, suggesting complexity science perspectives and computational modelling techniques such as social simulation.

In chapter 5, "Innovation policy modelling with SKIN", the editors of this book, **Petra Ahrweiler, Andreas Pyka and Nigel Gilbert**, bridge to the conceptual claims about what and how complexity science and social simulation can contribute to policy making in research and innovation. Their chapter introduces the SKIN platform as an agent-based model to simulate the effects and impacts of policy making on the structure, composition and outputs of research and innovation networks. The claims are supported with descriptions of four policy-relevant contributions of the SKIN platform: (i) scenario modelling of higher education policies for business innovation networks, (ii) scenario modelling of Irish MNC[1]-directed innovation policy for Ireland's indigenous industry networks, (iii) simulating the effects of different innovation management strategies of firms in the biotechnology-based pharmaceutical industry, and (iv) scenario modelling of European funding schemes and the effect of the size and geographical diversity of project teams. Using real-world datasets and in response to questions put forward by stakeholders, SKIN can provide precise, detailed information on the effects of specific policy instruments, on how and how well research and innovation networks operate, and how to understand and manage the relationship between research funding and policy goals. Importantly, the model allows experimenters to change policy parameters in the simulations. This allows use of the system as a tool for modelling and evaluating the results of specific interactions between policies, funding strategies and agents. Using the simulation, policy makers can observe and manipulate patterns of network evolution by varying simulation parameters. Because changing parameters within the model is analogous to applying different policy options in the real

[1] MNC: Multi-National Corporation

world, the model can be used to examine the likely real-world effects of different policy options before they are implemented. The chapter ends with assessing the experience with the model and its applications so far in terms of difficulties, limitations, risks and contingencies; and with comments on managing the expectations of stakeholders, general apprehensions around the predictability of future developments, data availability issues and validation questions.

The first one of the two chapters which describe modelling the effects and impacts of decision making and policy changes on the structure, composition and outputs of research and innovation networks is the one by **Harold Paredes-Frigolett, Luiz Flávio Autran Monteiro Gomes and Javier Pereira Retamales**. Their contribution, "Extending Agent-Based Modeling via Multicriteria Decision Analysis", refers back to the conventional approaches in innovation research presented in Chapters 3 and 4, and suggests potential intersections and interfaces between agent-based models with behavioural dynamics and variable-based approaches.

Diving fully into the issues of complexity, agent-based modelling, and innovation concerning the effects and impacts of policy changes is the next chapter contributed by **Cristina Ponsiglione, Ivana Quinto, and Giuseppe Zollo**, "An agent-based simulation model of Self-Sustaining Regional Innovation Systems". They conceptualise regional innovation systems as complex learning systems, and suggest an agent-based model as a simulation tool for policy advice aimed at analysing the conditions under which regional systems develop self-sustaining innovation cycles. Some simulation experiments verify the model's internal coherence and explore the behaviour of the system (in terms of learning, innovation capability, and resilience of the system) under different parameter settings. The problems of model validation are discussed: an empirical study of the Aerospace Industry of the Campania Region in Italy is currently under way to collect data for calibrating model parameters and validating simulation results. Chapter 7 illustrates that SKIN is not the only model applicable in the area of complexity science, social simulation and innovation, but that this area is a growing research field with many possible avenues for computational modelling applications.

Nevertheless, the SKIN model is the central tool for the modelling tasks in the case study the next chapters are dedicated to the research programme "**I**nnovation **P**olicy **S**imulation for the Smart **E**conomy", the IPSE project. Funded by the Irish Government, the strategic objective of IPSE is to provide insights into the need of the Irish economy to breed an innovation ecosystem with optimally structured university-industry-government networks. IPSE uses computational modelling, informed by large new datasets coming from empirical research, to investigate the actors, designs, processes, and policies of Irish innovation networks. The project is set up to develop and test policy strategies and options for anticipating and analysing new developments to help the recovery of the economy. Simulations focus on technology transfer issues and on commercialisation of research options in areas areas with high potential for innovation and economic growth.

The IPSE section begins with two chapters analysing Irish research and innovation policy. In "Exploring a neo-institutional approach to policy research - the politics of the emergence of a field of Science, Technology & Innovation in Ireland", **Camilla Noonan, Séamas Kelly, and Simeon Vidolov** explore the role of the OECD in shaping and directing Irish science, technology and innovation (STI) policies. Drawing on a sociological perspective on institutionalism, they argue that there have been at least two broad dimensions to the OECD's influence on Irish policy - governance by co-ordination and governance by opinion formation.

This sets the scene for chapter 9 by **Ciara Fitzgerald and Frederic Adam** on "Ireland's Technology Transfer Policy". Within the Irish context, the Strategy for Science Technology and Innovation (SSTI), 2006 – 2013, represents the government's plan for Irelands' universities to commercialise research in a competitive and dynamic knowledge-driven economy. The overarching vision of the SSTI is to ensure that 'Ireland by 2013 will be internationally renowned for the excellence of its research and will be to the forefront in generating and using new knowledge for economic and social progress within an innovation driven culture'. As a result of this strategy, research commercialisation and technology transfer are emerging as new missions for Irish Higher Education Institutes and Technology Transfer Offices. By reviewing the existing policy debates, the authors prepare the way for a better understanding of current policy decisions.

Next follows a chapter providing an example of the empirical work done in IPSE to calibrate the simulations. **Nola Hewitt-Dundas, Colm Burns and Gary Chapman** analyse in chapter 10 "Additionality of Incubator Support on Networks of University Spin-Out Firms", the network configuration of university spin-out firms, in two comparative contexts: a research intensive university *with* a university incubator on campus and a research intensive university *without* an incubator (either on-campus or off-campus), one located in Ireland, the other in Northern Ireland. This research addresses concerns about the high failure rates and no-to-low growth among university spin-outs. Universities have responded to this by investing in incubators. Yet how effective are incubators in supporting these firms? This is examined by the chapter in terms of the structural networks that spin-out firms form, the role of the incubator in this and the effect of this on the spin-out process. The aim of the investigation is two-fold: (i) to determine whether there is a structural difference in the network additionality of an incubator facility on spin-out firms and (ii) to explore the effect of an incubator on the early stages of firm development, particularly in terms of opportunity identification and entrepreneurial commitment.

Michel Schilperoord provides insights into the various modelling tasks within the IPSE project with his chapter “Start-ups when and where? Using the SKIN platform for modelling the birth of new companies”. The project focus - on technology transfer, commercialisation of research, and entrepreneurial activities - defined new requirements for developing some features of the SKIN platform, especially the process of how new firms come into being. Chapter 11 introduces a method of using SKIN for reasoning about the 'when' and 'where' of new start-up companies. The immediate objective is to model entrepreneurship by describing how entrepreneurs discover and evaluate new start-up opportunities, and how they create start-ups at fertile locations after testing the viability of the start-up opportunity in partnership with stakeholders in a competitive market that features thresholds for survival and growth. The method builds on new SKIN procedures for simulating start-up processes in two stages. In the first stage, entrepreneurs make a continuous valuation of their innovation hypothesis (IH) based on distance between their IH and the IH of their closest competitor in the market. This valuation mechanism implies that entrepreneurs with new and unique business ideas will value their IHs the highest, and will be the most likely to decide to 'go for it'. In the second stage, the entrepreneur creates a prototype of a new start-up company and the viability of the start-up opportunity is tested on the market. Only start-up prototypes that are able to survive this 'proto' stage will enter the market as real start-ups that can participate fully in the market. The SKIN market module provides the necessary mechanisms for obtaining market feedback on start-up prototypes. Initial results indicate that the method allows early identification of 'high potential' start-ups, since the entrepreneurs with the highest valued IHs (first stage) also tend to create the fittest prototype start-ups (second stage).

The final two chapters of the book return to some theoretical reflections, outlining areas for future research in complexity research and related modelling activities. In chapter 12, **Elena Pugacheva** contemplates “Collective Behaviour as a New Social Agent” and discusses how complexity theory might help in future to explain current phenomena of collective behaviour in the Ukraine and the Arab world using concepts such as synergy, emergence, self-organisation, and co-evolution. The last chapter, by **Özge Dilaver**, discusses epistemological and methodological issues in “Agenvironments? Towards simulating socially constructed complexity”. The chapter discusses what agent-based modelling might offer researchers for building better representations of socially constructed complexity. While agents and environment are often considered as separate design components, there are also discussions on interactions between agents through the environment, the role of the environment in enabling the pro-activity or purposefulness of agents, and the difference between how individual agents and the external observers perceive the environment. The chapter focuses on the social construction of environments, arguing that moving beyond strict distinctions between agents and the environment (agenvironments) may facilitate representing social construction in agent-based models.

The concluding essay by **Ben Vermeulen**, called “The merits of ABMs for policy evaluation”, reflects on the maturity and utility of the approach of combining complexity science and social simulation for research and innovation policy. Apart from the appeal of ABMs as the metaphors for actual real-world systems and inductive learning about possible mechanisms driving real-world phenomena when operationally designing them, there is a plethora of merits for policy evaluation that go beyond garnering a fundamental understanding. The essay starts with a juxtaposition of ABMs and other policy support tools and provides answers to some of the questions asked by stakeholders who are more familiar with those other tools (e.g. why use rule- rather than variable-based models, why use behavioural rather than econometric modelling and why are conventional equation-based models insufficient?). The remainder of the essay provides a detailed overview of three classes of benefit provided by agent-based modelling. First, ABMs can be calibrated to the empirical data of particular cases and can rescale themselves endogenously based on simulated events. Monte Carlo methods can be used to cope with unknown distributions and missing or sparse data. The downside is that modellers have to provide operationalisations and parameter settings for components that have no or an as yet unclear real-world counterpart, sometimes leading to lengthy simulation and modelling iterations. Second, all processes, events, decisions and flows in the artificial world can be fully controlled, recorded and experimentally studied, even those that are ordinarily unobservable or uncontrollable. This permits the study in detail of the connection of micro-level flows and decisions, non-linear interactions of agents at the meso-level with macro-level indicators and phenomena, and the feedback from macro- into micro-level behaviour. Third, many government policies (and agent strategies) are *ad hoc*, based, at best, on small pilots and without clear scientific support. There may be inconclusive or even invalidating evidence that particular policies should have been applied (e.g. it is by now recognised that the popular 'best practice' approach often neglects particularities). ABMs allow *ex ante* evaluation of policy interventions in a controlled environment, the tracing of structural interactions, and inductive-deductive discovery of non-linear effects. The author illustrates these benefits with examples taken from (SKIN-related) ABM work.

References

Castellani, B. and F. Hafferty (2009): Sociology and Complexity Science. A New Field of Inquiry. Berlin/Heidelberg: Springer.

PART I:

CHALLENGES OF RESEARCH AND INNOVATION POLICY

CHAPTER ONE

EUROPEAN AND NATIONAL INNOVATION AGENDAS

BENJAMIN SCHREMPF

Introduction

Technology policy is seen by all advanced economies as a means to accelerate and regulate the advancement of various technologies through innovation. Behind each technology policy there is a strategy, often referred to as 'Strategy for (Science,) Technology, and Innovation' (S(S)TI). This term also includes science and innovation as opposed to the more traditional term technology policy or strategy. Over the years a broader perspective was taken to achieve policies that influence knowledge generation, dissemination, and commercialisation in all areas including organisational change and marketable products.

S(S)TI usually includes measures to stimulate the generation of new ideas and knowledge at universities and in companies, the transfer of knowledge between actors, the commercialisation of knowledge in marketable products, and the protection of knowledge, for example through patents. The measures can be categorised in various ways, for instance into direct measures such as the funding of research through grants, and indirect measures such as tax credits for R&D expenditures.

Since technology and innovation are regarded as essential factors for economic prosperity, these strategies have received increased attention over the last few years in the wake of the financial and economic crisis. Many nations consider STI strategies as the basis for sustainable and long-term growth and necessary to overcome these crises. Furthermore, these strategies are also useful to help avoiding harmful developments in technology.

A sound S(S)TI first requires an in-depth analysis of the system which is to be influenced by the respective policy measures. It is crucial to understand the system, its actors, and their relations, as well as the boundaries of the system prior to introducing technology policy of any kind.

Therefore, all strategies are put into the perspective of the current economic situation, followed by a brief description of the main actors involved. The strategies for each country are then described in more detail, including the main goals and measures. Each of these strategy analyses closes with an outlook for each country and its major challenges. The following contains an overview of the S(S)TIs of the EU and five EU member states. The overview begins with the European Union and its overarching strategy, and then describes the strategies of in total five countries: Germany, the United Kingdom, Spain, Italy; Ireland's S(S)TI is introduced as the fifth country case, helping to put the following chapters about the IPSE (Innovation Policy Simulation for the Smart Economy) into context.

European Union

Economic and political situation

Even though the EU as a whole was hit severely by the financial and economic crisis unfolding in 2008 and 2009, differences within the Union are quite considerable. The Mediterranean countries, the UK, and Ireland suffered the most, which is reflected in their STI strategies. Most northern and central European countries were able to leave the economic turmoil behind relatively quickly. Unemployment ranges from 5% in Germany and Austria to about 25% in both Spain and Greece (Fig. 1.1), which is also reflected in GDP growth (Fig. 1.2).

Fig. 1.1: EU unemployment rates 2014. Source: Eurostat

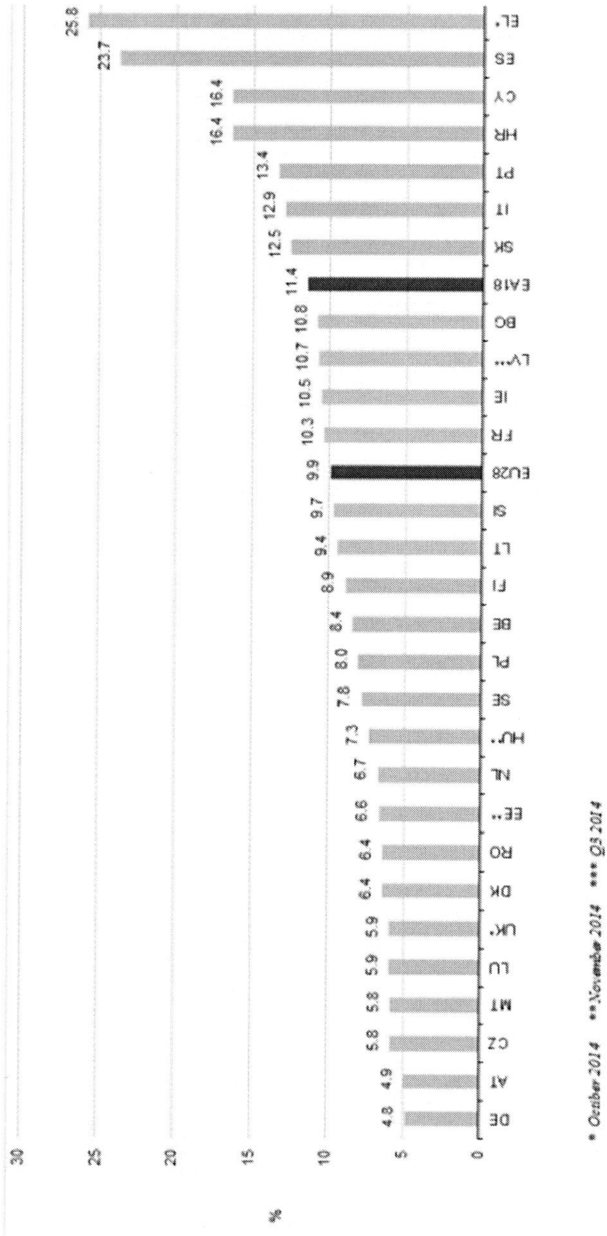

Fig. 1.2: GDP annual growth rate, selected countries. Source: Eurostat

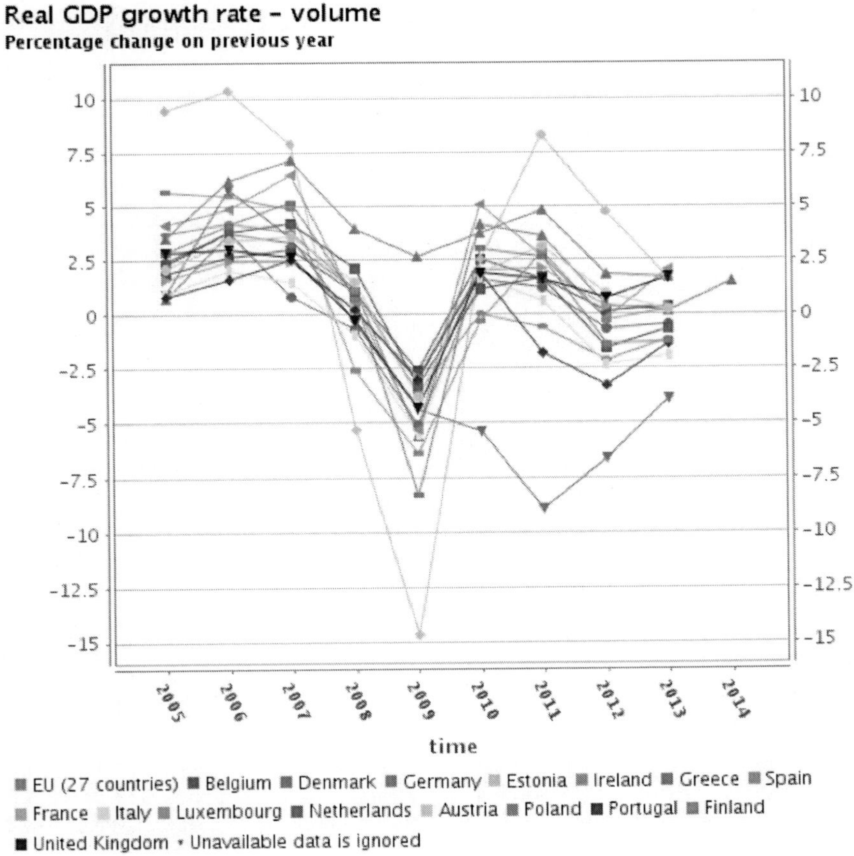

GEO/TIME	2002	2003	2004	2005	2006	2007	2008	2009	2010
European Union (27 countries)	1,88	1,87	1,83	1,82	1,85	1,85	1,92	2,02	2,01
Euro area (17 countries)	1,88	1,87	1,85	1,84	1,87	1,88	1,96	2,06	2,06
Belgium	1,94	1,87	1,86	1,83	1,86	1,89	1,97	2,03	2,01
Denmark	2,51	2,58	2,48	2,46	2,48	2,58	2,85	3,16	3,07
Germany (until 1990 former territory of the FRG)	2,5	2,54	2,5	2,51	2,54	2,53	2,69	2,82	2,8
Ireland	1,1	1,16	1,23	1,25	1,25	1,29	1,46	1,76	1,71
Spain	0,99	1,05	1,06	1,12	1,2	1,27	1,35	1,39	1,39
France	2,24	2,18	2,16	2,11	2,11	2,08	2,12	2,27	2,24
Italy	1,12	1,1	1,09	1,09	1,13	1,17	1,21	1,26	1,26
Netherlands	1,88	1,92	1,93	1,9	1,88	1,81	1,77	1,82	1,85
Austria	2,12	2,24	2,24	2,46	2,44	2,51	2,67	2,71	2,79
Poland	0,56	0,54	0,56	0,57	0,56	0,57	0,6	0,67	0,74
Portugal	0,73	0,71	0,74	0,78	0,99	1,17	1,5	1,64	1,59
Finland	3,36	3,44	3,45	3,48	3,48	3,47	3,7	3,94	3,9
Sweden	:	3,8	3,58	3,56	3,68	3,4	3,7	3,6	3,39
United Kingdom	1,8	1,75	1,69	1,72	1,74	1,77	1,78	1,85	1,8
Norway	1,66	1,71	1,57	1,51	1,48	1,59	1,58	1,78	1,69
Switzerland	:	:	2,82	:	:	:	2,87	:	:
United States	2,6	2,6	2,53	2,58	2,62	2,69	2,82	2,87	:
China (except Hong Kong)	1,07	1,13	1,23	1,32	1,39	1,4	1,47	1,7	:
Japan	3,12	3,14	3,13	3,31	3,41	3,46	3,47	3,36	:

Table 1.1: R&D spending as percentage of GDP, selected countries. Source: Eurostat

Institutions involved

The European Commission developed the Horizon 2020 strategy and the Innovation Union initiative.

Member States work together with the European Commission to develop a coherent S(S)TI for Europe.

Strategy overview

The Lisbon Strategy published in 2000 set out a vision for Innovation in the European Union. This included both an analysis of the current innovation needs in terms of societal changes (e.g. the dominance of the knowledge economy, demographic changes, etc.) and specific expenditure requirements to keep Europe a world leader in these fields of innovation. The projection at the time was that by 2010 R&D intensity (R&D expenditure as a percentage of GDP) in the EU should reach 3%. In 2010 that expenditure accounted for 2%, and the existing projections do not see any further increase (see Table 1.1). At the same time central government funds allocated to R&D showed a slight decrease from .77 [% of GDP] in 2009 to .76 in 2010. These discrepancies are due to the economic crisis, but they also set the stage for the current innovation dialogue in Europe and the Europe 2020 strategy (European Commission 2013b).

The '2020 Strategy for Europe' is the European Commission's strategy for growth. Within this strategy, the European Commission has set up the 'Innovation Union' Flagship Initiative (European Commission 2013c). As part of a joint vision and a common series of global challenges (climate change, energy scarcity, demographic change) and objectives, each country must specify its own objectives determined by their current situation and potential development. The strategy Europe 2020 has three priorities:

- **Smart growth**: generate value based on growth in knowledge and innovation. This will reinforce opportunities and social cohesion by making the most of education, research and digital economy potential;
- **Sustainable growth**: create a more competitive economy that is both connected with and friendly to the environment;
- **Inclusive growth**: strengthen the role of citizens in inclusive societies.

The Innovation Union will not only help tackle the identified global challenges, but it will also create growth. The initiative aims at a fundamental reform of the STI strategies of its member states. This will be achieved by the following measures:

1. Delivering the European Research Area (ERA)[1]:
    - facilitating cross-border research activities and remove regulatory obstacles;
    - coordinating European science projects in order to manage complexity of new technologies and profit from effects of scale.
2. Easier access to funding:
    - stimulating private investment on Research & Development (R&D) (the venture capital (VC) market of the EU is significantly smaller than the VC market of the US);
    - proposing new funding instruments by the Commission until 2014 in order to leverage private investment in R&D;
    - using funding to substitute private funding gap (due to financial crisis);
    - bridging the 'valley of death' between the phase-out of public funding and the not-yet forthcoming of private funding;
    - funding the expansion into other markets;
    - funding high-risk projects;
    - Competitiveness and Innovation Framework Programme (European Commission 2013a).
3. Establishment of a single European market for innovation:
    - making use of public procurement by EU institutions to stimulate innovation;
    - achieving more intelligent regulation ;
    - simplifying patent registration to cut cost for Intellectual Property Right holders (EU Patent).

The Innovation Union consists of a range of initiatives (for a full list, see: European Commission 2011), which should contribute to achieving the aims above:

- With the **'smart specialisation platforms'** (European Commission 2013d), the European Commission provides professional advice for EU member states and regions to help them design their STI strategies for smart specialisation. The smart specialisation approach aims at economic development

[1] The ERA was first introduced in the year 2000, and since then it has been the objective of a number of initiatives (e.g. Framework Programmes). With Innovation Union, the European Commission is planning to finalise the ERA.

through targeted support to Research and Innovation. It provides the basis for Structural Fund investments in Research and Innovation (R&I) (Cohesion Policy of the Horizon 2020 agenda).

- **European Partnerships** (European Commission 2012a): Initiated to deal with the 'Grand Challenges', these partnerships aim at bringing together all stakeholders involved to reach a critical mass. The partnerships, for instance, deal with the coordination of research efforts and help to develop norms.
- Promoting the **European Institute of Innovation and Technology** (EIT (European Commission 2012b)). The EIT provides a bridging function in Horizon 2020 from excellence-driven education, research and industry to innovation. It supports the development of innovation-driven solutions to societal challenges.

Challenges and outlook

Like most EU member states, the EU is also trying to cut its budget due to ongoing economic pressure. Since the new budget is still up for negotiation (European Parliament 2013), it remains to be seen how it will affect spending on R&D. Furthermore, as some goals in the Innovation Union agenda are ambitious (Blaauboer 2013), there is room for failure as partially happened to the Lisbon Agenda (European Commission 2010a; European Commission 2010b). National interest, as can be seen for instance in context with the realisation of the European Patent and the related discussion about language issues (Mullin 2012), is also a challenge.

Germany

Economic and political situation

Having experienced a sharp downturn in GDP in 2009, the German economy returned to reasonable growth in the following years, however at diminishing rates. The unemployment rate amounts to about 5% in 2014. Public investment in R&D sharply increased, whereas private investment remained stable in 2009 and increased in 2010, totaling about 2.9% of GDP in 2012 (Bundesministerium für Bildung und Forschung 2012a).

Institutions involved

Public support of science and R&D in Germany is a joint task of federal and regional institutions. The following focuses on the federal institutions involved:

- BMBF (Federal Ministry of Education and Research): primarily responsible for science and technology policy; implements several instruments such as grant-based project funding and institutional funding for public research organisations (e.g. Fraunhofer, Max Planck);
- BMWi (Federal Ministry of Economics and Technology): responsible for the implementation of industry-related research programs as well as collaboration between industry and Higher Educational Institutions (HEIs) – the commercialisation of R&D;
- German research foundation (DFG): runs research programs, grants funds mainly to academic research for research projects and infrastructure;
- KfW (German development bank): provides financial support for start-ups and small and medium enterprises (SMEs) - e.g. High-Tech start-up Fund.

Strategy overview

Research and Technology policy in Germany goes back to the 1960s. However, the High-Tech-Strategy (HTS 2010), published in 2006 (Bundesministerium für Bildung und Forschung 2012a), was the first national strategy for Germany developing a shared concept and vision including all relevant topics and encompassing all stakeholders involved in the innovation process. Those are HEIs, public research institutions, and industry, as well as the government and various ministries at the federal level. The strategy aimed at creating an innovation-friendly economic environment, and the activities proposed concentrated on the pooling of innovative power of science and industry, the improvement of conditions for SMEs and start-ups, the fostering of technology dissemination, the strengthening of international cooperation, and the investment in human capital.

The overall strategy priorities were – and still are *(see* Bundesministerium für Bildung und Forschung 2012a):

- to keep pace with global technology trends;
- to provide funding for cutting-edge public and private R&D and research;
- to reform the education system in order to tackle demographic change;
- to improve the link between industry and science.

Key technologies (medical technologies, transportations technologies, nano-technologies, biotech, material science, and environmental technologies) were identified as either being able to contribute significantly to the realisation of policy aims or as drivers of innovation for other technology fields.

In 2010, the German government published the HTS 2020 (Bundesministerium für Bildung und Forschung 2012b), which is based on the previous HTS, however refined and augmented by social dialogue (e.g. 'Dialog der Bundeskanzlerin' (The Federal Chancelor 2012) and Bürgerdialoge (Bundesministerium für Bildung und Forschung 2012c)) focused on five areas (see Fig. 1.3). The HTS 2020 is a demand-side strategy and it focuses on early interaction between potential users and developers of new technology. The strategy also aims at facilitating mutual learning and supporting the introduction of new technologies. It therefore contains lead market initiatives in five fields of action:

Fig. 1.3: Global challenges and fields of action of the HTS 2020. Source: Bundesministerium für Bildung und Forschung 2012a

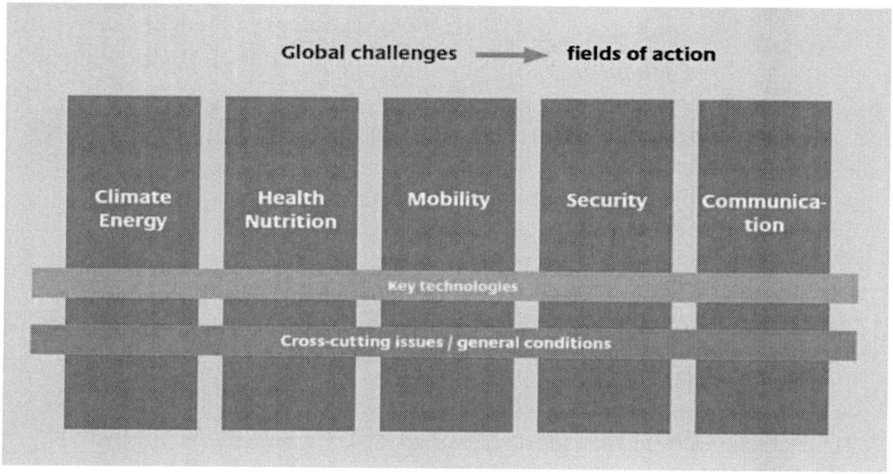

The fields are based on the main 'Global Challenges', which create a demand for innovative solutions, thus market potential. The strategy takes a mission-oriented approach, which orientates all research and innovation towards a number of missions. The most important challenges are specified in 'forward-looking projects' (FLP), lasting for up to 15 years. All projects are geared towards several lines of action (LOA) within these five areas:

- Climate/Energy: This field of action is motivated by climate change and the depletion of fossil fuels. Actions include: further support for cooperation between industry and the financial sector to develop better instruments to support climate protection; intensify international cooperation; promote energy efficiency measures and the use of more renewable energy. LOAs include: the 6th energy research programme, the framework programme on research for sustainable development, the Bio-economy framework programme, etc. FLPs are 'CO2-neutral, energy-efficient and climate-adapted cities' or 'Intelligent restructuring of the energy supply system'.

- Health/Nutrition: The focus here is on people's needs in view of the demographic change Germany has been facing: development of a new strategy for individualised medicine, support for company health management (esp. SMEs), and advancement of telemedicine to tackle a shortage of doctors. FLPs include: 'Treating illness more effectively with the help of individualised medicine', 'Better health through an optimised diet', and 'Living an independent life well into old age', alongside LOAs such as: individualised medicine, treatment of widespread diseases, strengthening prevention research, nutrition research and more.
- Mobility: Based on the assumption of a strong increase of traffic, priorities in this field of action include the development of fuel cells, battery technologies, intelligent traffic control, and the completion of Galileo (a satellite navigation system). The single FLP is 'A million electric vehicles in Germany by 2020'. LOAs include the mobility and transport technologies research programme, electric mobility, a general concept for the mobility of the future, the national aeronautics programme, and R&D projects for noticeable noise reduction in freight transport.
- Security: The protection of society and infrastructure from sabotage, organised crime, terrorism, and similar are key to this field of action. One FLP: 'More effective protection of communication networks'. LOAs include: protection of a modern democratic society, development of a clear competence profile (build up research infrastructure), development of security technologies, develop Germany into lead market for civil security solutions.
- Communication: As ICT is the basis for modern industry, the focus here is on: technological and legal advancement of internet-related developments, global standardisations, and a roadmap for embedded systems. FLPs are: 'Intelligent restructuring of the energy supply system', 'increasing internet use while decreasing energy consumption' and 'Making global knowledge digitally available and accessible'. The LOAs are: ICT Strategy 2010, IT summit (including e.g. smart grids and cloud computing), the IT security research program, etc.

Spanning these fields of action, support of R&D in key technologies and improvement of general conditions for innovation are also part of the strategy. The government also aims at expanding the strategy to the European level as the challenges identified are cross-national and should therefore be tackled on a supranational level.

The HTS 2010 furthermore outlines various cross-cutting issues and general conditions and names a number of measures and initiatives aiming at supporting research and innovation. Generally speaking, these include a positive innovation climate (see Innovationskraftwerk 2011) and planning security, better conditions for setting up businesses (including guidance and funding for spin-offs), and progressive participation in standard setting. On the educational level, HTS 2010 aims at the introduction of entrepreneurial training to become part of school curricula, vocational schools, and HEIs.

After the federal elections in fall 2013, the current federal government further developed the previous two editions of the HTS. The "New Hightech-Strategy" (Die Neue Hightech-Strategie, Bundesministerium für Bildung und Forschung 2015) now should bring together two earlier approaches focusing on the market potential of certain technologies (HTS 2006) and the tackling of societal needs with innovation (HTS 2010), respectively. This results in five pillars (see Fig. 1.4):

1. setting priorities in technology fields of great growth potentials;
2. improving transfer by better connecting science and economy on regional, national and international levels;
3. increasing innovation dynamics by supporting especially SMEs (see next section);
4. improving the regulatory framework for securing a qualified work force, financing of innovations and other prerequisites;
5. strengthening dialogue with society as a whole by improving general openness towards technology, citizen participation and social innovations.

Fig. 1.4: The five pillars of the new HTS. Source: Bundesministerium für Bildung und Forschung, 2015

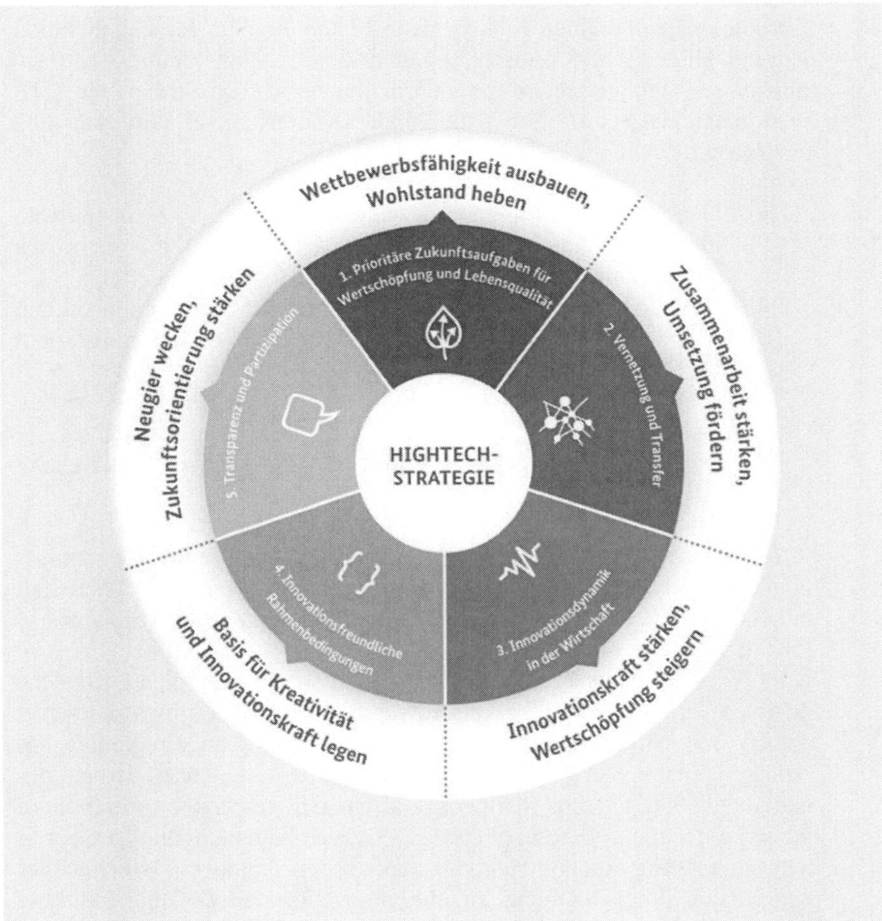

Due to their outstanding importance for the German economy, SMEs can also be considered to be a major focus. Measures include: support for funding of innovation (Innovation vouchers, High-Tech Start-up Fund, loan programmes, Central Innovation Programme for SMEs (ZIM)), access and availability of venture capital, workforce recruitment (e.g. Qualification Initiative for Germany 2008), access to knowledge and knowledge protection, pre-market support of research (IGF), commercialisation (e.g. trade fair support (Bundesministerium für

Wirtschaft und Technologie 2013a)), as well as easier access to public R&D programs (SME Innovative).

Considerable importance is also given to the support for collaboration between HEIs, public research organisations, and universities, and the transfer and application of knowledge. Important measures of the HTS 2020 in this respect are (see also: Bundesministerium für Wirtschaft und Technologie 2013c):

- 'Top Cluster Programme', which supports regional clusters, identified thematically by a bottom-up approach (Bundesministerium für Wirtschaft und Technologie 2015);
- 'Research Campus', which is funding long-term collaboration between HEIs, public research, and industry (Bundesministerium für Bildung und Forschung 2013);
- 'Innovation Alliance', which aims at bringing together existing top-level research in order to start new clustering processes (exemplary: Bundesministerium für Bildung und Forschung 2012d).

Moreover, innovation and public procurement, which indirectly supports industry by buying innovative products (Bundesministerium für Wirtschaft und Technologie 2013b), are beginning to play a bigger role than before.

In the German context, it is also important to note that apart from the federal government, all federal states have developed their own state-level strategy and policy. For instance, Sachsen-Anhalt (Landesregierung des Landes Sachsen-Anhalt 2014) and the Saarland (Landesregierung des Saarlandes 2007) focus their efforts on the respective presence of industrial sectors and research areas. Sachsen-Anhalt in this respect is home to a strong automotive components supplier industry, which serves as a major point of focus of the innovation strategy by the state government. In providing support for the establishment of an automotive related R&D centre, the state government tries to help interested firms develop new and more sophisticated products.

The Saarland state has defined three main sectors (Bio/Nanotechnology, IT/consulting, knowledge industries) and fosters the establishment of clusters around these industries. To achieve that, measures include the strengthening of industry-university relations, provision of a qualified work force, improvement of general investment conditions, and improvement of infrastructure.

Challenges and outlook

Even though spending on R&D remained stable during the crisis and increased afterwards, financial market turmoil still poses a major threat especially to SMEs and start-ups when it comes to risky investments (Rammer 2011). The venture capital market is still weak in Germany, despite several attempts to improve the situation (see e.g.: Poeverlein 2013). The shortage of qualified labor due to demographic developments already poses a problem to the innovative power of Germany. Immigration restrictions for the highly qualified are still a problem, as is the relatively low number of tertiary education graduates (Rammer 2011). In the wake of the 'Energiewende' (energy transition), energy costs, energy storage and availability are getting ever more important. The latter strategy towards the transition of the German energy system towards comprehensive sustainability was strengthened after the federal elections in September 2013.

United Kingdom

Economic and political situation

Due to the importance of the financial sector in the UK, the country was hit especially hard by the financial crisis. GDP growth has just picked up at notable rates in 2013 and even more so in 2014, and is expected to stay well above 2.5% in 2015 (OECD 2014c). During the recession the Government introduced severe cutbacks for almost all departments (emergency budget), however keeping the overall funding for science and research stable. Nevertheless, structural changes were made (see below). The current Government came to power in May 2010 and introduced the strategy subsequently outlined.

Institutions involved

- Technology Strategy Board: in effect the 'Innovation Agency' for the UK. Covers the entire UK, and is the only public sector body responsible for innovation. Prime channel for supporting business-led technology innovation. Develops technology strategies and makes choices on the allocation of funding;

- UK Finance for Growth Limited: company established by the government to manage its SME finance schemes and oversee all publicly funded VC schemes;
- Local Economic Partnerships: replaced Regional Development Agencies - consortia of local authorities responsible for economic development;
- Higher Education Funding Council: promotes and funds teaching and research;
- Research Councils UK: works together with higher education funding bodies and in discussion with individual universities and consortia.

Strategy overview

The government elected in 2010 published its "Innovation and Research Strategy for Growth" in 2011 (Department for Business, Innovation and Skills 2011a; Department for Business Innovation and Skills 2011b; and Cunningham et al. 2011). The main objective of the strategy is to create a coherent framework for the UK innovation system to improve the:

- identification of opportunities;
- building of capabilities and infrastructures;
- allocation of financial and skilled resources and coordination across all relevant actors.

The strategy is based on the recognition of Britain's pre-existing productive knowledge base and strength in world-class universities. The weaknesses in comparison with other top performing innovation-economies (USA, Japan, etc.), such as the lack of technical skills available in the workforce and the underdeveloped commercialisation of available knowledge as well as the general challenges all economies face, such as increased global competition and the increasing amounts of investments needed to do research, lead to a collection of activities, which are outlined in the strategy. The government mainly concentrates on tasks in the following areas:

- funding blue skies research as well as new discoveries and inventions;
- improving the interface between HEIs and businesses;
- delivering a better environment for commercialising research.

Though innovation and technology policy remained relatively stable over the years (Quantum Innovation Centre 2013), the new government made a number of important changes in three steps:

1. innovation support reductions, which included the closure of Regional Development Agencies (RDAs) and reductions in innovation & business support initiatives, simplification of the agencies and programs available;
2. Spending Review 2010: refocus of support and baseline budgets, e.g. reaffirm the 'ring-fenced' science and research budget, thus showing the importance of this area, and focus support via the Technology Strategy Board and Catapult Centres;
3. subsequent announcements of investment and initiatives, e.g. further funding for Catapult Centres, Grant for R&D, Innovation Vouchers and capital spending, and R&D tax credits (esp. for SMEs).

Acknowledging the great importance of innovation for long-term sustainable growth and in line with the need for short-term measures to boost the economy, the strategy consists of four major sections:

1. Discovery and Development

Due to limited resources in the wake of the financial crisis and the austerity budget, the strategy identifies a number of technologies on which the British government is focussing its efforts. The technologies, on the one, hand have to be promising in terms of actual and future market size, and on the other hand, the UK has to have sufficient expertise available within the country (science and industry) to be able to profit from further support adequately. The technologies identified are:

- life sciences (see also the UK life sciences strategy (Department for Business, Innovation and Skills 2011c), 'Biomedical Catalyst Fund' (Technology Strategy Board 2013));
- high-value manufacturing;
- nanotechnology;
- digital technologies;
- creative industries.

With 'Catapults' (e.g. High Value Manufacturing Catapult (Technology Strategy Board 2012) and Call Therapy Catapult), a network of technology transfer and innovation centers, access to expertise in HEIs, and access to research on and the development of marketable products are provided for companies in these important sectors. Additionally, emerging technologies as well as general-purpose technologies which are promising high market values and cross-sectoral applicability are supported through the investment in facilities. These are: synthetic biology, energy efficient computing, energy harvesting, and graphene.

2. Innovative businesses

This section of the "Innovation and Research Strategy for Growth" underlines the importance of business being innovative, thus raising productivity. In order to support companies to invest in adapting and developing their own complementary, non-technical innovations and intangible assets (skilled labor, design, business models, brandings), the strategy proposes a number of measures, including R&D tax credits (esp. for SMEs) and support for venture capital (e.g. 'Enterprise Capital Fund', 'UK innovation Investment fund (Erawatch, n.d.)', 'Business Growth Fund', 'Seed Enterprise Investment Scheme')). The Technology Strategy Board further supports collaborative R&D within knowledge transfer networks (e.g. connection through web platforms to access knowledge (Technology Strategy Board 2013b)) and knowledge transfer partnerships (project based). Support especially for SMEs is granted through 'Small Business Research Initiative' (which finances solutions by SMEs for government departments), the 'Grant for R/D' or 'SMART'. Also for SMEs, the 'Design for Innovation' should increase awareness of design and its importance for successful commercialisation. Focus is also laid on Intellectual Property (IP) and the support for SMEs to access (open access repository), protect and make full use of IP, as well as the provision of human capital with grants and new apprenticeship programs.

3. Knowledge and innovation

Due to the important role universities play in the innovation system and the importance of collaboration between HEIs and businesses, the strategy aims at strengthening this collaboration (Wilson 2012), e.g. through the Higher Education Innovation Funding and Innovation Vouchers (for SMEs). Furthermore, Technology Transfer Offices will be assisted in understanding how design can be of value to the commercialisation of research. The focus on design is due to the UK's strong position in the design sector. With the support for Research and Innovation Campuses (e.g. Babraham Research Campus, Norwich Research Park), Research

Clusters (Crowley 2011), and University Enterprise Zones (HM Treasury 2014) collaboration, commercialization, and the attraction of foreign research activities will be strengthened. Other measures include the 'Super-connected cities' initiatives, which will provide high-speed Internet for a number of cities with important research clusters, as well as funding for super-computing.

4. Global Collaboration:

Strong links, which already exist mainly to the US and within the EU, should be sustained and improved. Due to their increasing importance as export markets and sources of innovation and knowledge, links to China and India are a priority. The importance of links and collaborations is also based on shifts in the value chains of many industries. The UK tries to attract multinational enterprises (MNEs) to set up research and production facilities within the country and supports UK SMEs to establish international links. All measures are embedded in the strategic approach 'International Innovation and Research for the UK', which promotes UK business to access international markets. It also encourages researchers to establish collaboration, and it includes visa programmes and supports the engagement in EU programmes (Horizon 2020).

Challenges and outlook

The strategy incorporates a number of challenges and proposes solutions for near-future activities, including the further improvement of public data availability (e.g. from the National Health Service (NHS) (The Government of the United Kingdom 2011)), and the role of the government as lead-customer. Also, raising the general awareness of the importance of innovation and creating a more innovation-friendly environment by further cutbacks in regulations remain as issues.

Other challenges in the medium run can be seen in the effect of the increase of student fees on the number of third-level graduates, and the on-going financial crisis, and its effects on the government budget.

Spain

Economic and political situation

As many other EU members, Spain was hit hard by the economic downturn of 2009, with GDP shrinking by approximately 4% in 2009, and showing positive growth in 2014, the first time since the recession. Unemployment stands at approximately 25% and youth unemployment at more than 50% (OECD 2014b). In November 2011, a new government was elected.

Institutions involved

- Ministry of Economy and Competitiveness: responsible for design, planning and coordination of STI policy through Secretary of State for Research, Development, and Innovation (Ministerio de Economía y Competitividad 2013e);
- Council for Science Policy, Technology and Innovation: establishes the strategy and tries to increase efficient use of resources;
- Centre for Industrial Technological Development (CDTI): managed by the Ministry of Economy and Competitiveness, contributes to improving technological innovation of firms (applied research and technological services), channels funding for companies on national and international level;
- foundations: non-profit entities created by public or private sector, intermediary between R&D, science, technology, and business;
- university-enterprise foundations: created jointly by the universities and chambers of commerce to foster healthy relationships and collaborations between institutions;
- industrial liaison offices: work to identify technological needs of the business sector and to nurture technology transfer and commercialisation (European Commission, n.d.);
- not-for-profit institutions: these institutions, divided into three types, constitute another focal point of the science and technology system;
- scientific and technological parks: infrastructures acting as industrial development poles, SMEs and spin-offs emerge here;
- technological centres (RTOs) and technological innovation support centres provide companies with R&D and innovation

services and act as a support platform by generating technological know-how and facilitating its exploitation;

- European business and innovation centres: offering promoters' and entrepreneurs' advice and other forms of support, and monetary aids.

Strategy overview

The government elected in 2011 published a new strategy for science, technology, and innovation in February 2013 (Ministerio de Economía y Competitividad 2013a), replacing the prior government's strategies 'Estrategia Estatel de Innovación (e2i') of 2011 and 'Estrategia Nacional de Ciencia y Tecnología' of 2007 (Ministeria de Ciencia y Innovación 2011; Ministerio de Economía y Competitividad 2013b). The new strategy is more focused on generating social and economic effects than its predecessors. The new strategy has to be seen in the light of the severe economic crisis, and especially the very high rates of unemployment, affecting people of all educational levels.

The new government bases its strategy on the analysis of the Spanish research and innovation environment, which it says has improved in some aspects such as the number of scientific publications and the rate of GDP spent on R&D. However, some issues still remain. Therefore the STI is based on the following challenges:

1) still a relatively low level of R&D spending (1,33% of GDP in 2011);
2) low share of companies engaged in R&D (esp. SMEs) and a low share of medium and high-tech companies;
3) low share of employees engaged in R&D;
4) large persistent regional differences in R&D activities.

From this analysis, the government outlined four supreme objectives (see below) and 18 subordinate objectives, which are also depicted in Fig. 1.5.

Fig. 1.5: Objectives and priorities of the Spanish S(S)TI. Source: Ministerio de Economía y Competitividad 2013a

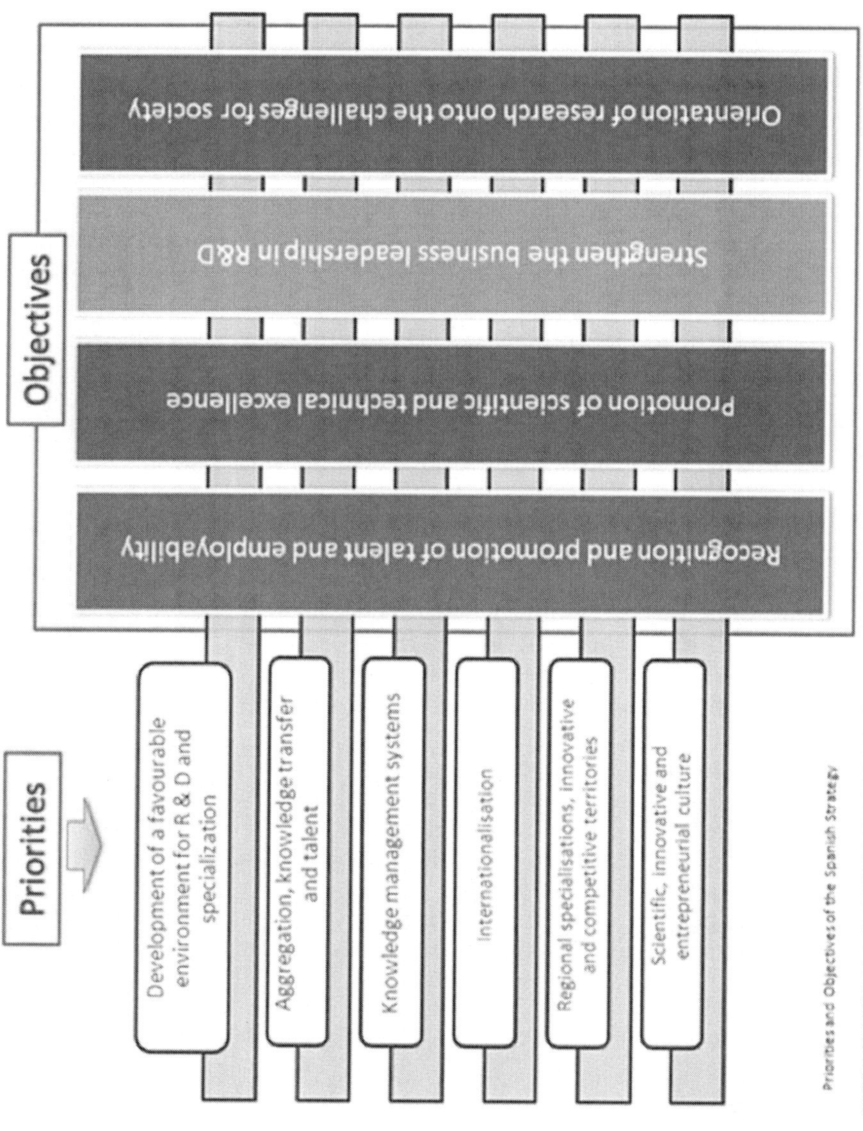

1. Recognition and promotion of talent and employability

This objective includes the promotion of education and the training of human resources, support for national and international mobility of researchers, and the encouragement of the employment of workforce trained in R&D. To tackle the imbalance between the number of PhDs available and the demand for scientific staff (even though the overall share in the population is still below EU average), supply and demand are meant to be better coordinated, industrial doctorates in collaboration with industry introduced, entrepreneurial skill training of researchers to be encouraged and curricula to be made a better fit to business needs. Furthermore, dual vocational training schemes will be set up.

2. Promotion of scientific and technical excellence

The goals of this objective are: generating cutting-edge knowledge, development of emerging technologies and leading or strengthening R&D institutions, as well as the consolidation of and the use of scientific and singular technologies. Measures are required to support interdisciplinary and collaborative research between the public and private sector (exploratory and precompetitive research, with priority on high industrial return) at the small scale where industrial interest and key sectors lie for the Spanish economy. General State Administration and the Autonomous Communities are to establish better coordination of activities, actions that strengthen the centers and units through recognition of and support for their R & D capabilities and international leadership potential. Finally, to facilitate and accelerate the translation of the results of R&D applied to products and services, it is necessary to have agents that facilitate transfer processes (technology centres and centres of innovation support, the science and technology parks, and technology transfer units). Full participation in the European Research Area (e.g. with the entire Spanish research infrastructure (Ministerio de Economía y Competitividad 2013c)), participation in international projects, and support of the "science industry" are also priorities.

3. Strengthen the business leadership in R&D

Objective 3 sees a need to promote the development of new technological solutions in all key sectors (the aerospace, energy, ICT, and pharmaceutical chemistry, and traditional sectors) with entrepreneurial approaches. Other measures are: fostering higher levels of business investment in R&D; promoting stability and sustainability of those investments, and increasing the number of companies engaged in R&D, (esp. SMEs); encouraging large Spanish and international companies to invest in Spain (R&D); promoting key enabling technologies; promoting R&D-oriented collaborative demands and enterprises, especially SMEs, in the implementation and funding of R&D and innovation, both technological and non-technological; stimulating large companies, which can be tractors for SMEs; developing the capacity of government to act as a driver for business innovation; managing the demand for products and services through innovative public procurement initiatives, and the promotion of key enabling technologies, because they have a big impact (areas such as micro and nano-electronics, photonics, nanotechnology, biotechnology, advanced materials and manufacturing systems). Finally, the aim is to strengthen the role and activities of technology centers and support centers for technological innovation, technology platforms, and science and technology parks in addition to the clusters and sector forums, as well as to remove obstacles that hinder PPP; also to ensure strategic management of IP and implementation of open innovation models.

4. Orientation of research towards the challenges for society

Objective 4 is concerned with challenges as follows, a list which includes some of its main activities: 1. Health, demographic change and wellbeing: make use of and collaborate with the Spanish public health system, collaborate with ICT sector; 2. Food safety and quality, productive and sustainable farming, sustainability of natural resources, marine and maritime research: healthier and more sustainable food production, use of technological developments incl. biotech. Promote innovation adoption by SMEs; 3. Energy - safe, sustainable and clean: 'Strategic Energy Technology Plan': sustainable energy production, renewable energy promotion; 4. Transport - smart, sustainable and integrated: sustainable mobility, safer and cleaner, better integrated transport; 5. Action on climate change and efficient use of resources and raw materials: stop deforestation, more recycling; 6. Social change and innovation: innovation has to protect historical, social and cultural heritage; 7. digital economy and society: Digital Agenda for Europe. Increase access to ICT and ICT use in business and government, training of skills; 8. Safety, security and defense: increase collaboration across borders.

All objectives are categorised into six priorities, and within each priority section a range of measures is outlined. Some of the most important measures are included in a short description of each priority area. The measures aim at reducing weaknesses and bringing more efficiency, flexibility and competitiveness to the system:

- development of a favorable environment for R & D and specialisation: (a) improve governance of public institutions of Science, Technology, and Innovation, encourage public-private partnerships, promote and facilitate private investment in R&D, (venture capital), support the creation of technology-based companies and the promotion of an entrepreneurial culture in universities (spin-offs), and use public procurement for innovation stimulation;
- aggregation, knowledge transfer and talent: promotion of research clusters and networks, interdisciplinary networking;
- knowledge management systems: identify research groups and innovative technologies with a high potential, develop systems for the collection, analysis, dissemination and protection of results, establish mechanisms for effective technology transfer and commercialization, and foster relationships between R & D centers, researchers, and companies;
- internationalisation of Spanish Science, Research and Innovation and its agents: improve international collaboration, especially with EU (Horizon 2020) and emerging countries, improve visibility of Spanish research and companies abroad;
- regional specialisations and development, innovative and competitive territories: collaboration and coordination of all efforts between the Autonomous Communities through 1) supporting activities in R&D aimed at the demands of the systems' agents; 2) the intensive use of ICT; and 3) the thrust of business development and competitiveness of SMEs;
- scientific, innovative, and entrepreneurial culture: creation of an enabling environment in which creativity and entrepreneurship are integrated as core values of the younger generation and act as levers of social change.

The development of the strategy includes the use of six coherent articulation mechanisms:

1. the responsibility of all levels of government in achieving the objectives and commitment to the priorities established;
2. open access to data and publications (shared repositories);
3. the development of an integrated information system;

4. rationalisation of public actions and administrative simplification;
5. the harmonisation of standards and assessment;
6. measures and instruments that raise business involvement in R&D, attracting investment in R&D from abroad.

Challenges and outlook

The key challenges are already mentioned in the strategy paper of 2011. It remains unclear whether they are sufficiently tackled by the strategy, for the following reasons:

- a growth model based on industries with low innovation;
- a financial sector that channels few resources to innovative companies and venture-capital activities;
- lack of coordination between the educational system and corporate needs;
- overly rigid public administration.

Overall, the strategy seems to be still at an early stage with many goals defined and activities proposed. A clearer outline of the measurements has been taken (Ministerio de Economía y Competitividad 2013d) but still seems to require more detailed planning. Evaluation of the strategy and its implementation is further challenged by the lack of clear budget planning, easy to access (Heijs 2011).

Italy

Economic and political situation

Like other countries, Italy was also severely hit by the financial crisis of 2008 and 2009. The unemployment rate surpassed 11% and after two years of modest GDP growth in 2010 and 2011, the economy slipped back into recession (OECD 2014a). As a special case, regional differences in Italy are extremely high between the northern and the southern part of the country, with the northern part being highly industrialised and the southern part living from agricultural and tourist income.

Institutions involved

- Ministry for Economic Development: supports and manages industrial innovation. Organised in departments: competitiveness promotion; development and cohesion; and market regulation;
- UVAL (Public Investment Evaluation Unit) at the Department of Development and Cohesion (MISE): plays an active role in supporting the implementation of the National Strategic Framework (NSF) and regional policy;
- Ministry for Education, University, and Research (MiUR): coordinates national and international scientific activities and distributes funding to universities and research agencies. MiUR establishes the means for supporting public and private research and technological development (RTD) funding, and coordinates preparation for the triennial National Research Programme (NRP);
- Agency for the Diffusion of Technologies for Innovation: inter-ministerial coordination of innovation policies reduces competence fragmentation among Ministries and regions. It aids cooperation between central government and the regions in the efficient use of available resources related to various technological innovation projects;
- Regional Innovation Agencies and Regional Competence Centres (RCCs): support the development of e-government and the information society at regional levels.

Strategy overview

The Italian S(S)TI strategy is outlined in the National Research Programme 'Programma Nazionale della Ricerca', PNR (Ministero dell'Istruzione, dell'Università e della Ricerca 2009; Researchitaly 2013a), the first being published for the years 2001-2003. The current strategy of 2011-2013 includes measures on the level of education, research, technology transfer, and intellectual property. The strategy is part of national reform efforts, which aim at turning Italy into a knowledge-based society in line with the Europe 2020 strategy (see above). Also in Italy, the S(S)TI is motivated by the argument that there is a need for a highly qualified workforce, and the case being made for common interests as well as investments in R&D in order to withstand economic turmoil. Gradually harmonising supply and demand for research between academia and industry by creating platforms as well as IT infrastructure, and opening up that infrastructure for the industrial sector to participate in, the strategy aims at raising the return on investment in science and innovation. All initiatives are concentrated on certain research areas in which Italy already has reached a competitive edge, and aim at further consolidating these areas. Additionally, strategic areas of interest were identified (climate and environment, energy, health, cultural heritage, security, urban areas).

Motivated by Italy's current economic problems, the PNR focuses on the young generation in industry and academia. Therefore the strategy incorporates measures for:

- creating and implementing a system to evaluate research projects;
- establishing structured career paths for young academics;
- supporting returning Italian scientists and integrating their scientific expertise;
- improving international scientific graduate schools in order to foster excellence and reduce the average age of graduate scientists.

A further goal is to populate the European Research Area with a growing number of young scientists capable of raising the level of competence and motivation in the private and public sector.

The 18 core activities within the seven objectives (see Fig. 1.6) of the PNR (Researchitaly 2013b) include the following:

1. creativity and excellence in all scientific areas: aims at supporting basic research at national research institutions for generating new knowledge with long-term effects;
2. basic research for enabling technologies: fosters interaction between universities, research institutions, ministries, industry, and regional governments for basic research in pervasive technologies with medium and long term effects;
3. innovative industries: direct interventions in projects involving the development of priority areas, supporting incubation of new high-tech companies in districts of regional and international importance;
4. integrated research projects supporting industry: involve fundamental research and industrial research, aimed at the development of products and services with impact on the medium - short term in collaboration with academia.

Fig. 1.6: Objectives of the Italian S(S)TI. Source: Researchitaly 2013a

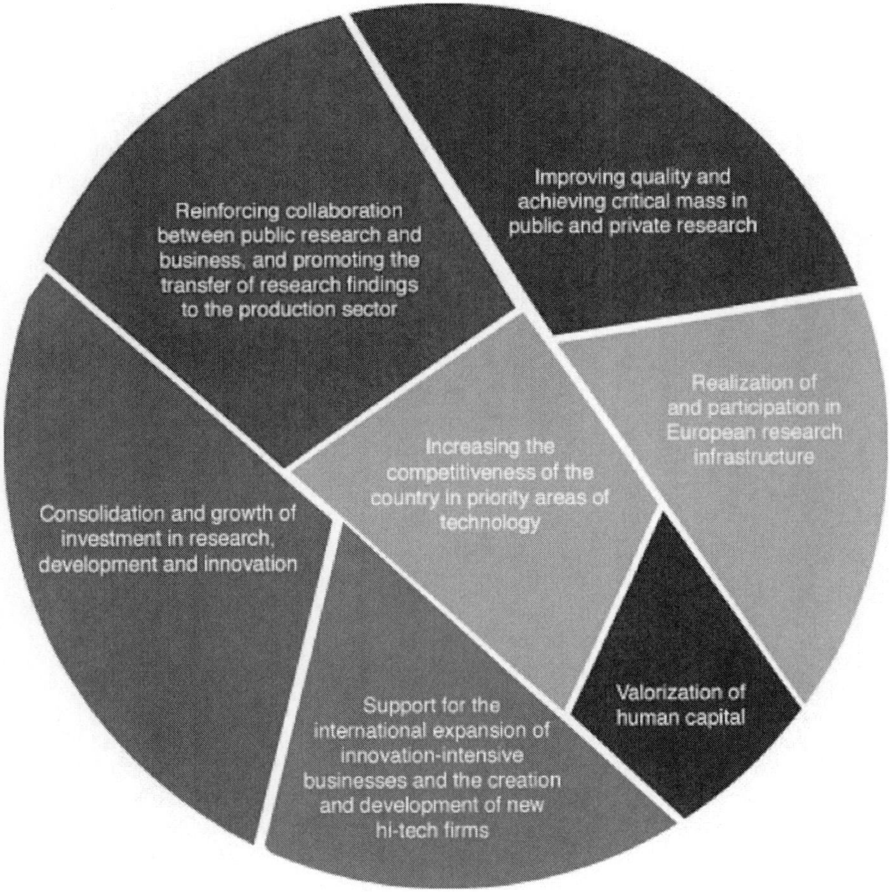

5. creation of new enterprises with high technological content: creation of enterprises with high technological content, spin-offs from universities and business networks;
6. national technology platforms: PNR fosters the emergence and consolidation of technology platforms while recognising their role in managing and evaluating the national research system;
7. districts with high technology: analysis and evaluation of districts and similar structures, aiming at enhancing their effectiveness; evaluation of their potential for reorganisation;

8. national centers of excellence: coordinating and connecting groups, skills, facilities, operated by a number of institutions;
9. young scientists: attracting and qualifying young people in scientific and technological research projects aimed at future employment in the R&D sector;
10. international doctoral schools: stimulating the foundation of international doctoral schools and suggesting the creation of doctoral programs focused on industrial R&D projects with industry involvement;
11. reorientation and recovery: introduces projects of reorientation and recovery of industrial research facilities, esp. training of staff, involvement of local institutions and the regional governments;
12. post-doctorates: support for large-scale experiments, repeated for limited periods of time, complemented by proposals for the adoption of procedures for tenure track;
13. infrastructure: defines the goals of internationalisation and specific interventions connected to the European ESFRI (European Commission 2013e) roadmap. Funding for R&D activities with national industries, construction of infrastructure;
14. Programma Operativo Nazionale (PON (PON 2004)): identifies optimal conditions in 'convergence regions' for the development and attraction of R&D investment, supports interaction between central and regional bodies, realisation of North-South cooperation to promote integration and knowledge transfer;
15. extension of the PON projects to other regions: involves the construction of cooperation between regions, promoting the integration and transfer of knowledge between technology-intensive areas and local development systems;
16. improving the Italian System of Research through internationalisation: full realisation of the European Research Area (ERA), support for commitment of bilateral and multilateral agreements, creation and updating of research infrastructures;
17. universities: assigns a value to the strategic public-private partnership for R&D, incentives for creation of transversal networks to overcome local or sectoral interests, stimulates synergies between universities and businesses;
18. research institutes: support for institutions supervised by the Ministry of Education for establishing international doctoral schools, attracting young researchers, patenting discoveries.

Additionally, the PNR aims at simplifying funding instruments and mechanisms as well as introducing monitoring measures for securing the efficient use of funds. The funds are provided by various sources such as the 'Ordinary fund for research institutes and bodies', 'research subsidy fund' or 'fund for investment in basic research'. The 'national operative programme' is another funding source funded by the EU with the objective of fostering convergence of regions (esp. southern Italy), via the Regional Innovation Strategies.

The PNR is augmented by several special programmes (Research Italy 2013c), such as the 'national Antarctic research programme', 'national aerospace research programme', and others. On top of that, other strategies such as the 'Industria 2015' strategy (Confederazione Italiana Sindicati Lavoratori, n.d.) are in place. Here, the government highlights the importance of company networks, innovating finance and Industrial Innovating Projects (PII). The strategy aims at supporting product development in the phase between basic research and the stage of having a marketable product. It finances operating prototypes, which solve specific, widespread problems (e.g. for the protection of cultural heritage: materials, diagnostic systems, sensors, etc.) (Ministero dell'Istruzione, dell'Università e della Ricerca 2011). The strategy also includes three main instruments:

- business networks (targeted at SMEs, contractual coordination);
- innovative finance (targeted at groups of firms, to leverage private funding (venture capital));
- Industrial Innovation Projects (in strategic areas, plurality of private and public actors, coordination among several ministries, mix of instruments (e.g. aid for research and product development, for SMEs expenditure linked to IP, etc.).

Overall, demand-side innovation policies are also in place; however they have only recently been introduced. Public procurement is also used for pre-commercial public procurement in order to stimulate innovation and promote environmentally sustainable procurement. Regulations and standardisations are used to encourage certain innovative behavior. Private demand is supported by tax incentives, awareness raising campaigns and catalytic procurement by the public sector. Additionally, lead-market initiatives are implemented and open innovation is supported.

In 2012, new legislation dealing with start-ups was set up (Ministerio dello Sviluppo Economico 2012). The legislation acknowledges that start-ups are key for developing a new business culture and are important for sustainable growth and technological development. The legislation for start-ups contains measures like costless registration at chambers of commerce, different labor law regulations, special taxation rules for the start-up itself as well as staff, priority access for start-ups to research facilities, tax credits, fast-track access to government grants, fast-failure regulation and resources for venture capital (through the Italian Investment Fund).

Challenges and outlook

The shift from incentives mainly centering around SMEs in traditional sectors to a more research-based approach to innovation, including innovation in other sectors, remains a challenge. As in most other European countries, the lack of venture capital available is problematic as well as the willingness of the private sector to invest in R&D. Funds dedicated for southern Italy should be revised for their effectiveness on innovation activity. The current unstable political situation after the elections in February 2013 also remains a challenge. Mobility of talents and the further improvement of technology transfer mechanisms should be tackled. More coordination at federal and regional government level seems to be necessary, including vertical integration (Potì and Reale 2011; Pro Inno Europe n.d.).

Ireland

Economic and political situation

The innovation policy and strategy of Ireland is strongly influenced by the on-going effects of the economic downturn since 2008. GDP between 2008 and 2010 fell by approx. 10% and growth rates remained flat until 2013. With 4.3% growth, the Irish economy expanded significantly in 2014. Peaking at approx. 15% (2012) and falling to 11.5%, unemployment started to improve (OECD 2014a). Gross government debt surpassed 130% of GDP (OECD 2014b). Research funding for higher education institutions (HEI) has been cut significantly, but funding for industry-HEI collaboration and applied research initiatives remains stable (Martin 2011). A new government was elected in February 2011, having considerably changed the Irish innovation policy since.

Institutions involved

- Forfás: Ireland's policy advisory board for enterprise, trade, science, technology, and innovation. Forfás provides independent and rigorous research, advice and support in the areas of enterprise and science policy. It plays an important role in the coordination of the agencies listed below;
- Enterprise Ireland: supports Irish companies in their export activities with financial resources and advice;
- Science Foundation Ireland: invests in academic research, provides grants, and supports cooperation between HEI, government, and industry;
- IDA (Industrial Development Agency) Ireland: responsible for the promotion and development of foreign industry in Ireland, focussing on the attraction of R&D facilities and European headquarters of companies and agencies;
- HEA (Higher Education Authority): planning and policy development body for the tertiary education sector and funding authority for the HEIs.

For a positioning of the respective institutions within the Irish research and innovation system, see Fig. 1.7.

Fig. 1.7: The Irish research and innovation system. Source: Own illustration according to Department of Jobs, Enterprise and Innovation 2014a

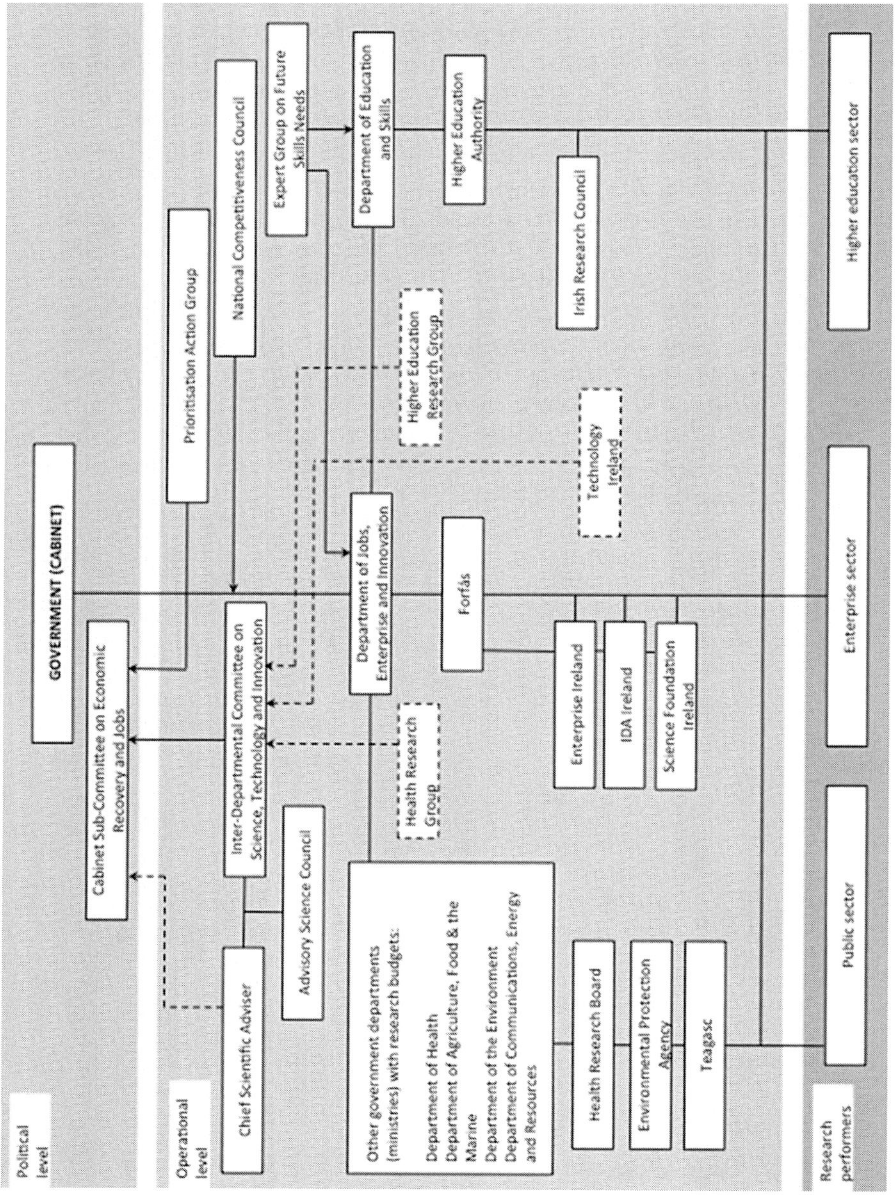

Strategy overview

Based on the vision of "Building Ireland's Knowledge Economy" (Forfás 2004) and the recommendations made by Forfás, the Irish government developed a Strategy for Science, Technology and Innovation 2006-2013 (The Irish Government 2006). The aim of the strategy is to make Ireland "internationally renowned for the excellence of its research" and to "be at the forefront in generating and using new knowledge for economic and social progress […]" (The Irish Government 2006, p. 8). The strategy comprises the following key elements:

- World Class Research: building of a critical mass of research teams across a number of disciplines to remain at world standard, encouraging researcher mobility between academia and enterprise as well as geographically (e.g. international experience).
- Capturing, Protecting and Commercialising Ideas and Know-How: enabling the strategic exploitation of know-how generated by HEIs.
- Support Research and Development for Enterprise, Innovation and Growth: increasing the number of firms undertaking R&D, supporting industry-HEI collaboration through accessible grants for R&D, supporting technology transfer and industry-led networks, establishing Competence Centres, improving taxation for R&D.
- Science Education and Society: reintroduction/reprioritisation of 'science' and connected subjects in curricula at primary and secondary education level.
- Research in the Public Sector: identification of sectors (agriculture and food, health, environment, marine and energy), which have the potential for innovation and improvement of the quality of life.
- All-Island (Ireland and Northern Ireland) and International Science Technology and Innovation: collaboration with Northern Irish institutes and further international collaboration (e.g. EU Framework Programmes, USA).

In the wake of the economic crisis, the government adapted the Strategy for Science, Technology and Innovation as published in 'Building Ireland's Smart Economy' (Department of the Taoiseach 2008), placing more importance on the commercialisation of knowledge. The aim of the strategy is the creation of the 'Innovation Island' through the following measures:

- supporting small domestic firms by direct (e.g. €500m venture fund) and indirect measures (e.g. favorable taxation of R&D spending, easier access to public procurement contracts);
- adapting the involved agencies' strategies. For instance, Enterprise Ireland should further strengthen industry-HEI collaborations through Competence Centres (see e.g. Collaborative Centre for Applied Nanotechnology 2012), Industry-Led Research networks, and innovation vouchers, focusing on the involvement of small Irish enterprises. Science Foundation Ireland should also be allowed to fund applied research and HEI-industry collaborations (Centres for Science, Engineering & Technology and Strategic Research Clusters).

In 2011 and 2012 two major reviews on the success of the strategy were published:

- The Research Prioritisation steering group (Forfás 2012), identified the main 14 focus areas (mainly in the ICT, health, pharmaceutical, biotech, renewable energy, and manufacturing sectors) in which publicly financed research should be based. These areas were identified by a number of indicators, such as their market potential for Irish companies and already existing expertise in Ireland. Based on the report, the RIS3 (Research and Innovation Strategies for Smart Specialisation) (Department of Jobs, Enterprise and Innovation 2014a) were developed for national and regional levels. In 2014 the first progress report (Department of Jobs, Enterprise and Innovation 2014b) was published.
- The second report (Minister for Jobs, Enterprise and Innovation 2012) proposed a framework that would ensure that all enterprises (small and large) can easily access intellectual property (IP) generated in the public sector on fair terms for all parties involved.

In 2011, the new government published its Programme of Government (The Irish Government 2011), highlighting some aspects of their Strategy for Science, Technology and Innovation in the national recovery plan. The plan reconfirmed the strategy of the smart economy report (The Innovation Taskforce 2010), but also incorporated recommendations from the above two reviews (Forfás 2012 and Minister for Jobs, Enterprise & Innovation 2012), in particular:

- R&D investment: within a budget of austerity this was underlined as an infrastructure investment priority;
- emphasis on commercialisation of research and support for start-ups;
- All Island Policy: Science Foundation Ireland funding may be granted to Northern Irish and other European Research Area based researchers;
- special focus on the games industry, as a particular strength of Ireland;
- public innovation support by enforced introduction of e-government measures and the use of cloud computing by government agencies;
- full commitment to the EU Innovation Union initiative (further elaborated in: Department of Jobs, Enterprise and Innovation 2013).

One of the major enhancements of the new government's strategy is the 'Agenda 2020' published in 2012 by the Science Foundation Ireland (SFI 2012). With its four objectives:

- to become the best science funding agency in the world;
- to be the exemplar in building partnerships between academia, business, philanthropy, and government;
- to have the most engaged and scientifically informed public;
- to present the ideal modern public service organization.

The strategy is set to make Ireland "the best country in the world for scientific research excellence and impact" (p. 2, SFI 2012).

Challenges and outlook

In a report on the innovation performance of Ireland (Forfás 2011), Forfás noted that Ireland has a high proportion of companies engaged in R&D and a high level of R&D expenditure. However, one of the main goals of the Strategy for Science, Technology and Innovation (to foster the collaboration between large multinational companies and small domestic firms) has not yet been reached. The main challenges, according to Forfás, are the ongoing economic and financial crisis, affecting the cost and availability of funding as well as the availability of a good ICT infrastructure. Additional problems may arise if the Irish corporation tax, which undisputedly presents a major factor for attracting multinational companies to Ireland, is challenged further by other EU member states. In 2013, the OECD (Haugh 2013) published a report on Ireland's efforts to generate growth from knowledge-based industries. Positive aspects in the report were

- the existence of sound conditions and conditions helpful to foreign direct investment;
- good infrastructure and universities;
- progress in building up scientific capabilities.

Restating the criticism of Forfás stated above (Forfás 2011), the report lists the following shortcomings of the Irish innovation policy:

- weak innovation capacity compared to other advanced OECD countries;
- need for a simpler and more effective innovation strategy with a reduction in agencies involved in innovation funding;
- lack of spillovers from multinational high-tech companies to domestic SMEs;
- improvement needed in other framework conditions such as access to non-bank finance, the insolvency regime, intellectual property rights, and broadband network.

Concluding remarks

Examining the different agendas for innovation, it is apparent that all nations reviewed as well as Europe as a whole are affected more or less severely by the economic downturn and the on-going financial crisis. While Germany managed to return to economic growth rather quickly while keeping unemployment under control, Ireland and the UK seem to have returned to growth recently, and southern Europe remains in recession, suffering from very high unemployment rates. All nations consider investing in R&D and fostering innovation as one of the most important instruments for returning to economic growth and maintaining prosperity.

Each country has set specific priorities, tackling the respective countries' most important problems. In many cases, this problem solving is combined with the attempt to capitalise further on already existing strengths. Italy, for example, explicitly supports innovations for investigating and preserving its cultural heritage; the UK emphasises its strength in the creative sector. With respect to the following chapters in this book, Ireland is of special interest. The country has managed to attract numerous multinational high-tech companies over the last decade. In fact, these companies have created numerous jobs for highly-trained employees, but hopes for an intense collaboration with the indigenous business sector and for spillover effects on both these two business sectors are yet to be fulfilled.

References

Web-sites referred to were all accessed on 4th or 5th February 2015, unless stated otherwise

Blaauboer, Rob. 2013. "Can Europe Really Become an Innovation Union". http://www.innovationmanagement.se/2010/11/11/can-europe-really-become-an-innovation-union/

Bundesministerium für Bildung und Forschung. 2012a. "Ideas. Innovation. Prosperity. High-Tech Strategy 2020 for Germany. http://www.bmbf.de/pub/hts_2020_en.pdf

—. 2012b. "Hightech-Strategie der Bundesregierung." http://www.hightech-strategie.de .

—. 2012c. Bürgerdialoge und Bürgerfoschung fördern - Hightech-Strategie der Bundesregierung. http://www.hightech-strategie.de/de/Buergerdialoge-und-Buergerforschung-foerdern-985.php

—. 2012d. Innovationsallianz "Lithium Ionen Batterie LIB 2015". http://www.bmbf.de/de/11828.php

Bundesministerium für Bildung und Forschung. 2012e. Federal Report on Research and Innovation 2012. Bundesministerium für Bildung und Forschung, Referat Grundsatzfragen der Innovationspolitik. Bonn, Berlin.

—. 2012f. Bundesbericht Forschung und Innovation 2012. http://www.bmbf.de/pub/bufi_2012.pdf

—. 2013. "Forschungscampus: öffentlich-private Partnerschaft für Innovationen." http://www.bmbf.de/de/16944.php

—. 2014. "Die Neue High-Tech Strategie". http://www.hightech-strategie.de

Bundesministerium für Wirtschaft und Technologie. 2013a. "BMWi - Veranstaltungen". http://www.bmwi.de/DE/Service/veranstaltungen,did=330026.html

—. 2013b. "Innovation im öffentlichen Beschaffungswesen."

http://www.bmwi.de/DE/Themen/Technologie/Rahmenbedingungen/innovation-beschaffungswesen.html
—. 2013c. "Rahmenbedingungen für Forschung und Innovation." http://www.bmwi.de/DE/Themen/Technologie/rahmenbedingungen.html
—. 2015 Clusterplattform Deutschland. http://www.clusterplattform.de/CLUSTER/Navigation/EN/Home/home.html
Collaborative Centre for Applied Nanotechnology. 2012. "CCAN - Putting Nanotechnology to work for Ireland's most innovative companies." http://www.ccan.ie
Confederazione Italiana Sindicati Lavoratori. n.d. "Industria 2015." http://www.cisl.it/sito-industria.nsf/b04ea0e73c450056c12576ba0034a30e/e40f5365300bcf65c125773e0033cbe3?OpenDocument
Crowley, Lizzie. 2011. "Streets Ahead - What makes a city innovative? Big Innovation Centre." Report, Lancaster University, The Work Foundation.
Cunningham, Paul, Thordis Sveinsdottir and Abdullah Gok. 2011. Mini Country Report United Kingdom - Thematic Report 2011 under Specific Contract for the Integration of INNO Policy TrendChart with ERAWATCH (2011-2012). Pro Inno Europe.
Department for Business, Innovation and Skills. 2011a. "Innovation and Research Strategy for Growth." https://www.gov.uk/government/uploads/system/uploads/attachment_data/file/32450/11-1387-innovation-and-research-strategy-for-growth.pdf
—. 2011b. "Innovation and Research Strategy for Growth." BIS Economics Paper No. 15.
—. 2011c. "Strategy for UK Life Sciences." https://www.gov.uk/government/uploads/system/uploads/attachment_data/file/32457/11-1429-strategy-for-uk-life-sciences.pdf
Department of Jobs, Enterprise and Innovation. 2013. "Horizon 2020 - EU Framework Programme for Research and Innovation (2014 – 2020) – Ireland's Strategy and Target for Participation." http://www.djei.ie/science/technology/strategypaper.pdf
—. 2014a. "Ireland's Smart Specialisation Strategy for Research and Innovation." http://www.djei.ie/science/technology/RIS3summary2014.pdf
—. 2014b. "National Research Prioritisation Exercise: First Progress Report, June 2014." http://www.djei.ie/publications/science/2014/NRPE_First_Progress_Report.pdf

Department of the Taoiseach. 2008. Building Ireland's Smart Economy. http://www.taoiseach.gov.ie/BuildingIrelandsSmartEconomy_1_.pdf

—. 2011. Innovation Taskforce - Work Completed. Accessed April 24 2013. http://www.taoiseach.gov.ie/eng/Work_Of_The_Department/Economic_and_Social_Policy/Innovation_Taskforce/

Erawatch. n.d. "Erawatch UK Innovation Investment Fund." http://erawatch.jrc.ec.europa.eu/erawatch/opencms/information/country_pages/gb/supportmeasure/support_mig_0038

European Commission. 2010a. "Lisbon strategy - towards a green and innovative economy." http://ec.europa.eu/archives/growthandjobs_2009/

—. 2010b. "Lisbon Strategy evaluation document." http://ec.europa.eu/europe2020/pdf/lisbon_strategy_evaluation_en.pdf

—. 2011. "Key initiatives - action points - Innovation Union." http://ec.europa.eu/research/innovation-union/index_en.cfm?pg=action-points&view=all

—. 2012a. "Commitment fiche - i3S." http://i3s.ec.europa.eu/commitment/43.html

—. 2012b. "European Institute of Innovation and Technology." http://i3s.ec.europa.eu/commitment/13.html

—. 2013a. "Competitiveness and Innovation Framework Programme (CIP)." http://ec.europa.eu/cip/index_en

—. 2013b. "Europe 2020 - Europe's growth strategy." http://ec.europa.eu/europe2020/index_en.htm

—. 2013c. "Innovation Union." http://ec.europa.eu/research/innovation-union/index_en.cfm

—. 2013d. "S3 Platform." http://s3platform.jrc.ec.europa.eu/de

—. 2013e. "ESFRI - Research Infrastructures - Research - European Commission." http://ec.europa.eu/research/infrastructures/index_en.cfm?pg=esfri

—. n.d. "CORDIS : Spain : The agents of the science and technology system." http://cordis.europa.eu/spain/agents_en.html

European Parliament. 2013. "European Parliament will not accept the EU long-term budget unless demands are met." http://www.europarl.europa.eu/news/en/headlines/content/20130313STO06477/html/EP-will-not-accept-the-EU-long-term-budget-unless-demands-are-met

Forfás. 2004. "Building Ireland's Knolwedge Economy - The Irish Action Plan for Promoting Investment in R&D." Report to the Inter-Departmental Committee on Science, Technology and Innovation.

http://www.djei.ie/publications/enterprise/2004/knowledgeeconomy.pdf
—. 2010. "Ireland's Nanotechnology Commercialisation Framework 2010-2014." http://www.forfas.ie/media/forfas310810-nanotech_commercialisation_framework_2010-2014.pdf
—. 2011. "Analysis of Ireland's Innovation Performance." http://www.forfas.ie/media/forfas110323-Analysis_of_Irelands_Innovation_Performance.pdf
—. 2012. "Report of the Research Prioritisation Steering Group." http://www.forfas.ie/publications/featuredpublications/title,8958,en.php
Haugh, David. 2013. "From Bricks to Brains: Increasing the Contribution of Knowledge-based Capital to Growth in Ireland", OECD Economics Department Working Papers, No. 1094, OECD Publishing.
Heijs, Joost. 2011. "Mini Country Report Spain - Thematic Report 2011 under Specific Contract for the Integration of INNO Policy TrendChart with ERAWATCH (2011-2012)." Pro Inno Europe.
HM Treasury. 2014. "Chancellor builds Northern Powerhouse with new funding for science and Atlantic Gateway in Liverpool." https://www.gov.uk/government/news/chancellor-builds-northern-powerhouse-with-new-funding-for-science-and-atlantic-gateway-in-liverpool
Innovationskraftwerk. 2011. "Innovationskraftwerk - Innovation in Deutschland - Land der Ideen." http://www.innovationskraftwerk.de/Plattform
Landesregierung des Landes Sachsen-Anhalt. 2014. "Regionale Innovationsstrategie Sachsen-Anhalt 2014-2020." http://www.mw.sachsen-anhalt.de/fileadmin/Bibliothek/Politik_und_Verwaltung/MW/Publikationen/RIS/Regionale_Innovationsstrategie_2014-2020_final.pdf
Landesregierung des Saarlandes. 2007. "Für alle, die Zukunft gestalten möchten: das Saarland - Innovationsstrategie bis 2015." http://www.saarland.de/31075.htm
Martin, Tom. 2011. "Mini Country Report Ireland - Thematic Report 2011 under Specific Contract for the Integration of INNO Policy TrendChart with ERAWATCH (2011-2012)." Pro Inno Europe.
Minister for Jobs, Enterprise and Innovation. 2012. "Putting public research to work for Ireland - Policies and procedures to help industry make good use of Ireland's public research institutions." http://www.djei.ie/publications/science/2012/Intellectual_Property_Protocol_Putting_Public_Research_to_Work_for_Ireland.pdf
Ministeria de Ciencia y Innovación. 2011. "Spanish innovation strategy." Ministeria de Ciencia y Innovación.

http://www.idi.mineco.gob.es/stfls/MICINN/Innovacion/FICHEROS/Spanish_Innovation_Strategy.pdf

Ministerio de Economía y Competitividad. 2013a. "Estrategia Española de Ciencia y Tecnología y de Innovación 2013-2020." http://www.idi.mineco.gob.es/portal/site/MICINN/menuitem.7eeac5cd345b4f34f09dfd1001432ea0/?vgnextoid=49c1a9d3a268c310VgnVCM1000001d04140aRCRD

—. 2013b. "Estrategia Estatal de Innovación E2I". http://www.idi.mineco.gob.es/portal/site/MICINN/menuitem.7eeac5cd345b4f34f09dfd1001432ea0/?vgnextoid=33a5c10fb468c310VgnVCM1000001d04140aRCRD

—. 2013c. "Mapa de ICTS." http://www.idi.mineco.gob.es/portal/site/MICINN/menuitem.7eeac5cd345b4f34f09dfd1001432ea0/?vgnextoid=2693ce5451f44410VgnVCM1000001d04140aRCRD

—. 2013d. "Plan Estatal de Investigación Científica, Técnica y de Innovación." http://www.idi.mineco.gob.es/stfls/MICINN/Investigacion/FICHEROS/Plan_Estatal_Inves_cientifica_tecnica_innovacion.pdf

—. 2013e. "Organismos Publicos y Entidades Dependientes." http://www.idi.mineco.gob.es/portal/site/MICINN/menuitem.7eeac5cd345b4f34f09dfd1001432ea0/?vgnextoid=2e4a44cb71b72210VgnVCM1000001d04140aRCRD

Ministerio dello Sviluppo Economico. 2012. "Executive summary of the new Italian legislation on startups." http://www.sviluppoeconomico.gov.it/images/stories/documenti/Exective_summary_ENG_FINAL.pdf

Ministero dell'Istruzione, dell'Università e della Ricerca. 2009. "PNR - Programma Nazionale della Ricerca 2011-2013." http://hubmiur.pubblica.istruzione.it/web/ricerca/pnr

—. 2011. "Programma Operativo Nazionale Ricerca e Competitività 2007-2013." http://www.ponrec.it

Mullin, Joe. 2012. "After decades of discussion, EU votes for unified patent system." http://arstechnica.com/tech-policy/2012/12/after-decades-of-discussion-eu-votes-for-unified-patent-system/

OECD. 2014a. "Italy – Economic forecast summary (November 2014)." http://www.oecd.org/eco/outlook/italy-economic-forecast-summary.htm

—. 2014b. "Spain – Economic forecast summary (November 2014)." http://www.oecd.org/eco/outlook/spain-economic-forecast-summary.htm

—. 2014b. "United Kingdom – Economic forecast summary (November

2014)."
http://www.oecd.org/eco/outlook/united-kingdom-economic-forecast-summary.htm
Poeverlein, Lino. 2013. Startupszene als Wirtschaftwunder? http://www.gruenderszene.de/allgemein/startups-rosler
PON – Programma Operativo Nazionale. 2011. "Programma Operativo Nazionale Ricerca e Competitività 2007-2013." http://www.ponrec.it
Potì, Bianca M. and Emmanuela Reale. 2011. "Mini Country Report Italy - Thematic Report 2011 under Specific Contract for the Integration of INNO Policy TrendChart with ERAWATCH (2011-2012)." Pro Inno Europe.
Pro Inno Europe. n.d. "Innovation and Innovation Policy in Italy." http://www.proinno-europe.eu/page/innovation-and-innovation-policy-italy
Quantum Innovation Centre. 2013. "Update on Innovation Policy in the UK."
http://www.quantumcentre.co.uk/update-on-innovation-policy-in-the-uk/
Rammer, Christian. 2011. "Mini Country Report Germany - Thematic Report 2011 under Specific Contract for the Integration of INNO Policy TrendChart with ERAWATCH (2011-2012)." Pro Inno Europe.
Researchitaly. 2013a. "Researchitaly - Italian Research just a klick away." https://www.researchitaly.it/en/understanding/
—. 2013b. "Programma Nazionale della Ricerca 2011- 2013." https://www.researchitaly.it/uploads/30/3b_Azioni_PNR.pdf
—. 2013c. "Research Italy - Special Programmes." https://www.researchitaly.it/en/researching/funding/programmes/special-programmes/
SFI – Science Foundation Ireland. 2012. "Agenda 2020." http://www.sfi.ie/assets/files/downloads/News%20and%20Events/AGENDA%202020.pdf
Technology Strategy Board. 2012. "HVM Catapult." https://hvm.catapult.org.uk
—. 2013a. Technology Strategy Board - Competitions - Biomedical Catalyst. https://interact.innovateuk.org/competition-display-page/-/asset_publisher/RqEt2AKmEBhi/content/biomedical-catalyst-feasibility-studies
—. 2013b. _connect Home - Open Innovation. https://connect.innovateuk.org
The Federal Chancelor. 2012. "Zukunftsdialog - About the Future Dialogue."
https://www.dialog-ueber-deutschland.de/EN/10-Dialog/_node.html
The Government of the United Kingdom. 2011. "Accelerating adoption of

innovation in the NHS." https://www.gov.uk/government/news/accelerating-adoption-of-innovation-in-the-nhs

The Innovation Taskforce. 2010. "Building Ireland's Smart Economy - A Framework for Sustainable Economic Renewal - Progress Report." http://www.taoiseach.gov.ie/BuildingIrelandsSmartEconomy_1_.pdf

The Irish Government. 2006. Strategy for Science, Technology and Innovation 2006-2013. http://www.djei.ie/publications/science/2006/sciencestrategy.pdf

—. 2011. "Programme for Government 2011 - 2016." http://www.taoiseach.gov.ie/eng/Work_Of_The_Department/Programme_for_Government/Programme_for_Government_2011-2016.pdf

Wilson, Tim. 2012. "A Review of Business–University Collaboration." https://www.gov.uk/government/uploads/system/uploads/attachment_data/file/32383/12-610-wilson-review-business-university-collaboration.pdf

CHAPTER TWO

SMART SPECIALISATION AND UNIVERSITIES: CHALLENGES AND OPPORTUNITIES IN THE 2014-2020 PROGRAMMING PERIOD

FRIGYES HAUSZ, VIRÁG ZSÁR
AND BÉLA KARDON

1. Introduction

The term Smart Specialisation got into the spotlight with the announcement in 2010 of the EU 2020 Strategy, the growth strategy of the European Union. When somewhat later Smart Specialisation Strategies – or more widely known as Research and Innovation Strategies for Smart Specialisation (RIS3) – had been proposed as an ex-ante conditionality for EU Structural Fund Programmes focussing on research and innovation in the programming period 2014-2020, the RIS3 concept became one of the most fashionable buzzwords of European Policy making. With this initiative, the concentration of public resources in knowledge investments on particular activities in order to strengthen comparative advantage in existing or new areas is no longer considered just as an option, but as a cornerstone of European research and innovation (R&I) policy.

The concept behind the term is – at least in its present form – relatively new[1]: the theoretical construct was first described by Dominique Foray and Van Ark in 2007, in a policy brief prepared for the Knowledge for Growth Expert Group (Foray and Van Ark, 2007 cited by Kempton et al.

---

[1] Although it was pointed out in earlier research (Charles et al., 2012, p. 5) that Smart Specialisation Strategies are quite similar to regional innovation strategies, there is an enhanced emphasis on the diversification of regions on the basis of existing strengths, and their cluster policy is more accentuated.

2013), an independent advisory group to Janez Potočnik, European Commissioner for Research.

The logic of the policy initiative that is now promoted by the Joint Research Centre of the European Union is simple: using a bottom-up approach, European regions are expected to identify their strengths and to constrain their R&I development plans to a limited number of streamlined directions. This concentration of development efforts is expected to foster economic growth and to promote innovation. The core principle of the RIS3 concept is the Entrepreneurial Discovery Process (EDP), which denotes a continuous trial and error process towards finding the strengths and specialisations of a given region. Although early versions of the RIS3 concept discussed R&I activity as a whole, the present policy briefs focus on the broad interpretation of innovation (business innovation, technological innovation, social innovation) and the role of enterprises (Iacobucci, 2012, 4). The current methodology presented by the Joint Research Centre (JRC) accentuates that prioritisation. It involves an interactive process, in which the private sector is discovering and producing information about new activities, and the government empowers actors that are most capable of realising potential.[2]

Although in Western European countries it is obvious that national R&I performance is greatly dependent on the performance of the entrepreneurial sphere, it will be demonstrated later that this is not entirely the case in Hungary, where in some regions R&I activity is solely represented by higher education institutions (HEIs) and SMEs cannot act as strategic enabler entities. This characteristic is presumably common in some regions in the countries of the former Eastern bloc. Although the role of universities is also strongly emphasised in RIS3 methodology[3], the possible development paths as to how higher education institutions could become engines of regional growth are not as meticulously described as the paths to SME-induced growth, and this is especially true in regions that are considered the poorest NUTS 2[4] regions of the EU. Moreover, it

[2] C.f.: http://s3platform.jrc.ec.europa.eu/documents/10157/63241/Foray_130124

[3] To mention but one: Kempton, Louise, John Goddard, John Edwards, Fatime Barbara Hegyi, and Susana Elena-Pérez. "Universities and Smart Specialisation." (2013)

[4]Nomenclature of Units for Territorial Statistics (NUTS) is a geocode standard for referencing the subdivisions of countries for statistical purposes. While NUTS 1 generally denotes major socio-economic regions such as countries, NUTS 2 usually means basic regions for the application of regional policies.

must be added that the relationship between policy objectives and the possible policy instruments is not entirely explored; and neither is the role of the stakeholders in the implementation of smart specialisation strategies (Navarro et al. 2011, 10).

The general aim of this chapter is to give a short overview of the RIS3 concept, exploring the issues that are related to the alignment of higher education development and science policy with Smart Specialisation, focusing on the role of the government. The intent here is not to give a detailed analysis of any of the specific tenets of the RIS3 concept, but to formulate – on the basis of earlier research and lessons learnt – a set of recommendations for governmental initiatives to support implementing smart specialisation.

By providing a case study of Hungary, the specific aim of this chapter is to propose answers to the following questions:

- How could higher education institutions play a pivotal role in implementing the smart specialisation concept?
- What are the crucial governmental measures to be taken to maximise the economic multiplier effect of higher education institutions?

In our view, in some cases higher education institutions should be considered not as mere facilitators of the RIS3 process, but rather as sole enablers in the R&I weak regions. In the poorest regions of the EU and Hungary, the lack of SMEs active in R&I renders the Entrepreneurial Discovery Process unachievable – R&I activity is represented by higher education institutions instead of in R&I-inactive enterprises. In such regions the RIS3 concept remains dysfunctional until higher education institutions exert their spill-over effect to the regional economy.

To answer the somewhat diffuse research questions listed above, this chapter will first explore the most important theoretical cornerstones of the RIS3 concept, with a special emphasis on the role of higher education institutions. Then a short overview of the Hungarian R&I system will follow, elucidating the possible misalignments of the general RIS3 concept and the special situation of R&I-weak poor regions. The discussion will continue with the positioning of higher education in the context of regional development, focussing on underdeveloped regions. Then we will move on to enumerate existing and proposed governmental measures to maximise the economic multiplier effect of higher education institutions. The paper will conclude with the formulation of recommendations concerning possible measures to extend the role of higher education in the smart specialisation process.

As the aim is not to provide a meticulous scientific analysis of the feasibility of RIS3 in Hungary, rather to provide additional information to support the implementation of the strategy, the use of scientific literature will not be exceedingly rigorous: theoretical ruminations on the economic foundations of the RIS3 concept will not be touched upon. The policy briefs on smart specialisation and works discussing the possible outcomes of RIS3 were consulted either on the homepage of the Smart Specialisation Platform[5] (http://s3platform.jrc.ec.europa.eu/home) or the homepage of the European Parliamentary Research Service (http://epthinktank.eu/2013/08/14/smart-specialisation/).

2. Theoretical Foundations of RIS3

The successful implementation of Smart Specialisation Strategies is expected to bring about an invigorated technological, economic, and social development of EU regions, and as a result to usher in the establishment of a unified European Research Area. A close look at the RIS3 concept reveals the main tenets of its working mechanism, which could be described as:

1. By focusing the use of resources and by avoiding spreading knowledge investments [including higher education, vocational training, public and private R&I spending, etc. (Iacobucci, 2012)], regional and national development policy becomes streamlined, and only those paths that are certain to contribute to the development of a region will be financially supported. By identifying specialisations, the profiles of European regions will be more recognisable, offering more opportunity for interregional cooperation.

---

[5] The Smart Specialisation Platform is an administrative unit, part of the European Commission's Joint Research Centre. The S3 Platform assists EU countries and regions to develop, implement and review their Research and Innovation Strategies for Smart Specialisation (RIS3). The aim of the S3 Platform is to provide information, methodologies, expertise and advice to national and regional policy makers, as well as promote mutual learning, trans-national co-operation and contribute to academic debates around the concept of smart specialisation.

2. By obliging countries to constrain the number of R&I development directions (by establishing RIS3 as an ex-ante conditionality for the use of Structural Funds for R&I ends in the 2014-2020 programming period) European Cohesion Policy becomes more transparent, enabling European Directorates General to monitor regional development more precisely.
3. The involvement of all the stakeholders in the drafting of RIS3, the selective strength of the regional market (EDP), and the simultaneous bottom-up (regional players) and top-down (governmental will) activity could guarantee a development strategy built upon an evidence-based choice of specialisations.

These working mechanisms of RIS3 are – as was pointed out by earlier works – generally based on two theoretical assumptions:

1. Achieving a critical mass of resources is crucial to maximise R&I performance and the productivity of its application.
2. Even if the RIS3 methodology enumerates more than options to identify strengths, it must be seen that regional specialisation is path-dependent; diversification of strengths could only be successful if development paths are related to the existing knowledge base. Therefore traditional R&I areas and currently emerging areas could be considered successful. (Asheim et al., 2011; Neffke et al., 2011 cited by Iacobucci, 2012)

Connected to the latter statement, as it was already pointed out in the introduction, the proposers of the Smart Specialisation concept based their theory on the requirement that the search for specialisations is not a bureaucratic process or an exercise of foresight ordered from a consulting firm. The main idea is the entrepreneurial process, in which the new knowledge produced relates to the already existing specialisations of the region (Foray, 2009). The role of the government therefore in the drafting and implementation of smart specialisation is not an authoritative one; RIS3 methodology sees governance rather as a facilitator of the specialisation process whose main tasks comprise: (1) ensuring incentives to encourage the entrepreneurial sphere that is involved in the discovery of specialisations; (2) the assessment of the value of identified specialisations; (3) identification and support of investments complementary to specialisations; (4) the termination of investments that turn out to be inappropriate (Foray, 2009).

Based on what was mentioned above, it is clear that the RIS3 concept presupposes the existence of an entrepreneurial sphere that is at least somewhat R&I intensive. Browsing the best-practice database of the Smart Specialisation Platform, one could find a great number of best practices describing the strategies of successful regions. Case studies, however, that focus on the poorest regions of the EU and their future potential are missing, and so are the policy instruments that could address the issue of these regions.

Based on GDP per capita data, four Hungarian NUTS 2 regions (Northern Hungary [9th], Northern Great Plain [11th], Southern Great Plain [12th] and Southern Transdanubia [16th] are among the poorest regions of the European Union.[6] These regions sometimes lack the R&I-active entrepreneurial sphere on which the RIS3 concept is built upon. As we will see, in these regions R&I activity is almost exclusively dependent on state-subsidised research units, mainly at higher education institutions. ***In these regions the R&I-neutral entrepreneurial sphere cannot set the paths for development; the emphasis must be placed upon higher education institutions and improvement of their economic multiplier effect; therefore governmental intervention and direction setting is necessary.***[7]

As we have covered the theoretical considerations of the RIS3 concept, we can move on to discussing the Hungarian R&I sphere.

3. R&I Structure in Hungary

Despite being one of Central East Europe's more successful competitors in the 7th Framework Programme for Research and Technological Development, the system of Hungarian R&I shows a fragmented picture from various viewpoints.

First, **the R&I performance of regions is extremely polarised** from more than one perspective. The geographical distribution of research units is highly uneven: 50% of Hungarian research units are situated in the most developed central region, especially in the capital Budapest (see Figure 2.1). The distribution of R&I units among the remaining regions is also remarkable: the second and third regions with the largest number of

[6] C.f.: http://ee24.com/digest/Report_2011.pdf

[7] The idea of granting governance more than a facilitative role has already been explored in Navarro et al. 2011.

research units are the largest university centres of the country. The R&I spending of NUTS 2 regions in Hungary shows an even greater asymmetry: 66% of national spending was concentrated in the Central-Hungarian Region in 2012 (see Figure 2.2.).

Figure 2.1

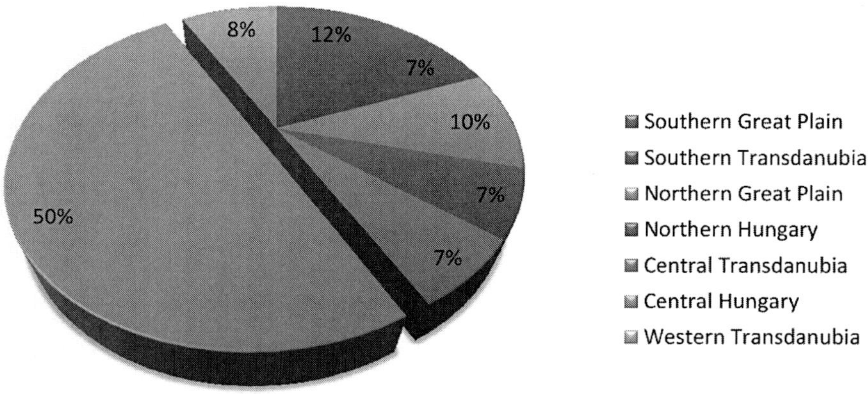

Figure 2.2

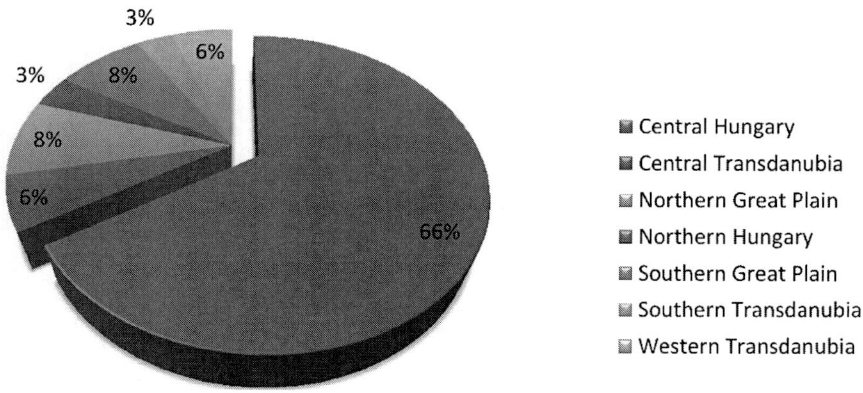

Speaking of the polarised nature of Hungarian R&I, another inherent characteristic feature must be touched upon, namely the sectorial distribution of research units. Figure 2.3 demonstrates the distribution of research units among enterprises (green), higher education institutions (red), and other state-subsidised research units, e.g. the Hungarian Academy of Sciences (blue). It can be seen that in a number of regions higher education institutions dominate the R&I scene (see Figure 2.3); the three most underdeveloped regions in Hungary - Northern Hungary, Northern Great Plain, Southern Great Plain - are largely characterised by their higher education institutions; they have two large universitas type institutions[8] with full training portfolios in Northern Great Plain and Southern Great Plain, and three smaller institutions with somewhat diffuse profiles in Northern Hungary.[9]

Figure 2.3

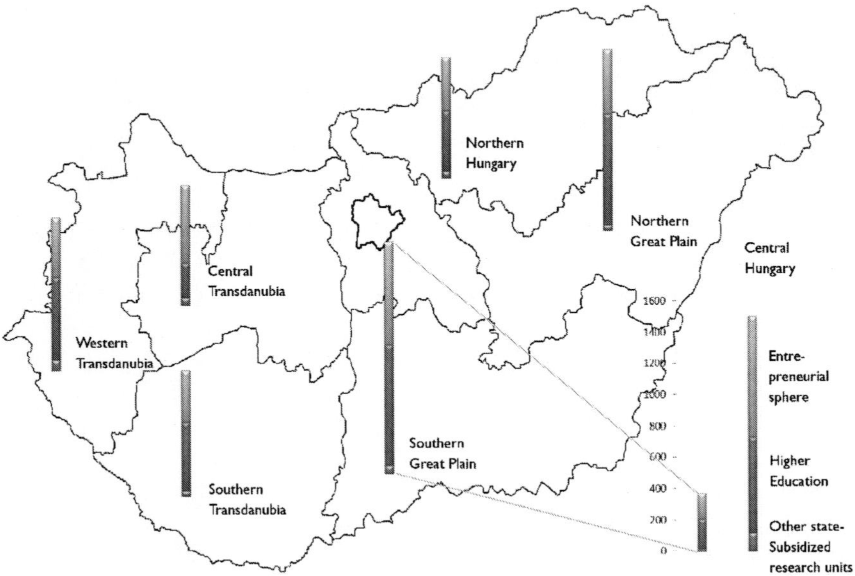

[8] The University of Szeged (Southern Great Plain), and the University of Debrecen (Northern Great Plain) are large Humboldtian institutions with full training portfolios, showing outstanding performance in medicine and natural sciences.

[9] The University of Miskolc that has a strong heavy industry focus, the Eszterházy Károly College in Eger that has one of the country's important teacher training centres, and the Károly Róbert College in Gyöngyös.

The extreme disparity between Central Hungary and the rest of the country has important implications for governmental development policy: as **Central Hungary** in the 2014-2020 programming period belongs to the most developed regions of the EU, it is now ineligible for Cohesion Policy funding. The task of supporting R&I investments in the region with the strongest technological and economic potential is now entirely a problem to be addressed by the national budget.

A glimpse at the entrepreneurial landscape of Hungary also provides some insights into the composition of its R&I system: the data of the Hungarian Central Statistical Office (HSCO) on the net income of SMEs active in the *Professional, scientific and technical activities* area (the category that best resembles R&I-active innovative SMEs[10]) reveals extreme differences between regions. The following table (Table 2.1) shows (1) the relevant income data of Hungarian NUTS 2 regions and (2) the percentage of regional income in the *Professional, scientific and technical activities* area compared to the total national income in the area, and (3) the percentage of regional income in the mentioned *Professional, scientific and technical activities* area compared to the regional income in all economic activities:

[10] The Hungarian classification closely follows the International Standard Industrial Classification of All Economic Activities, Rev.4 system (http://unstats.un.org/unsd/cr/registry/regcst.asp?Cl=27). It is important to mention that the category *Professional, scientific and technical activities* might not be the only one to denote innovative SMEs, (a good counterexample is the *information and communication activities* category), but for the sake of simplicity we chose the most pure category signifying almost surely an innovative SME.

Table 2.1

Activity	Central Hungary	Central Transdanubia	Western Transdanubia	Southern Transdanubia	Northern Hungary	Northern Great Plain	Southern Great Plain	Total
Professional, scientific and technical activities (Billion HUF)	1,874	127	111	99	65	106	117	2,499
All Activities (Billion HUF)	25,318	3,334	3,108	2,250	2,517	3,713	3,810	44,049
Proportion of regional income in the Professional, scientific and technical activities area compared to the national total income in the area	74.99%	5.08%	4.44%	3.96%	2.6%	4.24%	4.68%	100%
Proportion of regional income in the Professional, scientific and technical activities area compared to the national total income in all areas (%)	4.25%	0.29%	0.25%	0.22%	0.15%	0.24%	0.27%	100%

The relatively low income of R&I-intensive SMEs in the poorest regions could hint at their irrelevancy, even at a regional level. The entrepreneurial discovery process in such an environment would not be effective enough as there are not enough players submitted to market selection.

Having seen the extreme disparities in the Hungarian R&I system and the relative weakness of the R&I-active entrepreneurial sphere in certain regions, the question can be formulated:

What are the possible development paths for these underdeveloped regions with the underdeveloped entrepreneurial sphere?

The answer is relatively simple: as higher education coverage of Hungarian regions is relatively good, and higher education institutions are always considered as centres of knowledge, ***specialisations could be adjusted to the strengths of higher education institutions.*** Where the selective power of the market cannot drive the entrepreneurial discovery process, the true aim is ***to improve the economic multiplier effect of institutions and to increase the knowledge spill-over effect of academia***. If the aim is the improvement of higher education to invigorate the regional economy, the most important issues to consider in the light of the smart specialisation concept are the following:

- To maximise the support of development, synergies funds must be established;
- As governmental intervention in these regions is stronger, national development goals must be aligned with international development aims;
- The selection of specialisations induced by higher education must be based on evidence (real strengths must be selected) and special emphasis must be laid upon the relationship between industry and higher education.

In the following pages, we will try to explore these issues touching upon possible governmental initiatives.

4. Governance and higher education in the light of RIS3

Before doing so, some important features of the economic impact of public research and higher education institutions, including references to the Hungarian state-of-the-art, will be highlighted. Public research, i.e.

research primarily funded with public money and carried out by public research institutions (PRIs) and research universities, plays an extremely important role in innovation systems by ensuring the provision of new knowledge (OECD 2012, 177). What is more, universities have a potentially pivotal role to play in the social and economic development of their regions (JRC 2013, 2). At this point it is worth taking into consideration the example of the relationship between Silicon Valley and Stanford University; namely, on the one hand, that governmental support is of utmost importance in research funding (around 80 % of total funding of the University) rather than revenues from the industry; on the other hand, the most important contribution of Stanford in generating an outstanding percentage of innovations in Silicon Valley is the skilled labour force rather than the technology transferred (Clement 2013).

Consequently, among the three main activities of universities, namely education, research and the third mission, which aims to answer the societal challenges of the 21st century, even if education can be operated on business principles, higher education institutions should be supported to conduct excellent research and achieve their third mission through basic and/or applied research, letting alone research belonging to national interests.

Despite the crisis, governmental spending on R&D has increased since 2008 in many OECD countries (Austria, Germany, Poland, Czech Republic, etc.); but this is not the case in Hungary, where investment in R&D by the government is modest and is stagnating.[1]

One can argue in favour of more funding for higher education research if its benefits are proven. According to the recommendations for the implementation and monitoring of Hungary's Science Policy Strategy (HETFA 2013), the effects of higher education can be measured by the following aspects: (1) emission of skilled workforce, i.e. number of graduates, ratio of graduated people employed by STI sphere, value of degree, etc., (2) scientific excellence, i.e. volume and quality of publications and patents, scientific cooperation, (3) cooperation with industry, i.e. Intellectual Property Rights (IPR), knowledge transfer, boosting innovation, as well as (4) macroeconomic effects such as innovation capacity of the national economy, productivity, etc.

[1] See OEDC STI country profile on Hungary:
http://www.oecd.org/sti/outlook/e-outlook/sticountryprofiles/hungary.htm

Consequently, measurement of the economic effect of higher education institutions and research conducted intramurally requires a many-folded approach. Out of the aspects listed above, the example of Silicon Valley and Stanford highlights that it is important to examine at least the ratio of skilled people and their work status following their studies, as well as innovation-related indicators. Though many of these indicators are not measured yet, some examples can provide an overview of the state-of-the-art in Hungary. According to the OECD country profile, Hungary's skills levels and human resource indicators are low. The ratio of young people (aged 20-29) who attained tertiary education is below the EU average (3.3 % in Hungary compared to 4.3% in EU28). Additionally, the ratio of young people (aged 25-34) who completed PhD studies is also below the EU average (0.04% in Hungary; 0.1 % in EU27). Compared to this, employment rates of young people (20-34) who have completed tertiary grade are almost around the EU average (74% for Hungary, 74.3% for EU28)[2]. Innovation-related indicators describing the performance of the higher education system are far below the EU average: i.e. the ratio of companies introducing innovative products or services (44% in Hungary compared to 82% of EU average); SMEs introducing innovative products or services (16.8% in Hungary compared to 38.4 % of EU average) (Innobarometer 2009).

Though this is not an exclusive list of indicators of higher education, nevertheless all of them suggest that there is room (and also economic need) for improvements in the sector. The study, however, does not aim to suggest that governmental support alone can solve the problems; rather its goal is to introduce those measures which can multiply governmental funding. Therefore it is important to examine other possible funding sources, since research and innovation activities are supported at EU level also.

Possible ways of synergy tracking

The relevance of the topic is considered not only important but also timely. The need for exploitation of synergies for research and innovation support is not recent; however it only became an explicit need and part of the EU legislation during the planning and finalisation of the funding instruments of the 2014-2020 Multiannual Financial Frame in order to achieve greater impact.

---

[2] EUROSTAT statistics

To build on synergies, national governments have to

(1) align their priorities to these frameworks (top-down approach);
(2) ensure that the exploitation of EU funds by research entities is maximised (bottom-up approach);
(3) identify real strengths of higher education institutions and improve knowledge-triangle-type cooperations between higher education and the industry.

The first and second recommendation regards the exploitation of national and EU funding, whereas the third point focuses on the sustainability of HEI research.

(1) Align national priorities to EU programmes relating to R&I

This top-down approach requires that during the planning of the European Structural and Investment Funds (ESIF) programmes, Member States (MSs) shall pay attention not only to the entrepreneurial discovery process executed in the frame of smart specialisation strategies but also to the priorities of other EU instruments, such as Horizon 2020, Erasmus +, European Transnational Cooperation Programmes, Creative Europe, Connecting Europe Facility, etc. This means that unnecessary overlaps among supported actions shall be avoided, whereas instruments shall be harmonised and made mutually amplifying (EC 2014). ***Operational programmes (OPs) elaborated at national level for the use of ESIF funds are advised therefore to be oriented to EU programmes in terms of content and selection, but also in cost models.***

Possible ways of harmonising the **content** of relevant EU and national programmes can be briefly summarised as follows:

- **Horizon 2020** (H2020) aims to support frontier research, collaborative research projects, and mobility of excellent researchers within and beyond the EU. It focuses mainly on piloting various research and innovation schemes which may later be applied in projects financed by ESIF. H2020 is open to excellent researchers and research groups who aim to conduct research of European interest. **ESIF** therefore shall support the establishment of R&I infrastructure and equipment on the one hand; on the other hand it shall also support the improvement of skills and of human capital, training, and business advisory

activities with the overarching goal of enhancing cohesion among regions of the EU at different development stages, as well as providing the necessary basic conditions for researchers to take part in H2020. Additionally, knowledge transfer and business innovation are also in ESIF's focus; provided that these developments are in line with the regional smart specialisation strategy.
- **COSME** is the new programme for the Competitiveness of Enterprises and Small and Medium-sized Enterprises. It focuses on funding projects strengthening the competitiveness and sustainability of the Union's enterprises, particularly SMEs, and encouraging, entrepreneurial culture and promoting the creation and growth of SMEs. Complementarily, **ESIF** largely aims to improve R&I capacities and R&I eco-systems with the objective of regional growth and place-based economic transformation towards higher added value and more knowledge-intensive activities.
- **ERASMUS +** aims to improve education and skills, modernise education and training systems and foster cross-sector cooperation. In such actions, **ESIF** funds can be used to improve education and training systems, as well as R&I capacities and R&I ecosystems on a regional basis.
- **Connecting Europe Facility** aims to facilitate the interoperability of public IT services and applications at transnational level. Parts of Digital Services Infrastructure (DSI) are composed of EU and national components. **ESIF** funded services could be set up complementarily or build on existing DSI to save costs, reduce time-to-market and increase interoperability.

The harmonisation of different programmes suggests applying **cost models** of EU programmes in the financial management and reporting procedures of national programmes. Since important simplification efforts took place at EU level, managing authorities at national level could take over the transparent and well-functioning cost models of EU programmes with which many applicants are already familiar or must be familiar if they apply for EU funds. Even so, the work of auditors could be eased in this way, especially if it comes to projects supported from more than one programme.

Additionally, the **support for failed H2020/COSME projects** (meeting the necessary criteria but not receiving funds) is also encouraged in the frame of ESIF. This would mean that projects both of national and European interest would be funded by ESIF. However, this means that national OPs shall be opened up for transnational cooperation in line with S3 strategies – which became possible in the 2014-2020 multiannual framework period.[3]

The problem is evidently the fact that the guide on enabling synergies among ESIF, H2020, and other R&I related programmes was being issued when regional or national smart specialisation strategies elaborating regional strengths and weaknesses, as well as Partnership Agreements highlighting the national priorities and Operational Programmes gathering various interventions, were drafted and finalised. National authorities not familiar with the functioning of EU programmes lack the time and experience to align and fine-tune both the goals and the other schemes (cost models, transnational coverage, etc.) in national programmes. Apart from major infrastructure projects, such considerations were hardly taken into account. For instance, in the case of Hungary only the Human Resource Development OP and the Integrated Transport Development OP refer to the possibility of transnational actions. Therefore it is the task of the upcoming period to do the harmonisation in the process of doing. As a result, ***there is a need for ongoing, better and more strategic coordination of funding programmes at national and EU levels***.

(2) Maximise the exploitation of EU funds

According to the general approach of European research and innovation policy, there are a number of requirements to be met by potential applicants for EU grants. Among others, these include scientific and technological excellence, quality and efficiency regarding the implementation and management of proposed projects, potential impact through development, publication, and use of project results, possession of adequate infrastructure, etc.

---

[3] See Art. 96(3)d of ESF regulation (Regulation (EU) N°1304/2013 of the European Parliament (EP) and of the Council of 17/12/2013- OJ L 347/470 of 20.12.2013) allowing that up to 3% of the budget of a European Social Fund (ESF) operational programme or ESF part of a multi-fund OP may be allocated to operations located outside the programme area, provided that it concerns the thematic objective 'promoting sustainable and quality employment and supporting labor mobility' or 'investing in education, training and vocational training for skills and life-long learning', and provided that the relevant monitoring committee has given its agreement to the operation or types of operations concerned.

In addition, to meet these criteria, there are a number of factors which influence the level of participation of research entities of a country. First, there are socio-economic factors, such as personnel and monetary capacities of the country, management skills of researchers and their excellence. Second, peculiarities of the national RTDI systems are also significant, i.e. the efficiency of converting research results into marketable products or the existence and the implementation of an R&I strategy.

Based on analysis of the participation of Central East European countries in the research and development Framework Programmes, which are financed by the EU, the following general statements can be concluded:

- The more resources a country spends on R&I, the more successful its participation in the Framework Programme (FP);
- The more national funding programmes are available as part of GERD[4], the easier researchers and developers can access it;
- The more familiar a country's institutions are with the FPs, measured by the average number of projects participating in them per institution and country, the higher the number of applications;
- The capabilities to apply for or acquire FP projects increases with the number of projects participated in and thereby enriching the knowledge and experience of the participants (Rauch and Sommer 2012).

With regard to the participation of Hungarian HEIs in FP7, it can be stated that there are only a few entities (12 out of 79) which were successful in participating in projects granted (Budapest University of Technology and Economics, Central European University, University of Debrecen, etc.); they take part in the majority (63%) of projects (254 out of 406) in which Hungarian HEIs are involved. The budget received by these HEIs amounts to €54,631 k, which is 77% of grants received by all HEIs in FP7. Their success rate varies between 7.7% and 66.7% with an average of 21.3%, which exceeds the average success rate of all kinds of Hungarian applicant entities (20.6%).[5] These statistics suggest that generally, major universities have the human and infrastructural capacities, similar to the international network to continuously take part in project preparation. Project preparation requires an important investment of resources, which is generally recovered in one case out of five.

---

[4] Gross domestic expenditure on R & D

[5] Data gathered from e-CORDA database.

Figure 2.4

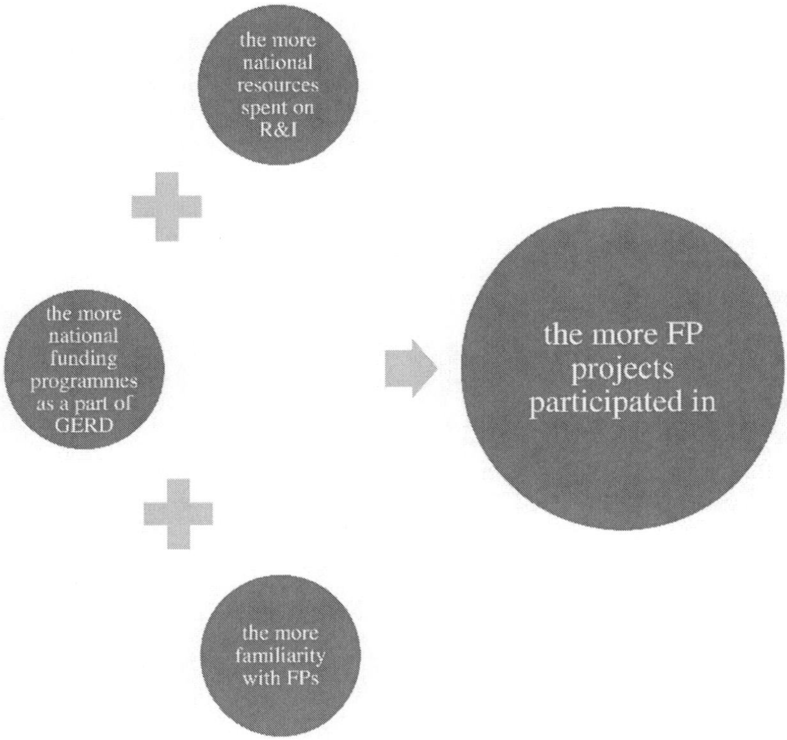

Consequently, this bottom-up approach suggests that it is not enough to harmonise the programmes at EU and national levels; it is also of utmost ***significance to provide support for higher education institutions to meet the criteria of FP participation and improve their participation rate. These resources may come either from the national budget or from ESIF, as is shown in Figure 2.5.***

With regard to recent years, in Hungary there were quite a number of such instruments albeit with limited budgets. Regarding the first case, namely **programmes financed from the national budget,** the former Hungarian Scientific and Research Fund (OTKA), and the Research, Technological and Innovation Fund (KTIA) can be mentioned.

OTKA supported[6] basic research on the criteria of excellence and significance at international level. The activities of KTIA were more diverse; on the one hand, it provided national top-ups of cooperation projects in the frame of BONUS, co-funding for ERA-NETs, EUROSTARS, EUREKA programmes, etc.; on the other hand, it managed European Research Council (ERC) grants at national level, mobility programmes, bilateral S&T cooperation programmes, as well as large-scale international projects.

Figure 2.5

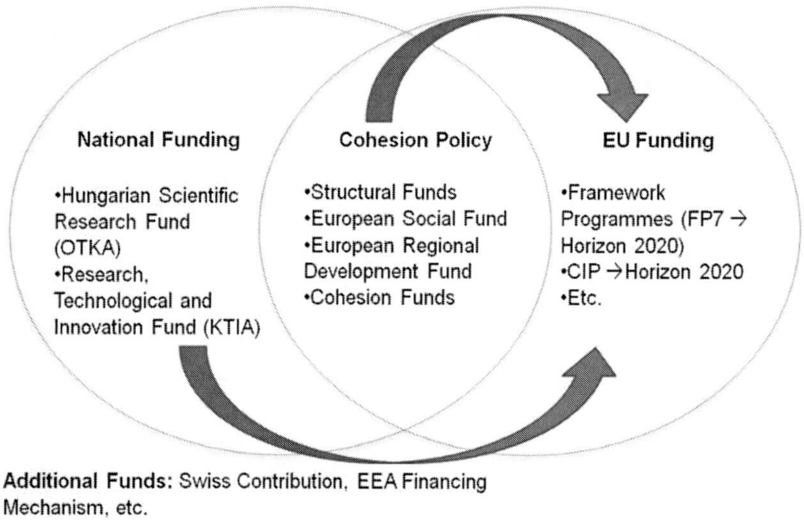

These national instruments were of utmost importance in funding excellent research as well as enabling accession to international grant schemes and preparing the research community for international RTDI culture, standards, and requirements. However they have several disadvantages, such as the lack of long-term strategies, high dependence on decision-makers and personal connections, delays in contracting and administrative burdens, etc.

---

[6] Currently, due to the reorganisation of the Hungarian research and innovation support system, OTKA is being integrated into the National Research, Development and Innovation Office (NKFIH).

Nevertheless, it must be stressed that ***higher education institutes do need these instruments*** in the future especially in three fields: first, ***providing co-funding*** for ERA-NET, EUROSTARS and EUREKA type activities; second, ***facilitating networking of researchers at international level*** (i.e. attendance at scientific conferences, brokerage events, mobility programmes, etc.); third, ***making visible excellent research and its results*** (supporting publications in leading scientific journals, etc.). Harmonising cost models with EU programmes would be an additional benefit for grantees.

With regard to **Cohesion Policy instruments,** a number of good practices in the field of funding higher education research can be mentioned from the previous (2007-2013) financial period. Both the Economic Development OP and Social Infrastructure OP provided resources to establish internationally competitive scientific and innovation capacities. Also, several actions supported the development of a knowledge-based society in the frame of the Social Renewal OP (e.g. supporting basic research in HEIs, ICT research and training, mobility programme for incoming and outgoing students, researchers, etc.).

These programmes were considered ***significant in human capacity building but also in research infrastructure development***. However, researchers had to face several obstacles such as delays in contracting, administrative burdens in financial management and reporting, etc. Participating institutions encountered delays in the delivery of subsidies, securing in-kind contribution, etc.

Other instruments of Cohesion Policy (i.e. European Transnational Cooperation Programmes, Cross-Border Cooperation Programmes, and Instrument for Pre-Accession) had R&I-relevant priorities important for higher education institutions too, facilitating their regional or cross-border networking and pilot activities as well as innovation-oriented activities. Several higher education institutions took part in such projects, reinforcing their transnational networks and contacts with other public entities. Administrative burdens, problems with in-kind contribution, and delays in the delivery of grants hindered their participation in such programmes.

Following this short review of previous instruments, as detailed above**, Cohesion Policy is covering important R&I aspects in the current funding period (between 2014 and 2020) too**. The challenge from the point of view of the bottom-up approach is how HEIs can benefit most from these instruments to maximise their economic impact. To do so, they will need to ***conduct ongoing synergy-tracking activities at project level*** and combine funding scenarios which were enabled among the various EU funds.

Generally the following synergies can be exploited:[7]

- **Horizon 2020**: funding from ESIF can be received either to (1) prepare a project which shall be submitted to H2020, (2) to conduct a parallel project or (3) the same project to amplify impact or (4) a subsequent project. ESIF could also finance projects which are considered excellent but do not receive grants from H2020 due to budgetary limits.
- In the case of **Erasmus +,** ESIF can be used to complement Erasmus + funding for outgoing students/trainees/apprentices at national or regional level by providing additional grants to individuals not in receipt of Erasmus + grants.
- **Connecting Europe Facility**: ESIF can complement CEF investment through national/regional projects linked to CEF platforms.

The above-mentioned synergy-tracking activity necessitates a deep knowledge of the various R&I supporting programmes (including their content, cost models, eligible cost items, etc.), which can hardly be found in HEIs currently. However, in Hungary the lack of research project managers is an important hindrance to successful exploitation of R&I related funds. ***Training for researchers or related staff at universities could be also covered by ESIF.***

However, it is important to note that all project proposals under ESIF have to be in line with the RIS3 of the given region, which significantly limits the opportunities available for HEIs. Then the need for the harmonisation of financial rules must be stressed again to decrease the complexity and the clash of rules in the implementation of a major project granted by various programmes.

[7] COSME and CreativeEurope are not dealt with since they are not available for higher education institutions but only for individuals.

Figure 2.6

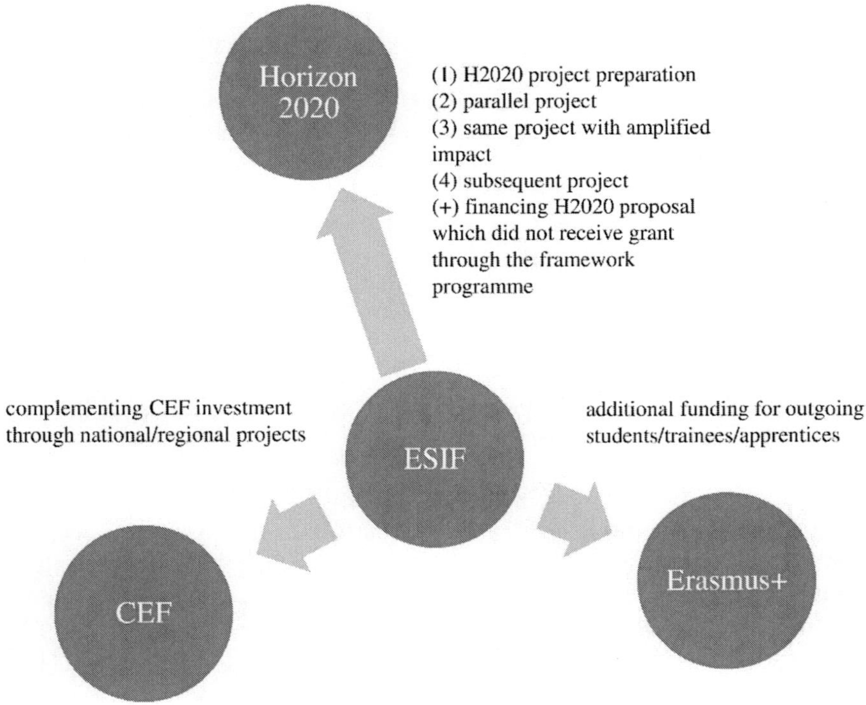

Last but not least it must be admitted that receiving funding only on a project basis has several disadvantages, i.e. it can push HEIs to become project opportunistic and reactive; and it can cause permanent uncertainty for researchers and research centre managers, which does not agree with long-term development of HEI research. Projects generally imply a demanding and burdensome framework of administrative processes and rules that are difficult to navigate and meet, and are often incompatible with the internal systems and processes of universities as well as the requirements of 'traditional' funders of academic research.

Two main aspects derive from this statement: first, ***development actions shall be built up and implemented in a well-structured way***. Second, ***governmental support is needed to bridge the intervals between subsequent projects.***

With regard to the first statement, a complex development approach in HEIs funded by ESIF shall provide support for them to shove off from the project-opportunistic character of HEI research funding. This means that different parts of a research programme such as research infrastructure, the research group, participation at conferences, etc. shall be financed and developed in the frame of an integrated development programme in line with the development strategy of universities instead of multiple projects.

Since ESIF funds are limited and subject to change each funding period, in the long-term ***it is suggested there should be secure government financing to higher education institutions rather than financing only on a project basis***. This approach is also important to finance those needs of HEIs which cannot be financed by EU or other programmes.

(3) Identifying real strengths of higher education institutions and improving knowledge-triangle-type cooperation between higher education and the industry

In a healthy market environment, most successful specialisations emerge automatically, as selection happens on the basis of excellence, cost efficiency, and marketability. In those regions, where competition among research-intensive SMEs is not significant, alternative selection methods must be utilised to define specialisations. As research in such regions is mainly represented by higher education institutions, excellent institutional R&I endeavors with the highest potential market value must be selected. The market value of institutional research activity is easy to determine from the volume of industrial R&D contracts.

As a complementary method, bibliometric tools could be used to identify the research strengths of a given region. Scrutinising the metadata of the largest scientific databases[8] and filtering them on institutional and regional level could show the publication productivity (number of publications) and the publication impact (number of citations) of an institution in the different branches of science. The research performance in some cases can help to delineate the development paths of a region.

It must be noted, however, that high quality research does not always signify marketable research; in order to amplify the economic multiplier effect of higher education institutions, ***governmental initiative must be***

[8] i.e. Web of Science and Scopus

taken to build profitable partnerships between the academic sphere (universities and other state-subsidised research units) and the industrial and entrepreneurial spheres. Although blue skies research is one of the most important tasks of higher education, in poor regions higher education institutions must transform into workhorses of regional development, and must focus on easily marketable applied research and on increased transfer of technology as well as on training tailored to the market needs of the region.

Currently knowledge transfer faces several obstacles in Hungary, which (1) are partly inherent historical obstacles (i.e. lacking central organisation, no intention to share business partners), (2) partly derive from the lack of entrepreneurial attitude (i.e. answering demands from industry is below the dignity of researchers), or (3) partly come from macroeconomic factors such as regulatory framework and market environment (i.e. insufficient funding of technology transfer, no adjustment of imported technology transfer models to national characteristics).

Instead of using ESIF funds to launch industrial parks which are unable to develop once the funding ends, the relationship between universities and business shall be improved on the basis of the regional innovation strategy. In line with the findings of the study prepared by the Joint Research Centre (JRC) on the possible role of HEIs in regional smart specialisation, we can underline the following issues:

- Universities shall seek more of a development role in shaping and supporting regional businesses, institutions, capacities and networks.
- Businesses shall absorb university research to proceed with the implementation of S3 strategies.
- Universities could be engaged more locally by providing training and other kinds of services to regional businesses (JRC 2013).

These activities would not only reinforce the cooperation between HEIs and industry but would also provide a more important role for universities in increasing the outcome of development in the frame of RIS3.

5. Conclusions

To sum up, the aim of the chapter was to provide a short overview of the concept of Regional Innovation Strategies, including the possible alignment of higher education development and science policy. Two major issues were analysed briefly, namely (1) the possible role of HEIs in the implementation of RIS3 and (2) the necessary governmental measures to maximise the economic multiplier effect of education institutions.

Due to the fact that in many of the poorest regions of the European Union higher education institutions represent the only R&I potential instead of the entrepreneurial sphere, HEIs shall take a pivotal role and improve their economic effect in line with the RIS3 strategy. However, to maximise their economic impact, higher education research needs public funding.

During the 2014-2020 funding programmes, the European Union encourages the use of various instruments in boosting R&I. This requires a synergy tracking approach which consists of the following aspects:

(1) Operational programmes elaborated at national level for the use of ESIF funds are advised to be orientated towards EU programmes in terms of content and selection as well as in cost models. This requires ongoing, better, and more strategic coordination of funding programmes at national and EU levels.
(2) Higher education institutions shall be supported to meet the criteria of FP participation and improve their participation rate. Their successful participation requires the following activities: co-type activities; networking of researchers at international level; making visible excellent research and its results; and developing high quality infrastructure. Resources may come either from national budgets or from ESIF.
(3) Since higher education institutions are incited to exploit various funding sources in order to conduct their research, they are supposed to manage synergy tracking activities, which require skilled project manager staff. Training for this staff should also be supported by ESIF.
(4) To shove off from project opportunism and secure a stable environment for HEI research, development actions in the higher education sector shall be built up and implemented in a well-structured way. Governmental support is needed to bridge the intervals between successive projects.
(5) Governmental initiatives must be taken to build profitable partnerships between the academic sphere (universities and other state subsidised research units), industry, and the entrepreneurial sphere.

References

Asheim, B. T., Ron Boschma and Phil Cooke. 2011. "Constructing Regional Advantage: Platform Policies Based on Related Variety and Differentiated Knowledge Bases". Regional Studies 45, 893–904.

Charles, David, Frederike Gross and John Bachtler. 2012 "Smart specialisation and cohesion policy – a strategy for all regions?". IQ-Net Thematic Paper No. 30(2), Tampere.

Clement, J-L. 2013. EU-Ukraine STI Cooperation – Paving the way for Joint activities. Enhancing Bilateral Cooperation? Presentation held on 21 May 2013, Kiev, Ukraine. http://bilat-ukr.eu/_media/Annex_9_J_L_Clement_France.pdf

European Commission (EC). 2014. Enabling synergies between European Structural and Investment Funds, Horizon 2020 and other research, innovation and competitiveness-related Union programmes - Guidance for policy-makers and implementing bodies. Luxemburg: European Commission

Foray, Dominique. "Understanding smart specialisation." The Question of R&D Specialisation, JRC, European Commission, Directorate General for Research, Brussels (2009): 19-28.

HETFA. 2013. Stratégiai irányok meghatározása, javaslat a tudománypolitikai stratégiára. Kutatási zárójelentés. Budapest: Oktatási Hivatal

Iacobucci, Donato. 2012 "Developing and implementing a smart specialisation strategy at regional level: some open questions" c.MET Working papers. 12/2012.

Innobarometer 2009 – Analytical Report. Conducted by Gallup Organization upon the request of DG Entreprise and Industry. Luxemburg: European Commission

Joint Research Centre (JRC). 2013. Universities and Smart Specialisation. Scientific and Policy Reports: S3 Policy Brief Series: 3.

Kempton, Louise, John Goddard, John Edwards, Fatime Barbara Hegyi, and Susana Elena-Pérez. "Universities and Smart Specialisation." (2013). accessed: 05-01-2015. URL: http://s3platform.jrc.ec.europa.eu/documents/10157/a180cb45-b272-455b-9211-3e351a6626d3

Navarro, Mikel, Mari Jose Aranguren Querejeta, and Edurne Magro. 2011. "Smart Specialisation Strategies: The Case of the Basque Country". Orkestra Working Paper Series in Territorial Competitiveness Number 2011-R07 accessed:15-1-2015. URL: http://i3s.ec.europa.eu/commitment/30/download/5256.html;i3sid=2x3l

TTzVBkpSqzhfJ4v1SLwW1kZJJsh2fJBpynkMGxYQ1FYrnhTG!93932101
Neffke, Frank, Martin Henning, and Ron Boschma. "How do regions diversify over time? Industry relatedness and the development of new growth paths in regions." Economic Geography 87.3 (2011): 237-265.
Nemzeti Innovációs Hivatal (NIH). 2012. A Kutatás és Technológiai Innovációs Alap által finanszírozott pályázati portfólió hasznosulásának elemzése. Budapest: Nemzeti Innovációs Hivatal
OECD. 2012. Science, Technology and Industry Outlook 2012. Paris: OECD Secretariat
—. STI country profiles. Hungary. http://www.oecd.org/sti/outlook/e-outlook/sticountryprofiles/hungary.htm
Rauch, M., Sommer-Ulrich, J. 2012. Participation of the Central and Eastern European EU Member States in the 7th Framework Programme: Analysis, Evaluation, Recommendations. Leipzig: Fraunhofer MOEZ
Reports for the government prepared by the president of OTKA. OTKA website. http://www.otka.hu/otka-rol/kormanyjelentesek

PART II:

APPLYING CONVENTIONAL QUANTITATIVE METHODS IN INNOVATION RESEARCH

CHAPTER THREE[1]

THE INTERPLAY BETWEEN ENVIRONMENTAL AND QUALITY/LEAN PRACTICES IN SUPPLY CHAINS

GEORGE ONOFREI, EAMONN AMBROSE, FRANK WIENGARTEN AND BRIAN FYNES

Introduction

Environmental concerns and disasters such as the BP oil spill have brought environmental management to the centre stage in operations and supply chain management. To some extent discussions about whether or not to invest in environmental practices have been replaced by discussions about how to gain greater benefits from them. In the recent annual "Sustainability & Innovation Global Executive Study", Haanaes et al. (2011) reported that despite the effects of the financial crisis and the slowing economy, sustainability investments have increased significantly. This increase in investments has been matched by an increased interest in sustainability among the academic community. Initially, both practitioners and researchers sometimes considered sustainability a management fad. However, more recently Lubin and Esty (2010) concluded that sustainability will profoundly change the way companies conduct their business. Managers as well as researchers have reported various financial and non-financial benefits through sustainability initiatives such as operational performance improvements, increase in share prices, improved brand reputations, enhanced stakeholders/investors relations, and even increased innovativeness (Russo and Fouts, 1997; Christmann, 2000; Pagell et al., 2004; Svensson, 2007; Pagell and Gobeli, 2009). However,

[1] The authors acknowledge Emerald Group Publishing Ltd.'s support for the publishing rights.

while the advantages of investing in environmental practices are apparent, some managers still find it difficult to articulate a business case for it.

Nonetheless, while the hype surrounding sustainability efforts has focused managerial attention on environmental investments, traditional investments in practices, such as quality and lean, are still ranked high on the managerial agendas (Rigby and Bilodeau, 2009). The supply chain and operations benefits of lean and quality practices such as JIT (just-in-time), kaizen, TQM (total quality management), Six Sigma, and similar practices have been widely reported. The successful implementation and execution of these programs can still provide companies with a competitive edge. However, what is known to a lesser extent is how investments in lean and quality practices interact with each other in a changing business environment characterised by a shift towards investments in sustainability practices. This research tries to fill this gap in the literature by exploring the following research question: can the efficacy of investments in quality and lean practices be increased through investments in environmental practices in the supply chain? A positive answer to this question would provide an additional business case for environmental investments. In other words, if environmental practices “fit in” with existing quality and lean practices, an additional benefit from becoming green would be experienced. The notion of ‘fit’ is explored through interaction effects, underpinned through the resource based view (RBV) and concept of complementarity.

Literature and hypotheses

The objective of this literature review is to reflect on and analyse the current body of research exploring the relationships between quality/lean and environmental practices, and their effects on supply chain performance. First, literature exploring the individual effects of the selected practices on supply chain performance will be reviewed. Second, similarities between these practices will be explored to analyse their combined effect on supply chain performance. Based on this literature review, hypotheses will be developed and subsequently tested in the following sections.

The impact of quality practices on supply chain performance

Quality management programmes and practices have defined decades of research in operations management. Quality management practices and programmes such as TQM, Six Sigma, statistical process control, and external certification programs, such as the ISO 9000 series, have been extensively implemented and researched (Choi and Eboch, 1998). According to Sroufe and Curkovic (2008) a properly implemented quality management system (QMS) assists companies in meeting short-term regulatory and performance goals, and in the long-term it can serve as the foundation to establish a companywide long-term strategic view on quality. Previous empirical research suggests that quality management improves various aspects of firm performance (Kaynak, 2003). Specifically, quality management programmes can improve customer satisfaction, operational performance, and also financial performance (Choi and Eboch, 1998; Withers and Ebrahimpour, 2002).

Researchers have also considered the specific impact of quality management practices within a supply chain context (Romano and Vinelli, 2001; Foster et al., 2011; Vanichchinchai and Igel, 2011). Traditionally quality management has predominantly taken either an internal or an external view of quality, focusing on processes or on the customer. However, research on quality issues in the supply chain context requires taking a systematic approach, merging these views as they internalise upstream and downstream processes with their own (Foster, 2008). Kaynak and Hartley (2008) called for more quality management research in the supply chain domain. Since competition has moved beyond the single firm to the supply chain, quality managers must integrate their firms' quality practices with their customers and suppliers. Companies that succeed in doing so will become more competitive (Kaynak and Hartley, 2008). Previous research has generally confirmed performance improvements through quality management practices within the supply chain context (Romano and Vinelli, 2001; Foster et al., 2011).

Kaynak and Hartley (2008) assessed specific performance benefits through applying TQM in the supply chain context. Their results indicate that the success of quality management for a firm depends not only on internal quality practices but also on customer focus and supplier quality management. Looking specifically at the impact of TQM on supply chain performance, Vanichchinchai and Igel (2011) identified that TQM has a significant, direct, positive impact on supply chain performance. Based on these previous findings and focusing specifically on operational supply chain performance, we posit the following hypothesis:

H1. Investments in quality practices have a positive impact on operational supply chain performance.

The impact of lean practices on supply chain performance

The term "lean" manufacturing is used to refer to a production system pioneered by Toyota that focuses on the elimination of any type of waste (Holweg and Pil, 2001; Holweg, 2007). In the lean context, waste refers to overproduction, waiting time, inventory, defective goods, or any other factor that can disrupt the even flow of goods along the transformation process (Cusumano, 1994). Lean manufacturing can be broadly described as a manufacturing system that encompasses a variety of practices such as work teams, quality management, cellular manufacturing, pull system production, just-in-time (JIT), and set-up time reduction (Cua et al., 2001; Shah and Ward, 2003; Simpson and Power, 2005).

Previous research has repeatedly reported operational performance improvements through lean (e.g. Sakakibara et al., 1997; Fawcett and Myers, 2001; Swink et al., 2005; Ward and Zhou, 2006). However, lean practices do not only have significant impacts on manufacturing but also on the management and performance of supply chains (Lamming, 1993; Aronsson et al., 2011). According to Simpson and Power (2005), the success of lean manufacturing depends on the coordination of the supply chain, which is directly related to the management of the customer-supplier relationship. McIvor (2001) explains that for minimal inventory and early detection of defects, kanban systems are required. For this, suppliers need to work closely with buyers to both deliver frequently and eliminate the need for quality controls. Furthermore, assemblers involve suppliers early in the new product design, who in turn organise their supply base into a tiered hierarchical structure. Similarly, it has been reported that lean initiatives lead to closer coordination with suppliers and buyers, reduce business risks by joint R&D, decrease inventories through information sharing, enhance product quality, and provide more stable supply prices (Hines, 1996; Levy, 1997; So and Sun, 2010). As such, the reduction of waste and the achievement of lean practices can be closely linked to supplier involvement. Subsequently, lean practices such as customer satisfaction, supplier involvement and development and the underlying philosophies are expected to have a positive impact on the performance of the supply chain. Accordingly, the following hypothesis is proposed:

H2. Investments in lean practices have a positive impact on operational supply chain performance.

The impact of environmental practices on supply chain performance

Social and environmental changes have led to a managerial rethinking of the necessity for a firm to be not only sustainable from a performance viewpoint, but also from a social and environmental perspective (e.g. De Brito et al., 2008). As a result, stakeholders now increasingly tend to judge the success of a company no longer solely in terms of financial performance aspects, but also in terms of social and environmental performance (O'Brien, 1999; Linton et al., 2007; Montabon et al., 2007; Golicic et al., 2010; Parmigiani et al., 2011). Companies are increasing their efforts and investments towards practices related to energy savings, the usage of renewable energy, reduction of waste, pollution prevention, and recycling efforts to conduct business without compromising the ability of future generations to meet their own needs (WCED, 1987; Linton et al., 2007). However, from a practitioner's viewpoint the need to become environmentally sustainable needs to be balanced by the need to be economically sustainable. Previously, researchers as well as practitioners often viewed environmental investments as a financial burden. It was generally accepted that environmental investments did not necessarily pay off, neither in the short- nor in the long-term (Hoffman et al., 1999; Morris and Su, 1999). It has been argued that the investments in new machines and facilities outweigh their potential benefits (Walley and Whitehead, 1994). However, it has been recently acknowledged that becoming environmentally sustainable can reduce material and production costs, reduce transportation and logistics costs, increase product quality, reduce warehouse costs, and even increase innovativeness (Russo and Fouts, 1997; Christmann, 2000; Pagell et al., 2004; Svensson, 2007; Pagell and Gobeli, 2009).

Some researchers have investigated sustainability issues within the context of supply chain management (Linton et al., 2007; Pagell et al., 2007; Pagell et al., 2010). The majority of sustainable supply chain studies assess various aspects of sustainability in terms of procurement in general and supplier selection and management in particular (e.g. Svensson, 2007; Walker and Brammer, 2009; Ehrgott et al., 2011). Pagell et al. (2007) for example tested the efficacy of environmental investments in the context of supply chain management in terms of supplier relationships. They found mixed results in terms of environmentally based performance impacts on cost and quality. A recent study by Paulraj (2011) assessed the relationship between various resources and capabilities on sustainable supply chain management and organisational sustainability. Besides others, Paulraj (2011) identified that strategic purchasing is a key capability for the success of sustainable supply chains.

Previous research has demonstrated that sustainability aspects in procurement and supplier management clearly impact on various aspects of the supply chain. However, this only represents a limited view of supply chain management and performance. Despite these research efforts it is still relatively unclear how environmental investments impact the supply chain as a whole, and not only from a demand side perspective. It is therefore expected that investments in environmental practices not only improve various performance aspects with the demand side, but also with the production and supply side of supply chain performance. Accordingly, we posit the following hypothesis:

H3. Investments in environmental practices have a positive impact on operational supply chain performance.

Environmental practices and the quality/lean practices – supply chain performance relationship

The proposed synergetic relationship between environmental and quality/lean practices can be underpinned by the resource-based view (RBV) in general and the concept of complementarity in particular. The RBV takes an internal resource based focus on a firm's value creation (Barney, 1991). The RBV provides practical guidance about the identification of value-adding firm resources. Resources are defined as all assets, capabilities, organisational processes, firm attributes, information, knowledge, etc., controlled by a firm, enabling the firm to conceive of and implement strategies that improve its performance (Daft, 1989, cited in Barney, 1991). Wernerfelt (1984) noted that a resource can be viewed as anything that may provide strength or weakness to the possessing firm.

In addition, it comes as a sustainable competitive advantage (SCA) when other firms are unable to duplicate the benefits of this strategy (Barney, 1991). Subsequently, resources need to exhibit the following attributes to be a source of SCA: valuable, rare, imperfectly imitable, and non-substitutable (Bowman and Collier, 2006). Operations management programs and practices such as quality, environmental, and lean viewed from a RBV perspective might not entirely fulfil the requirements to be a source of sustainable competitive advantages (Barney, 1991). They might certainly be of value, but the continuous standardisation effort through, for example, the ISO series or TQM and Six Sigma, makes them transferable and, to a certain degree, substitutable across companies. However, through combining these practices they might be of greater value not only to a company's operation, but also to its supply chain. There are noticeable similarities between the three focal practices of this study. Various researchers have remarked on the palpable similarities between quality and environmental management practices in terms of managerial tools and underlying philosophies (Curkovic et al., 2000; Rusinko, 2005; Curkovic et al., 2008). Rusinko (2005) for example identified the following common beliefs and shared principles between quality management and sustainability: long-run focus – economic and social, continuous improvement, employee empowerment, integrated perspective, multifunctional approach, and participation by the whole value chain. Curkovic et al. (2000) empirically confirmed structural similarities and parallels between environmental responsible manufacturing and TQM. There is also an extant body of literature comparing the similarities of external certification programmes, such ISO 9001 to exemplify quality practices, and ISO 14001 to exemplify environmental practices (Hunt and Auster, 1990; Klassen and McLaughlin, 1993; Curkovic et al., 2000; Sroufe and Curkovic, 2008). Having a well-defined quality management programme enhances the chance of success of implementing an additional environmental management system such as ISO 14001 (Curkovic et al., 2000). Industry efforts have also acknowledged the importance of integrating management systems and practices especially regarding ISO certifications such as ISO 9001 in terms of quality and ISO 14001 in terms of environmental certification systems (Klassen and McLaughlin, 1996; ISO, 2008; Nawrocka et al., 2009). For example the PAS 99 framework has been published for companies to identify and benefit from their various management systems and practices that they are likely to have implemented simultaneously (Leopulos et al., 2010).

Kleindorfer et al. (2005) established a link between lean and environmental practices in operations management. Synergies between both programmes in terms of waste reduction can enable companies to gain greater performance improvements through both programs (Yang et al., 2011). Other studies by King and Lenox (2001) and Rothenberg et al. (2001) also confirmed similarities between lean and green operations. However, they also found that gaining performance benefits through combining both programs is a difficult task for operations managers.

It has been highlighted that based on the RBV and previous literature, the sustainable performance enhancing ability of operations management programmes, such as environmental, lean, and quality management, has not yet been fully explored. In other words, the impact of quality and lean practices on performance might be complemented by environmental practices, resulting in a complementary performance enhancing relationship. According to Teece (1986), complementarity refers to how one resource might influence another, and how this relationship affects a firm's competitive position or performance. From a theoretical viewpoint this relationship can be further explored through the concept of complementarity and specifically through the notion of fit (Fiedler, 1964; Nadler and Tushman, 1980; Drazin and Van de Ven, 1985). Fit can be defined as the degree to which the needs, demands, goals, objectives, and/or structures of one component are consistent with those of another component (Nadler and Tushman, 1980).

The literature has shown that environmental practices can complement quality and lean practices in a supply chain context. It is not only the case that many principles and practices are overlapping, but also that the underlying philosophies between all three approaches are comparable. A focus on eliminating waste is the core of the lean movement and at the same time the core of environmental practices. Focusing on quality also entails the notion of waste, but it comprises much more. The definition of quality has changed over the years, and it is arguable that products as well as processes nowadays need to be environmentally sustainable to be considered being of quality by the producer and customers. Accordingly, based on the previous literature and the theoretical underpinnings drawn from the RBV and the concept of complementarity, it can be argued that the performance impact of lean and quality practices can be supported and enhanced through investing in environmental practices. Consequently, we propose the following hypotheses:

H4a,b. Investments in quality (a) and lean practices (b) have a stronger positive impact on operational supply chain performance when combined with high levels of investments in environmental practices.

Figure 3.1 graphically illustrates and summarises the relationships between the practices and supply chain performance expressed through the proposed hypotheses. Quality and lean practices are the independent variables that are proposed to improve supply chain performance (H1 and H2). Environmental practices are also expected to improve supply chain performance (H3) and also moderate the impact of quality and lean practices on performance (H4a and H4b). The subsequent sections report the empirical results of testing this model with its associated hypotheses.

Figure 3.1 Research model

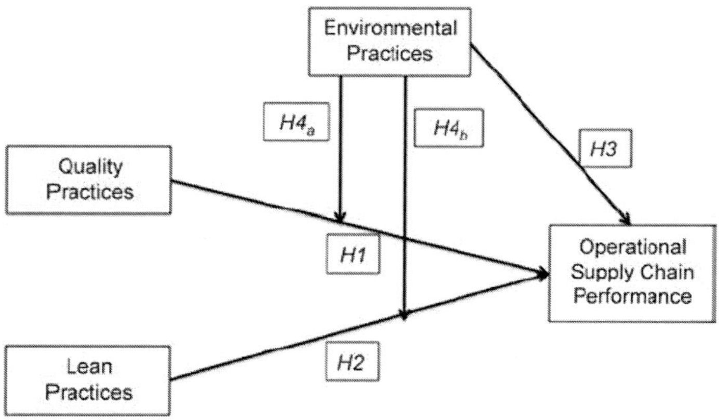

Research method

Questionnaire and data collection

To test the research question as to whether or not the efficacy of quality and lean practices can be increased through environmental investments in the supply chain, data collected by the Global Manufacturing Research Group was utilised. GMRG is a group of well-respected operations management scholars that has been collecting cross-country data related to various operations and manufacturing topics. The GMRG aims to improve the research field through the development of theory and dissemination of its results. Standardised survey instruments that were developed and redefined at annual meetings by GMRG members were administered by members of the research group in their respective countries. The standardised questionnaire is translated back and forth into the native language of the country and English, ensuring the equivalency, validity, and reliability of the translated surveys (Power et al., 2010).

The GMRG has collected data since 1985, continuously evolving and improving the survey instrument in four collection rounds. For this study data collected from the fourth round was utilised. Data were collected between 2006 and 2008 (Whybark, 1997; Whybark et al., 2009). The level of analysis was the plant level, and the target respondents were plant managers. These key informants were deemed to have comprehensive knowledge related to the management and operation of the plant. However, the manager was also advised to seek input from other functions if necessary (Schoenherr, 2011). Within each country the individual GMRG member determined the most appropriate means of collecting the survey data (Whybark, 1997; Whybark et al., 2009). The majority of the data was collected electronically via e-mail or web survey. However, other methods such as telephone, mail, or face-to-face interviews were also utilised. The data collected from various countries were grouped by a central coordinator and subsequently distributed to the participating scholars. The GMRG database is a unique set of global data that can be used to analyse operations and supply chain management practices and viewpoints (Power et al., 2010).

To test whether or not the efficacy of investments in quality and lean practices can be increased through investments in environmental practices in the supply chain, data collected from the following European countries has been analysed: Austria, Croatia, Finland, Germany, Ireland, Italy, Poland, Sweden, and Switzerland. This sample frame provided a rich source of information regarding the practices' relationships with supply chain performance within a European context. Subsequently, this allowed for making generalisations about the results throughout Europe and across these countries, which can be viewed as an advantage in comparison to single country studies. Regions such as Europe are becoming more and more integrated and cohesive. Table 3.1 provides an overview of the dataset in terms of country of origin, company size, and industry. A total of 522 usable responses were used to test the previously stated hypotheses.

Measures

Quality practices were measured by considering the plant's level of quality practices investments within the previous two years (Appendix, Table AI). Specifically, respondents were asked to indicate the extent to which their plant had invested resources (money, time, and/or people) in these initiatives in the previous two years. The measures related to quality practices have been extensively used and tested in previous research (Kull and Wacker, 2010; Power et al., 2010; Pagell et al., 2013; Wiengarten et al., 2011). The quality practice scale as well as the lean and environmental practice scale ranged from one to seven, where one indicates not at all and seven to a great extent (Whybark et al., 2009). Lean practices were measured by considering the plant's level of lean practice investments within the previous two years. (Appendix, Table AI). Respondents were asked to indicate the extent to which their plant had invested resources (money, time, and/or people) in these initiatives in the previous two years. The measures related to lean practices have also been extensively used and tested in previous research (Shah and Ward, 2003; Ketokivi and Schroeder, 2004; Ward and Zhou, 2006; Jayaram et al., 2008).

Similarly, environmental management practices or initiatives were measured by considering the plant's level of environmental investments within the previous two years (Schoenherr, 2011) (Appendix, Table AI). Respondents were again asked to indicate the extent to which their plant had invested resources (money, time, and/or people) in these initiatives in the previous two years. The measures related to environmental practices have also been extensively used and tested in previous research (Yang et al., 2010; Pagell et al., 2013; Schoenherr, 2011; Wiengarten et al., 2012).
Supply chain performance was conceptualised at the operational level using various indicators representing supply chain performance (Kroes and Ghosh, 2010). Operational supply chain performance is defined in terms of rejects and delivery performance (Swafford et al., 2006). It has been assessed using multiple items measuring the purchasing, manufacturing, and supply stages (Appendix, Table AI). Respondents were asked to indicate the plant's operational supply chain performance in terms of delivery timeliness, rate of returns, and scrap rate as percentages at each of the aforementioned stages. The measures related to operational supply chain performance have also been extensively used and tested in previous research (Lee, 2004; Swafford et al., 2006; Kroes and Ghosh, 2010). As investments in quality, lean, and environmental practices follow certain learning curves, a two year amortisation timeframe was applied (Whybark et al., 2009).

Table 3.1 Sample Descriptive

Country of Origin: Western Europe	N	Industry	N	Size: Number of Plant Employees	N
Austria	17	Food & Drink	40	< 50	166
Croatia	82	Textiles, Apparel & Footwear incl. Leather Goods	22	51 - 100	132
Finland	139	Wood Products incl. Furniture	34	101 - 500	176
Germany	59	Paper & Printing	27	501-1000	30
Ireland	51	Petroleum, Chemicals, Pharmaceuticals, Plastics & other Man Made Fibre Products	50	>1000	18
Italy	54	Primary Metals	14		
Poland	57	Fabricated Metal Products except Machinery & Transportation	92		
Sweden	32	Electronic Equipment including Computers, Measuring Devices & Optical Equipment	153		
Switzerland	31	Transportation Equipment	24		
		Stone, Clay, Glass & Concrete	33		
		Other	33		
Total	**522**				

Finally, firm size and industry were used as control variables. The survey items are listed in Table 3.2 and in the Appendix (Table AI). Shah and Ward (2003) highlighted the importance of controlling for the effects of size and industry in empirical research in general and involving lean in particular. Therefore, in order to increase the generalizability of the results, size and industry were included. Subsequently, the results will be representable across all industries and company sizes within this sample.

Table 3.2 Construct measurement items

Construct	Variable	Loading	*t*-value	Std. Error	R^2
Investments in Quality practices α=.721	ISO 9000	.59	18.75	.17	.32
	Supplier Certification	.56	24.66	.094	.46
	Statistical Process Control	.71	27.18	.091	.54
	Six Sigma	.62	22.42	.12	.39
Investments in Lean practices α=.712	Cellular Manufacturing	.54	16.42	.14	.22
	JIT	.67	23.12	.12	.44
	Manufacturing throughput time reduction	.66	21.51	.081	.43
	Set-up time reduction	.62	22.27	.097	.42
Investments in Environmenta l practices α=.751	ISO 14000	.60	21.44	.15	.34
	Pollution Prevention	.74	28.78	.089	.60
	Recycling Of Materials	.61	22.17	.092	.40
	Waste Reduction	.63	22.41	.079	.40
Operational Supply Chain Performance α=.708	Rejects of incoming material	.84	34.14	.031	.74
	Rejects during processing (scrap rate)	.76	34.13	.032	.71
	Rejects at final inspection	.68	23.51	.032	.45
	Returns from the customer	.64	28.41	0.30	.62
	Plant's customer orders late delivery	.73	30.11	.031	.59
	Plant's purchase orders delivered late by suppliers	.75	29.01	0.41	.65

Factor analysis: validity and reliability

Content and face validity were affirmed and examined through the involvement of numerous senior international operations management researchers and extensive testing in the development and design stages. In addition, all items are grounded in the operations literature to ensure a certain degree of content and face validity (Power et al., 2010). Confirmatory factor analysis (CFA) was conducted using LISREL (a software tool to analyse structural equation models) to assess additional validity and reliability characteristics of the measure. The CFA results are listed in Table 3.2 in terms of their factor loadings, t-values, standard errors, and R^2s. It is also important to address incremental and absolute fit issues. A comparison of the following goodness-of-fit values against those in Hu and Bentler (1998) indicate that this model is satisfactory (RMSEA = 0:049; RMSEA 90 per cent conf. interval (0.041; 0.053); RMR = 0:12; GFI = 0:97; AGFI = 0:96; NNFI = 0:98; CFI = 0:98; IFI = 0:98; RFI = 0:96).

In addition, the ratio of chi-square to degrees of freedom of 2.85 (X^2/df) is well below the commonly desired threshold of 3 (MacCallum, 1986; Byrne, 1998). Subsequently, it can be concluded that the measurement items represent the underlying factor structure in a conclusive manner (Bollen, 1989). Convergent validity is the degree to which individual items measure the same underlying construct. Subsequently, it signifies the extent to which the measurement items represent the construct. Convergent validity has been assessed and confirmed through comparing the coefficients and standard error of the items. Results in Table 3.2 indicate that each coefficient was greater than twice its associated standard error (Anderson and Gerbing, 1988). Finally, discriminant validity measures the extent to which items intended to only measure one latent variable do not at the same time measure a different latent variable (De Vellis, 1991). Discriminant validity was confirmed through testing inter-factor correlations (De Vellis, 1991). Results in Table 3.3 indicate that inter-factor correlations were in an acceptable range. Additionally, Cronbach alpha values have been calculated to test the reliability (internal consistency) of the proposed latent variables. The Cronbach alpha values in Table 3.2 are all above the commonly used cut-off value with a minimum of 0.708 indicating reliable measures (Nunnally, 1978).

Table 3.3 Inter-Factor correlations

Factors	Mean	(1)	(2)	(3)	(4)
Investments in Quality Practices (1)	3.07	1			
Investments in Lean Practices (2)	3.59	.511**	1		
Investments in Environmental Practices (3)	3.71	.559**	.479**	1	
Operational Supply Chain Performance (4)	34.2 %	.207**	.218**	.183**	1
**Correlation is significant at the .001 level (2-tailed)					

Common method variance, which can be referred to as the variance that is linked to the measurement method rather than to its constructs, has been evaluated (Podsakoff et al., 2003). Common method variance was assessed through rerunning the CFA with an additional unmeasured factor. Results indicate that all measurement items continued to load on their originally assigned latent variables. It can therefore be concluded that common method variance is not of significance in this dataset (Podsakoff et al., 2003). Finally, since the dataset used in this study was collected in multiple countries, conceptual issues with regards to measurement equivalence had to be addressed. Subsequently, it had to be ensured whether or not the constructs via their related scales are invariant across countries (Malhotra and Sharma, 2008). Measurement equivalence refers to whether or not measurement items, under varying conditions and phenomena, yield the same attributes. It is critical to assess measurement invariance across groups in order to be able to make valid scientific claims and to arrive at scientific conclusions (Malhotra and Sharma, 2008). Only if measurement equivalence is ensured across countries, then the collected datasets can either be combined or compared with each other. A number of recent studies have confirmed measurement equivalence in the GMRG dataset through various tests (e.g. Schoenherr and Narasimhan, 2012; Wiengarten et al., 2011). The interested reader may therefore be referred to these sources, and it can be concluded that measurement equivalence has been repeatedly established in the GMRG sample. Additional information is presented in the Table 12.4.

Table 3.4 provides a country specific sample overview of the analysed and confirmed investments in quality, lean, and environmental practices (i.e.

mean values and standard deviation). The country-specific mean and standard deviation values are listed for quality, lean, and environmental practices.

Table 3.4 Measurement specific sample overview

Country of Origin	Quality Practices (Mean/S.D)	Lean Practices (Mean/S.D)	Environmental Practices (Mean/S.D)
Austria	3.58/ 1.63	4.15/ 1.40	3.62/ 1.48
Croatia	3.77/ 1.42	4.08/ 1.10	4.21/ 1.30
Finland	2.51/ .91	3.58/ 1.06	3.71/ 1.30
Germany	2.73/ 1.50	3.47/ 1.30	3.18/ 1.38
Ireland	3.88/ 1.31	3.76/ 1.33	4.36/ 1.30
Italy	3.04/ 1.36	3.60/ 1.20	3.69/ 1.21
Poland	3.15/ 1.37	2.59 1.12	3.09/ 1.51
Sweden	3.00/ 1.15	3.81/ 1.06	3.98/ 1.37
Switzerland	3.05/ 1.62	3.65/ 1.40	3.29/ 1.59

Results

To address the research question of whether or not the efficacy of investments of quality and lean practices can be increased through investments in environmental practices, a series of OLS regression analyses were carried out. The analysis was conducted in two separate models reflecting the two interaction terms (i.e. quality practices and environmental practices; lean practices and environmental practices). In the first step of the OLS analysis, the control variables industry and firm size were introduced, in the second step quality practices (Model I) and lean practices (Model II), and environmental practices, and in the third step the interaction term (Model I: Quality and environmental practices;

Model II: Lean and environmental practices). Before carrying out the OLS analysis, the data characteristics were tested in terms of linearity and multicollinearity (Kennedy, 1999). Firstly, the variance inflation factors (VIFs) were calculated and listed in Table 3.5. The resulting VIFs indicate that multicollinearity is not apparent. Additional results regarding the condition indices confirmed this result (Belsley et al., 1980).

Table 3.5 OLS analysis

	Model I: Quality Practices	Model II: Lean Practices
Variable	Std. Estimate	Std. Estimate
Control Variables:		
Firm size	.003	.005
Industry	-.005	-.012
Independent Variables:		
Quality Practices	.193**	
Lean Practices		.171**
Moderator: Environmental Practices	.098	-.066
Interactions:		
Quality-Practices X Environmental-Practices	.119**	
Lean Practices X Environmental-Practices		.091*
Step 1: Adjusted R^2/ Sig. F change	.011 .003	.012 .003
Step 2: Adjusted R^2/ Sig. F change	.044 .000	.046 .000
Step 3: Adjusted R^2 (incl. Interaction Term)/ Sig. F change	.047 .010	.049 .003
Max VIF	1.581	1.509
Notes: * Sign. at the .05 level; ** Sign. at the .001 level		

In H1 it was hypothesised that investments in quality practices have a significant and positive impact on operational supply chain performance. Previous empirical research has highlighted that investments in quality practices can have significant effects on the quality of processes within and between organisations (Choi and Eboch, 1998). Results presented in Table 3.5 indicate that, as expected, investments in quality practices such as ISO 9000, supplier certification, statistical process control and Six Sigma do significantly improve operational supply chain performance (B = 0.193; $p < 0.001$) (B represents the associated beta-value).

In H2 it was hypothesised that investments in lean practices have a significant and positive impact on operational supply chain performance. Previous empirical research has highlighted that investments in lean practices have a significantly positive effect on various dimensions of operational supply chain performance (Cocks, 1996). Results presented in Table 3.5 highlight that as expected investments in quality practices, such as cellular manufacturing, JIT, manufacturing throughput time reduction and set-up time reduction, do indeed significantly improve operational supply chain performance (B = 0.171; $p < 0.000$).

In the third hypothesis it was proposed that investments in environmental practices have a significant and positive impact on operational supply chain performance. Previous empirical research has highlighted that investing in environmental practices can have significant positive effects on various forms of firm performance (Pagell et al., 2004; Svensson, 2007; Pagell and Gobeli, 2009). However, results presented in Table 3.5 indicate that investments in environmental practices such as ISO 14000, pollution prevention, recycling of materials, and waste reduction do not improve operational supply chain performance in the (I) quality practices model (B = 0.098; $p = 0.065$) and (II) lean practices model (B = 20.066; $p = 0.079$). This result is certainly contrary to recent literature. However, it is worthwhile noting that our performance measure solely captures the dimensions of delivery and quality (i.e. rejects).

In the fourth and final hypothesis, it was proposed that investments in quality and lean practices have a stronger positive impact on operational supply chain performance when combined with high levels of investments in environmental practices. To analyse these potential synergetic effects, interaction terms were calculated, modelling environmental practices as the moderating variable.

H4a tests for synergetic effects between environmental and quality practices. Adding the two-way interaction term to the OLS Model I contributed to a significant change in the variance explained (R^2 adj: =

0.047, $p = 0.01$), and the interaction term was significant ($B = 0.119$, $p < 0.001$). To interpret this finding, the significance of the slopes was calculated at low (one SD below the mean) and high (one SD above the mean) levels of environmental investments (Aiken and West, 1991; Preacher et al., 2006). The results reveal that investments in quality practices were more strongly associated with operational supply chain performance when investments in environmental practices were high ($B = 0.29$; $p<0.001$) than when environmental investments were low ($B = 0.15$; $p<0.05$). In other words, investments in quality practices do have a higher payoff rate in terms of operational supply chain performance when the company is also investing in environmental practices. Therefore, synergetic effects between environmental and quality practices were detected.

H4b tests for synergetic effects between environmental and lean practices. Adding the two-way interaction term to the OLS Model II contributed to a significant change in the variance explained (R^2 adj: = 0.049, $p = 0.003$), and the interaction term was significant ($B = 0.091$, $p< 0.05$). To interpret this finding, the significance of the slopes was calculated again at low and high levels of environmental investments (Aiken and West, 1991; Preacher et al., 2006).

The results reveal that investments in lean practices were more strongly associated with operational supply chain performance when investments in environmental practices were high ($B = 0.32$; $p<0.001$) than when environmental investments were low ($B = 0.13$; $p<0.05$). In other words, investments in lean practices do have a higher payoff rate in terms of operational supply chain performance when the company is also investing in environmental practices. Therefore, synergetic effects between environmental and lean practices have also been detected.

Discussion

The objective of this paper is to investigate whether or not the efficacy of investments in quality and lean practices can be increased through complementary investments in environmental practices in the supply chain. In undertaking this investigation, five hypotheses were developed and tested. In the first hypothesis it was proposed that quality management practices have a positive impact on operational supply chain performance. Empirical results confirmed this hypothesis. The result of the second hypothesis also confirmed that lean practices also have a positive impact on operational supply chain performance. The third hypothesis was rejected, which indicates that environmental investments do not significantly improve operational supply chain performance. However, as mentioned previously, we solely conceptualise operational supply chain performance in terms of the quality (i.e. rejects) and delivery dimensions. Based on the complementarity aspect of the RBV, the fourth hypothesis proposed potential synergetic effects between environmental and lean/quality practices. The fourth hypothesis, which was nested into (a) and (b) sub-hypotheses, was confirmed, which indicates that the impact of quality and lean practices on operational supply chain performance can be significantly enhanced through high levels of investments in environmental practices.

These empirical findings have some important implications for theory, but possibly more so from a practitioner's perspective. From a theoretical perspective, the results confirm the concept of complementarity that has been proposed in the realm of the RBV (e.g. Teece, 1986). While the performance enhancing ability of manufacturing practices, such as quality and lean, certainly have a significant impact on operational supply chain performance, they do so to a greater extent while complemented by environmental investments. To some extent this does confirm the RBV in the sense that manufacturing practices are of value. However, their value might be limited due to standardisation and transferability. Nevertheless, truly sustainable resource value can be created through the unique combination of lean/quality practices with environmental practices (Barney, 1991). Furthermore, this research confirms previous findings in that lean and quality practices are beneficial not only from an internal manufacturing perspective but also from a supply chain perspective. This research therefore confirms the works of Kaynak and Hartley (2008), Vanichchinchai and Igel (2011) and the like, suggesting that quality management cannot only have internal performance benefits but also supply-chain-wide benefits. Similar claims have been made in relation to lean practices (Lamming, 1993). This research contributes to this body of literature by confirming the importance of lean practices from a supply chain perspective. Previous research indicates that environmental investments in general are beneficial for the performance of a company (Russo and Fouts, 1997; Christmann, 2000; Pagell et al., 2004; Svensson, 2007; Pagell and Gobeli, 2009). Recent research in particular has been very optimistic in terms of the performance enhancing abilities of environmental practices (Pagell and Gobeli, 2009). However, our results indicate the need for a much more nuanced view on this topic. In terms of operational supply chain performance, measured through rejects and delivery performance, environmental investments do not seem to be of significant importance.

However, previous research has predominantly focused on the impact of environmental investments on internal manufacturing-based operational performance in terms of cost, quality, delivery, and flexibility (e.g. Wiengarten et al., 2012). Operational supply chain performance adds another dimension to this discussion. The findings of this paper suggest that within a supply setting environmental investments take on a different role. Rather than having a direct impact on operational supply chain performance, they act as a moderator and complement addition management practices such as lean and quality. As such, this finding does not suggest that environmental practices are not important for the success of a supply chain. Moreover, environmental practices take on a different role in this setting as they support traditional manufacturing practices such as quality and lean. This is the main contribution of this research as it might explain some of the earlier negative empirical findings with regard to environmental practices – performance relationships (Hoffman et al., 1999; Morris and Su, 1999).

This theoretical contribution also serves as the base for the main practical contributions. Previous research has continuously highlighted that companies are exposed to increased pressure from various stakeholders to become “green”. However, in order to become sustainable, not only from an economic viewpoint, but also from an environmental one, requires extensive investments in processes, machineries, facilities, etc. The majority of today’s companies certainly have quality and lean practices in place. The results of this research provide decision-makers with evidence that the success of these practices can be enhanced through investing in environmental practices. In other words, these findings serve as an additional source of information, providing a different perspective on the particular benefits of environmental practices.

Although this may be one of a few studies that could not detect any performance benefits related to environmental investments, it does not dismiss its sustainable importance from an economic perspective. Moreover, this study has explored a different role for environmental practices. Environmental practices take a supporting role for lean and quality practices. This should not make them less attractive for supply chain managers; it only suggests a different role, which may require a different managerial approach. Synergies can be achieved through combining environmental with lean and quality practices. These various practices should therefore no longer be viewed in isolation. An integrated managerial approach to these practices is required to improve the supply chain to a significant extent. This subsequently results in social implications or implications for public policy. Building the case for increasing environmental investments through rules and regulations is certainly one approach to increase the company's level of investment in these practices. However, these results could be used to reinforce this approach through encouraging "voluntary" environmental investments. Being able to communicate to companies that investing in environmental practices leads to a more efficient use of "traditional" manufacturing practices provides additional incentives and motivations. Therefore, managers might start thinking about additional environmental investments that even exceed regulatory requirements.

Conclusion

This research contributes to the recent discussion on the role of environmental practices for the success of traditional manufacturing practices such as quality and lean in supply chain settings. Synergetic effects between quality/lean and environmental management practices have been identified. Moreover, these results provide additional arguments as to why companies should start investing in environmental practices.

Nevertheless, this research has its limitations. First, the utilised dataset is unlikely to be a truly random sample of the selected population in the included countries. Second, since the data is of a cross-sectional nature, it is relatively difficult to evaluate genuine causality. This leaves room for speculation as to whether some portion of the interaction effect is based on some sort of learning effect due to implementing various programmes simultaneously. However, respondents were asked to indicate their level of investments within the previous two years and their current operational supply chain performance. Thirdly, the dataset is limited to plants situated in the relatively well-developed manufacturing environments of Western Europe. Possibly, the identified synergetic effects are only present in these areas, and the proposed model may behave differently for plants situated in less-developed countries. Finally, since this study relied on survey data, not every aspect of quality, lean, and environmental practice that companies implement may have been captured. However, the selected practices can be viewed as being representative. Similarly, the measures related to supply chain performance are only at the operational level, which limits the generalizability of the results. In addition, they are limited in the sense that they only capture performance improvements in terms of delivery and quality (i.e. rejects). Consequently, the presented results have to be interpreted carefully-framed in the realm of the specific measures utilised in this study. Despite these limitations, this paper makes some important contributions to research and practice.

From an academic perspective this research does not confirm numerous previous articles identifying that investing in environmental practices improves firm performance (Russo and Fouts, 1997; Christmann, 2000; Pagell et al., 2004; Pagell and Gobeli, 2009). Specifically, operational supply chain performance has been applied as the dependent variable to assess its performance impact. Nevertheless, it has been identified that environmental practices are important and crucial support mechanisms for more traditional and existing practices, such as lean and quality practices. While their importance for the supply chain is indisputably confirmed by this research, their pivotal role can even be increased. Through simultaneously investing in environmental practices, the efficacy of quality and lean practices can be significantly increased within the supply chain context. The importance of this finding should not only be arbitrated from an academic perspective but also even more so from a practitioner's perspective.

The recent downturn in the global economy has surely increased the rigour and intensity of company-wide spending audits when it comes to relatively innovative practices such sustainability management. Finding conclusive economic arguments for environmental investments might certainly not be an easy task. However, the synergetic effects identified here might provide managers with additional arguments and reasons to invest in environmental practices. These practices in isolation, on their own, might have limited capabilities in terms of improving operational supply chain performance. However, they do interact with quality and lean practices to improve a firm's operational supply chain performance. This finding is of significant importance when making an informed decision about environmental practices within the supply chain context.

Acknowledgement

The author gratefully acknowledges the financial support from the Irish Government's Programme for Research in Third Level Institutions (PRTLI 5) project grant entitled 'Innovation Policy Simulation for the Smart Economy (IPSE)'.

References

Aiken, L.S. and West, S.G. (1991), Multiple Regression: Testing and Interpreting Interactions, Sage Publications, Newbury Park, CA.

Anderson, J.C. and Gerbing, D.W. (1988), "Structural equation modeling in practice: a review and recommended two-step approach", Psychological Bulletin, Vol. 103 No. 3, pp. 411-23.

Aronsson, H., Abrahamsson, M. and Spens, K. (2011), "Developing lean and agile health care supply chains", Supply Chain Management: An International Journal, Vol. 16 No. 3, pp. 176-83.

Barney, J. (1991), "Firm resources and sustained competitive advantage", Journal of Management, Vol. 17 No. 1, pp. 99-120.

Belsley, D.A., Kuh, E. and Welsch, R.E. (1980), Regression Diagnostics, John Wiley & Sons, New York, NY.

Bollen, K.A. (1989), Structural Equations with Latent Variables, John Wiley & Sons, New York, NY.

Bowman, C. and Collier, N. (2006), "A contingency approach to resource-creation processes", International Journal of Management Reviews, Vol. 8 No. 4, pp. 191-211.

Byrne, B. (1998), Structural Equation Modelling with Lisrel, Prelins, and Simplis: Basic Concepts, Applications, and Programming, Lawrence Erlbaum Associates, Hillsdale, NJ.

Choi, T.Y. and Eboch, K. (1998), "The TQM paradox: relations among TQM practices, plant performance, and customer satisfaction", Journal of Operations Management, Vol. 17 No. 1, pp. 59-75.

Christmann, P. (2000), "Effects of 'best practices' of environmental management on cost advantage: the role of complimentary assets", Academy of Management Journal, Vol. 43 No. 4, pp. 663-80.

Cocks, P. (1996), "Partnership in pursuit of lean supply", Purchasing and Supply Management, February, pp. 32-3.

Cua, K., McKone, K. and Schroeder, R.G. (2001), "Relationships between implementation of TQM: JIT and TPM and manufacturing performance", Journal of Operations Management, Vol. 19 No. 6, pp. 675-94.

Curkovic, S., Sroufe, R. and Landeros, R. (2008), "Measuring TQEM returns from the application of quality frameworks", Business Strategy and the Environment, Vol. 17 No. 2, pp. 93-106.

Curkovic, S., Melnyk, S.A., Handfield, R.B. and Calantone, R.J. (2000), "Investigating the linkage between total quality management and environmentally responsibly manufacturing", IIEE Transactions on Engineering Management, Vol. 47 No. 4, pp. 444-64.

Cusumano, M. (1994), "The limits of lean", Sloan Management Review, Vol. 35 No. 4, pp. 27-32.

Daft, R. (1989), Organization Theory and Design, International Thomson Publishing, Mason, OH.

De Brito, M.P., Carbone, V. and Blanquart, C.M. (2008), "Towards a sustainable fashion retail supply chain in Europe: organisation and performance", International Journal of Production Economics, Vol. 114 No. 2, pp. 534-53.

De Vellis, R.F. (1991), Scale Development: Theory and Applications, Sage, Newbury Park, CA.

Drazin, R. and Van de Ven, A. (1985), "Alternative forms of fit in contingency theory", Administrative Science Quarterly, Vol. 30 No. 4, pp. 514-39.

Ehrgott, M., Reimann, F., Kaufmann, L. and Carter, C.R. (2011), "Social sustainability in selecting emerging economy suppliers", Journal of Business Ethics, Vol. 98 No. 1, pp. 99-119.

Fawcett, S.E. and Myers, M.B. (2001), "Product and employee development in advanced manufacturing: implementation and impact", International Journal of Production Research, Vol. 39 No. 1, pp. 65-79.

Fiedler, F. (1964), "A contingency model of leadership effectiveness", Advances in Experimental Social Psychology, Vol. 1 No. 1, pp. 149-90.

Foster, S.T. (2008), "Towards an understanding of supply chain quality management", Journal of Operations Management, Vol. 26 No. 4, pp. 461-7.

Foster, S.T. Jr., Wallin, C. and Ogden, J. (2011), "Towards a better understanding of supply chain quality management practices", International Journal of Production Research, Vol. 49 No. 8, pp. 2285-300.

Golicic, S.L., Boerstler, C.N. and Ellram, L.M. (2010), "'Greening' transportation in the supply chain", MIT Sloan Management Review, Vol. 51 No. 2, pp. 46-55.

Haanaes, K., Balagopal, B., Arthur, D., Kong, M.T., Velken, I., Kruschwitz, N. and Hopkins, M.S. (2011), "First look: The second annual sustainability and innovation survey", MIT Sloan Management Review, Vol. 52 No. 2, pp. 77-83.

Hoffman, A.J., Gillespie, J.J., Moore, D.A., Wade-Benzoni, K.A., Thompson, L.L. and Bazerman, M.H. (1999), "A mixed-motive perspective on the economics versus environment debate", American Behavioral Scientist, Vol. 42 No. 8, pp. 1254-76.

Holweg, M. (2007), "The genealogy of lean production", Journal of Operations Management, Vol. 25 No. 2, pp. 420-37.

Holweg, M. and Pil, F. (2001), "Successful build-to-order strategies start with the customer", Sloan Management Review, Vol. 43 No. 1, pp. 74-83.

Hines, P. (1996), "Purchasing for lean production: the new strategic agenda", Journal of Supply Chain Management, Vol. 32 No. 1, pp. 2-10.

Hu, L. and Bentler, P.M. (1998), "Fit indices in covariance structure modelling: sensitivity to under-parameterized model misspecification", Psychological Methods, Vol. 3 No. 4, pp. 424-53.

Hunt, C.B. and Auster, E.R. (1990), "Proactive environmental management: avoiding the toxic trap", Sloan Management Review, Vol. 31 No. 2, pp. 7-18.

ISO (2008), The ISO survey of certifications – 2008, ISO, Geneva, available at: www. iso.org

Jayaram, J., Vickery, S. and Droge, C. (2008), "Relationship building, lean strategy and firm performance: an exploratory study in the automotive supplier industry", International Journal of Production Research, Vol. 46 No. 20, pp. 5633-49.

Kaynak, H. (2003), "The relationship between total quality management practices and their effects on firm performance", Journal of Operations Management, Vol. 21 No. 4, pp. 405-35.

Kaynak, H. and Hartley, J.L. (2008), "A replication and extension of quality management into the supply chain", Journal of Operations Management, Vol. 26 No. 4, pp. 468-89.

Kennedy, P. (1999), A Guide to Econometrics, Blackwell Publishers, Oxford.

Ketokivi, M. and Schroeder, R.G. (2004), "Manufacturing practices, strategic fit and performance: a routine-based view", International Journal of Operations & Production Management, Vol. 24 No. 2, pp. 171-91.

King, A. and Lenox, M. (2001), "Lean and green? Exploring the spillovers from lean production to environmental performance", Production and Operations Management, Vol. 10 No. 3, pp. 244-56.

Klassen, R.D. and McLaughlin, C.P. (1993), "TQM and environmental excellence in manufacturing", Industrial Management & Data Systems, Vol. 93 No. 6, pp. 14-22.

Klassen, R.D. and McLaughlin, C.P. (1996), "The impact of environmental management on firm performance", Management Science, Vol. 42 No. 8, pp. 1199-214.

Kleindorfer, P.R., Singhal, K. and Van Wasssenhove, L.N. (2005), "Sustainable operations management", Production and Operations

Management, Vol. 14 No. 4, pp. 482-92.
Kroes, J.R. and Ghosh, S. (2010), "Outsourcing congruence with competitive priorities: impact on supply chain and firm performance", Journal of Operations Management, Vol. 28 No. 2, pp. 124-43.
Kull, T.J. and Wacker, J.G. (2010), "Quality management effectiveness in Asia: the influence of culture", Journal of Operations Management, Vol. 28 No. 3, pp. 223-39.
Lamming, R. (1993), Beyond Partnership: Strategies for Innovation and Lean Supply, Prentice Hall, New York, NY.
Lee, H.L. (2004), "The triple – a supply chain", Harvard Business Review, Vol. 82 No. 10, pp. 102-12.
Leopulos, V., Voulgaridou, D., Bellos, E. and Kirytopoulos, K. (2010), "Integrated management systems: moving from function to organisation/decision view", The TQM Journal, Vol. 22 No. 6, pp. 594-628.
Levy, D.L. (1997), "Lean production in an international supply chain", Sloan Management Review, Winter, pp. 94-102.
Linton, J.D., Klassen, R. and Jayaraman, V. (2007), "Sustainable supply chains: an introduction", Journal of Operations Management, Vol. 25 No. 6, pp. 1075-82.
Lubin, D.A. and Esty, D.C. (2010), "The sustainability imperative", Harvard Business Review, Vol. 88 No. 5, pp. 42-50.
McIvor, R. (2001), "Lean supply: the design and cost reduction dimensions", European Journal of Purchasing and Supply Management, Vol. 7 No. 4, pp. 227-42.
MacCallum, R. (1986), "Specification searches in covariance structure modelling", Psychological Bulletin, Vol. 100, pp. 107-20.
Malhotra, M.K. and Sharma, S. (2008), "Measurement equivalence using generalizability theory: an examination of manufacturing flexibility dimensions", Decision Sciences, Vol. 39 No. 4, pp. 643-69.
Montabon, F., Sroufe, R. and Narasimhan, R. (2007), "An examination of corporate reporting, environmental management practices and firm performance", Journal of Operations Management, Vol. 25 No. 5, pp. 998-1014.
Morris, M.W. and Su, S.K. (1999), "Social psychological obstacles in environmental conflict resolution", American Behavioral Scientist, Vol. 42 No. 8, pp. 1322-49.
Nadler, D. and Tushman, M. (1980), "A model for diagnosing organizational behaviour", Organizational Dynamics, Vol. 9 No. 2, pp. 35-51.
Nawrocka, D., Brorson, T. and Lindhqvist, T. (2009), "ISO 14001 in

environmental supply chain practices", Journal of Cleaner Production, Vol. 17 No. 16, pp. 1435-43.

Nunnally, J.C. (1978), Psychometric Theory, McGraw Hill, New York, NY.

O'Brien, C. (1999), "Sustainable production – a new paradigm for a new millennium", International Journal of Production Economics, Vol. 60-61 No. 1, pp. 1-7.

Pagell, M. and Gobeli, D. (2009), "How plant managers' experiences and attitudes towards sustainability relate to operational performance", Production and Operations Management Journal, Vol. 18 No. 3, pp. 278-99.

Pagell, M., Krumwiede, D.W. and Sheu, C. (2007), "Efficacy of environmental and supplier relationship investments – moderating effects of external environment", International Journal of Production Research, Vol. 45 No. 9, pp. 2005-28.

Pagell, M., Wiengarten, F. and Fynes, B. (2013), "Institutional effects and the decision to make environmental investment", International Journal of Production Research, Vol. 51 No. 2, pp. 427-46.

Pagell, M., Wu, Z. and Wasserman, M.E. (2010), "Thinking differently about purchasing portfolios: an assessment of sustainable sourcing", Journal of Supply Chain Management, Vol. 46 No. 1, pp. 57-73.

Pagell, M., Yang, C., Krumwiede, D.K. and Sheu, C. (2004), "Does the competitive environment influence the efficacy of investments in environmental management?", Journal of Supply Chain Management, Vol. 40 No. 3, pp. 30-9.

Parmigiani, A., Klassen, R. and Russo, M. (2011), "Efficiency meets responsibility: configuring an accountable and responsible supply chain", Journal of Operations Management, Vol. 29, pp. 212-23.

Paulraj, A. (2011), "Understanding the relationship between internal resources and capabilities, sustainable supply chain management and organizational sustainability", Journal of Supply Chain Management, Vol. 47 No. 1, pp. 19-37.

Podsakoff, P.M., MacKenzie, S.B., Lee, J.Y. and Podsakoff, N.P. (2003), "Common method biases in behavioural research: a critical review of the literature and recommended remedies", Journal of Applied Psychology, Vol. 88 No. 5, pp. 879-903.

Power, D., Schoenherr, T. and Samson, D. (2010), "The cultural characteristic of individualism/collectivism: a comparative study of implications for investments in operations between emerging Asian and industrialized Western countries", Journal of Operations Management, Vol. 28 No. 3, pp. 206-22.

Preacher, K.J., Curran, P.J. and Bauer, D.J. (2006), "Computational tools for probing interaction effects in multiple linear regression, multilevel modelling, and latent curve analysis", Journal of Educational and Behavioral Statistics, Vol. 31 No. 4, pp. 437-48.

Rigby, D. and Bilodeau, B. (2009), Management Tools and Trends 2009, Bain & Company, London.

Romano, P. and Vinelli, A. (2001), "Quality management in a supply chain perspective: strategic and operative choices in a textile-apparel network", International Journal ofOperations & Production Management, Vol. 21 No. 4, pp. 446-60.

Rothenberg, S., Pil, F.K. and Maxwell, J. (2001), "Lean, green, and the quest for superior performance", Production and Operations Management, Vol. 10 No. 3, pp. 228-43.

Rusinko, C.A. (2005), "Using quality management as a bridge to environmental sustainability in organizations", SAM Advanced Management Journal, Vol. 70 No. 4.

Russo, M. and Fouts, P. (1997), "A resource-based perspective on corporate environmental performance and profitability", Academy of Management Journal, Vol. 40 No. 3, pp. 534-59.

Sakakibara, S., Flynn, B.B., Schroeder, R.G. and Morris, W.T. (1997), "The impact of just-in-time manufacturing and its infrastructure on manufacturing performance", Management Science, Vol. 43 No. 9, pp. 1246-57.

Schoenherr, T. (2011), "The role of environmental management in sustainable business development: a multi-country investigation", International Journal of Production Economics, Vol. 140 No. 1, pp. 116-28.

Schoenherr, T. and Narasimhan, R. (2012), "The fit between capabilities and priorities and its impact on performance improvement: revisiting and extending the theory of production competence", International Journal of Production Research, Vol. 50 No. 14, pp. 3755-37775.

Shah, R. and Ward, P.T. (2003), "Lean manufacturing: context, practice bundles, and performance", Journal of Operations Management, Vol. 21 No. 2, pp. 129-49.

Simpson, D.F. and Power, D.J. (2005), "Use the supply relationship to develop lean and green suppliers", Supply Chain Management: An International Journal, Vol. 10 No. 1, pp. 60-8.

So, S. and Sun, H.Y. (2010), "Supplier integration strategy for lean manufacturing adoption in electronic-enabled supply chains", Supply Chain Management: An International Journal, Vol. 15 No. 6, pp. 474-87.

Sroufe, R. and Curkovic, S. (2008), "An examination of ISO 9000:2000 and supply chain quality assurance", Journal of Operations Management, Vol. 26 No. 4, pp. 503-20.

Svensson, G. (2007), "Aspects of sustainable supply chain management (SSCM): conceptual framework and empirical example", Supply Chain Management: An International Journal, Vol. 12 No. 4, pp. 262-6.

Swafford, P.M., Ghosh, S. and Murthy, N. (2006), "The antecedents of supply chain agility of a firm: Scale development and model testing", Journal of Operations Management, Vol. 24 No. 2, pp. 170-88.

Swink, M., Narasimhan, R. and Kim, S.W. (2005), "Manufacturing practices and strategy integration: effects on cost efficiency, flexibility, and market-based performance", Decision Sciences, Vol. 36 No. 3, pp. 427-75.

Teece, D.J. (1986), "Firm boundaries, technological innovation and strategic planning", in Thomas, G.L. (Ed.), The Economics of Strategic Planning, D.C., Heath, Lexington, MA, pp. 187-99.

Vanichchinchai, A. and Igel, B. (2011), "The impact of total quality management on supply chain management and firm's performance", International Journal of Production Research, Vol. 49 No. 11, pp. 3405-24.

Walker, H. and Brammer, S. (2009), "Sustainable procurement in the United Kingdom", Supply Chain Management: An International Journal, Vol. 14 No. 2, pp. 128-37.

Walley, N. and Whitehead, B. (1994), "It's not easy being green", Harvard Business Review, Vol. 72 No. 3, pp. 46-51.

Ward, P. and Zhou, H. (2006), "Impact of information technology integration and lean/just-in-time practices on lead-time performance", Decision Sciences, Vol. 37 No. 2, pp. 177-203.

Wernerfelt, B. (1984), "A resource-based view of the firm", Strategic Management Journal, Vol. 5 No. 2, pp. 171-80.

Whybark, C. (1997), "GMRG survey research in operations management", International Journal of Operations & Production Management, Vol. 17 No. 7, pp. 686-96.

Whybark, C., Wacker, J. and Sheu, C. (2009), "The evolution of an international academic manufacturing survey", Decision Line, May, pp. 17-19.

Wiengarten, F., Pagell, M. and Fynes, B. (2012), "Supply chain environmental investments in dynamic industries: comparing investment and performance differences with static industries", International Journal of Production Economics, Vol. 135 No. 2, pp. 541-51.

Wiengarten, F., Fynes, B., Pagell, M. and de Burca, S. (2011), "Exploring the impact of national culture on investments in manufacturing practices and performance: an empirical multi-country study", International Journal of Operations and Production Management, Vol. 31 No. 5, pp. 554-78.

Withers, B. and Ebrahimpour, M. (2002), "ISO 9000 certification: the financial performance implications", Total Quality Management, Vol. 18 No. 4, pp. 217-31.

World Commission on Environment and Development (WCED) (1987), Our Common Future, Oxford University Press, Oxford.

Yang, C.L., Lin, S.P., Chan, Y.H. and Sheu, C. (2010), "Mediated effect of environmental management on manufacturing competitiveness: An empirical study", International Journal of Production Economics, Vol. 123 No. 2, pp. 210-20.

Yang, M.G., Hong, P. and Modi, S.B. (2011), "Impact of lean manufacturing and environmental management on business performance: an empirical study of manufacturing firms", International Journal of Production Economics, Vol. 129 No. 2, pp. 251-61.

Appendix

Table AI Survey instrument

Investments in manufacturing practices							
In the last two years, to what extent has the plant invested resources (money, time and/or people) in programs in the following areas? (range: 1 = not at all; 4 = to some extent; 7 = to a great extent)							
ISO 9000	1	2	3	4	5	6	7
Supplier Certification	1	2	3	4	5	6	7
Statistical Process Control	1	2	3	4	5	6	7
Six Sigma	1	2	3	4	5	6	7
Cellular Manufacturing	1	2	3	4	5	6	7
JIT	1	2	3	4	5	6	7
Manufacturing throughput time reduction	1	2	3	4	5	6	7
Set-up time reduction	1	2	3	4	5	6	7
ISO 14000	1	2	3	4	5	6	7
Pollution Prevention	1	2	3	4	5	6	7
Recycling Of Materials	1	2	3	4	5	6	7
Waste Reduction	1	2	3	4	5	6	7
Operational supply chain performance (Recoded into positive outcomes)							
What are the plant's approximate reject/return percentages at each of the following stages?							
Percent rejects of incoming material							
Percent rejects during processing (scrap rate)							
Percent rejects at final inspection							
Percent returns from the customer							
What percentage of the plant's customer orders is delivered late?							
What percent of the plant's purchase orders do suppliers deliver late?							
Control variables							
Please identify the industry sector that describes your business activity							
Approximately how many total employees work for the plant?							

CHAPTER FOUR

APPROPRIATION REGIMES AND FIRM PERFORMANCE IN INCUMBENT SERVICES FIRMS

PETER MCNAMARA, CATHAL RYAN, DARRAN JONES AND CAMILLA NOONAN

Introduction

This chapter offers insights for service firm innovators into the mechanisms that are most effective in appropriating an economic return from innovations that create new service products and the processes that underpin the design and delivery of such services. We assume that a primary purpose of innovations, be they innovations in the processes that generate a service or an innovation in a service being offered to customers, is to capture profits for the firm. Practical examples of a service innovation in our study would be the introduction of a new communications support system for customers, a new type of working capital bank loan product for business customers, or a new engineering consulting service for road infrastructure contractors. Process improvements might include creating systems in a consulting firm to more efficiently train new graduates in client engagement, improvements to the process of credit approval by a bank, or a new audit design process by an accountancy firm.

A recent review of the literature on appropriation regimes (James, Leiblein and Lu 2013) demonstrates that much is known about the relationship between four individual appropriation regimes, namely patents, secrecy, lead time, and complementary assets, and also about manufacturing settings. Less is known about how different appropriation regimes are bundled together to collectively impact on protecting profits of innovation and also more generally about service firm appropriation regimes. James et al (2013) recommend that researchers seek to fill these gaps using CEO or R&D function surveys that explore combinations of appropriation mechanisms and how these impact on profit protection in multiple settings. This chapter addresses this call to action. Our first contribution is therefore to identify clusters of appropriation mechanisms that bundle together into distinct appropriation regimes, which are conceptually and statistically valid, and then to test their individual and interactive relationship with firm performance.

We surveyed 622 service firms with more than 50 employees located on the island of Ireland, obtaining a response from 188 CEO/business level senior management, to estimate how effective a series of mechanisms was to protect the profit streams that flowed from innovations to service offerings as well as from innovation in the processes that are used to design and deliver services. These firms were typically incumbents, with an installed base of customers, and hence their innovations sought to retain installed customers in the face of competition while growing into new markets. We explore the four appropriation regimes noted by James et al (2013). We expand on these, which results in a clustering of five appropriation regimes. Our work addresses mechanisms that protect both service products and process innovations, thus bringing together in one service industry survey multiple appropriation regimes across the spectrum of innovation activity. We found that profit streams of service offerings were protected by the stability of their legal protections (copyrights, patents, and trade secrecy) and by the coherence of their market offering (reputation regarding quality, compatibility with existing services, and marketing support staff). Process innovations were protected by legal stability: process commercialisation protections (accreditation of the process, branding, and long term contracts with customers), and internal resource supports (dedicated project management, supportive organisational culture, and compatibility with existing processes).

Using a ten-item scale of firm profitability, we observed that both the appropriation regimes of legal product stability and an internal process resource are negatively associated with profit streams: they may create innovations, but they fail to protect profit streams. Effective appropriation regimes that protect innovation profits were: the product commercialisation appropriation regime for the service offering (reputation for quality, dedicated marketing staff, and compatibility with existing products), process commercialisation appropriation regimes (helping the process to be recognised as quality by external customers and orientated to their needs) and legal protection of the process from imitation. Our study highlights that purely legal methods to protect the profit streams of an innovation have limited impact; however, appropriation regimes deploying a mix of legal and non-legal mechanisms do protect profits flowing from service 'product' and process innovations. A moderating effect was observed but only in limited circumstances; thus many of these appropriation regime clusters were found to have independent and not interactive impacts on profit streams.

This study has three research questions. First, how to identify conceptually and empirically valid clusters of appropriation mechanisms in practice. Second, how do these clusters, which we refer to as appropriation regimes, impact firm performance? Third, how do moderations between appropriation regimes impact firm performance? These research questions are important to theory as they seek to fill gaps in the relevant body of literature, and to industry as the answers to these questions could provide a road map for managers wishing to maximise returns from innovations. We use a unique survey dataset from CEO/Head of Business Unit respondents across the Irish services industry to address these questions.

The remainder of this chapter is divided into five parts. The first part consists of a literature review, which seeks to generate valid hypotheses. It will be seen that appropriation mechanisms can be divided into legal and non-legal appropriation regimes, and this structure forms the basis for our hypotheses.

The second part outlines the research methodology that has been used. The research design can be classified as exploratory, with a quantitative exploration, i.e. a cross-sectional design of a single cross section. A postal survey approach was deemed best fit for reasons outlined within. Finally, the dependent, independent, and control variables are discussed.

The third part details our first contribution to the relevant body of literature. We provide five conceptually and empirically valid appropriation regime bundles. Each of these appropriation regime clusters consists of three individual mechanisms that protect the profits of innovations from imitation by rivals. These appropriation regime clusters are: product legal stability, product commercialisation, process internal focus, process commercialisation, and process lead stability.

The fourth part outlines the testing of our performance hypothesis, where we detail the individual and interactive relationships between these five appropriation regime clusters and firm performance.

The fifth part discusses our results and outlines our contributions, limitations, and directions for future research.

Part I: Literature Review and Hypothesis Development

Introduction to Innovation, Appropriation and Firm Performance

We use a broad definition of innovation, "Innovation is an application of knowledge to produce new knowledge" (Drucker, 1993). Not all innovations are commercially successful, and therefore innovators can be classified as firms who are first to commercialise a new product or process in the market (Teece, 1986). This study concentrates on both service 'product' and process innovations: service product innovations are outputs or services that are introduced for the benefit of customers or clients; process innovations in contrast are tools, devices, and knowledge in throughput technology that mediate inputs and outputs and are new to an industry, organisation, or subunit, (Gopalakrishnan and Damanpour, 1997). However, it is important to note that process innovations can often lead to product innovations (Mansfield et al., 1977). A process innovation could increase the effectiveness of a software package for instance, resulting in reduced processing time (which is a product innovation).

Many authors have found innovations to have a direct impact on firm performance (Teece, 1986; Bresnahan et al., 1997; Cho and Pucik, 2005; Greenhalgh et al., 2004; Koellinger, 2008; Levin et al., 1987). In particular, product innovations contribute to economic progress by expanding the range of products available to customers and by improving the performance dimensions of existing products (perhaps through complementary benefits), (Bresnahan et al., 1997; Tushman and Anderson, 1986; McGahan and Silverman, 2006). Process innovations can benefit through cost-cutting measures, offering new services to customers, and improving product innovations (Mansfield et al., 1977; Rosenkranz, 2003).

Innovation can also be seen to fit into the resource-based view of the firm, in which resources are stocks of available factors owned or controlled by the firm (Amit and Schoemaker, 1993). A key underpinning to the resource base view is the principle that sustainable competitive advantage can be achieved through resources that are inimitable, rare, valuable, and non-substitutable; or, in other words, resources that are in some way superior to those of competitors (Barney, 1991; Grant, 1991; Penrose, 1959; Peteraf, 1993; Wernerfelt, 1984). These characteristics can be achieved through innovation (Cho and Pucik, 2005). Therefore, it is very important for firms to protect their innovations in order to achieve a return on investment in innovation. Arrow argued that innovators require a period of transitory market power to create such a return (Arrow, 1962). Building on the contribution of Arrow, others also argue that returns from innovation are only sustainable up until the point that competitors will be able to copy the innovation and the complementary assets required (Beath, Katsoulacous and Ulph, 1995; Gotz, 1999; Koellinger, 2008; Sherry and Teece, 2004; Geroski, Machin and Vanreenen, 1993). Such instances are common and are often caused by spillovers (McGahan and Silverman, 2006), and consequently, the timing of an innovation also influences the expected payoff, (Koellinger, 2008).

Firms seek to protect their innovations through means such as appropriation regimes – "a regime of appropriability refers to the environmental factors, excluding firm and market structure, that govern an innovator's ability to capture the profits generated by an innovation" (Teece, 1986). We take a broad view of appropriation regimes, and thus include the traditionally researched ones such as patenting, commercial secrecy, and complementary assets, but take a more finely-grained perspective and also include the following in our study: complexity of the service 'product', compatibility with existing service 'products', marketing staff, quality of service 'products', non-compete clauses, and external accreditations such as quality marks (Levin et al., 1987; Teece, 1986; Arundel, 2001; Rogers, 1983; Hooley et al., 2005; Cho and Pucik, 2005; Samila and Sorenson, 2011). These can allow an innovator a period of transitory market power and reduce spillovers, thereby helping to maximise returns from innovation.

The impact and effectiveness of methods of appropriability vary across industries and within industry (Teece, 1986; Levin et al., 1987; Koellinger, 2008; Arundel, 2001; Teece, 2006). Consequently, generalizations from the relevant body of literature have been difficult, and there are many inconsistencies. Wolfe commented in 1994 that the most consistent theme found in innovation literature is that its research results have been inconsistent (Wolfe, 1994). From a search of the literature it appears little has changed since Wolfe's study. Some have tried to form theories of intellectual property and innovation but have been unsuccessful (Andersen and Konzelmann, 2008). Jones et al (2013) have undertaken a large review of this literature, and yet inconsistencies in what regimes matter at all, which matter most, and how they combine to protect profits are all issues that remain in the literature. Amara et al (2008) note that, "Few studies have examined the question of how several protection methods are used in complementarity to prevent imitation from competitors", a point very much echoed by the conclusions and suggestions for further research of Jones et al (2013) a few years later.

Our study seeks to make a contribution to this literature by clustering, using a systematic method, and different appropriation mechanisms into distinct regimes, which will be composed of legal, non-legal, and mixed (containing legal and non-legal mechanisms) regimes. These clusters will then be tested to assess their impact on firm performance. It is hoped that by distinguishing among the clusters, determinants of performance in an innovation context can be observed. The moderating effect between regimes on firm performance has not been widely researched. Therefore, as process innovations can often lead to product innovations (Mansfield et al., 1977), this study focuses on both process innovations and service 'product' innovations in order to test for moderating effects.

The rest of this part of our chapter will review the current literature on appropriation mechanisms that are included in this study (brief definition, benefits, and any relevant limitation of each), which can be classified as legal and non-legal (Amara et al., 2008, Andersen and Konzelmann, 2008).

Four Legal Appropriation Mechanisms

We measure the relationship between four legal appropriation regimes and protection of profits, namely: patents, trade secrets, copyright, and non-compete clauses. In theory, such methods provide a reliable legal protection from imitation by other firms (Amara et al., 2008; Jones et al., 2013). In practice, however, firms may find legal enforcement of these rights problematic (Arundel and Kabla, 1998, Cho and Pucik, 2005). Reasons why legal rights may be difficult to enforce include but are not limited to: lacking the resources to enforce rights, the length of time it takes to enforce rights in court versus the limited time to exploit an opportunity commercially, competing legal rights from other firms which make determination of who owns what complex in the eyes of the courts, complexities over international legal property rights, and complexities of jurisdictions of enforcement, limited damages from infringement of rights versus the commercial gains from using the legally protected knowledge.

Patents

Patents are partial and temporary monopolies that are granted to inventors under a given set of conditions, (Coriat and Orsi, 2002). The awarding of a temporary monopoly gives an innovator the opportunity to gain a return on innovation. Some studies have shown that patented innovations are positively related to financial market value (Reitzig, 2004). However, many other studies have confirmed empirically that patents do not operate in practice as they do in theory (Teece, 1986, Levin et al., 1987, Arundel, 2001, Cho and Pucik, 2005). The main limitation of patenting is the release of information by publishing a patent and competitors being able to legally "invent around" patents, (Levin et al., 1987; Arundel, 2001; Arundel and Kabla, 1998). Even without the release of information, once products or services have been released to the market they can be reverse engineered, (Arundel, 2001). The protection provided by a patent is very much dependent on the legal system of the country in which it originates (Ceccagnoli 2009). In cases were patent appropriability is weak, firms can lose the benefits of their own innovations to competitors; but on the flip side, they can gain from the innovations of their rivals by being able to integrate their own inventions with advances from other innovators (McGahan and Silverman, 2006).

Product patents have been shown to be more effective than process patents (Levin et al., 1987). Evidence suggests firms believe product patents are useful in protecting innovations (Arundel, 2001), with the propensity rates for product patents increasing since the 1990s with an average of 35.9% of products patented but with large deviations across industry (Arundel and Kabla, 1998). Patents are not only useful in their traditional sense of merely protecting the innovation but also in acting as a signal of a firm's expertise, which in turn can attract investors and trading partners, (Mazzoleni and Nelson, 1998; Arundel, 2001). Others have attributed the increase in patenting to an essential increase in "patentable innovations" (Kortum and Lerner, 1999 i.e. completely new products/processes rather than small incremental changes to existing products, (Arundel, 2001).

Trade Secrecy

In a comprehensive review of the appropriation regime literature by Jones et al (2013), patenting was the most researched regime, closely followed by its mirror mechanism of protecting innovations, namely secrecy. A patent offers a limited exclusive use of an innovation in return for public disclosure of the methodology underpinning the invention. It requires in essence that imitators could copy the idea based on the patent documentation. In contrast, innovations could be deliberately protected from imitation by rivals by the firm, making a reasonable effort to keep the method of invention secret from the outside world. Firms that do not wish to disclose information can use trade secrets as a viable alternative (Arundel, 2001; Teece, 1986; Hannah, 2005). Friedman et al (1991) define a trade secret as “an item of information - a customer list, business plan, or manufacturing process - that has commercial value and that the firm possessing the information wants to conceal from its competitors in order to prevent them from duplicating it”. The enforcement and underlying legislation regarding trade secrecy mainly comes from case law but also has protection under patent law and competition law (Lavery, 1996).

Trade secrets work best when a firm can release its innovation to customers and still keep the underlying technology secret (Teece, 1986). Trade secrets perform best when tacit knowledge, or knowledge that is unarticulated and tied to the senses, movement skills, physical experiences, intuition, or implicit rules of thumb (Nonaka and von Krogh, 2009) are being secured (Bharadwaj et al., 1993). Secrecy protects innovations from expropriation, but this also leads to a key limitation: secrecy makes it difficult for customers and other trading partners to assess the quality of a supplier’s products (Terlaak and King, 2006). Secrecy also creates an information asymmetry between the firm that holds the secret knowledge versus those that do not. If this secret knowledge is commercially valuable then it can be used to create higher profits, or more formally it allows for abnormally high economics rents (Liebeskind, 1997).

Arundel (2001) found trade secrecy was more effective than patents in protecting process innovations and that trade secrecy works best for process innovations rather than for product innovations. Trade secrets provide a valuable source for product protection, especially given that not all innovations can be patented due to their very nature (Liebeskind, 1997). Trade secrets can also be used in tandem with other mechanisms (Friedman et al., 1991; Arundel, 2001; Teece, 1986; Arora, 1997). Recent reviews of the literature observe that disclosure of information, for example through a patent, is more likely to be effective in high technology industries, where the costs of disclosing inaccurate information are high and the protection of patenting is strong, whilst trade secrecy is more likely to be valuable in industries where disclosure protections are uncertain (Jones et al. 2013). The nature of service industries is often that there is considerable interaction with the customer and that innovation is not strictly technical; thus trade secrets are likely to be an effective method of appropriation.

Copyright

Copyright is a legal term describing rights given to the authors and creators of work such as computer programmes, original databases, broadcasts, and recordings (Irish Copyright and Related Rights Act, 2000). This legislation grants authors the exclusive right to prohibit or authorise others to copy their work, perform their work, make their work available to the public, or make an adaption to their work for a period between 50-70 years (Irish Copyright and Related Rights Act, 2000). This means, by effectively leasing it to another party, a firm can profit from an innovation even if they decide not to pursue it further. Copyright is generally associated with product innovations rather than process innovations (Samuelson, 2007); however, for completeness we also test it for process protection.

Copyright has been shown to be an effective protector of the returns from innovation (Teece, 1986), but, similar to patents, it is enforcement of such rights that is important. The view has been long held that the "case for copyright protection is weak" (Breyer, 1970). Nevertheless, in regions such as Europe, copyright industries are increasingly well protected due to their contribution to service economies (Media Group, 2003). The effectiveness of the copyright system is also influenced by predominant norms, values, and beliefs in cultural expressions and ideas (Andersen and Konzelmann, 2008). One of the main limitations of copyright regards the transaction costs incurred to obtain the copyright itself and challenges in enforcement of such rights.

Non-Compete Clauses

Non-compete clauses are covenants in employment contracts that specify a post-employment period of time during which individuals are restricted from competing with their former employers (Samila and Sorenson, 2011; Stuart and Sorenson, 2003). They are used mainly to protect intellectual property, trade secrets, honour customer confidentiality, human capital, and business relationships (Samila and Sorenson, 2011; Valiulis, 1985) and are increasingly used, particularly for middle management and technical workers (Samila and Sorenson, 2011; Marx et al., 2009; Stuart and Sorenson, 2003; Franco and Mitchell, 2008).

Where enforced, non-compete clauses effectively give the employer property rights over tacit knowledge, avoiding information spillover to competitors and the subsequent diffusion of innovation (Gilson, 1999). There is scepticism in the literature surrounding whether non-compete clauses can be readily enforced (Samila and Sorenson, 2011; Franco and Mitchell, 2008). One of the major problems that have been noted is the unwillingness of governments and courts to enforce these clauses. Enforcement of non-compete clauses can conflict with wider societal economic goals of free movement of labour, thus limiting enforcement of these clauses in practice (Samila and Sorenson, 2011). Several studies have shown that the success of Silicon Valley and the failure of Massachusetts Route 128 were due to the differential enforcement of non-compete clauses (Gilson, 1999; Samila and Sorenson, 2011).

Taken as a whole, the above discussion leads us to hypothesise positive relationships between legal appropriation regimes and profit protection.

> Hypothesis 1a: Service '*Product' legal* appropriation regimes will have a positive effect on firm performance.

> Hypothesis 1b: *Process legal* appropriation regimes will have a positive effect on firm performance.

Eleven Non-Legal Appropriation Mechanisms

Non-legal appropriation regimes lack formal legal protection but are often embedded in the daily routines of firms (Andersen and Konzelmann, 2008), making them effective means by which an innovation is protected. We study eleven appropriation mechanisms. Overall these could be classified as a combination of complementary assets and lead or first mover advantages that have been conceptually highlighted in the literature (Jones et al 2013) but not combined together in a single study. These appropriation mechanisms are: external accreditation, reputation regarding quality,dedicated marketing staff, dedicated project management staff, organisational culture, long term contracts with customers, branding, first mover advantages, participation of customers, compatibility with existing products and services, and complexity of copying the process or service.

A service 'product' is also an experience good, in that the quality of the service is not fully known to the customer until after consumption. Do we really know the quality of our bank until we face a problem as either a saver or borrower? It is only when a problem arises that the customer knows if the bank will deliver on its promises to repay depositors, to assist borrowers, to be prudent for regulators. Does a consultancy customer know the value of advice until the advice is put to the test, which often comes after the point of consumption? For example we do not know the value of legal service advice until we have cause to test the strength of our contracts when difficulties arise, such as when a property purchaser is challenged over the title of their lands. Do we really know that a communications system is effective until at a future point it crashes in the face of high usage and we have cause to rely upon the service support claims of the provider? A key appropriation mechanism for innovations may therefore be the signals that are provided as to the quality of a service experience. There are multiple mechanisms through which the quality of a service experience can be communicated, including accreditation of the service by an external (honest) broker, reputation in the market for the quality of the service, branding (that signals trust in the service), participation of customers (that signals customer involvement in development, hence they have prior experience of testing the experience claims of the product). Each of these mechanisms is thus tested in this study and collectively they are an appropriation regime for an experience good. Additionally, we test other non-legal mechanisms as noted above and detailed below.

External Accreditation

External accreditations such as ISO, quality marks, and industry awards can act as a signal of quality to customers and business partners (Tsekouras et al., 2002; Lima, Resende and Hasenclever, 2000; Milgrom and Roberts, 1986; Terlaak and King, 2006; Beatty and Smith, 1987) and act as an appropriation mechanism by distancing a firm from competitors (Semadeni, 2006). Some studies found an association between accreditation and performance (Tsekouras et al., 2002; Terlaak and King, 2006; Darnall and Edwards; 2006; Lafuente et al., 2010), but others found no such relationship or indeed a negative one, (Lima et al., 2000; King and Lenox, 2002).

One common theme across the literature is that external accreditation can be used as a signalling tool to attract customers, investment, and business partners, which has been found to have a significant impact on firm performance (Milgrom and Roberts, 1986). Some authors have even suggested that firms may use ISO 9000 as their primary instrument for signalling quality to their customers (Cole, 1998). Possessing certain types of certification can often be a critical requirement to enter into particular buyer-supplier relationships (Terlaak and King, 2006) and can reduce customer search, (Beatty and Smith, 1987).

The main weakness of using external accreditation is that often tacit knowledge contained within the firm needs to be codified to enable the creation of a quality management document in order to achieve certain standards. This takes time and increases the risk of information spillover as tacit knowledge becomes codified.

Reputation Regarding Quality

A broad definition of quality is one whereby the attributes of quality associated with performance include reliability, conformance, durability, serviceability, aesthetics, and perceived quality (Garvin, 1984). Cho and Pucik (2005) conducted a comprehensive study on the impact of quality on performance, some of their main findings discussed below. Quality is generally perceived as a dynamic threshold that firms must meet in order to satisfy customers and is a key determinant in returns generated from an innovation (Cho and Pucik, 2005). The impact of innovativeness on profitability has also been found to be mediated by quality (Cho and Pucik, 2005). Similar to external accreditation, a reputation regarding quality helps to distance a firm from its competitors. Other studies have also found a positive relationship between quality reputation and return (Phillips, Chang and Buzzell, 1983; Schoeffl et al., 1974) and also a positive relationship between stock return and changes in quality perceptions (Aaker and Jacobson, 1994).

Dedicated Marketing Staff

Marketing staff can be viewed as the knowledge bridge between the market and the process of innovation. Dedicated marketing staff can take the time to analyse a market and to understand its structures, needs, challenges, and methods of extracting value. They can infuse the innovation process with this market knowledge, ensuring that when an innovation arrives in the market, it has a greater chance of fitting the needs and structures of the market and thus extracting profits.

The impact of different marketing resources on firm performance has been a significant theme in marketing literature (Bharadwaj et al., 1993; Day, 1994; Hunt and Morgan, 1995; Webster, 1992; Hooley et al., 2005). Marketing resources are "defined as any attribute, tangible or intangible, physical or human, intellectual or relational, that can be deployed by the firm to achieve a competitive advantage in its markets" (Hooley et al., 2005). Marketing capabilities can protect returns from innovations since leveraging marketing resources place a firm in a stronger position to succeed in the marketplace (Srivastava, Shervani and Fahey, 1998; Hooley et al., 2005). As recent studies have shown, marketing capabilities have a greater impact on performance than R&D or operations capabilities (Krasnikov and Jayachandran, 2008).

Dedicated Project Management

Dedicated project management staff working on and supporting an innovation product or process can act as a bridge between knowledge of technology and the market, facilitating smooth implementation of a project along the innovation and commercialisation cycle. This ought to assist the firm in improving the efficiency and speed of the innovation process and ensuring coordination between the technical and market needs of an innovation.

Project management is another capability that can be associated with successful innovation and is a method of isolating a firm from imitation. Project management can be defined as "the application of processes, methods, knowledge, skills and experience to achieve the project objectives" (Association for Project Management, 2016). The core characteristics of this definition are time, cost, and quality, known as the Iron Triangle (Larson, 2011). These aspects of project management help to protect the returns from an innovation, given they all have a cost or resource constraint element attached to them. The reasoning behind this is that project management allows for greater efficiencies in these areas (Larson, 2011). In process innovations, a key role of the project management team is to oversee the implementation of a new process innovation and its assimilation with existing processes. Without this assimilation a process innovation would be a silo and therefore would not be able to reach its full potential. Consequently, a dedicated project management team plays a key role in achieving returns from process innovations.

Organisational Culture

Organisational culture can be defined as "the specific collection of values and norms that are shared by people and groups in an organisation and that control the way they interact with each other and with stakeholders outside the organisation" (Charles, 2001). A firm's culture can allow its operations to flow smoothly and can be considered as a source of sustainable competitive advantage allowing a firm to obtain an abnormal level of profit, (Barney, 1986). This is because culture is embedded in the very fibre and being of a firm, thus making it difficult if not impossible to to imitate by other firms. Organisational culture can be seen to protect the returns from innovation by protecting tacit knowledge based upon which innovations are created and exploited by firms.

Long Term Contracts with Customers

Long term contracts have become important mechanisms through which firms exchange products, services, and knowledge (Lane and Lubatkin, 1998; Argyres and Mayer, 2007). These contracts have a number of benefits as they "facilitate easier and more frequent communication and information exchange, more effective monitoring of production processes, economies of scale in production, elimination of expenses associated with frequent rebidding for contracts, early supplier involvement leading to faster product development, and mutual cooperation in order fulfilment" (Cohen and Agrawal, 1999). These allow for a minimisation of total costs including production costs, transaction costs (Williamson, 1971), and supply chain costs (Bassok and Anupindi, 1997). To date, long-term contracts have not been widely investigated as an appropriation mechanism, but it is felt that the cost and revenue advantages gained by having long term contracts aid the protection of profit from innovations.

Brand

Branding can be a source of competitive advantage. A brand can be legally protected, but this is not the core of its value-creating potential. Rather, a brand can come to communicate to customers the essence of innovation (rather than technical detail) and can act as a method of protecting innovation (Teece, 2006). Trademarks can also be a source of competitive advantage and can be a visual representation of the firm's brand (Olins, 2008; Cohen, 1986). Information on the impact of branding and trademarks on protecting the returns from innovation are limited. "The subject of branding is virtually never raised in the books and articles on innovation ... However, a brand strategy can be critical to the success of an innovation, particularly in the long-term" (Aaker, 2007). Branding and trademarks can help firms to differentiate their offerings from those of their competitors and in some cases can convey a sense of innovation where in fact no innovation has taken place (Carpenter et al., 1994). Consequently, it can be observed that branding and trademarks have significant potential in the protection of innovation.

First Mover Advantages

The advantages being first in developing a process or product can include higher market share, brand recognition, and penetration, which are mainly created by technology leadership, pre-emption of assets, and buyer switching costs (Lieberman and Montgomery, 1988, Lieberman and Montgomery, 1998). First movers bear the costs and risks associated with initial research and development, building market infrastructures and acceptance of a new process or product. Second movers can face lower costs by imitating or learning from the R&D of the first mover and thus avoid their failures. Second movers in essence can free-ride on the achievements of the first mover, who has resolved the challenges of technological and market uncertainty and shifts in technological or customer needs (Lieberman and Montgomery, 1988; Lieberman and Montgomery, 1998).

Participation of Customers in Process and Product Innovation

Customers can contribute in two ways: as information providers or co-developers (Fang, 2008; Lengnickhall, 1996). In either role customers can provide information regarding market demand, which can lead to demand-driven innovation, which has greater likelihood of being accepted by the market. Indeed, acceptance of an innovation by customers is essential for the success of an innovation (Luo et al., 2007). Participation of customers also has other benefits such as decreasing time to market, improving quality, and decreasing costs (Fang, 2008, LengnickHall, 1996).

Compatibility with Existing Products/Services

From a customer perspective, any product offered by a firm will only be successful if it meets the needs and wants of customers (Bharadwaj et al., 1993; Cho and Pucik, 2005). A new innovation that is compatible with existing complementary products and services should have a greater chance of succeeding when compared to an innovation that lacks compatibility with complementary products (Greenhalgh et al., 2004; Rogers, 1983).

From a firm perspective, compatibility with existing products/services has an additional determinant of success as production and distribution channels may already be established (Greenhalgh et al., 2004). Compatibility can also increase buyer switching costs for customers and therefore protect not only the current innovation but also past innovations. However, increasing switching costs to a high degree can also lock out new services. The compatibility of innovations with existing products and services can play a crucial role in the development of a sustainable, competitive advantage as innovation can often be path-dependent, (Hutzschenreuter and Guenther, 2009).

Complexity of Copying a Service or Process

Complexity can be seen as the extent to which an innovation is perceived by customers and other external parties – as relatively difficult to understand and use (Rogers, 1983; Tornatzky and Klein, 1982; Wolfe, 1994; Zaltman, Duncan and Holbeck, 1973). Complex innovations are defined by a number of characteristics including: degree of customised components, extent of interactions to manage between these components (parts coupling), technological novelty, the breadth of knowledge and skills required, intensity of user involvement, intensity of other supplier involvement, and the degree of new knowledge involved in production (Hobday, 1998, Novak and Eppinger, 2001).

Literature on the impact of complexity on firm performance is scarce. One exception is the work of Arundel, who states that 14.1% of firms use product complexity as their primary appropriation regime (Arundel, 2001). Complexity is not a uniform good as the greater the perceived complexity of a good by customers, the less likely they are to adopt the product (Greenhalgh et al., 2004; Rogers, 1983). Complex products can also cause problems in production and distribution processes when compared to "simple" products, and they can also increase transaction costs (Hobday, 1998; Novak and Eppinger, 2001). Therefore, complexity can be seen as a high risk appropriability strategy in securing returns from innovation.

Based on the evidence reviewed above, we argue that, broadly speaking, non-legal appropriation mechanisms have a positive effect on firm performance.

> Hypothesis 2a: Service '*Product' non-legal* appropriation regimes will have a positive effect on firm performance.

Hypothesis 2b: *Process non-legal* appropriation regimes will have a positive effect on firm performance.

Although appropriation mechanisms can be classified as legal and non-legal, it is anticipated that complementary, mixed clusters may emerge. Such "mixed" appropriation regimes have been observed by Amara et al. (2008), who also investigated service industries. James et al. (2013) argue that future research ought to consider the impact of mixed appropriation regimes on firm performance and the above evidence would point to positive impacts.

Hypothesis 3: *Mixed appropriation* regimes will have a positive effect on firm performance.

Further, to the best knowledge of the authors, and indicated by the literature review of James et al (2013), moderation of appropriation regimes has not been widely tested in the literature. This is surprising given the number of instances in which a process innovation leads to a product innovation (Mansfield et al., 1977). Thus, in response to the calls of James et al (2013), we also consider interactive impacts of appropriation regimes upon each other.

Hypothesis 4: Appropriation regimes will *moderate* each other and will have a positive effect on firm performance.

Part II: Research Methodology

James et al (2013) argue that future development of the literature on the relationship between appropriation regimes and firm performance would be fruitfully served through survey designs that collect original datasets from CEOs or heads of the innovation function and through survey designs which explore how appropriation mechanisms are combined in the field to protect innovations. We designed a survey that asked CEOs (or the head of a subsidiary) two basic questions:

1. "How effective are the following mechanisms in protecting the profit stream from your service/product innovations?", using a 6-item Likert scale (from very ineffective to very effective) of our 16 mechanisms outlined earlier (with the same question asked for process innovations).
2. "With regard to your firm's main marketplace, how would you score your business performance over the last one year relative to your

closest direct competitors?", providing 10 pre-validated measures of firm performance and using a 6-item Likert scale (from much weaker than competitors to much stronger than competitors).

Sample Description: Our Firms and Respondents

We drew our sample of CEO/Managing Director/Head of Subsidiary respondents from the Kompass directory of Irish firms, surveying all firms classified as private sector services – 622 firms (specifically excluding public sector, manufacturing, transportation, agricultural, extractive industry, or entertainment industries) – with more than 50 employees.

We obtained responses from 180 firms, which came from 14 different service sectors. These were classically incumbent firms. Seven industries represented 82% of respondents: Financial Services (26%), Computing and Software (13%), Engineering Services (11%), Communications (11%), Consultancy (6%); Legal Services, Accounting, Healthcare (5% each respectively). The average age of our firms was 35.3 years (median 21 years), with average sales of € 506 million (median € 13.75 m), an average of 70.25% of sales within the domestic market (median 90%); average employee numbers of 316 inside Ireland (median 111) and 7571 outside Ireland (median 2). 37% of them were wholly Irish owned, whilst the remainder were international firms. When asked what percentage of their sales came from products three or fewer years old, 49% of respondents indicated approximately 10%, with 72% of the total sample responding that sales from new products was 30% or less. This is not surprising: given that these were incumbent firms, we would expect most of their service 'products' to be incremental rather than entirely new.

Our respondents had an average of 14.5 years experience in their industry (21.7 years median) and an average of 13.5 years service inside their firm (median 20 years). 70% of the respondents were the CEO or Managing Director of the firm, 23% held a Senior Executive function (e.g. head of division) and 7% were Chief Financial Officers. Thus we can say that our respondents were likely to have a high level of knowledge of their firm and sector, making it likely they both understand the mechanisms that protect innovations in their firm from imitation by rivals and also to have knowledge of the relative performance of their firm. We undertook a similar study using a sample of manufacturing firms (not reported in this chapter), and comparing the two, we see that the service firms are on average larger in terms of sales, but more focused on sales within Ireland.

The survey was pre-tested with ten respondents and underwent a number of revisions to ensure both clarity of the questions asked in the eyes of respondents and face validity with colleagues expert in this field of study. The final survey was distributed along with a cover letter and a free post return envelope as these had been shown to increase response rates (Czaja and Blair, 2005, Dillman, 2007). Further, a donation of €1.00 was also made to the Simon Community (a homeless charity) for every completed survey in order to incentivise recipients to respond. The survey was distributed to 622 firms and achieved a response rate of 30% with 188 surveys returned. 60% of the total responses came within the first three weeks of mailing the survey. To increase the initial response rate, we sent a reminder postcard three weeks after posting the survey, a second questionnaire and cover letter five weeks into the study, and a reminder phone call to address any issues the respondents might have with the survey in week seven. We ceased collection of surveys after ten weeks from the initial posting to respondents. After accounting for missing data and deleting outliers, our final sample included 170 surveys. A copy of the survey is available from the first author of this chapter upon request.

Measures – Dependent Variable

The dependent variable is firm performance. Informal discussions with business leaders in Ireland confirmed that there would be a reluctance to provide actual profit figures even to our survey design that assured respondent confidentiality. Prior research has demonstrated strong association between actual performance of a firm and responses from firms on their relative performance compared to competitors (Morgan and Strong, 2003). An excellent review of the performance literature (Combs, Crook and Shook, 2005) argues that firm performance is multi-dimensional, being a mix of three elements: accounting returns, growth, and stock market performance and also underpinned by operational performance including marketing performance. As many of our firms were not stock market listed, our measure of performance seeks to measure accounting returns (profitability and firm size), growth, and some elements of operational performance (namely customer satisfaction and customer retention). Thus, our measure of firm performance is an additive measure of ten pre-validated scale measures from the literature of firm performance: profitability; growth; firm size, and efficiency.

We used an eight-item scale of firm performance as discussed by Morgan and Strong (2003) to measure most of our items: business performance, market share, customer satisfaction, competitive position, customer retention, sales growth, return on investment, and overall firm performance. This scale was augmented with two additional items in the form of "Net profits" and "Profit margin", which measure relative financial performance. These variables were added to improve the accuracy of the dependent variable and are discussed by Combs et al. (2005). These ten performance variables were measured using a six-item Likert scale with the help of which the respondent was asked to rate their own firm's performance on each of the ten items, from much weaker than competitors (1) to much stronger than competitors (6). There was nonon-applicable option in these performance questions. Forced choice is appropriate as these respondents ought to have a knowledge of the performance of their firm on all ten dimensions.

To ensure the four dimensions of the dependent variable were valid, an exploratory factor analysis (EFA) was conducted on the ten items, to test factor loading for unique communality. Varimax rotation was used with four factors to be extracted. The results can be seen in Table 4.1 and the loading is consistent with Combs et al (2005), as the four dimensions are clearly measured.

Table 4.1: Dependent Variable (10 item scale Cronbach Alpha of .886)

Dependent Variable Scale Items	Factors 1	2	3	4	Cronbach Alpha	Dimensions Measured
Profit margin	.884				.886	Profitability
Net profits	.836					
Return on investment	.829					
Overall firm performance	.538					
Sales growth		.866			.795	Growth
Market share growth		.810				
Market share			.868		.781	Size
Sales volume			.699			
Customer Satisfaction				.895	.776	Efficiency
Customer retention				.857		

The factor analysis produced four distinct factors with strong communality, which were significant with a unique communality above .7 and a residual error of 42%: thus the factor analysis is valid (Field, 2009). In order to test the internal consistency of the ten-item scale, a Cronbach's Alpha reliability analysis was conducted, which provided an alpha of .886. This signifies that these items are correlated with each other (Welch and Comer, 1988; George, 2000), thus providing a reliable scale for measuring firm performance. Further, each of the individual dimensions has a consistent Cronbach's Alpha above 0.7, which is classified as acceptable (George, 2000).

Measures – Independent Variables

The survey contained two distinct sections for service 'product' and process appropriation regimes. Recipients were asked on a six-item Likert scale how effective each appropriation mechanism is in protecting their service 'product'/process innovations. A 'non-applicable' option was available for each of these questions as there is widespread evidence in the literature that firms use a selection of appropriation mechanisms, dependent upon their resources, capabilities, and industry circumstances (James et al. 2013). We used exploratory factor analysis to identify clusters of appropriation regimes, which encouragingly fell into groupings that are logical in the context of prior literature. By using data reduction, exploratory factor analysis (EFA), and principal component analysis (PCA), the data was reduced and the variable items were clustered on the basis of unique communality. The specific independent variables can be seen in the results section.

Measures – Control Variables

This study controlled for firms sales, firm age, total number of firm employees, and the percentage of domestic sales. Each continuous control variable (except % sales) was converted into a log to manage skew. These controls were selected because each has an impact on the four dimensions of the dependent variable, as discussed previously.

Part III: Appropriation Regime Clusters

An Exploratory Factor Analysis was conducted to determine if appropriation mechanisms are individual, or if firms' behaviour is to bundle them into groups that create distinct appropriation regimes. We did this analysis to advance the literature as suggested by James et al. (2013), who argue that through surveys we need to explore whether or not appropriation mechanisms are used as distinct bundles in the strategic action of firms. Varimax rotation was used due to the theoretical unrelated nature of each variable item and that varimax will maximise the dispersion of the loading on each factor (Field, 2009). The number of factors to be extracted was not specified; however, it was specified that eigenvalues above 1 were to be extracted (Field, 2009). Variables were also excluded due to having unique communality below .5 as recommended by Field (2009). This enabled the extraction of two service 'product' and three process clusters based on the following criteria from Table 4.2.

Table 4.2: Criteria to extract appropriation regime clusters

Unique Communality with other variables of	above 0.5	(Field, 2009)
Reproduction correlation residual of	below of 50%	(Field, 2009)
Kaiser-Meyer-Olkin Measure of Sampling Adequacy	above 0.5	(Kaiser, 1974)
No variable item correlation of	above 0.9	(Field, 2009)
Significance of loading onto the components	above 0.512	(Stevens, 2002)

To test the validity of these clusters, a Cronbach's Alpha and a Confirmatory Factor Analysis (CFA) were also conducted. The results of this analysis are discussed below. We will provide justification for why these appropriation mechanisms ought to be considered separate regimes and name them distinctly. The EFA produced legal and non-legal regimes as well as one mixed regime. We will subsequently test each of these appropriation regimes for their individual and interactive relationship with firm performance as per our hypothesis.

Service 'Product' Appropriation Regime Clusters

Statistical Development

Table 4.3 shows the extracted factors with their corresponding names, factor score, and Cronbach Alphas. Cluster 1, legal stability, has a good alpha of .846, which suggests that these item variables are highly correlated (Welch and Comer, 1988). Cluster 2, service 'product' commercialisation, has a more marginal alpha at .685, however it is still valid (Welch and Comer, 1988).

Table 4.3: Service 'Product' Appropriation Regime Clusters

Product Clusters	Cluster Name	Factors 1	Factors 2	Cronbach Alpha
Patents	Legal Stability	.936		.846
Copyright		.918		
Trade Secrecy		.732		
Compatibility with existing products/services	Product Commercialisation		.823	.685
Dedicated marketing staff			.801	
Reputation regarding quality			.699	

The Nature of Service 'Product' Appropriation Regimes

1. Service Product Legal Stability – Patents, Copyright, Secrecy

Patents, copyrights, and secrecy are all legal appropriation regimes that afford a firm a level of institutional protection, allowing for some stability in protecting innovations. Such stability arises naturally, as once these mechanisms are installed, they are static and self-sufficient: protection arises from their implementation, with no further management or monitoring required. Very close comparisons have been made between patents and secrecy, and they are often used in tandem (Friedman et al., 1991; Arundel, 2001; Teece, 1986; Arora, 1997). For example patents can be used to protect certain aspects of an innovation, and secrecy can be used to protect other aspects of the same service 'product' innovation that may not be of a patentable nature. Indeed, copyright can be used to protect the original expression of the innovation, and patent can be used to protect the idea or the concept of the innovation. Dosi (1988) also found that patenting is a complementary appropriability mechanism which does not seem to have a central mechanism - with some exceptions (for example, chemicals and pharmaceutical products). Therefore, other regimes are often required to complement patents, and our study demonstrates that firms combine these with secrecy and copyright.

2. Service 'Product' Commercialisation – Compatibility, Dedicated Marketing Staff, Reputation for Quality

Commercialisation is the procedure "to cause something having only a potential income-producing value to be sold so as to yield income or raise capital" (Jolly, 1997). In contrast to service 'product', legal stability merely protects the actual innovation itself from imitation, whereas service 'product' commercialisation directly seeks to gain a return from innovation through the utilisation of dedicated marketing staff, using compatibility with existing products and services, and a reputation for quality.

A dedicated marketing team can be used to signal the quality attributes of innovations, which can lead to a reputation regarding quality. This reputation can attract customers, resulting in increased firm performance. Compatibility with existing products and services widens the customer appeal base of a product innovation (New and Westbrook, 2004). By providing compatible products to customers, switching costs are increased, which can increase customer retention. Complementary service 'products' may be easier for marketing staff to sell into the market place, as distribution and marketing channels already exist. The complementary effects of these mechanisms help to achieve a return from innovation by actually commercialising the service 'product' and bringing it to market.

Process Appropriation Regime Clusters

Statistical Development

Table 4.4 shows the extracted factors with their corresponding names, factor scores, and Cronbach's Alphas. Process appropriation regime cluster 1, Internal Focus, has a good Alpha at .831, which suggests that these item variables are highly correlated (Welch and Comer, 1988). Process appropriation regime cluster 2, Process Commercialisation, and process appropriation regime cluster 3, Legal Lead Stability, have more satisfactory Alpha at .696, and .684 respectively, and these remain statistically valid (Welch and Comer, 1988).

Table 4.4: Process Clusters

Process Clusters	Cluster Name	Factors 1	2	3	Cronbach Alpha
Organisation Culture	Internal Focus	.835			
Project Management		.830			
Compatibility with existing products/ services		.781			
External Accreditation	Process Commer cialisatio n		.769		
Brand/ Trademark			.750		
Long term contracts with customers			.567		
Trade Secrecy	Legal Lead Stability			.825	
Patents				.719	
Complexity				.665	

The Nature of Process Appropriation Regimes

1. Process Internal Focus – Organisational Culture, Dedicated Project Management, Compatibility

Process internal focus is put forward as an appropriation regime that can be used for process innovations where the benefit created does not necessarily directly impact in ways that are immediately visible to the customer. It can result in cost efficiencies (such as more efficient project management of an innovation), improved innovation processes (through a culture that supports innovation), improved access to markets through compatibility with other processes within the firm or its customers, or perhaps a combination of these. For example, a process innovation that improves internal IT support (such as a new method of remote access) is of benefit to the firm in terms of improving efficiency of sharing knowledge and speed of processes, but might not be directly visible to customers.

Project management allows for greater efficiencies by effectively managing and monitoring cost, time, stakeholders, and quality standard constraintswhen implementing the process innovation. By being compatible with existing processes, the implementation becomes easier and indeed efficiencies can be increased for existing processes through complementary benefits. However, in order for efficiencies to be realised, the firm's organisational culture needs to be open to, and accepting of, new internal process innovations. These efficiencies allow for lower costs to be achieved, resulting in a platform for increasing the return from innovation.

2. Process Commercialisation - External Accreditation, Trademark/Brand, Long-Term Contracts with Customers

Similar to service 'product' commercialisation, process commercialisation seeks to gain a direct return from innovation by creating a branded process that is validated with external accreditations. Such a validated brand can be used in the securing of long-term contracts that help to protect the returns from innovation into the future by reducing transaction costs and ensuring a revenue stream. The accredited brand can differentiate the firm from competitors and can even help to associate the process with that particular firm. These mechanisms in complement increase the barriers to imitation for competitors and thus protect returns from innovation.

3. Process Legal Lead Stability – Trade Secrecy, Patents, Complexity

Process legal lead stability is similar to service 'product' legal stability, with the difference being that complexity is substituted for copyright. Copyrights are generally associated with service 'product' innovations, and their omission here is consistent with the literature (Samuelson, 2007). As noted previously, patents involve the release of information about a particular process. A process that is complex may be observed, but others may lack the capabilities or required understanding to replicate it. Consequently, the use of complexity in tandem with patents can protect innovation to a greater degree. Trade secrets and complexity are believed to be related for a similar reason. Secrecy works best when the underlying technology or process can be used without the customer or rivals understanding how. A key way to achieve this outcome is through complexity or casual ambiguity.

Part IV: Appropriation Regime Clusters and Firm Performance

Hypothesis Testing

Table 4.5 provides our correlation matrix and Table 4.6 the regression models that test our hypothesis. The correlation table shows that there is a significant linear relationship between firm performance and all of the appropriation regime clusters. Our dependent variable is the ten-point additive scale of firm performance. Our independent variables are the five appropriation regime clusters, each being additive scales of three items. All of the control and independent variables were mean-centred to control the Variance Inflation Factor (VIF) in the regression model, which kept them below the minimum threshold of 10 (Kutner, Nachtsheim and Neter, 2004). Mean centring is also necessary for performing interactions. A potential problem of multicollinearity arose given the high correlation of 0.71 between service 'product' 1, legal stability, and process 3, legal lead stability. These fall below the threshold of 0.9 as set out by Field (2009), thus it is appropriate to include these in our model. However, due to reliability concerns, these independent variables will not be interacted with each other as this could skew the model.

A Casewise diagnostic was performed which showed the data was being influenced by some outlier cases. Therefore, the top 2.5% and the bottom 2.5% of performers were removed. A Cook's Distance showed that one case was exerting significant influence over the model as it had a score of 1.65, which is a cause for concern (Field, 2009), and therefore this case was removed. The models represent a good fit for the data by explaining up to 30.8% of firm performance with an adjusted R-squared of 18.5.

Model 1 contains control variables only, with models 2 to 5 testing the hypotheses. Each regression contained two interactions only. Individual regimes in interactions cannot be duplicated as this would skew findings. Hypothesis 1a predicts that service 'product' legal appropriation regime will be positively related to firm performance. Model 2 shows service 'product' appropriation regime cluster 1, legal stability, is a positive, but non-significant, contributor to firm performance. This suggests that service 'product' legal stability is not significantly related to firm performance. However, when the process appropriation regimes are introduced in model 3, the service 'product' legal regime becomes significant and negative ($p < 0.10$). This suggests there is a negative effect on firm performance when in the presence of the process appropriation regimes and Hypothesis 1a is not supported.

Hypothesis 1b predicts process legal appropriation regimes will have a positive effect on firm performance. As discussed in the justification, no purely legal process regimes were found during the EFA, thus Hypothesis 1b could not be tested. A mixed legal/non-legal regime for process innovations was extracted and is discussed in Hypothesis 3.

Hypothesis 2a predicts that non-legal service 'product' appropriation regimes have a positive effect on firm performance. Models 2-5 show service 'product' commercialisation to be positively significant at both the .01 and .05 levels. Thus they provide support for Hypothesis 2a. Hypothesis 2b predicts that non-legal process appropriation regimes have a positive effect on firm performance. Models 3-5 show internal focus to have a negative effect on firm performance at a significant level of .05. Conversely, models 3-5 show process commercialisation to have a positive effect on firm performance at significant levels of .05 and .10. Therefore, partial support is found for Hypothesis 2b.

Hypothesis 3 predicted that mixed appropriation regimes have a positive effect on firm performance. Models 3-5 show process 3, legal lead stability (patents, trade secrecy, and compatibility), has a positive effect on firm performance at the .01 significance level. Indeed, process legal lead stability has the greatest contribution to the model, therefore providing support for Hypothesis 3.

Hypothesis 4 predicts that appropriation regimes will moderate each other and will have a positive effect on firm performance. It is only possible to have two moderations in the model as duplication of individual elements of moderations would bias the results. Due to the high correlation between service 'product' legal stability and process legal lead stability, these were not moderated as they would have biased the regression model. All possible combinations were tested in the regression (but not reported in this chapter). It was found that the following two interactions provided the most significant results: service 'product' commercialisation x process commercialisation, and service 'product' legal stability x process 1 internal focus.

Table 4.5: Correlations

	Mean	Std Dev.	N	1	2	3	4	5	6	7	8	9	10	11
1. Firm performance	42.42	7.66	170	1.00										
2. Log of Sales (log mean = 16.64)	0.00	0.94	146	0.07	1.00									
3. Log of Firm Age (log mean 3.12)	0.00	36.26	166	0.01	0.16**	1.00								
4. % domestic sales (71.04%)	0.00	36.26	163	0.04	-0.01	0.30***	1.00							
5. Log of Employees (log mean 5.65)	0.00	2.08	156	0.02	0.33***	0.03	-0.08	1.00						
6. Service 'Product' legal stability (Copyright, Patents, Trade Secrets; mean =4.17)	0.00	2.08	98	0.13*	-0.03	-0.37*	-0.40*	-0.07	1.00					

7. Service 'Product' Internal Focus (Reputation for Quality, Dedicated Marketing, Compatibility with existing services; mean = 2.84)	0.00	4.17	142	0.31***	-0.12**	-0.15**	-0.15**	0.11	0.24*	1.00				
8. Process Internal Focus (project management, organisational culture, compatibility with existing services; mean = 12.34)	0.00	2.74	122	0.18***	0.04	-0.26	0.14*	0.05	0.05	0.42**	1.00			
9. Process Commercialisation (External Accreditation, Brand/Trademark, Long Term Contracts with Customers; mean = 9.46)	0.00	3.92	101	0.24***	0.01	-0.02	0.07	0.06	0.33***	0.24**	0.60***	1.00		

10. Process Legal Lead Stability (Trade Secrecy, Patents, Complexity; mean = 8.42)	0.00	3.73	92	0.30***	0.18*	-0.30***	-0.30***	0.10	0.71***	0.24**	0.38**	0.35*	1.00	
11 Service 'Product' X Process Commercialisation	2.65	10.89	94	-0.22**	0.02	0.07	0.15*	0.03	-0.13	-0.34***	-0.19**	0.10	-0.16*	1.00
12. Service 'Product' Legal Lead Stability X Process Internal Focus	0.51	14.68	79	-0.02	0.10	0.16*	0.14	-0.01	-0.07	-0.05	0.16	-0.02	0.08	0.53*

Significance: * p<0.10; ** p<0.05; *** p<0.01; all independent and control variables are mean centered to control for VIF, thus mean = 0. The raw mean score for each variable is reported in brackets, column 1.

Table 4.6: The Impact of Appropriation Regimes Upon Firm Performance

	Model 1	Model 2	Model 3	Model 4	Model 5
Constant	42.418***	42.418***	42.418***	42.821***	42.823***
Log of Sales	0.314	0.465	0.242	0.25	0.249
Log of Firm Age	-0.167	0.325	0.39	0.283	0.267
Percentage of Sales Domestic	0.009	0.027	0.018	0.021	0.021
Log of Employees	-0.21	-0.368	-0.652	-0.667	-0.667
Product Cluster1, Legal Stability Copyright, Patents & Trade Secrecy		0.215	-0.787*	-0.868**	-0.87**
Product Cluster 2, Product Commercial-isation Reputation regarding quality, Dedicated marketing staff & Compatibility with existing products/services		0.916***	1.122***	0.973**	0.975**
Process Cluster 1, Internal Focus Project management, Organisational culture & Compatibility with existing products/services			-0.916**	-1.093**	-1.103**
Process Cluster 2, Process Commercial-isation External accreditation, Brand/Trademark			0.609*	0.786**	0.793**

& Long term contracts with customers					
Process Cluster 3, Legal Lead Stability Trade Secrecy, Patents & Complexity			1.206***	1.218***	1.215***
Process 2 x Product 2 Process commercialisation x Product Commercialisation				-0.152*	-0.154
Product 1 x Process 1 Legal stability x Internal Focus					0.006
Adjusted R2 F change significance	-0.052 0.943	0.057 0.014	0.157 0.025	0.185 0.093	0.170 0.926

Model 4 shows service 'product' commercialisation, moderated with process commercialisation, is negatively related to firm performance at the .10 significance level. Model 5, however, shows no significance for this main effect or the interaction between service 'product' 1, legal stability, and process 1, internal. However, to fully interpret the moderation between service 'product' and process commercialisation, the moderation must be graphed, as per Figure 4.1.

Figure 4.1: Moderation Graph

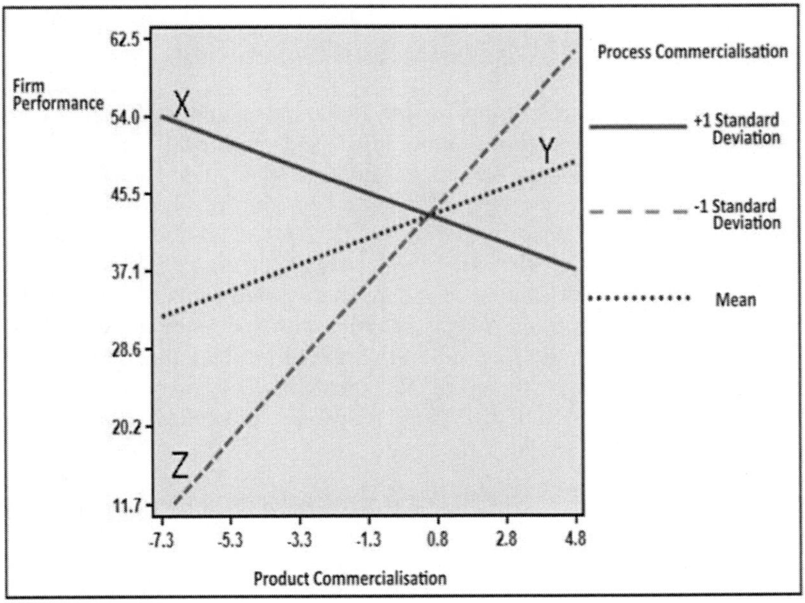

Line X depicts firms who reported process commercialisation at one standard deviation above average effectiveness in protecting profits from innovation. In this case, as service 'product' commercialisation effectiveness increased, firm performance decreased. Line Y depicts firms which found process commercialisation as having average effectiveness at protecting profits from innovation. In this case, as service 'product' commercialisation increased, firm performance increased. Line Z depicts firms which found process commercialisation had one standard deviation less than average effectiveness at protecting profits from innovation. In this case as the effectiveness of service 'product' commercialisation increased, firm performance increased. Figure 4.1 allows the following conclusions to be drawn: higher levels of effectiveness of one regime in conjunction with lower levels of effectiveness of the other regime can lead a firm to expect above average performance. However, this is primarily experienced at extreme levels of effectiveness and therefore in general an interaction between these regimes results in below average firm performance. This suggests that this moderation should be balanced carefully in order to achieve higher than average firm performance. Therefore, partial support is found for Hypothesis 4.

Part V: Discussion and Conclusions

This chapter sought to fill gaps in the literature on innovation and firm performance by investigating how legal and non-legal appropriation regimes, and interactions between them, impact firm performance. Previous studies have largely concentrated on the impact of individual mechanisms on firm performance (Arundel, 2001; Cho and Pucik, 2005; Wolfe, 1994; James et al. 2013), with Amara et al. (2008) being one notable exception. Our sample of incumbent service firms offers insights into the process of appropriating a return from experience goods, whilst prior research has heavily focused on the role of product innovations. Our first contribution was therefore the grouping of mechanisms into appropriation regimes and justifying these on a theoretical basis in the context of incumbent service firms.

The literature has delivered mixed results on the impact of legal mechanisms on firm performance. This study has shown that a purely service 'product' legal appropriation regime has a negative impact on firm performance, but a process legal lead regime has a positive impact on firm performance. This would seem to suggest that for incumbent service firms, where there is a distinctly experience-good dimension to the process of competition, legal mechanisms need to be augmented with complementary non-legal mechanisms in order to be effective protectors of the returns from innovation. This finding has implications for theory and for practitioners. Our results show that a mixture of legal and non-legal mechanisms has the greatest impact on firm performance, and therefore having a balance between legal and non-legal mechanisms has a greater impact on firm performance.

Further, a key insight from this study is to see the clear role of commercialisation appropriation regimes, where there are embedded experience-good signalling mechanisms such as external accreditation, reputation for quality, and embedding in an experience eco-system of compatible services. Service 'product' commercialisation was the only service 'product' regime found to have a positive impact on firm performance, illustrating the importance of non-legal regimes in protecting 'product' innovations relative to the more frequently researched legal regimes. Commercialisation was also shown to be important for protecting process innovations as it had a positive effect on firm performance. In fact, the notion of commercialisation of an innovation is an important concept. Legal regimes may protect an innovation from imitation, whereas commercialisation regimes actively seek to gain a return from an innovation.

Process, internal focus, was put forward as a regime that protects processes that are not directly visible to customers as a service feature, and was found to be negatively related to firm performance. It may be the case that these processes are necessary for the business to operate, but they do not add to the firm's customer value proposition. However, the theoretical underpinnings of this need to be investigated further, perhaps on a qualitative basis, in order to validate and explain this finding.

Another contribution of this paper to the literature is the moderation effects of appropriation regimes. We sought to find if moderating effects between service 'product' and process regimes would have a positive impact on firm performance. The results of such would provide guidance to firms for protecting the returns from an innovation that has both process and service 'product' innovations associated with it. One moderating effect was observed, the interaction between process and service 'product' commercialisation, which was found to have a negative effect on firm performance. However, further analysis showed a positive effect could be achieved when higher levels of effectiveness of one regime are present in conjunction with lower levels of effectiveness of the other regime. Thus, the balance of these regimes is important.

Finally, the study also provided a new ten-item scale for the dependent variable, firm performance, which can be used in subsequent studies.

Limitations and Further Research

We used a survey design, and whilst this brings the benefit of live company data, it lacks the ability to be used as an interactive tool for policy formation in the way that simulation methods can. We suggest that this work could be used as a primer for exploring the relationships between strength of appropriation regime, firm performance and the innovation options available to both firms and policy makers. How might policy makers seeking to influence service innovation activity by firms change the incentives to innovate by changing appropriation regimes? What might be the consequences of a change in appropriation regimes upon expected firm performance? How might a change in a legal appropriation regime interact with non-legal dimensions of appropriation regimes? Might small changes by policy makers have an asymmetric impact, positive or negative, on the performance expectations of firms? These and other questions cannot be addressed by this survey data, but could be explored by simulation methods.

The dataset used for the analysis was collected during a time of unprecedented economic boom in Ireland (2004) and thus may reduce the generalisability to today's much changed Irish economy. It contained a significant number of financial services firms (26%) and firms heavily reliant upon domestic sales. During the economic recession of 2008-2013, the financial services industry contracted severely and the domestic economy had several years of decline. We did in robustness testing include a control for financial services in our model. The significance and sign of all variables in the model remained unchanged in the presence of a financial services control variable. Thus we believe our results to be robust to influences of financial services. Our aim was not, however, to create generalisable results for the Irish economy, but rather first and foremost to develop clusters of appropriation regimes, and only then to explore their relationship to profit protection. The quantum of profits may have changed during the deep recession of 2008-2013, but we argue that the nature of relationships between appropriation regimes and profit protection is likely to be robust. This is a single country study and thus may not be generalisable in other contexts; however, we do note that the legal framework for commercial transactions in Ireland is largely set within the wider context of European Union law. Our survey does have responses from 14 sectors and as such is not a single-industry study. Therefore we believe it more likely that our study does have generalisable findings in terms of clusters of appropriation regimes across a range of service industries.

Our results may be less generalisable outside the small-country context of the European Union. Emerging markets may have weaker enforcement contexts for legal appropriation mechanism than a setting such as the EU (Feldstein and Fabozzi, 2008). As an emerging market economy grows and becomes more developed, research into how firms in that market are protecting their innovations could provide additional insight into the protection of innovation. Our study was placed in the resource-based view of the firm, but the signalling effects of mechanisms were mentioned throughout. Future research investigating protection in the context of signalling theory could provide interesting results.

During the course of robustness testing, a conformity factor analysis was conducted to test for the presence of common method variance (CMV; see Podsakoff et al. 2003 for a review of this issue). The results (not reported in this chapter) showed that CMV may be present. Chang, van Witteloostuijn and Eden (2010) outline the problem and some classical methods to manage CMV in single-respondent studies. Two of their remedies include careful construction of the questionnaire to ensure that the respondents clearly understand the questions asked (hence our efforts in initial design of the survey and re-design following consultation with ten initial respondents and colleagues), and assurance of anonymity (which was assured in our study cover letter). They also noted that more complex models that have moderation arguments (so long as these are conceptually reasonable) are less likely to be subject to CMV in practice. Our study employed moderators, which were significant, thus making CMV less likely to be present in our analysis.

The analysis looked at how effective certain mechanisms are at protecting profits from innovations. The survey did not measure "usage", and therefore this study is unable to fully explain if certain ineffective or indeed effective mechanisms are being used. This could also help develop a stronger argument for moderating effects.

A cross-sectional study such as ours can neither provide insights into the evolution of appropriation regimes within firms or sectors over time, nor can it explore potential mediating relationships between, for example, legal and non-legal appropriation regimes. Future research could examine the possibility of these effects using a longitudinal study, though the challenge of survey firm 'mortality' is a practical challenge of such a study. Further, future research is required to look at individual innovations that have both service 'product' and process innovations associated with them. This would provide a greater context for investigating mediating effects.

Acknowledgements

The authors would like to acknowledge research assistance from Claire-Louise Davey, Kurt Harding, and Adele Miley, each of whom helped at various stages of the data collection and analysis process. Our survey was part of a research project entitled 'Business Performance:

Does Innovation Matter', partially funded by the Management Subject Area of UCD Business Schools.

The authors gratefully acknowledge the financial support from the Irish Government's Programme for Research in Third Level Institutions (PRTLI 5) project grant entitled 'Innovation Policy Simulation for the Smart Economy (IPSE)'.

References

Aaker, D. 2007. Innovation: Brand it or lose it. California Management Review, 50(1): 8-24.

Aaker, D. A. & Jacobson, R. 1994. The financial information content of perceived quality. Journal of Marketing Research, 31, 191-201.

Amara, N., Landry, R. & Traore, N. 2008. Managing the protection of innovations in knowledge-intensive business services. Research Policy, 37, 1530-1547.

Amit, R. & Schoemaker, P. J. H. 1993. Strategic Assest and Organisational Rent. Strategic Management Journal, 14, 33-46.

Andersen, B. & Konzelmann, S. 2008. In search of a useful theory of the productive potential of intellectual property rights. Research Policy, 37, 12-28.

Argyres, N. & Mayer, K. J. 2007. Contract design as a firm capability: An integration of learning and transaction cost perspectives. Academy of Management Review, 32, 1060-1077.

Arora, A. 1997. Patents, licensing, and market structure in the chemical industry. Research Policy, 26, 391-403.

Arrow, K. 1962. Economic Welfare and the Allocation of Resources for Invention: In R Nelson, (editor) The Rate and Direction of Inventive Activity, Princeton, Princeton University Press.

Arundel, A. 2001. The relative effectiveness of patents and secrecy for appropriation. Research Policy, 30, 611-624.

Arundel, A. & Kabla, I. 1998. What percentage of innovations are patented? Empirical estimates for European firms. Research Policy, 27, 127-141.

Association for Project Management (2016). What is Project Management. https://www.apm.org.uk/WhatIsPM#WhatisPM. Accessed 12 February 2016.

Barney, J. 1991. Firm resources and sustained competitive advantage. Journal of Management, 17, 99-120.

Barney, J. B. 1986. Organizational culture. Can it be a source of sustainable competitive advantage? Academy of Management Review, 11, 656-665.

Bassok, Y. & Anupindi, R. 1997. Analysis of supply contracts with total minimum commitment. IEEE Transactions, 29, 373-381.

Beath, J., Katsoulacous, Y., Ulph, D. 1995. Game-theoretic approaches to the modelling of technological change. In: Stoneman, P. (Ed.), Handbook of the Economics of Innovation and Technological Change, Oxford/Cambridge Blackwell.

Beatty, S. E. & Smith, S. M. 1987. External search effort. An investigation across several product categories. Journal of Consumer Research, 14, 83-95.

Bharadwaj, S. G., Varadarajan, P. R. & Fahy, J. 1993. Sustainable competitive advantage in service industries. A conceptual model and research propositions. Journal of Marketing, 57, 83-99.

Bresnahan, T. F., Stern, S. & Trajtenberg, M. 1997. Market segmentation and the sources of rents from innovation: Personal computers in the late 1980s. Rand Journal of Economics, 28, S17-S44.

Breyer, S. 1970. Uneasy case for copyright – study of copyright in books, photocopies, and computer programs. Harvard Law Review, 84, 281-351.

Carpenter, G. S., Glazer, R. & Nakamoto, K. 1994. Meaningful brands from meaningless differentiation. The dependence on irrelevant attributes. Journal of Marketing Research, 31, 339-350.

Chang, S., van Witteloostuijn, A. & Eden, L. 2000. From the editors: Common method variance in international business research. Journal of International Business Studies, 41: 178-184.

Cho, H. J. & Pucik, V. 2005. Relationship between innovativeness, quality, growth, profitability, and market value. Strategic Management Journal, 26, 555-575.

Cohen, D. 1986. Trademark Strategy. Journal of Marketing, 50, 61-74.

Cohen, M. A. & Agrawal, N. 1999. An analytical comparison of long and short term contracts. IEEE Transactions, 31, 783-796.

Cole, R. E. 1998. Learning from the quality movement: What did and didn't happen and why? California Management Review, 41(1), 43-73.

Combs, J., Crook, T. & Shook, C. 2005. The dimensionality of organisational performance & its implications for strategic management research. Research Methodology in Strategy & Management, 2, 259-286.

Coriat, B. & Orsi, F. 2002. Establishing a new intellectual property rights regime in the United States - Origins, content and problems. Research Policy, 31, 1491-1507.

Czaja, R. & Blair, J. 2005. Designing Surveys: A guide to decisions and procedures, California Pine Forge Press.

Darnall, N. & Edwards, D. 2006. Predicting the cost of environmental management system adoption: The role of capabilities, resources and ownership structure. Strategic Management Journal, 27, 301-320.

Day, G. S. 1994. The capabilities of market driven organizations. Journal of Marketing, 58, 37-52.

Dillmann, D. A. 2007. Mail and Internet Surveys: The tailored design method, New Jersey, Wiley.

Dosi, G. 1988. Sources, procedures, and microeconomic effects of innovation. Journal of Economic Literature, 26, 1120-1171.

Drucker, P. 1993. Post-Capitalist Society, New York, Harper-Collins.

Fang, E. 2008. Customer participation and the trade-off between new product innovativeness and speed to market. Journal of Marketing, 72, 90-104.

Feldstein & Fabozzi 2008. The Handbook of Municipal Bonds, John Wiley and Sons.

Field, A. 2009. Discovering Statistics Using SPSS, Third Edition. London, Sage.

Franco, A. M. & Mitchell, M. F. 2008. Covenants not to compete, labor mobility, and industry dynamics. Journal of Economics & Management Strategy, 17, 581-606.

Friedman, D. D., Landes, W. M. & Posner, R. A. 1991. Some economics of trade secret law. Journal of Economic Perspectives, 5, 61-72.

Garvin, D. A. 1984. What does product quality really mean? Sloan Management Review, 26, 25-43.

George, D. 2000. SPSS for Windows Step by Step: A Simple Guide and Reference, London, Allyn & Bacon.

Geroski, P., Machin, S. & Vanreenen, J. 1993. The profitability of innovating firms. Rand Journal of Economics, 24, 198-211.

Gilson, R. J. 1999. The legal infrastructure of high technology industrial districts: Silicon Valley, Route 128, and covenants not to compete. New York University Law Review, 74, 575-629.

Gopalkrishnan, S. & Damanpour, F. 1997. A review of innovation research in economics, sociology and technology management. Omega-International Journal of Management Science, 25, 15-28.

Gotz, G. 1999. Monopolistic competition and the diffusion of new technology. Rand Journal of Economics, 30, 679-693.

Grant, R. M. 1991. The resource-based theory of competitive advantage. Implications of strategy formulation. California Management Review, 33, 114-135.

Greenhalgh, T., Robert, G., Macfarlane, F., Bate, P. & Kyriakidou, O. 2004. Diffusion of innovations in service organizations: Systematic review and recommendations. Milbank Quarterly, 82, 581-629.

Hannah, D. R. 2005. Should I keep a secret? The effects of trade secret protection procedures on employees' obligations to protect trade secrets. Organization Science, 16, 71-84.

Hobday, M. 1998. Product complexity, innovation and industrial organisation. Research Policy, 26, 689-710.

Hooley, G. J., Greenley, G. E., Cadogan, J. W. & Fahy, J. 2005. The performance impact of marketing resources. Journal of Business Research, 58, 18-27.

Hunt, S. D. & Morgan, R. M. 1995. The Comparative Advantage Theory of Competition. Journal of Marketing, 59, 1-15.

Hutzschenreuter, T. & Guenther, F. 2009. Complexity as a Constraint on Firm Expansion Within and Across Industries. Managerial and Decisions Economies, 30.

Irish Copyright and Related Rights Act 2000. Irish Statue Book number 28 of 2000. Available from http://www.irishstatutebook.ie/eli/2000/act/28/enacted/en/print

James, S., Leiblein, M. & Lu, L. 2013. How firms capture value from their innovations. Journal of Management, 36(5): 1123-1155.

Jolly, V. K. 1997. Commercializing new technologies - Getting from mind to market, Harvard Business Press.

Kaiser, H. F. 1974. Index of factorial simplicity. Psychometrika, 39, 31-36.

King, A. & Lenox, M. 2002. Exploring the locus of profitable pollution reduction. Management Science, 48(2), 289-299.

Koellinger, P. 2008. The relationship between technology, innovation, and firm performance - Empirical evidence from e-business in Europe. Research Policy, 37, 1317-1328.

Kortum, S. & Lerner, J. 1999. What is behind the recent surge in patenting? Research Policy, 28, 1-22.

Krasnikov, A. & Jayachandran, S. 2008. The relative impact of marketing, research-and-development, and operations capabilities on firm performance. Journal of Marketing, 72, 1-11.

Kutner, M., Nachtsheim, C. & Neter, J. 2004. Applied Linear Regression Models, McGraw-Hill Irwin.

Lafuente, E., Bayo-Moriones, A. & Garcia-Cestona, M. 2010. ISO-9000 Certification and Ownership Structure: Effects upon Firm Performance. British Journal of Management, 21, 649-665.
Lane, P. J. & Lubatkin, M. 1998. Relative absorptive capacity and interorganizational learning. Strategic Management Journal, 19(5), 461-477.
Larson, E. A. G. 2011. Project Management: The Managerial Process, Singapore, Gray Larson.
Lavery, P. 1996. Commercial Secrets: The action for Breach of Confidence in Ireland, Dublin, Round Hall Sweet and Maxwell.
Lengnickhall, C. A. 1996. Customer contribution to quality: A different view of the customer-oriented firm. Academy of Management Review, 21, 791-824.
Levin, R. C., Klevorick, A. K., Nelson, R. R. & Winter, S. G. 1987. Appropriating the returns from industrial research and development. Brookings Papers on Economic Activity, 783-831.
Lieberman, M. B. & Montgomery, D. B. 1988. First mover advantages. Strategic Management Journal. 9 (Summer): 41-58.
Lieberman, M. B. & Montgomery, D. B. 1998. First-Mover (dis)Advantages: Retrospective and link with the resource-based view. Strategic Management Journal, 19, 1111-1125.
Liebeskind, J. P. 1997. Keeping organizational secrets: protective institutional mechanisms and their costs. Industrial and Corporate Change, 6, 623–663.
Lima, M. A. M., Resende, M. & Hasenclever, L. 2000. Quality certification and performance of Brazilian firms: An empirical study. International Journal of Production Economics, 66, 143-147.
Lindell, M. K. & Whitney, D. J. 2001. Accounting for common method variance in cross-sectional research designs. Journal of Applied Psychology, 86, 114-121.
Luo, L., Kannan, P. K. & Ratchford, B. T. 2007. New product development under channel acceptance. Marketing Science, 26, 149-163.
Mansfield, E., Rapoport, J., Romeo, A., Wagner, S. & Beardsley, G. 1977. Social and private rates of return from industrial innovations. Quarterly Journal of Economics, 91, 221-240.
Marx, M., Strumsky, D. & Fleming, L. 2009. Mobility, Skills, and the Michigan Non-Compete Experiment. Management Science, 55, 875-889.

Mazzoleni, R. & Nelson, R. R. 1998. The benefits and costs of strong patent protection: a contribution to the current debate. Research Policy, 27, 273-284.

McGahan, A. M. & Silverman, B. S. 2006. Profiting from technological innovation by others: The effect of competitor patenting on firm value. Research Policy, 35, 1222-1242.

Media Group 2003. The Contribution of Copyright and Related Rights to the European Economy - Report for the European Commission.

Milgrom, P. & Roberts, J. 1986. Price and advertising signals of product quality. Journal of Political Economy, 94, 796-821.

Morgan, R. E. & Strong, C. A. 2003. Business performance and dimensions of strategic orientation. Journal of Business Research, 56, 163-176.

New, S., Westbrook, R. 2004. Understanding supply chains: concepts, critiques, and futures, Oxford University Press.

Nonaka, I. & von Krogh, G. 2009. Tacit Knowledge and Knowledge Conversion: Controversy and Advancement in Organizational Knowledge Creation Theory. Organization Science, 20, 635-652.

Novak, S. & Eppinger, S. D. 2001. Sourcing by design: Product complexity and the supply chain. Management Science, 47, 189-204.

Olins, W. 2008. The Brand Handbook, Thames and Hudson.

Penrose, E. 1959. The Theory of the Growth of the Firm, New York, Wiley.

Peteraf, M. A. 1993. The cornerstones of competitive advantage. A Resource Based View. Strategic Management Journal, 14, 179-191.

Phillips, L. W., Chang, D. R. & Buzzell, R. D. 1983. Product quality, cost position and business performance. A test of some key hypothesis. Journal of Marketing, 47, 26-43.

Podsakoff, P. M., MacKenzie, S. B., Lee, J. Y. & Podsakoff, N. P. 2003. Common method biases in behavioral research: A critical review of the literature and recommended remedies. Journal of Applied Psychology, 88, 879-903.

Reitzig, M. 2004. Improving patent valuations for management purposes - validating new indicators by analyzing application rationales. Research Policy, 33, 939-957.

Rogers 1983. Diffusions of Innovations, New York, Free Press.

Rosenkranz, S. 2003. Simultaneous choice of process and product innovation when consumers have a preference for product variety. Journal of Economic Behavior & Organization, 50, 183-201.

Samila, S. & Sorenson, O. 2011. Noncompete Covenants: Incentives to Innovate or Impediments to Growth. Management Science, 57, 425-438.

Samuelson, P. 2007. Why copyright law excludes systems and processes from the scope of its protection. Texas Law Review, 85, 1921-1977.

Schoeffl.S, Buzzell, R. D. & Heany, D. F. 1974. Impact of Strategic Planning on Profit Performance. Harvard Business Review, 52, 137-145.

Semadeni, M. 2006. Minding your distance: How management consulting firms use service marks to position competitively. Strategic Management Journal, 27, 169-187.

Sherry, E. F. & Teece, D. J. 2004. Royalties, evolving patent rights, and the value of innovation. Research Policy, 33, 179-191.

Srivastava, R. K., Shervani, T. A. & Fahey, L. 1998. Market-based assets and shareholder value: A framework for analysis. Journal of Marketing, 62, 2-18.

Stevens, J. P. 2002. Applied multivariate analysis statistics for the social sciences. Hilsdale NJ, Erlbauum.

Stuart, T. E. & Sorenson, O. 2003. Liquidity events and the geographic distribution of entrepreneurial activity. Administrative Science Quarterly, 48, 175-201.

Teece, D. J. 1986. Profiting from technological innovation. Implication for integration, collaboration, licensing and public-policy. Research Policy, 15, 285-305.

Teece, D. J. 2006. Reflections on "Profiting from Innovation". Research Policy, 35, 1131-1146.

Terlaak, A. & King, A. A. 2006. The effect of certification with the ISO 9000 Quality Management Standard: A signalling approach. Journal of Economic Behavior & Organization, 60, 579-602.

Tornatzky, L. G. & Klein, K. J. 1982. Innovation characteristics and innovation adoption-implementation. A meta-analysis of findings. IEEE Transactions on Engineering Management, 29, 28-45.

Tsekouras, K., Dimara, E. & Skuras, D. 2002. Adoption of a quality assurance scheme and its effect on firm performance: A study of Greek firms implementing ISO 9000. Total Quality Management, 13, 827-841.

Tushman, M. L. & Anderson, P. 1986. Technological discontinuities and organizational environments. Administrative Science Quarterly, 31, 439-465.

Valiulis, A. 1985. Covenants Not to Compete: Forms, Tactics, and the Law, New York, John Wiley and Sons.

Webster, F. E. 1992. The changing-role of marketing in the corporation. Journal of Marketing, 56, 1-17.

Welch, S. & Comer, J. 1988. Quantitative methods for public administration: Techniques and applications, Dorsey Press.

Wernerfelt, B. 1984. A Resource-Based View of the Firm. Strategic Management Journal, 5, 171-180.

Williamson 1971. Vertical Integration of Production – Market Failure Considerations. American Economic Review, 61, 112-127.

Wolfe, R. A. 1994. Organizational Innovation – Review, Critique and Suggested Research Directions. Journal of Management Studies, 31, 405-431.

Zaltman, G., Duncan, R., & Holbeck, J. 1973. Innovations and Organizations, New York,

PART III:

COMPLEXITY SCIENCE, SOCIAL SIMULATION AND INNOVATION

CHAPTER FIVE[1]

POLICY MODELLING OF LARGE-SCALE SOCIAL SYSTEMS: LESSONS FROM THE SKIN MODEL OF INNOVATION[2]

PETRA AHRWEILER, ANDREAS PYKA AND NIGEL GILBERT

Introduction

What and how can modelling and simulation contribute to policy making in complex environments like research and innovation? Policy makers regularly complain about the difficulties in promoting innovation in the knowledge economy. Worldwide, every year, governments spend billions on promoting innovation. For example, the EU spent €7.3B in 2009 on research, innovation, and competitiveness, and the EU may increase their overall funding level by 46% under the new funding scheme Horizon 2020 from 2014 to 2020. Innovation policymakers, business managers, and the public often expect that such investments in R&D, higher education institutions, science-industry networks, etc. will immediately produce a flow of products and processes with high commercial returns. The disappointments and legitimation problems when they do not are considerable and show the limits of conventional steering, control, and

[2] The analogy is not exact, for the kene units can represent items of tacit knowledge (which can therefore not be made explicit as IPC codes) and can also represent non-technical knowledge, such as business strategies, marketing techniques and management competences, none of which are patentable.

policy functions. Innovation managers mention a frustration with the messy and complicated features of the innovation process, which simply does not seem to pay off. However, policy informatics offers the promise of new approaches to understanding innovation and decision making about policies to enhance innovation.

Without a doubt socio-economic systems are confronted with a high degree of complexity when it comes to the development of new knowledge, its diffusion, and its commercial application in innovation. In the case of innovation, agents are confronted with *true uncertainty* that makes any forecasts and predictions impossible. Any analytical approach that tries to offer guidance and support for political decision makers has to acknowledge this intermingling of rich complexity and uncertainty. Policy consulting in the past has relied on the idea of a linear sequential innovation process with the invention and innovation phases strictly separated. Consequently, the complex interactions of heterogeneous actors were de-emphasised by assuming the actors to be endowed with an Olympic rationality that allowed them to apply an optimisation calculus to their decisions. However, since the 1980s, the weaknesses of this approach have become obvious. Not only are different systems related and their actors not endowed with homogenous knowledge, but also the simplifying assumptions that were necessary to maintain predictability of the analytic model stripped it of its usefulness to provide genuine, novel insights into innovation policy.

New approaches enable the modelling of innovation policy initiatives to take into account more parameters and perform simulations to forecast potential impacts of proposed innovation policy measures. A conceptual framework that combines the application of empirical research, computational network analysis, and agent-based modelling allows for a more integrated and comprehensive understanding of innovation policymaking than has hitherto been achieved. The approach could ultimately create methodological foundations for the sustainable transformation of research and innovation landscapes.

The thoughtful use of a computational systems approach, in our case agent-based modelling (ABM), can be used to identify and understand the effects of innovation policy strategies and their associated knowledge dynamics. In contrast to conventional methods of social research, this method is capable of dealing with the high complexity and non-linearity of the processes under study. ABM users can address questions that involve different levels of the innovation ecosystem: from start-up firms (micro level) to academic-industry partnerships (meso level) to whole sectors or regions (macro level). ABMs can be informed by large empirical data sets. These factors motivated the model that we have developed and applied over the last decade. *S*imulating *K*nowledge Dynamics in *I*nnovation *N*etworks (SKIN) is a multi-agent AMB model used to understand innovation policy initiatives that contain heterogeneous agents that act and interact in a large-scale complex and changing social environment.

This chapter first describes the details of the SKIN model and explores the development processes associated with modelling large-scale social systems. Then it explores four policy-relevant applications of the model. To communicate the value to policy informatics of this approach, each of the applications are broken down into its intended purpose, unique features, how the experiment or activities were conducted, and the specific type of outcomes produced by the application. The chapter concludes with reflections on how the model has been received by the policy-making community over a decade of use and development, including its successes, limitations, and contingencies.

What is the SKIN Model?

Simulating Knowledge Dynamics in Innovation Networks (SKIN) is an agent-based model used to understand innovation policy initiatives that contain heterogeneous agents that act and interact in a large-scale complex and changing social environment. The agents represent innovative actors who try to sell their innovations to other agents and end-users but who also have to buy raw materials or more sophisticated inputs from other agents (or material suppliers) to produce their outputs. This basic model of a market is extended with a representation of the knowledge dynamics in and between the agents. Each agent tries to improve its innovation performance and its sales by improving its knowledge base through adaptation to user needs, incremental or radical learning, and co-operation and networking with other agents.

SKIN is grounded in empirical research and theoretical frameworks from innovation economics and economic sociology. It is the result of a number of projects stretching over twelve years that combined empirical research into innovation networks with agent-based simulation. The work started with the European Union (EU) project "Simulating Self-Organising Innovation Networks" (SEIN). This project combined four empirical case studies in different sectors of technological innovation and in different EU member states with agent-based simulation of these case studies. The results of the SEIN project are summarised in Pyka and Kueppers (2003) and Gilbert, Pyka, and Ahrweiler (2003) as well as described in this chapter. The model was used by the European Commission for scenario modelling of current and future innovation policy strategies (Ahrweiler, de Young, & Windrum 2003).

The current SKIN model builds on the procedures designed initially to fit the biotechnology-based pharmaceutical industry in Europe since this sector is an example par excellence of a knowledge-intensive industry. The following is a streamlined description of the model that highlights its key components and capacities.[3]

The Agents

A core concept of a model of innovation networks is knowledge. Accordingly, one of the first modelling tasks is to find an appropriate knowledge representation. The approach to knowledge representation used in our model is similar to Toulmin's (1967) evolutionary model of knowledge production. This model identified concepts, beliefs, and interpretations as the "genes" of scientific/technological development evolving over time in processes of selection, variation, and retention. Ackermann (1970) interpreted the works of Kuhn and Popper according to this perspective allowing for different selection systems. In the SKIN model, an analogical concept, the "kene," is used to represent the aggregate knowledge of an organisation (Gilbert, 1997).

The individual knowledge base of a SKIN agent, its kene, contains a number of "units of knowledge." Each unit in a kene is represented as a triple consisting of a firm's capability C in a scientific, technological, or business domain, its ability A to perform a certain application in this field, and the expertise level E the firm has achieved with respect to this ability. In the artificial space of a model, kenes could consist of arbitrary bit sequences of indefinite length. However, we need to portray the knowledge of the artificial agents in a way that allows comparison with

[3] The description summarises the details of the model and of the empirical research that was continued in the bi-national research project of the British ESRC and the German DAAD "Comparing German and UK biotechnology-based pharmaceuticals: Simulating Knowledge Dynamics in Innovation Networks," (Ahrweiler, Gilbert, and Pyka 2006).

empirical actors. Therefore, the composition of kenes is inspired by the International Patent Classification (IPC). The IPC provides a hierarchical system of language-independent symbols for the classification of patents according to the different areas of technology to which they apply. IPC Codes of patents allow the assignment of technological fields and competences by providing so-called concordance tables (cf. Schmoch et al., 2003) to identify industrial sectors. In this sense, the IPC Codes can be considered as coordinates of an empirical knowledge space that correspond approximately to the "units of knowledge" in the kenes.

Other Agents that Form the Market

Since actors in empirical innovation networks of knowledge-intensive industries interact on both the knowledge and the market levels (cf. Garcia et al., forthcoming b: 2), we need a representation of market dynamics in the SKIN model.

Each firm agent, when it is set up, has a stock of initial capital. The agent needs this capital to produce for the market and to finance its R&D expenditures; it can increase its capital by selling products. The amount of capital owned by a firm is used as a measure of the size of the firm and additionally influences the amount of knowledge (measured by the number of units in its kene) that the firm can maintain. In many knowledge-intensive industries, we find both large and small actors (e.g. large pharmaceutical firms and the biotech start-ups, and the former national monopolists and high technology specialists in the ICT industries, cf. Pyka & Saviotti, 2005). We assume that large diversified firms are characterised by a larger knowledge base as compared with smaller specialised companies (cf. Brusoni et al., 2001). To represent this, most firms are initially given the same starting capital allocation in the model, with a few allocated extra capital.

Firms apply their knowledge to create innovative products that have a chance of being successful in the market. The underlying idea of an innovation, the 'innovation hypothesis', is the source an agent uses for its attempts to make profits in the market. The innovation hypothesis determines the required inputs and the nature of the firm's product.

To be able to engage in production, all the inputs need to be obtainable on the market, i.e. provided by other firms or available as raw materials. If the inputs are not available, the firm is not able to produce and has to give up this attempt to innovate. If there is more than one supplier for a certain input, the agent will choose the one at the cheapest price and, if there are several similar offers, the one with the highest quality. If the firm can go into production, it has to find a price for its product, taking into account the input prices it is paying and a possible profit margin. Using a price adjustment mechanism, agents are able to adapt their prices to demand and, in doing so, learn from feedback. In making a product, an agent applies the knowledge in its innovation hypothesis, and this increases its expertise in this area. This is the way that learning by doing/using is modelled.

The expertise levels of the units in the innovation hypothesis are increased, and the expertise levels of the other units are decremented. Expertise in unused units in the kene is eventually lost and the units are then deleted from the kene; the corresponding abilities are "forgotten" or "dismissed" (e.g. Hedberg, 1981). Thus, in trying to be successful on the market, firms are dependent on their innovation hypothesis, that is, on their kene. If a product does not meet any demand, the firm has to adapt its knowledge to produce something else for which there are customers (e.g. Duncan, 1974). A firm has several ways of improving its performance, either alone or in co-operation, and in either an incremental or a more radical fashion.

Learning and Co-operation: Improving Innovation Performance

The SKIN model, inspired by the literature on organisational learning, takes many of the ideas of the Argyris and Schön (1996) framework and uses them to examine the assumption that, in the words of de Geus (1997), the greatest competitive advantage for any firm is its ability to learn (Gilbert, Ahrweiler & Pyka, 2007). Firm agents can:

- use their capabilities (learning by doing/using) and learn to estimate their success via feedback from markets and clients (learning by feedback), as already mentioned above, and/or
- improve their own knowledge incrementally when the feedback is not satisfactory to adapt to changing technological and/or economic standards (adaptation learning, incremental learning).

If a firm's previous innovation has been successful (i.e. it has found buyers), the firm will continue selling the same product in the next round, possibly at a different price depending on the demand it has experienced.

However, if there were no sales, the firm considers that it is time for change. If the firm still has enough capital, it will carry out “incremental” research (R&D in the firm’s labs). Performing incremental research (cf. Cohen and Levinthal 1989) means that a firm tries to improve its product by altering one of the abilities chosen from the units in its innovation hypothesis while sticking to its focal capabilities. Alternatively, if making losses and under pressure, firms can radically change their capabilities to meet completely different client requirements (e.g. innovative learning, radical learning).

A firm may also consider partnerships (e.g. alliances, joint ventures, etc.) to exploit external knowledge sources. The decision whether and with whom to co-operate is based on the mutual observations of the firmswhich estimate the chances and requirements coming from competitors, possible and past partners, and clients. Bolton, Katoka and Ockenfels (2005), writing from a theoretical viewpoint, and Mitchelet (1992), using empirical evidence, show that greater mutual information, where firms know their partner’s history of co-operation, improves the conditions for co-operation.

The model allows for choosing between two partner search strategies (Powell et al. 2005), both of which compare the firm’s own and the possible partner’s capabilities. Applying the conservative strategy, a firm will be attracted to a partner that has similar capabilities; using a progressive strategy, the attraction is based on the difference between the capability sets.

Previously good experience with former contacts generally augurs well for renewing a partnership. For example, the findings of Garcia et al. concerning the interaction patterns between public research centres and industrial firms confirm that “prior formal relationships are a fundamental element for collaboration… Strong ties (past relationships) appear to be more fundamental in building university-industry ties” (Garcia et al. forthcoming a: 2f). This is mirrored in the model: to find a partner, the firm will look at previous partners first, then at its suppliers, customers and finally at all others. If there is a firm sufficiently attractive according to the chosen search strategy, it will stop its search and offer a partnership. If the potential partner wishes to return the partnership offer, the partnership is set up.

If the firm's last innovation was successful (i.e., the value of its profit in the previous round was above a threshold) and the firm has some partners at hand, it can initiate the formation of a network. This can increase its profits because the network will try to create innovations as an autonomous agent in addition to those created by its members and will distribute any rewards back to its members who, in the meantime, can continue with their own attempts, thus providing a double chance for profits. If a network is successful, it will distribute any earnings above the amount of the initial capital to its members; if it fails and becomes bankrupt, it will be dissolved. If a sector is successful, new firms will be attracted into it, representing Schumpeterian competition by imitation.

Innovation Policy Initiatives

Using the simulation, policy makers can observe and manipulate patterns of network evolution by varying simulation parameters. Since changing parameters within the model is analogous to applying different policy options in the real world, the model can be used to examine the likely real-world effects of different policy options before they are implemented. Using real-world datasets and responses to questions put forward by stakeholders, the following four applications were developed. Collectively, they begin to demonstrate how SKIN can meet multiple policy needs because it can provide precise, detailed information on the effects of specific policy instruments, on how well research and innovation networks operate, and how to understand and manage the relationship between research funding and policy goals.

Four Innovation Policy-Relevant SKIN Applications

This section discusses four recent applications of the SKIN model: (i) modelling the impact of university links on business innovation networks, (ii) scenario modelling of an individual case with a country's, Ireland's, MNC-directed innovation policy for indigenous industry networks, (iii) simulating the effects of different innovation management strategies of firms in an individual context, the biotechnology-based pharmaceutical industry, and (iv) scenario modelling of European funding schemes concerning size and geographical diversity of project teams.

Modelling the Impact of University Cooperation for Business Innovation Networks

Purpose

What role do university-industry links play in innovation generation and diffusion? The first SKIN application presented here (Ahrweiler, Pyka and Gilbert 2011) focuses on R&D co-operations between universities and industry. These partnerships transfer technology from academic institutions to companies and, in doing so, spread knowledge through the population. There are some empirical studies investigating the knowledge flows from universities to firms (Agrawal and Henderson 2002, Siegel et al. 2003). The success and failure of technology transfer activities have also been studied (Henderson et al. 1998, Thursby and Kemp 2002, Chapple et al. 2005). However, most of these studies report measurement difficulties due to the unobservable nature and non-linear properties of knowledge flows. The advantage of using an agent-based model is that although our hypotheses focus on the same unobservable knowledge flows in university-industry networks to which this body of literature refers, we can observe simulated knowledge flows in the model.

R&D and industrial policy assume that university-industry links are the fuel of knowledge-based economies. Public spending on university-industry collaborations is therefore considerable. Policymakers (and the public) expect that current investments in academic research and university-industry networks will produce a flow of new and innovative products and processes with high commercial returns in science-based firms and a positive impact on labour markets. However, empirical evidence demonstrating the direct commercial profitability of the "science connection" is scarce.

Additional Features

For this application, two new agent types, university agents and spin-off companies, were added to the basic SKIN model as described in section 2 above. Like the firm agents, university agents have an individual knowledge base (kene). Since the university agents have significant technological capabilities, abilities, and expertise, their kenes are twice as long as those of the firm agents. University agents do research, form R&D partnerships with firms, and participate in larger networks. If a university agent is successful (see below), it breeds a firm (university spin-off). This is an enterprise that can buy, sell, and produce. A spin-off's kene is a clone of the university's innovation hypothesis. If a spin-off is created, a university loses one unit of its kene and gets a new random one (to represent the turnover of researchers); all expertise levels of the spin-off are reduced by one unit. Unlike the firm agents, university agents in the extended SKIN model are non-profit organisations (they do not produce for the market, they do not sell) with stable public core funding. Their success is measured by the economic gains of their firm partners.

Experiments

We compared a scenario with and a scenario without university agents to test whether firms that interact with universities develop more products and have more commercial success; whether having universities among the co-operating actors raises the knowledge/competence level of the whole population (i.e. whether we see more variety at the knowledge level, whether we see increased innovation performance overall, and whether we see increased diffusion in terms of quantity and speed); whether firms interacting with universities will be more attractive to other firms when new partnerships (commercialising, financing, R&D collaboration with other firms) are considered; and whether firms interacting with universities can better adapt to changing environmental conditions.

Outcomes

Performing experiments on the simulation provides new insights that potentially contribute to the formation of a more widely accepted perspective on the effects of university-industry relationships. We can show that there is indeed no linear and immediate relationship between increased knowledge inputs and economic profits – our experiments reproduced the ambiguous evaluations of empirical studies. Firms interacting with universities cannot adapt to changing environmental conditions any better than their counterparts without university affiliation. The average lifetime of firms interacting with universities is no greater than those that do not. There seems to be a slight trend towards higher innovation performance in the scenario with universities, but it is not statistically significant. Neither does an increased amount of knowledge automatically lead to increased innovation performance and thus to economic success.

Nevertheless, having co-operating universities raises the knowledge and competence levels of the whole population of actors, increases the variety of knowledge among the firms, and increases innovation diffusion in terms of quantity and speed. Furthermore, firms interacting with universities are more attractive for other firms when new partnerships are considered. Although no direct relation between university contributions and economic success can be found, the agent-based simulation confirms that university-industry links improve innovation diffusion and collaborative arrangements in innovation networks.

Scenario Modelling of Irish MNC-Directed Innovation Policies

Purpose

In this SKIN application, we investigated the effects of the presence and embeddedness of Multi-National Corporations (MNCs) in networks of innovation (Ahrweiler, Schilperoord, Gilbert and Pyka 2012). New products and processes can result from the ongoing interactions of innovative organisations such as universities, research institutes, firms such as MNCs and SMEs, government agencies, venture capitalists and others.

By looking at knowledge flows and capital stocks, we wanted to investigate whether the mere presence of MNCs is beneficial for innovation networks and whether there is an additional advantage if these MNCs are engaged in collaborative R&D with other players in the network. We examined the role of MNCs for innovation networks from the perspective of their subsidiaries′ host countries. The simulation was grounded in the empirical example of Ireland, enabling us to analyse the role of MNCs in the Irish indigenous industry.

Scenario modelling of the role of MNCs for host countries is highly policy-relevant: in Ireland, there has been a growth in the high-technology industry sectors but this has only been fostered by foreign-owned MNCs. The MNCs are still poorly integrated into Irish networks, clusters, and innovation centres. Accordingly, Ireland almost has a dual economy, composed of SMEs with weak R&D and innovation performance, and MNCs with cutting-edge technology providing a substantial contribution to the wealth of the country. To prevent MNCs from leaving Ireland in favour of competing manufacturing locations and to help the indigenous industry benefit from MNCs, Irish policymakers have been trying to convince MNCs to locate their R&D in Ireland and to cooperate with Irish organisations (SMEs, universities etc.) in innovation networks. Agent-based modelling can contribute to assessing the impacts and effects of these policies by modelling scenarios that correspond to Irish MNC policy options.

Additional Features

In the adapted model for this application, MNCs are normal SKIN agents producing (manufacturing) and selling products to customers with inputs from suppliers. They can employ all the learning and networking activities usually available to SKIN agents. In addition to these attributes, MNC agents have large knowledge bases, and high capital stocks, which give them a better chance of entering foreign markets and marketing new technologies due to their commercialisation experience and distribution networks.

Experiments

For the experiments, we operationalised the policy questions in relation to the Irish economy: how important is the knowledge integration function of MNCs as knowledge hubs and financial magnets for regional innovation networks? Does a firm population containing MNCs perform better in terms of knowledge diffusion and innovation performance than a uniform-size population of small and medium firms? What are the effects of MNC presence and activities on the knowledge level of the firm population?

To deal with these questions, we constructed two different comparisons. First, we compared a model with MNC agents to a model without MNC agents. Second, we compared a model containing MNC agents in R&D cooperation with the indigenous industry to a model where MNCs just follow go-it-alone innovation strategies while all other firms in that scenario can cooperate with each other. Go-it-alone innovation strategies are the features described above as incremental and radical learning, which can be performed in the R&D labs of a firm without having to cooperate with external partners. Cooperation includes all features described above as partnerships and networks.

The starting configuration of the experiments was set up to mirror the conditions in the Irish economy (Forfás Central Statistics Office, Statistical Release March 2009). Modelling results were validated against empirical findings from Irish data.

Outcomes

Our results strongly confirmed the current Irish MNC policy strategies. Just attracting and retaining MNCs provides increasing capital availability and innovation performance for the indigenous industry. Surprisingly, even the mere presence of MNCs in the indigenous economy raises the knowledge flows in the host country's industry because firms can more safely engage in R&D and market activities. This is intensified when MNCs engage in local learning activities and embed themselves into the R&D network of regional innovation. The agent-based simulation confirmed that MNCs in R&D collaboration with the indigenous innovation network improve the knowledge and competence level of the whole industry and the innovation diffusion and collaborative arrangements in the host country.

Simulating the Effects of Different Learning Strategies

Purpose

This SKIN application (Gilbert, Pyka and Ahrweiler 2007, 2010) is about simulating the effects of different learning activities of firms in the biotechnology-based pharmaceutical industry (go-it-alone strategies such as incremental and radical learning, and learning through R&D partnerships, and innovation networks). According to the organisational learning literature, the greatest competitive advantage a firm has is its ability to learn. The SKIN model is applied here to simulate learning competence in firms to improve policies and management decisions for supporting innovation.

The results of this application were closely observed by a large multi-national corporation in the UK pharma industry, because this company's management was about to decide on the future cooperation and embeddedness strategies of their enterprise within the surrounding industry. Tracking the performance of an agent through the simulation that had similar properties to this company but applied different combinations of learning and cooperation strategies provided interesting policy and management insights into how to navigate in complex innovation networks and how to improve one's position in the network to exploit its resources to the best advantage.

Additional Features

This application did not require any features to be added to the basic model outlined in section 2.

Experiments

Experiments consisted in testing different combinations of learning and cooperation strategies against a baseline scenario where firms were not able to learn or to cooperate at all.

Outcomes

The simulation experiments underlined the importance of innovation and learning. They demonstrated the importance of finding new capabilities from outside the firm, either through partnering or radical research. They also showed that the simpler forms of organisational learning, such as learning by doing and learning by feedback, are of limited value by themselves in the highly dynamic environment of modern knowledge-based market sectors, although they are of significance when combined with other forms of learning.

The observing pharma company was interested to see that its preferred go-it-alone strategies were indeed sufficient for satisfactory innovation performance; however, that performance could be improved by additionally allowing partnerships and networks with the surrounding industry. The model also demonstrated the possibilities opened up by simulation for carrying out experiments on a model that would be impossible to perform in the real world. Clearly, it would not be practicable to constrain actual firms in their learning capacities to study the effect on their success and determine the causal consequences, still less to do this for a whole market sector. But as this application has shown, it is possible and revealing to do so on a model of a sector.

Scenario Modelling of European Funding Schemes

Purpose

This SKIN application investigated the interaction between the political governance, structures, and functions of R&D collaboration networks that are induced by policy programmes, in particular the networks that have emerged in the seven European Framework Programmes. The goal was to identify ways to evaluate efficient network structures for R&D collaboration networks and to develop policy designs for their creation.

Additional Features

SKIN was adapted to the context of EU-funded research networks so that agents are R&D organisations. Instead of triples, kenes consist of quadruples: Research Direction (RD), Capabilities (C), Abilities (A), and Expertise (E). The research direction (RD) represents the general knowledge orientation, ranging from completely theoretical knowledge (i.e. basic research) to exclusively applied research. These research directions allow for a differentiation between university and firm actors.
The capabilities (C) represent different knowledge areas and technological disciplines e.g. biochemistry, telecommunication, or mechanical engineering. For modelling purposes the number of different capabilities has to be chosen to be large enough to cover all potential research areas in the European Framework Programmes. The market of the basic SKIN model is "switched off".

The behaviours of the agents follow the empirical understanding of processes of network formation and evolution in the Framework Programmes:

- Definition of **incentives and rules** for R&D collaboration: the EU provides funding for collaborative research. The rules are defined in the Framework Programmes (e.g. rules for project consortia, research topics, time span of the FP etc.).
- **Consortium formation / partner choice**: the actors (research institutes, firms etc.) form project consortia. Partner choice mechanisms apply.

- **Proposal production**: the actors collaboratively produce proposals, which are first representations of the (collaborative) knowledge of consortium partners. The consortium submits the proposal to the Commission.
- **Proposal selection**: the Commission evaluates the proposals according to a template that emphasises: contents (programme match), quality, and architecture of consortium (e.g. minimum number of members, industry involvement etc.). The Commission selects projects to fund. The availability of funding limits the number of projects.
- **R&D cooperation**: the projects start to work, i.e. they are involved in research and cooperative learning activities. In the end they produce deliverables (e.g. a number of publications, patents, reports).
- **Performance evaluation**: the Commission changes its work programme taking into account the success of projects. The process repeats.

The following flowchart summarises this cycle (Scholz, Nokkala, and Ahrweiler 2010).

Figure 5.1

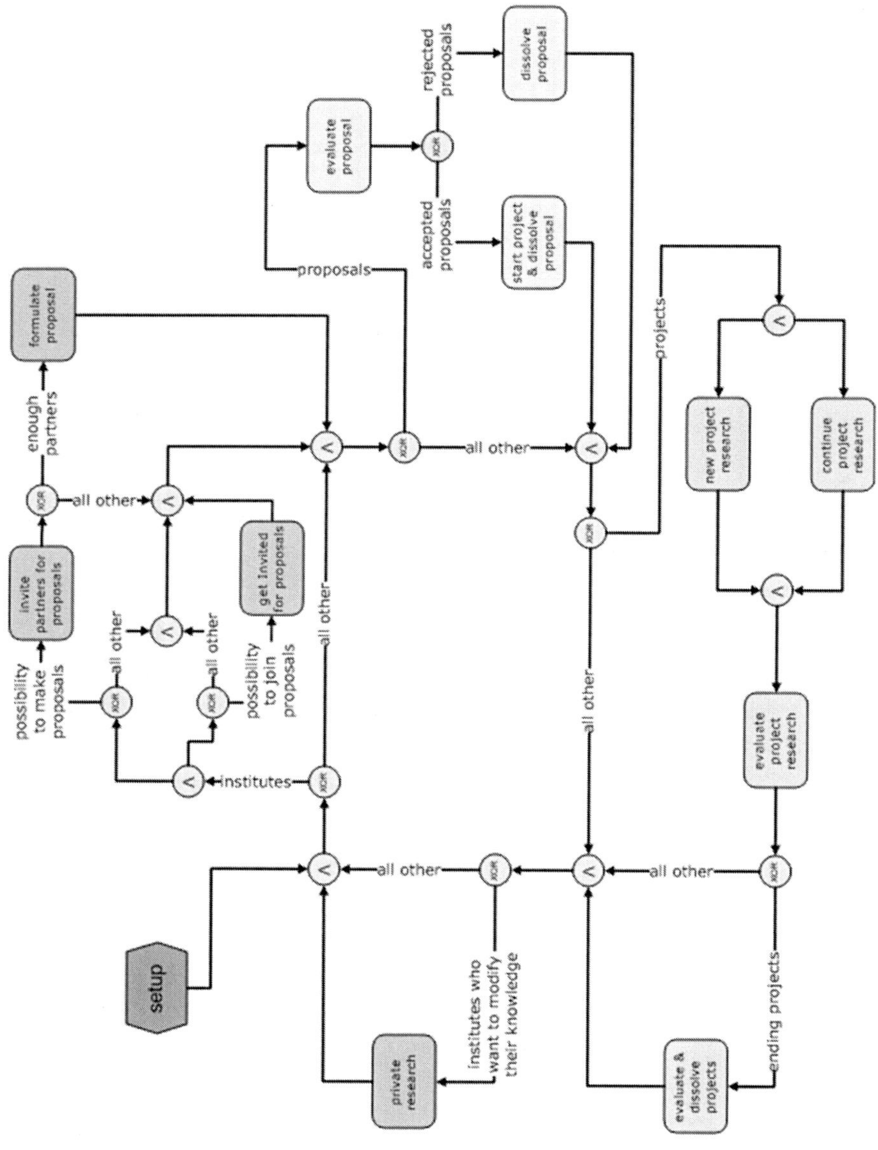
setup
private research
institutes who want to modify their knowledge
all other
institutes
possibility to make proposals
invite partners for proposals
all other
enough partners
formulate proposal
possibility to join proposals
get invited for proposals
proposals
evaluate proposal
accepted proposals
rejected proposals
start project & dissolve proposal
dissolve proposal
projects
new project research
continue project research
evaluate project research
ending projects
evaluate & dissolve projects

Experiments

This application works with a baseline scenario, which reproduces the network structures of FP6, obtained using the calibration data and policy rules of that particular Framework Programme. The policy experiments were designed as an implementation of new rules into the baseline scenario. To analyse the impact of the policy experiments on the evolution of the research networks, we compared network structures and network performances. For example, one experiment dealt with an increase in the minimum number of teams participating in a research project, and a second one suggested a scenario including large projects and with geographical location added as one of the selection criteria used by the European Commission to select projects. With large projects, for example, we implement the policy rule that project consortia have to be larger than 2.5 times a normal project and the consortia members have to be from at least 4 different geographical areas.

Outcomes

The simulation showed that having bigger consortia and increased geographical diversity within consortia diminishes project output and performance – both in quantity and quality. The model demonstrated that it can act as an in silico laboratory for policy instruments. It allows experimentation with a variety of policy parameters to investigate both their effectiveness and their consequences on the creation and behaviour of collaborative networks.

By offering a conceptual framework for the combined application of empirical research, computational network analysis, and agent-based modelling, these applications of the same basic model show that SKIN is a powerful new tool that allows a more integrated and comprehensive understanding of innovation policymaking than has hitherto been possible.

Assessing the Experience with the SKIN Model

In this section, we assess our experience with the model and its applications in terms of its successes, limitations, and contingencies. This concerns managing expectations of stakeholders, general apprehensions around the predictability of future developments, data availability issues, and validation questions.

The Scope of the Model

The SKIN model, like any model, is an abstraction of reality. Not every aspect of innovation networks can be included; if that were possible, the resulting model would be so complicated that nothing of value could be learned from it. The art of modelling is to include only the essentials, no more, no less. Hence, each of the examples of the application of SKIN could be criticised for failing to model some relevant characteristics: it is not until the model is validated against the empirical world that we can assess whether it has been over-simplified. For example, the extent of heterogeneity between universities is not well represented in the model of university-industry links described in section 2.1. Adding such heterogeneity, for example to the balance of universities' teaching and research, or to the extent of their entrepreneurial culture, could add realism and accuracy to the model at the price of considerable complication and the need for additional data for calibration. Similarly, in the model of Irish MNCs, further development would be needed to recognise their heterogeneity as integrated players, global innovators, implementers and local innovators (Gupta and Govindarajan 1991, 1994).

The Data Base

Applying the SKIN model to specific policy topics, such as the four ones described in section 2, requires not only the adaption of the model to assign the appropriate attributes and behaviours to the agents, but also the calibration of the model to the situation being simulated. For example, design and calibration of the model of European funding schemes (section 2.4) required both a detailed analysis of FP6 funding policies and data about the partners involved in FP6 project consortia. The adequacy of the simulation depends on the reliability of the data that is available for calibration. Such data can be hard to obtain or difficult to process into a form suitable for analysis. In the case of the model of European funding schemes, significant effort was required to 'clean' the data on project consortia because, for instance, organisation names changed from year to year, and some companies were merged into new ones.

The Policy Questions

The versions of the SKIN model described in section 2 were developed to provide answers to policy questions. However, determining what the policy questions should be was often not as simple as one might expect. A host of issues can arise. Whose questions are to be answered? This requires identifying relevant 'stakeholders'. Which questions do these stakeholders want answering? Our experience suggests that policy makers often do not have clearly articulated policy questions already formulated, and there may need to be lengthy discussion before their general interest in a topic can be honed down to a specific question. Furthermore, the questions may not be amenable to answering using simulation models, or may depend on normative concepts that defy clear definition. For example, one of the objectives of the European funding scheme model (section 2.4) was to assess the effect of various policy changes on 'network performance'. But what policymakers meant by 'performance' was not well defined and required some work to operationalise in a form that policymakers could relate to.

An additional issue was managing expectations of the policymakers about what simulation models of complex social phenomena could achieve. The SKIN model contains numerous stochastic elements, with the result that it gives slightly different results for every run. Therefore, point predictions are not possible. More seriously, since the model is non-linear, small changes to parameters can have major effects on the results. Thus, at best, the model can be used to examine broad scenarios and to assess the likely effects of policies in qualitative terms, but it does not provide the certainty and precision that policy makers would ideally like.

Conclusion

In this chapter we have shown that our observations do not necessarily lead to the rejection of a scientific analysis of innovation processes. We have introduced an agent-based model that places the network organisation of innovation processes at its centre. Network organisation means that single actors consciously choose their connections to other agents. Some might be refused and others dissolved in the case of failure or lack of trust. The ties are a necessary condition for knowledge to flow among agents.

We applied the network model to four very different cases to show how this modelling tool can be used to derive policy and strategic conclusions. The first case deals with university-industry networks, which are central to innovation policies. The connection of basic researchers with applied researchers should guarantee fast knowledge and technology transfer and consequently a higher level of competitiveness and improved economic performance. The results of the experiments show that there is no simple relationship between basic and applied research. Instead, the interaction processes are more subtle, and the positive effects indirectly emerge from the increased variety in knowledge and the improved capabilities of the involved agents. The second case focuses on the actors in a sectorial innovation system. Large Multinational Enterprises interact with specialised local firms and thereby encourage economic development. The experiments identify targets and mechanisms through which economic policy can improve the chances of a country in the catching-up process of coping with global competition. The third variant of the model is used to disentangle the complexities of learning processes in firms. These are empirically unobservable, but can be measured in the artificial world of the model. The model having been designed to suit the particularities of the biopharmaceutical industry, we were able to improve understanding of innovation and cooperative behaviour in this sector. Results are not only relevant to innovation policy but also to informing firms' strategy development. The two final examples described in this chapter could be considered to be policy engineering. The agent-based simulation model was adapted to the characteristics of the European research networks generated in the Framework Programmes. The variables are calibrated with rich empirical information, and the model is trained to reproduce the historical path of the emergence of the European research area. Potential effects of new policy designs that modify the size, spread of disciplines and nationality requirements on this European research landscape are then analysed.

Employing agent-based models, in our case ones focusing on mutual knowledge exchange and learning in research and innovation networks, is a method that allows the modelling of the interactions between heterogeneous agents confronted with uncertainty. The examples given in this chapter also illustrate the flexibility of this class of models. The basic mechanisms of knowledge exchange and knowledge creation remain similar in the different cases. However, the agents are modified to suit the applications with regard to their sizes, location, and knowledge. The chapter also demonstrates that agent-based simulation models can be adapted to address the information interests of different target groups (e.g. firms and policy makers).

Agent-based simulation models allow for the analysis of dynamic and historical processes using so-called in-silicio experiments. Because they can be calibrated and trained with empirical information, they improve the understanding of the mechanisms and dynamics that have shaped past developments. The results of a scenario analysis using such models need, however, to be interpreted keeping in mind the epistemological disclaimer, that point predictions of the future are impossible. What the results do tell us is, on the one hand, the mechanisms and dynamics that the modellers think are relevant to explain past developments. On the other hand, it tells us that extensions to the future can only show that certain development paths might lead to bottlenecks and should be avoided and that, due to the non-linear interactions, certain self-organising and therefore surprising drastic changes are possible. Because of this epistemological caveat, modellers as well as policy makers have to keep in mind that agent-based simulation models are not predicting precise developments, although they can identify general trends including the possibility of surprises. In other words, agent-based simulation models help to support the instinctive design of policy instruments. Even if the veil of ignorance cannot be lifted, at least it becomes more transparent.

References

Ackermann, R. (1970). The philosophy of science. New York: Pegasus.

Agrawal, A., & Henderson, R. (2002). Putting patents in context: Exploring knowledge transfer from MIT. Management Science, 48, 44-60.

Ahrweiler, P., Schilperoord, M., Gilbert, G. N., & Pyka, A. (2012). Simulating the role of MNCs for knowledge and capital dynamics in networks of innovation. In M. Heidenreich (Ed.), Innovation and institutional embeddedness of companies (pp. 141-168). Cheltenham, UK: Edward Elgar.

Ahrweiler, P., Pyka, A., & Gilbert, G. N. (2011). A new model for university-industry links in knowledge-based economies. Journal of Product Innovation Management, 28(2), 218-235.

Ahrweiler, P., Gilbert, N., & Pyka, A. (2006). Institutions matter, but ... organisational alignment in knowledge-based industries. Science, Technology and Innovation Studies, 2, 3-18.

Ahrweiler, P., de Jong, S., & Windrum, P. (2003). Evaluating innovation networks. In A. Pyka & G. Kueppers, Innovation networks: Theory and practice. Cheltenham, UK: Edward Elgar Publishers.

Argyris, C., & Schoen, D. A. (1996). Organizational learning: A theory of action perspective. Reading, MA: Addison-Wesley.

Bolton, G.E., Katoka, E., & Ockenfels, A. (2005). Co-operation among strangers with limited information about reputation. Journal of Public Economics, 89, 1457-1468.

Brusoni, S., Prencipe, A., & Pavitt, K. (2001). Knowledge specialisation, organizational coupling and the boundaries of the firm: Why firms know more than they make? Administrative Science Quarterly, 46: 597-621.

Cantner, U., & Pyka, A. (1998). Absorbing technological spillovers: Simulations in an evolutionary framework. Industrial and Corporate Change, 7, 369- 397.

Chapple, W., Lockett, A., Siegel, D., & Wright, M. (2005). Assessing the relative performance of U.K. university technology transfer offices: Parametric and non-parametric evidence. Research Policy, 34, 369-384.

Cohen, W. M., & Levinthal, D. (1989). Innovation and learning: the Two faces of RD. The Economic Journal, 99, 569-596.

de Geus, A. (1997). The living company. London: Brealy.

Duncan, R. B. (1974). Modifications in decision structure in adapting to the environment: Some implications for organizational learning. Decision Sciences, 5, 705-725.

Garcia, R., Dunn, D. T., & Smith, L. A. (forthcoming a). Boundary spanners and social networks surrounding research centers. Partners for Innovation Program. [Working Paper: NSF 04-556.]

Garcia, R., Dunn, D. T., & Smith, L. A. (forthcoming b). Performance of knowledge interactions between public research centers and industrial firms: An application for Spanish public research centers based on project-level data. [Working Paper.]

Gilbert, G. N. (1997). A simulation of the structure of academic science. Sociological Research Online, 2. Retrieved from http://www.socresonline.org.uk/socresonline/2/2/3.html.

Gilbert, G. N., Pyka, A., & Ahrweiler, P. (2003). Simulating innovation networks. In A. Pyka & G. Kueppers (Eds.), Innovation networks: Theory and practice (pp. 169-196). Cheltenham, UK: Edward Elgar.

Gilbert, G. N., Ahrweiler, P., & Pyka, A. (2007). Learning in innovation networks: Some simulation experiments. Physica A, 378, 100-109.

Gilbert, G. N., Ahrweiler, P., & Pyka, A. (2010). Learning in innovation networks: Some simulation experiments. In P. Ahrweiler (Ed), Innovation in complex social systems. London: Routledge.

Gupta, A. K., & Govindarajan, V. (1991). Knowledge flows and the structure of control within multinational corporations. Academy of Management Review, 16(4), 768-792.

Gupta, A. K., & Govindarajan, V. (1994). Alternative value chain configurations for foreign subsidiaries: Implications for coordination and control within MNCs. In H. Thomas, D. O'Neal, & R. White (Eds.), Building the strategically responsive organization (pp. 375-392). Chichester, UK: John Wiley.

Hedberg, B. (1981). How organizations learn and unlearn. In P. C. Nystrom & W. H. Starbuck (Eds.), Handbook of organizational design. Oxford: Oxford University Press.

Henderson, R., Jaffe, A., & Trajtenberg, M. (1998). Universities as a source of commercial technology: A detailed analysis of university patenting, 1965-1988. Review of Economics and Statistics, 80(1), 119-127.

Knight, F. H. (1921). Risk, uncertainty and profit. Chicago.

Michelet, R. (1992). Forming successful strategic marketing alliances in Europe. Journal of European Business, 4, 11-15.

Pavitt, K. (1987). The objectives of technology policy. Science and Public Policy, 14, 182-188 (Reprinted in Pavitt, K. (1999). Technology, management and systems of innovation. Cheltenham, UK: Edward Elgar.).

Powell, W. W., White, D. R., Koput, K. W., & Owen-Smith, J. (2005). Network dynamics and field evolution: The growth of inter-organizational collaboration in the life sciences. American Journal of Sociology, 110, 1132-1205.

Pyka, A., & Kueppers, G. (2003). Innovation networks: Theory and practice. Cheltenham, UK: Edward Elgar.

Pyka, A., & Hörlesberger, M. (2004). A neurological view on the technological brain of a firm. Mimeo: Austrian Research Centers.

Pyka, A., & Saviotti, P. P. (2005). The evolution of R&D networking in the biotech industries. International Journal of Entrepreneurship and Innovation Management, 5(1/2), 49-68.

Schmoch, U., Laville, F., Patel, P., & Frietsch, R. (2003). Linking technological areas to industrial sectors. Final Report to the European Commission. DG Research.

Scholz, R., Nokkala, T., Ahrweiler, P., Pyka, A., & Gilbert, N. (2010). The agent-based Nemo Model (SKEIN) – Simulating European Framework Programmes. In P. Ahrweiler (Ed.), Innovation in complex social systems. London: Routledge.

Siegel, D. S., Waldman, D., Atwater, L., & Link, A. N. (2003). Commercial knowledge transfers from universities to firms: Improving the effectiveness of university-industry collaboration. Journal of High Technology Management Research, 14, 111-133.

Teece, D. (1987). Capturing value from a technological innovation. In B. R. Guile et al. (Eds.), Technology and global industry. Washington, DC: National Academic Press.

Thursby, J., & Kemp, S. (2002). Growth and productive efficiency of university intellectual property licensing. Research Policy, 31, 109-124.

Toulmin, S. (1967). The philosophy of science: An introduction. London: Hutchinson.

Winter, S. G. (1984). Schumpeterian competition in alternative technological regimes. Journal of Economic Behaviour and Organization, 5, 237-261.

CHAPTER SIX

EXTENDING AGENT-BASED MODELING VIA MULTICRITERIA DECISION ANALYSIS

HAROLD PAREDES-FRIGOLETT,
LUIZ FLÁVIO AUTRAN MONTEIRO GOMES
AND JAVIER PEREIRA RETAMALES

Introduction

Although well-established as a research methodology in the natural sciences and engineering, agent-based modeling and simulation has recently emerged as a highly promising research methodology in the social sciences. The field of computational social simulation holds the promise of unleashing the power of modeling social systems as they function in the real world. Despite the advances in this field in recent years, there are still important limitations as to the complexity of the models that can be simulated using this technique. In the field of innovation, these shortcomings become evident when we consider the complexity of innovation networks and the role they play in driving processes of innovation in knowledge-intensive industries (Ferrary and Granovetter, 2009). These shortcomings can be classified in three main areas:

1. *Knowledge acquisition*: acquiring knowledge from structured and semi-structured sources to come up with large knowledge bases containing the knowledge diffused in knowledge-intensive industries (Gordon and Schubert 2010, 2014; Schubert 2002; Singh 2005; van Durme and Schubert 2008; van Durme, Quian and Schubert 2008; van Durme, Michalak, and Schubert 2009);
2. *Knowledge representation*: developing languages able to represent the knowledge diffused in innovation networks in such a way that artificial agents can use this knowledge for strategic

decision-making (Baader et al. 2003; Baader, Horrocks, and Sattler 2007; Lenat and Feigenbaum 1987; Lenat and Guha 1990, 1993; Levesque and Brachmann 1987; Sowa 1991, 1992, 2000, 2008, 2011; Sowa and Majumdar 2003; Schubert 2014);

3. *Knowledge discovery*: providing tools for automatic knowledge extraction so that agents can make decisions under uncertainty during simulations and produce new knowledge.

The aim of this chapter is to make a contribution in the third area listed above by exploring how artificial agents can make decisions under uncertainty in a way that more closely mimics decision-making processes in the real world.

The chapter is organized as follows. In Section 2, we introduce three basic agent-based models of the links between research institutions and industry that show the canonical way in which strategic decision-making has been addressed in previous work in the area of agent-based modeling and innovation networks. In Section 3, we formally define the decision-making processes entailed in the agent-based models introduced in Section 2 from a multicriteria decision analysis standpoint. In Section 4, we present a multicriteria decision analysis method to be used in concert with the agent-based models presented in Section 3. In Section 5, we present our conclusions and ideas for future work.

The Agent-Based Models

The agent-based models introduced in this section show the canonical way in which strategic decision-making is commonly approached in agent-based modeling. In particular, we will present how strategic decisions pertaining to such areas as budget allocation, consortium formation, sponsoring, and licensing are made in agent-based models that deal with the relationships between research institutions and industry.

The Agent Types

The study of the links between research institutions, particularly universities, and industry has produced a large body of work and the nature of these links is well understood today (Poyago-Theotoky et al. 2002). This body of work has led to a number of studies that use agent-based modeling to simulate the way these relationships work (Ahrweiler, Pyka and Gilbert 2011; Pyka, Gilbert and Ahrweiler 2007).

The agents we will consider correspond to research institutions, small and medium-sized enterprises, and large diversified companies.

Research Institutions (RIs): Research institutions correspond to universities, research centers linked to universities, independent research centers from the public and private sector that rely on public funding to conduct research and development activities, and research centers that perform contract research and development for clients and partners from industry or the public sector. Following these previous approaches, we assume that research institutions engage in these research projects with other research institutions, small and medium-sized enterprises, and large diversified companies. We also assume that research institutions do not engage in the productization or commercialization of their research output, although they can license the intellectual properties (IPs) they produce either to small and medium-sized enterprises or to large diversified firms or spin-out companies. In the latter case, research institutions would transfer these IPs to their spin-out companies in exchange for equity, licenses, or a combination of both.

Small and Medium-Sized Enterprises (SMEs): Small and medium-sized companies correspond to enterprises from the private sector that typically have only one strategic business unit and serve one specific market. Small and medium-sized enterprises have a more specialized knowledge stock and they do not have the vast amounts of capital stock typically available to large diversified companies. Some of these small and medium-sized companies drive radical innovation in emerging markets, which can lead to processes of high value creation and disruption within an industry. This makes them ideal candidates to receive venture capital investment. Small and medium-sized enterprises can engage in research projects as active members of the research team, but they differ from research institutions in that they can also license intellectual properties (IPs) from either research institutions, other small and medium-sized enterprises, or large diversified companies. Although some of these small and medium-sized enterprises could also sponsor research, they typically do not have the capital at their disposal to sponsor large research and development projects. From a radical innovation standpoint, small and medium-sized enterprises are important nodes in an innovation network because they do not have the dilemma of creative destruction typically associated with large diversified companies. In fact, most radical innovations in knowledge-intensive industries are driven by small and medium-sized enterprises.

In many knowledge-intensive industries, small and medium-sized enterprises driving radical innovation need to receive vast amounts of venture capital to fund processes of market expansion and acceleration with the ultimate goal of consolidating a leadership position in the markets they serve. Successful small and medium-sized enterprises that go down this path will typically end up executing an exit scenario. The quintessential exit scenario for small and medium-sized enterprises is an initial public offering (IPO). Sometimes a large diversified company proposes the strategic acquisition of a successful small and medium-sized enterprise in order to tap into a new emerging market or to neutralize a potential future competitor. This is often an interesting exit scenario for small and medium-sized enterprises that fail to execute an IPO. Small and medium-sized enterprises that fail to execute an exit and are in financial distress can attempt to execute a management buy-out, an asset acquisition, or an outright acquisition by another small and medium-sized enterprise or a large diversified company.

Large Diversified Companies (LDCs): Large diversified companies differ from small and medium-sized enterprises in that they have several strategic business units serving different markets. Some of them could also serve different industries. They have large amounts of knowledge and capital stock at their disposal and they usually have a research and development division as a functional area serving the research and development needs of more than one of their business units. Unlike small and medium-sized enterprises, large diversified companies are not eligible as investment opportunities for venture capital firms, although their business units might become an acquisition target for another large diversified company. Like research institutions and small and medium-sized enterprises, large diversified companies can engage in research projects with research institutions, small and medium-sized enterprises, and large diversified companies. Like small and medium-sized enterprises, large diversified companies can also license IPs from research institutions, small and medium-sized enterprises, or other large diversified companies. Unlike research institutions and most small and medium-sized enterprises, though, large diversified companies can also engage with research institutions and small and medium-sized enterprises as sponsors of research and development projects with the aim of becoming beneficiaries or licensees of the IPs produced by the projects they sponsor. As sponsors, large diversified companies will typically engage with research institutions and small and medium-sized enterprises as members of consortia, usually contributing financial backing and requirements.

Large diversified companies often engage in intrapreneurial activities, spinning out companies and providing them with both capital and knowledge stock in the form of IP. In several industries, large diversified companies can also act as venture capitalists themselves through a separate corporate entity or unit specially dedicated to investing in small and medium-sized enterprises employing business models that are strategically aligned with the core business of their strategic business units. Typically, large diversified companies fund and take an equity position in small and medium-sized enterprises driving radical innovation in the same way a venture capital firm does. Unlike venture capital firms, large diversified companies do so not based on the potential financial reward that can be achieved through successful exit scenarios of their portfolio companies. Large diversified companies differ from venture capital firms in that their primary aim is to increase the demand for the products and services they market. To this end, they help their portfolio companies accelerate their market expansion, increasing the demand for their own products and services in the process.

The Dynamics of Agent-Based Models

In this subsection, we present three flow charts describing the dynamics of the agent-based models corresponding to research institutions, small and medium-sized enterprises, and large diversified companies. In the flow charts shown in this section, the white rectangle with rounded corners represents the initialization module, the white rectangles represent inputs, the gray rectangles represent outputs, the white diamonds represent decision gates, the white ellipses represent alternatives, and the gray boxes with rounded corners represent actions.

Figure 6.1 shows the flow chart of the agent-based model corresponding to research institutions.

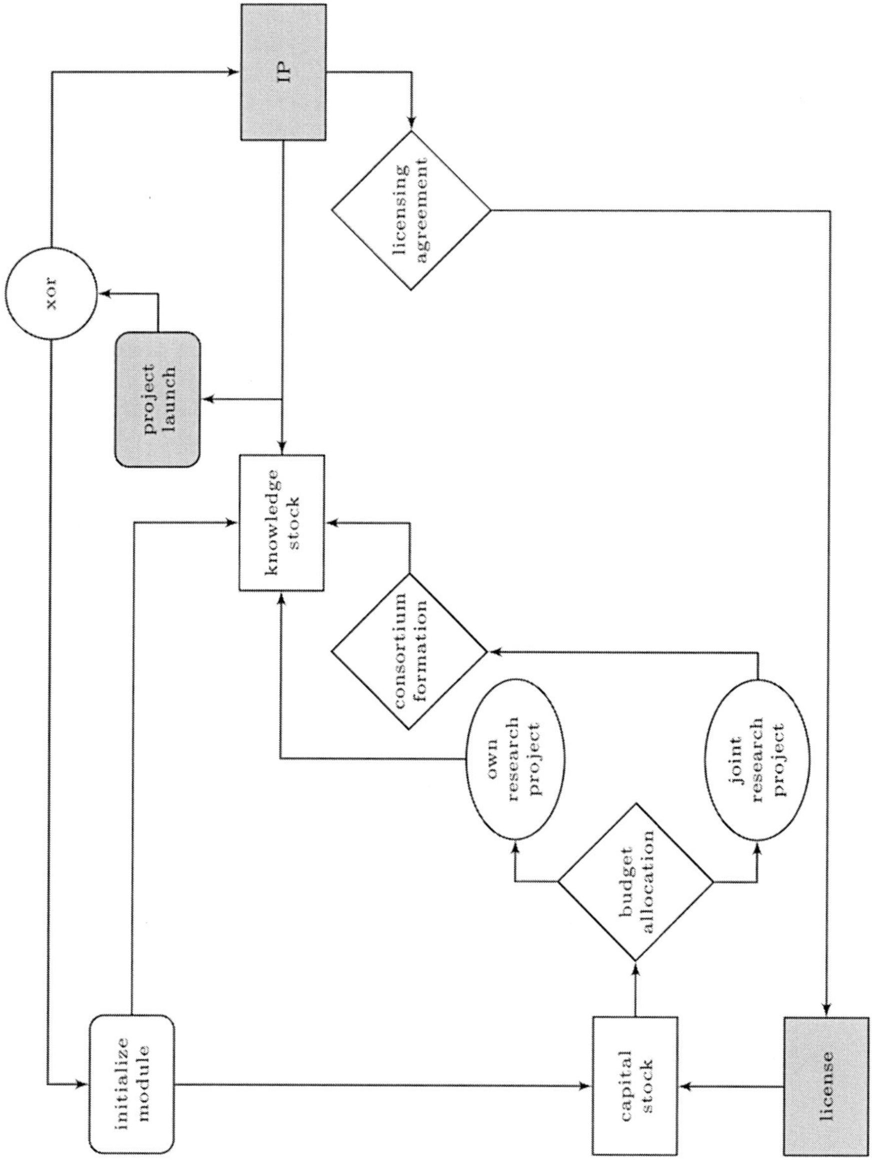

Figure 6.1: Agent-based model flow chart for research institutions. Source: Based on Triulzi, Scholz and Pyka 2011, p. 12.

Research institutions build their own research groups or form research consortia with other research institutions, small and medium-sized enterprises, or large diversified companies. The projects launched as a result of these research activities may produce IPs that will increase the knowledge stock of research institutions. Research institutions can also engage in licensing agreements with small and medium-sized enterprises and large diversified companies. Though research institutions do not engage in productization and commercialization agendas, the licenses they obtain from their licensing agreements will contribute to increasing their capital stock.

Figure 6.2 shows the flow chart of the agent-based model corresponding to small and medium-sized enterprises (SMEs).

Small and medium-sized enterprises build their own research groups or form research consortia with research institutions, other small and medium-sized enterprises, or large diversified companies. The projects launched as a result of these research activities may produce IPs that will increase the knowledge stock of small and medium-sized enterprises.

Unlike research institutions, small and medium-sized enterprises can license IPs from research institutions, from other small and medium-sized enterprises, and from large diversified companies to build solutions and launch them as innovations in the market. Unlike research institutions, small and medium-sized companies engage in productization and commercialization agendas as shown by the actions "solution building" and "market launch" shown in Figure 6.2. These actions can lead to solutions deployed in the market, which can eventually lead to innovations that increase the capital stock of these agents.

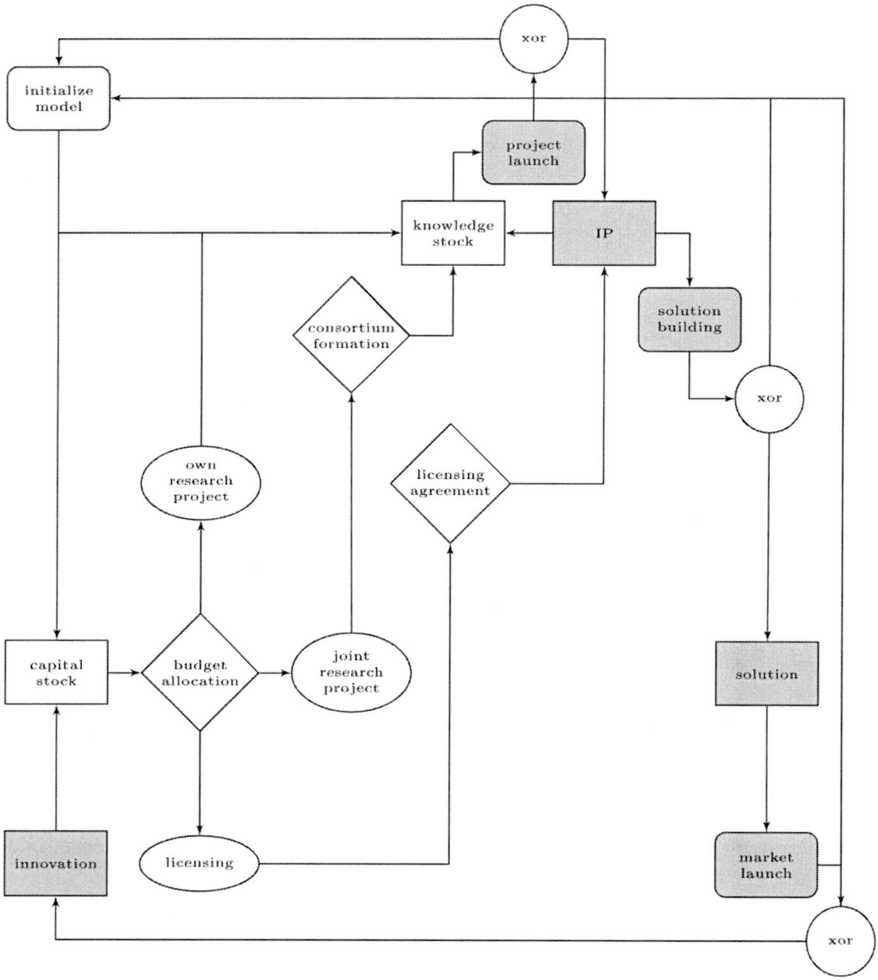

Figure 6.2: Agent-based model flow chart for small and medium-sized enterprises. Source: Based on Triulzi, Scholz and Pyka 2011, p. 12.

Figure 6.3 shows the flow chart of the agent-based model corresponding to large diversified companies (LDCs).

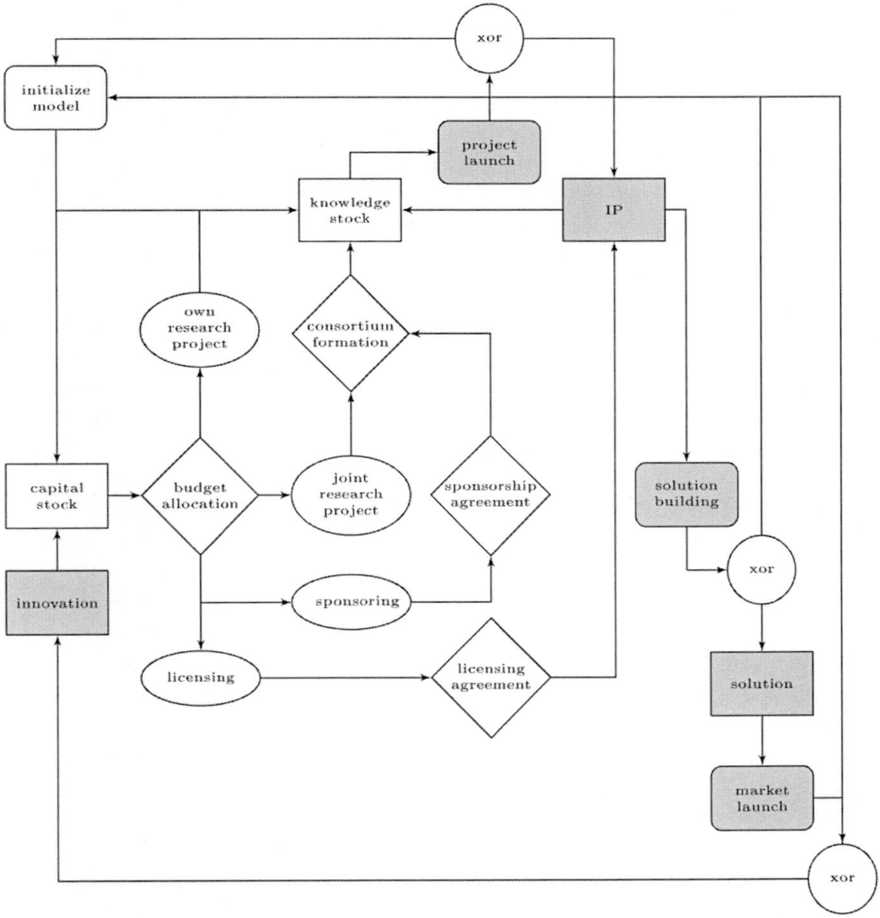

Figure 6.3: Agent-based model flow chart for large diversified companies. Source: Based on Triulzi, Scholz and Pyka 2011, p. 12.

Large diversified companies build their own research groups or form research consortia with research institutions, small and medium-sized enterprises, or other large diversified companies. The projects launched as a result of these research activities may produce IPs that will increase the knowledge stock of large diversified companies. Like small and medium-sized enterprises, large diversified companies can license IPs from research institutions, small and medium-sized enterprises, and other large diversified companies and they can also productize and commercialize solutions in the market. These solutions can lead to innovations that can increase the capital stock of these agents. Large diversified companies differ from small and medium-sized enterprises, though, in that they can also sponsor the research projects of research institutions and small and medium-sized enterprises. These sponsored projects will produce new IP, which large diversified companies will typically co-own and exploit in order to build new solutions and launch them as innovations in the market.

Conventional Decision-Making Approaches

In this section, we showcase some typical approaches to decision-making in agent-based modeling. We use the links between research institutions and industry partners in innovation networks of knowledge-intensive industries as application domain.

Decision Gate 1 (Budget Allocation): Let us begin by considering the first decision gate in the agent-based models shown in Figures 6.1 through 6.3. This first gate corresponds to the budget allocation decision problem. In the case of the agent-based model for agents of type 1 (research institutions) shown in Figure 6.1, there are only two possible alternatives at this gate, internal research projects and joint research projects. For agents of type 2 (small and medium-sized enterprises), the agent-based model in Figure 6.2 shows licensing as another alternative available to small and medium-sized enterprises. For agents of type 3 (large diversified companies), the agent-based model in Figure 6.3 shows sponsoring as yet another alternative available to large diversified companies.

A common approach to addressing this decision problem would consist in initializing all agents with a certain amount of capital stock and then defining randomly the percentage of the total capital stock to be allocated to all of these alternatives in each period (Ahrweiler, Pyka and Gilbert 2011; Pyka, Gilbert and Ahrweiler 2007; Triulzi, Scholz and Pyka 2011). Usually, this percentage would be either kept in subsequent rounds or it would be adjusted in future rounds depending on innovation performance expressed in terms of research or innovation output achieved. The next decision at this gate would be to decide how to divide that percentage between the alternatives available. Although agents in the real world would address this budget allocation problem using more complex decision analysis methods, this percentage is often defined randomly in agent-based modeling as well. In fact this decision is highly complex, involving a number of different criteria under high strategic uncertainty.

A more realistic approach would involve considering the following criteria: (i) the size of the capital stock available; (ii) the risk associated with the project; and (iii) the strategic alignment of the project with the strategic objectives of the organization that innovates. A random allocation policy is obviously quite a departure from the decision-making processes followed by agents in the real world. To compensate for this, agent-based models usually adjust their random allocation process to incorporate "market feedback" (Triulzi, Scholz and Pyka 2011). Such adjustments try to emulate the budget allocation of the most successful agents in subsequent periods. These types of adjustments are difficult to reconcile with the mechanisms used by real agents because information about internal allocation policies directly affecting innovation performance is not only not public but it is also strictly confidential. Consequently, competing agents in the real world will hardly be in a position to imitate the budget allocation patterns of the most successful companies in their respective industries because they would not have access to such confidential information.

Decision Gate 2 (Consortium Formation): Let us now consider the second decision gate in the agent-based models shown in Figures 6.1 through 6.3. This second gate corresponds to the consortium formation decision problem. All agents can establish consortia with agents of any type. A typical approach to addressing this decision problem would consist in randomly defining the type of projects in which agents get involved. Some authors have addressed this problem by proposing a conservative strategy whereby agents form consortia with firms whose knowledge bases are more similar (Balconi et al. 2009; Guezguez, Nesta and Saviotti 2009; Triulzi, Scholz and Pyka 2011). These authors suggest that this conservative strategy is more attuned to the need to produce incremental innovations. Agents favoring the formation of consortia with agents whose knowledge bases are more different would then pursue a more aggressive strategy. It is then argued that this aggressive partnering strategy would be preferred so as to produce radical innovations. Therefore, a logical approach to addressing the problem at the decision gate 2 could consist in dividing the agents in two populations, one population of agents pursuing incremental innovation and partnering with more similar agents and another one pursuing more radical innovation and partnering with more dissimilar agents. Usually, the instantiation of these two populations is performed randomly.

We might argue that these strategies for the formation of research consortia do not reconcile with evidence provided by technology managers in a variety of knowledge-intensive industries. In fact, even for incremental innovations, small and medium-sized enterprises as well as large diversified companies tend to form these consortia based on complementarities rather than on similarities. In fact, one of the main mantras of successful innovation team formation is that of looking for a complementor and not for a substitute when it comes to building successful innovation teams (Carlson and Wilmot, 2006). In some of the SKIN implementations put forth thus far (Ahrweiler, Pyka and Gilbert 2011; Pyka, Gilbert and Ahrweiler 2007) the strategy of forming teams based on the similarities and dissimilarities of the knowledge bases contained in the agents' kenes has been used.

We put the case that the use of multicriteria decision analysis methods to address the problem at this decision gate 2 would lead to a more comprehensive approach to forming innovation teams based on a variety of often conflicting criteria. This metric of distance between the agent's knowledge bases is just one of a number of criteria for successful innovation team formation. In fact, the problem of forming consortia is an area that requires the consideration of a number of often conflicting criteria.

Decision Gate 3 (Licensing): Let us now consider the third decision gate in the agent-based model corresponding to small and medium-sized enterprises shown in Figure 6.2 and the agent-based model corresponding to large diversified companies shown in Figure 6.3. This licensing decision can also be made via more sophisticated decision-making processes than those currently *en vogue* in the agent-based modeling research community. We need to make the distinction, though, between research institutions producing intellectual properties (IPs) as a result of basic or applied research, on the one hand, and small and medium-sized enterprises and large diversified companies, on the other. Research institutions act rather like potential licensors of IP using push models of technology transfer. The licensing decisions pertaining to these push models are usually less complex and they are usually made by a dedicated technology licensing office. Since universities and their technology licensing offices are not designed to assume the agency and monitoring costs associated with early-stage technology innovation projects, the issue of long-term profitability is usually less of a concern. This makes the negotiation of IP licensing terms between universities, on the one hand, and small and medium-sized enterprises and large diversified firms, on the other, more straightforward. Depending on the industry, though, most of these deals are negotiated by the researchers that were involved in the joint creation of the IPs with other members of an initial skeleton management team. To make such negotiations straightforward, the most entrepreneurial research universities around the world tend to provide the research team and the entrepreneurs involved with standard terms that are very favorable and are designed to push technology out of laboratories. The licensing situation for small and medium-sized enterprises and large diversified companies, as either licensors or licensees, is usually more complex as licensing terms are usually subject to a process of negotiation involving a number of different alternatives and criteria.

The way artificial agents go about making licensing decisions and producing outcomes such as licenses has also been handled in a straightforward manner in the agent-based modeling research community. Usually, it is assumed that a certain percentage of projects end up successfully by producing the intended outcomes and that a certain percentage of those outcomes results in licenses that will drive revenues for the licensor. These percentages are often determined randomly as empirical data for calibration purposes is often hard to obtain due to the confidential manner in which this information is handled by small and medium-sized enterprises and large diversified companies in knowledge-intensive industries.

Licensing decisions in agent-based modeling can be greatly improved if more complex methods of analysis such as those usually used by managers at small and medium-sized enterprises and large diversified companies were to be implemented *in silico* in an agent-based model. Decisions pertaining to licensing terms and potential licensors are often very complex, involving several licensing options and conflicting criteria. Multicriteria decision analysis methods are often used by managers at small and medium-sized enterprises and large diversified companies to define a ranking of potential licensing alternatives from different licensees according to a number of different criteria.

Decision Gate 4 (Project Sponsorship): Let us now consider the project sponsorship decision at the fourth decision gate in the agent-based model for large diversified companies shown in Figure 6.3. Sponsorship is a problem that only agents of type 3, namely, large diversified companies, need to address. Large diversified companies would typically sponsor research institutions and small and medium-sized enterprises. The decision processes associated with sponsoring projects are even more susceptible to being addressed using multicriteria decision analysis. The reason for this is the potentially large number of alternative projects to sponsor and the variety of criteria that need to be taken into account in order to select the best projects.

To illustrate this type of decisions, we consider how this sponsoring problem was addressed by a recent SKIN implementation of the university-industry links in the biotechnology and pharmaceutical industries (Triulzi, Scholz and Pyka 2011). The approach taken by these authors consisted in addressing the sponsorship problem by considering two rankings, a first ranking of large diversified companies sorted according to their available sponsorship budget, and a second ranking of research institutions (universities) sorted according to the number of patents held. To simplify matters, these authors assumed that all university projects seeking sponsorship had equal cost. The sponsorship problem was then implemented using a simple matching procedure whereby the large diversified company with the highest remaining sponsorship budget would fund the university with the highest number of patents held.

Though approaches such as this constitute an attempt to add complexity to the decision-making challenges faced by artificial agents in an agent-based model, they still are quite a departure from the way these decisions are handled by large diversified companies in the real world. In the procedure described above, only a single criterion, i.e. the number of patents held by the university, was used to make a strategic sponsorship decision. In making such strategic decisions, other criteria such as the actual strategic fit between the sponsor's strategic objectives and the actual objectives pursued by the research agenda of the agents seeking sponsorship, the ability of the actual research team members to execute, the actual amount of funds needed, and the duration of the project are relevant criteria that also need to be taken into account when making such project-sponsoring decisions.

The sponsorship strategy of large diversified companies is in actuality a special form of a technology transfer strategy called technology pull. This strategy is not very popular with research institutions, especially those that are part of research universities. University-linked research institutions use push models of technology transfer that do not drive research and innovation agendas starting from the important needs of small and medium-sized enterprises and large diversified companies. The resulting lack of strategic alignment between research institutions linked to universities and large diversified companies leads to a situation in which the objectives pursued by the research team become the most important criterion to consider when making project-sponsoring decisions. Research in the area of technology transfer can benefit from multicriteria decision analysis due to the number of alternatives and criteria available to analyze these complex project-sponsoring decisions.

Extending SKIN via Multicriteria Decision Analysis

Previous work in the area of agent-based modeling and innovation networks has modeled the decisions an artificial agent can make based on inputs, decisions, actions, and outcomes. In the previous section, we have made a case for the incorporation of more complex decision-making methods in agent-based modeling. In particular, we have made a strong case for the adoption of multicriteria decision analysis methods. With this objective in mind, we propose a model that lies at the intersection of agent-based modeling and multicriteria decision analysis and allows artificial agents to make decisions based on multiple criteria at each of the decision gates in an agent-based model.

The Decision-Making Process

The decision-making process of agents at each of the gates in an agent-based model follows the phases of a decision-aiding process proposed by Bouyssou et al., 2006:

1. *The Problem Formulation*: Let γ be the triplet $\gamma = \langle \mathrm{D}, \mathrm{V}, \Pi \rangle$, where D is a set of gates in an agent-based model, V is a set of points of view, and Π is a procedure stating what to do with the elements of D.
2. *The Evaluation Model*: Let Γ be the tuple $\Gamma = \langle \mathrm{A}, \mathrm{C}, \mathrm{U}, \mathrm{L} \rangle$, where A is set of alternatives at a decision gate derived from D, C is a set of criteria derived from V allowing the evaluation of elements of A, U is a model of the uncertainty associated with the information we deal with in $\mathrm{A} \times \mathrm{C}$, and L is an aggregation

logic determining the way this information is to be operationalized in order to solve the decision-making problem Π.

3. *The Recommendation*: Finally, agents make a decision at a decision gate in D, that is, they have to select an alternative in the set A based upon the recommendation produced by the aggregation logic L considering the criteria in C.

The Aggregation Logic

When facing a number of different alternatives, the decisions agents make during a simulation round are the result of the aggregation logic L. This logic can take several forms depending on the nature of the problem Π. Usually, L will correspond to either a screening, a sorting, or a classification problem. A screening problem will arise whenever agents need to reduce a large number of alternatives to a reduced number containing the best alternatives. A sorting problem in contrast covers the more common situation in which agents need to rank alternatives according to a set of predefined criteria. The third family of problems consists in the agents assigning alternatives to already-established groups or classes. Of all these three families of problems, the most commonly dealt with in agent-based modeling and simulation is the sorting problem. In fact, previous work in agent-based modeling has generally relied upon ranking alternatives with the aim of selecting those with the highest ranking (often subject to some constraints).

We are interested in modeling situations in which agents have more than one criterion to rank alternatives at a decision gate. In such cases, we can approach this problem as a multicriteria decision analysis problem following the general model presented above. Multicriteria decision analysis methods can be used to assist an artificial agent in making strategic decisions involving several alternatives and criteria at a decision gate. These methods aim to assist agents in evaluating the alternatives based on the criteria defined.

Defining the Agent-Based Decision-Making Problem

Let us consider the set $A = \{a_1, \dots, a_n\}$ of n alternatives at a decision gate $d \in D$ in an agent-based model and the set $C = \{c_1, \dots, c_m\}$ of m criteria used to rank the alternatives in the set A. The agent-based modeler will need to implement a ranking algorithm of the alternatives in A using the set of predefined criteria in the set C. The solution to the decision-making problem at a decision gate d will then consist in choosing the alternatives with the highest ranking. Often in agent-based modeling, these alternatives will need to comply with a set of predefined constraints. In this case, only those alternatives satisfying the constraints will be valid alternatives in the set A to be ranked using the criteria in the set C.

Choosing a Multicriteria Decision Analysis Method

Discrete multicriteria decision analysis methods have been put forth and are used to solve complex decision making problems (Balenžentis, Balenžentis and Brauers 2012; Balezentiene and Kusta 2012; Ginevičius, Podvezko and Raslanas 2008; Vaidogas, Zavadskas and Turskis 2007). To solve the ranking problem in our application domain, we have chosen TODIM[1] as a multicriteria decision analysis method, as introduced in (Gomes and Lima 1991). This decision is based on two main features of the TODIM method: (i) TODIM uses the notion of positive and negative utility contributed by each criterion and (ii) TODIM models the risk aversion of agents, as opposed to multicriteria decision methods such as PROMÉTHÉE (Brans and Mareschal, 1990).

The TODIM Method

Founded on Prospect Theory (Kahneman and Tversky 1979; Tversky and Kahneman 1992), TODIM was put forth in the early nineties (Gomes and Lima 1991). Today, different extensions of the TODIM method exist for application domains such as real estate evaluation (Gomes, Gomes and Maranhão 2009; Gomes, Gomes and Rangel 2009; Moshkovich, Gomes and Mechitov 2011; Moshkovich et al. 2012), business planning (Rangel, Gomes and Moreira 2009; Rangel, Gomes and Cardoso 2011), energy resource management (Gomes, Gomes and Rangel 2009, Gomes, Gomes and Maranhão 2010), hospital management (Nobre, Trotta and Gomes 2012), and road planning (Gomes and Lima 1991).

TODIM can handle either hybrid or fuzzy data (Chen et al. 2010; Fan et al. 2013; Krohling and de Souza 2012). The value function of TODIM mirrors the value function of Cumulative Prospect Theory (Tversky and Kahneman 1992) in that it computes gains and losses with respect to a

[1] TODIM is a Portuguese acronym which stands for Interactive and Multicriteria Decision Making

reference point. This is based on the gain and loss attitude of agents for each criterion (Gomes and Lima 1991, 1992; Gomes, Gomes and Maranhão 2009, Gomes, Gomes and Rangel 2009; Nobre, Trotta and Gomes 2012). A global multi-attribute value function aggregates gains and losses for all criteria. This is performed using an additive difference function. This function adds up arguments in favor of and against an alternative, building a pairwise comparison to all other alternatives, as PROMÉTHÉE does (Brans and Mareschal, 1990). In this way, TODIM accounts for dominance relations among all pairs of alternatives.

Applying TODIM

Let us consider $A = \{a_1, \dots, a_n\}$ as the set of *n* alternatives at a decision gate $d \in D$ to be ranked and $C = \{c_1, \dots, c_m\}$ the set of m criteria. The evaluation of the alternatives in relation to all criteria is a matrix of evaluation containing numerical values. Verbal scales can be converted to cardinal values for qualitative criteria, if required. Let $P = [p_{nm}]\mathrm{P} = [\mathrm{P_{nm}}]$, where $p_{nm} \in [0,1]$, be the matrix of normalized scores of all alternatives against criteria. To implement "different flavors" of agents of a given agent type, we introduce inter-criteria information. To this end, we first introduce the importance of each criterion $c_i \in C$, expressed as w_i. We then define a *reference criterion* as the one with the highest importance, let us say c_r. Then, the relative weight of each criterion becomes $w_{ir} = w_i / w_r$ and the following utility function can be calculated:

$$\phi_i(a_j, a_k) = \begin{cases} \sqrt{\frac{w_{ir}(p_{ji} - p_{ki})}{\sum_{i=1}^{m} w_{ir}}} & if\ (p_{ji} - p_{ki}) > 0 \\ 0 & if\ (p_{ji} - p_{ki}) = 0 \\ -\frac{1}{\vartheta}\sqrt{\frac{(\sum_{i=1}^{m} w_{ir})(p_{ki} - p_{ji})}{w_{ir}}} & if\ (p_{ji} - p_{ki}) < 0 \end{cases} \qquad (1)$$

The pairwise comparison function ϕ_i models the agent's preferences. Depending on whether $p_{ji} - p_{ki}$ is positive or negative, gains or losses are experienced and the concave or convex form of ϕ_i represents the aversion or propensity to risk by agents. In the convex part, the attenuation factor of losses ϑ shapes the negative part of ϕ_i. A global dominance relation between each pair of alternatives (a_j, a_k) is then calculated as follows:

$$\delta(a_j, a_k) = \sum_{i=1}^{m} \phi_i(a_j, a_k) \qquad (2)$$

To come up with a global value, (2) is aggregated as follows:

$$\xi_j = \frac{\sum_{k=1}^{n} \delta(a_j, a_k) - min_j \sum_{k=1}^{n} \delta(a_j, a_k)}{max_j \sum_{k=1}^{n} \delta(a_j, a_k) - min_j \sum_{k=1}^{n} \delta(a_j, a_k)} \qquad (3)$$

Expression (3) represents a normalized global performance for the alternative a_j when compared against all other alternatives. Determining ξ_j leads to the ranking of all alternatives available at a decision gate in an agent-based model.

Using TODIM in Agent-Based Modeling

The way artificial agents deal with complex decision-making in agent-based modeling can mimic the way agents go about making strategic decisions in the real world. The multicriteria decision analysis method introduced above provides a tool for artificial agents to evaluate complex decisions in agent-based models. The function ξ_j in (3) gives us a ranking of alternatives an artificial agent can use to make a decision at a decision gate during an agent-based simulation round. Given a decision gate in the agent-based model, the ranking is built according to a predefined set of criteria that is common to all agents of a certain type. In the model presented in this section, agents of the same type may make different decisions according to the importance (the weights) they assign to the different criteria.

Conclusions and Future Work

The work reported in this chapter covers uncharted territory at the intersection of agent-based modeling and multicriteria decision analysis. To our knowledge, the use of multicriteria decision analysis methods is a novelty in the agent-based modeling research community. In our view, this line of research is important because it allows us to build agent-based models that more closely mimic the way agents make complex decisions in the real world. This is relevant because – to the extent that artificial agents are endowed with the ability to make more complex decisions – the complexity of the resulting models will contribute to filling the gaps between the real world and artificial worlds, thereby contributing to a broader acceptance of agent-based modeling as a research methodology in the social sciences.

In this chapter, we have shown how the problem of strategic decision-making can be approached by artificial agents using a multicriteria decision analysis method that implements a ranking algorithm. The ranking algorithm is required in order to sort the alternatives artificial agents face at a decision gate in agent-based models according to a predefined set of criteria for each agent type in the model. Although the set of criteria is fixed for each agent type and each decision gate, the set of weights attached to the set of criteria can vary across the same type of agents at a decision gate, thus allowing us to capture the more realistic scenario in which agents behave differently depending on the relevance assigned to each criterion. This introduces additional complexity for the agent-based modeler in terms of defining the set of criteria per agent type and per decision gate in each of the agent-based models and the set of weights associated with the set of criteria defined. The set of criteria and the weights can be calibrated in the agent-based models using empirical data.

We have shown how multicriteria decision analysis methods can be used in agent-based models to implement decision-making processes that can be construed as a ranking problem. But the range of decision problems spans a wide variety of filtering, sorting, and classification problems. In actuality, there is a comprehensive body of work in the multicriteria decision analysis research community that can be put to work in the area of agent-based modeling and simulation in order to implement decision problems above and beyond ranking (sorting).

From a computational implementation standpoint, this gain in complexity poses some challenges. It remains to be tested how well agent-based models that implement multicriteria decision analysis methods will scale as the number of agent types, agents, decision gates, alternatives, and criteria grows. This can become an obstacle to building large agent-based models endowed with multicriteria decision capabilities for real-world applications such as those encountered in innovation networks.

Future work will focus on compiling a set of filtering and classification problems often made by agents in innovation networks in the real world, modeling them as multicriteria decision analysis problems, and implementing them in agent-based models. We will also work on implementing algorithms based on metaheuristics to overcome potential scalability problems. The ultimate goal of this ambitious research agenda is to propose a theory of formal agent-based models and languages so that agent-based models and their implementation *in silico* can become technically feasible for commercial-grade applications not only in the area of innovation networks but in other areas of the social sciences as well.

Acknowledgements

The work reported in this chapter has been partially funded by the GREAT project of the European Commission (www.great-project.eu). Support has also been provided by a grant from Universidad Diego Portales (ONTOCODEX Project) in Chile and a grant from CNPq in Brazil under Research Project No. 305732/2012-9.

References

Ahrweiler, P., Pyka, A. and Gilbert, N. 2011. "A new model for university industry links in knowledge-based economies." Journal of Product Innovation Management, 27: 218-235.

Baader, F., Calvanese, D., McGuinness, D.L., Nardi, D. and Patel-Schneider, P.F. 2003. The Description Logic Handbook: Theory, Implementation, Applications. Cambridge, UK: Cambridge University Press.

Baader, F., Horrocks, I. and Sattler, U. 2007. "Description Logics." In Handbook of Knowledge Representation, Chapter 3, 135–179. Amsterdam: Elsevier.

Balconi, M., Palamara, G., Saviotti, P. and Zuchella, A. 2009. "The role of cognitive and geographic distance in the networks of Italian Biotechnology firms." In Proceedings of the European Association for Evolutionary Political Economy (EAEPE) Conference 2009. Amsterdam, The Netherlands.

Balezentiene, L. and Kusta, A. 2012. "Reducing greenhouse gas emissions in grassland ecosystems of the Central Lithuania: multi-criteria evaluation on a basis of the ARAS method." Scientific World Journal, published online.doi: 10.1100/2012/908384.

Balenžentis, A., Balenžentis, T. and Brauers, W.K.M. 2012. "MULTIMOORA-FG: A Multiobjective decision making method for linguistic reasoning with an application to personnel selection." Informatica, 23 2: 173-190.

Bouyssou, D., Marchant, T., Pirlot, M., Perny, P., Tsoukias, A. and Vincke, P. 2006. Evaluation and Decision Models with Multiple Criteria: New York: Springer.

Brans, J.P. and Mareschal, B 1990. The PROMÉTHÉE methods for MCDM, the PROMCALC GAIA and BANDADVISER software. In Readings in Multiple Criteria Decision Aid, edited by Bana e Costa, C.A., 216-252. Berlin: Springer.

Carlson, C. and Wilmot, W. 2006. The Five Disciplines for Creating What Customers Want: Crown Publishing Group, New York.

Chen, F.D., Zhang, X., Kang, F., Fan, Z-P. and Chen, X. 2010. "A Method for Interval Multiple Attribute Decision Making With Loss Aversion." In Proceedings of the 2010 International Conference of Information Science and Management Engineering, 453-456. Hangzhou, China: IEEE Computer Society.

Fan, Z-P., Zhang, X., Chen, F.D. and Liu, Y. 2013. "Extended TODIM method for hybrid MADM problems." Knowledge-Based Systems, 42: 40-48.

Ferrary, M. and Granovetter, M. 2009. "The role of venture capital firms in Silicon Valley's complex innovation network." Economy and Society, 38: 326-359.

Ginevičius, R., Podvezko, V. and Raslanas, S. 2008. "Evaluating the alternative solutions of wall insulation by multicriteria methods." Journal of Civil Engineering and Management, 14 4: 217-226.

Gomes, L.F.A.M. and Lima, M.M.P.P. 1991. "TODIM: Basics and application to multicriteria ranking of projects with environmental impacts." Foundations of Computing and Decision Sciences, 16 4: 113-127.

Gomes, L.F.A.M. and Lima, M.M.P.P. 1992. "From modeling individual preferences to multicriteria ranking of discrete alternatives: A look at prospect theory and the additive difference model." Foundations of Computing and Decision Sciences, 17 3: 171-184.

Gomes, L.F.A.M., Rangel, L.A.D. and Maranhão, F.J.C. 2009. "Multicriteria analysis of natural gas destination in Brazil: An application of the TODIM method." Mathematical and Computer Modeling, 50 1-2: 92-100.

Gomes, L.F.A.M., Gomes, C.F.S. and Rangel, L.A.D. 2009. "A comparative decision analysis with THOR and TODIM: rental evaluation in Volta Redonda." Revista Tecnologia, 30 1: 7-11.

Gomes, C.F.S., Gomes, L.F.A.M. and Maranhão, F.J.C. 2010. "Decision analysis for the exploration of gas reserves: merging TODIM and THOR." Pesquisa Operacional, 30 3: 601-617.

Gordon, J. and Schubert, L.K. 2010. "Quantification sharpening of commonsense knowledge." In: Commonsense Knowledge Symposium (CSK-10), AAAI 2010 Fall Symposium Series, 27-32. Arlington (VA), USA: The Association for the Advancement of Artificial Intelligence.

Guezguez, H., Nesta, L. and Saviotti, P. 2009. "Complementary and Similar Competences as Determinants of Alliance Formation in the Biopharmaceutical Industry." In Proceedings of 6th European Meeting of Applied Evolutionary Economics (EMAEE 2009), Max-Planck Institute of Economics, Jena, Germany.

Kahneman, D. and Tversky, A. 1979. "Prospect theory: An analysis of decision under risk." Econometrica, 47 2: 263-292.

Krohling, R.A. and de Souza, .T.M. 2012. "Combining prospect theory and fuzzy numbers to multi-criteria decision making." Expert Systems with Applications, 39 13: 11487-11493.

Lenat, D. and Feigenbaum, E. 1987. "On the thresholds of knowledge." In Proceedings of the 10th International Joint Conference on Artificial Intelligence (IJCAI-87), 1173-1182. Milan, Italy: Morgan Kaufmann.

Lenat, D. and Guha, R. 1990. Building Large Knowledge-Based Systems. Reading, MA: Addison Wesley.

Lenat, D. and Guha, R. 1993. "Review of Building Large Knowledge-Based Systems: Representation and Inference in the Cyc Project." Artificial Intelligence, 61:95-104.

Levesque, H. and Brachmann, R., 1987. "Expressiveness and tractability in knowledge representation and reasoning." Computational Intelligence, 3: 78-93.

Moshkovich, H., Gomes, L.F.A.M. and Mechitov, A.I. 2011. "An integrated multicriteria decision-making approach to real estate evaluation: The case of the TODIM method." Pesquisa Operacional, 31 1: 3-20.

Moshkovich, H.M., Gomes, L.F.A.M., Mechitov, A.I. and Rangel, L.A.D. 2012. "Influence of models and scales on the ranking of multiattribute alternatives." Pesquisa Operacional, 32 3: 523-542.

Nobre, F.F., Trotta, L.T.F. and Gomes, L.F.A.M. 1999. "Multi-criteria decision making—an approach to setting priorities in health care." Statistics in Medicine, 18 23: 3345-3354.

Poyago-Theotoky, J., Beath, J. and Siegel, D. 2002. "Universities and fundamental research: Reflections on the growth of university-industry partnerships." Oxford Review of Economic Policy, 18: 10-21.
Pyka, A., Gilbert, N. and Ahrweiler, P. 2007. "Simulating knowledge generation and distribution processes in innovation collaborations and networks." Cybernetics and Systems, 38: 667-693.
Rangel, L.A.D., Gomes, L.F.A.M. and Moreira, R.A. 2009. "Decision theory with multiple criteria: an application of ELECTRE IV and TODIM to SEBRAE/RJ." Pesquisa Operacional, 29 3: 577-590.
Rangel, L.A.D., Gomes, L.F.A.M. and Cardoso, F. P. 2011. "An application of the TODIM method to the evaluation of broadband Internet plans." Pesquisa Operacional, 31 2: 235-249.
Schubert, L.K. 2002. "Can we derive general world knowledge from texts?" In Proceedings of 2nd International Conference on Human Language Technology Research, 94-97. San Francisco (CA), USA: Morgan Kaufmann Publishers.
—. 2014. "NLog-like inference and commonsense reasoning." In Semantics for Textual Inference, edited by Zaenen, A. and Condoravdi, C. Stanford (CA), USA: CSLI Publications.
Singh, J. 2005. "Collaborative networks as determinants of knowledge diffusion patterns." Management Science, 49: 351-365.
Sowa, J. 1991. Principles of Semantic Networks: Explorations in the Representation of Knowledge. San Mateo (CA), USA: Morgan Kaufmann Publisher.
—. 1992. "Conceptual analysis as a basis for knowledge acquisition." In The Psychology of Experts: Cognitive Research and Empirical AI, edited by Hoffman, R.R., 80-96. New York (NY), USA: Springer.
—. 2000. Knowledge Representation: Logical, Philosophical, and Computational Foundations. Pacific Grove (CA), USA: Brooks Cole Publishing Company.
—. 2008. "Conceptual graphs." In Handbook of Knowledge Representation, 213-237. Amsterdam: Elsevier.
—. 2011. "Future directions for semantics systems." In Intelligence-based Systems Engineering, Chapter 2, 23-47. Berlin: Springer.
Sowa, J. and Majumdar, A. 2003. "Analogical reasoning." In Conceptual Structures for Knowledge Creation and Communication, LNAI 2746, 16-36. Berlin: Springer.
Triulzi, G., Scholz, R. and Pyka, A. 2011. "R&D and knowledge dynamics in university-industry relationships in biotech and pharmaceuticals: an agent-based model." FZID Discussion Paper 33-2011,

Forschungszentrum für Innovation und Dienstleistungen, University of Hohenheim, Stuttgart, Germany.

Tversky, A. and Kahneman, D. 1992. "Advances in prospect theory, cumulative representation of uncertainty." Journal of Risk and Uncertainty 5 4: 297-323.

Vaidogas, E.R., Zavadskas, E.K. and Turskis, Z. 2007. "Reliability measures in multicriteria decision making as applied to engineering projects." International Journal of Management and Decision Making, 8 5-6: 497-518.

van Durme, B. and Schubert, L.K. 2008. "Open knowledge extraction through compositional language processing." In Symposium on Semantics in Systems for Text Processing (STEP 2008), 239-254. Venice, Italy: Springer.

van Durme, B., Quian, T. and Schubert, L.K. 2008. "Class-driven attribute extraction." In Proceedings of the 22nd International Conference on Computational Linguistics (COLING 2008), 921-928. Manchester, UK: The Association for Computational Linguistics.

van Durme, B., Michalak, P. and Schubert, L.K. 2009. "Deriving generalized knowledge from corpora using WordNet abstraction." In Proceedings of the 12th Conference of the European Chapter of the Association for Computational Linguistics, 808-816. Athens, Greece: The Association for Computational Linguistics.

Chapter Seven

An Agent-based Simulation Model of Self-Sustaining Regional Innovation Systems

Cristina Ponsiglione, Ivana Quinto and Giuseppe Zollo

1. Introduction

In the last three decades, scholars, social scientists, economists, experts and policy makers have proposed different theoretical approaches (local productive systems, milieux innovateurs, regional clusters, learning regions, etc) to frame and study the topic of how and why localised systems of heterogeneous agents (firms, research organisations, institutional actors....) are able to foster learning, innovation, and economic growth of territories and regions. These different perspectives, in turn, have been the rationales behind diverse policy approaches to regional innovation (Laranja, Uyarra, and Flanagan, 2008).

Due to the emergence of successful regional clusters of firms in numerous regions around the world (i.e. Silicon Valley, Third Italy, etc) as well as the failure of some regional development models and policies, the concept of Regional Innovation Systems (henceforth RISs) has gained increasing popularity (Asheim and Coenen, 2005; Doloreux and Parto, 2005; Enright, 2001). In the literature, RISs have been defined as "a territorially embedded institutional infrastructure which supports innovation within the production structure of a region" (Asheim and Coenen, 2005; Doloreux, 2002; Doloreux and Parto, 2005). Put differently, RISs are composed of two sub-systems, namely the productive sub-system and the institutional one, which continually interact and mutually reinforce each other. According to this theoretical framework, regions are seen increasingly as designated loci of innovation, interaction, and competitiveness in a globalised economy (Doloreux and Parto, 2005; Asheim and Coenen, 2005; Quatraro, 2009).

Unfortunately, several studies (RIS, 2009; 2012; 2014) have shown that RISs with similar industrial structures and characteristics can differ greatly from each other even in terms of innovation and competitive performance. Saxenian (1994) in her studies starts to point out how and why a set of people and collective actors with their interactions could explain the success stories of the most innovative regions in the world. She claims that it is exactly such irreducible complexity of interactions which explains why local innovative and productive systems are impossible to replicate (Saxenian, 1994). In accordance with this, scholars and experts (Fortis and Quadrio Curzio, 2002; Garnsey, 2002; Holland, 2002; Lombardi, 2003; Longhi, 2002; Squazzoni and Boero, 2002; Testfastion, 2002) deal with productive-economic innovative systems (e.g. industrial districts, milieux innovateurs, local productive systems, regional clusters) as Complex Adaptive Systems (CAS). More recently, Pilotti, Sedita and Noni (2013) claim that a new perspective is emerging in the analysis of local productive-economic systems in which the central point is the framing of these systems as generated from complex interactions among internal and external elements. In other words, such complexity could explain the existence of differences among the worldwide regions in terms of innovation, economic development and growth.

Despite the main concepts of complexity science being used from a theoretical point of view to characterise territorial innovation systems, we claim that these concepts are poorly explored from a practical point of view. Filling this gap requires specific theoretical and methodological approaches in order to understand and possibly influence the emergence, the reinforcing, or the restructuring of certain desired patterns in territorial innovation systems.

Additionally, most research on RISs is focused on high-tech systems in large regions, usually characterised by the presence of effective institutional infrastructures and strategic actors enabling innovation processes. By contrast, medium-low innovative regions have attracted much less interest in the literature. We think that there is an important gap existing in the current literature considering both the European Commission indications and what is occurring around the world. This is the premise of our research.

In order to address these issues concerning regional innovation, in this chapter we propose a computational laboratory called CARIS (Complex Adaptive Regional Innovation System), which is able to support policy-makers in defining proper regional innovation policies. In particular, the agent-based model, core of the computational laboratory, has been built to explore in a systematic way how to develop a Regional Innovation System (RIS) in lagging regions of Europe.

Agent-Based Modelling (ABM) is considered as one of the methodological approaches most suited to analyse CASs (Heath, Hill and Ciarallo, 2009) and, more recently, it has been increasingly recognised as a useful tool to support policy making in different fields and at different levels (OECD, 2009; Brenner and Werker, 2009). The CARIS laboratory is built upon the claim that complexity and social simulations can be used to support policy-makers in defining proper and more effective innovation policies. Once fully developed and validated, the CARIS laboratory should help researchers, practitioners, and policy-makers to answer the following questions: What are the current level and the critical mass of local resources and competencies able to sustain the RIS? How far is the current pattern from a self-sustaining innovative pattern? How effective are current innovation policies and measures? What are the most effective policies to reassess the current pattern?

The chapter is organised as follows. In section 2, a literature review on Regional Innovation Systems is presented. In section 3, the conceptual framework of RIS as Complex Adaptive System is described. Section 4 illustrates the adopted methodological approach. Then, the CARIS conceptual and formal model developed in Netlogo language (available on request) is thoroughly discussed. Finally, results of internal validation of the model and statistical tests are presented, and further developments are discussed.

2. Regional Innovation Systems: the state-of-art

The concept of RISs has been gaining increasing attention not only from academic researchers and scholars but also from policy makers (Asheim, Boschma and Cooke, 2011; Doloreux, 2002; Doloreux and Parto, 2004). Additionally, compelled by the economic crisis and by the increased intensity of international competition, policy-makers have added a regional dimension in the definition of innovation policies (Fritsch and Stephan, 2005; Werker, 2006) and have paid much attention to RIS literature. As a consequence, the RIS approach has been increasingly recognised as a promising analytical framework to better analyse and understand the innovation process in a regional economy (Asheim et al., 2003; Asheim, Boschma and Cooke, 2011).

In the literature, RISs are defined as a set of economic, political, and institutional relationships in a specific geographic area, which generates an interactive learning process that, in turn, enables the production, diffusion, and use of specific knowledge and skills (Maillat, 1998; Cooke, Uranga, and Etxebarria, 1998; Asheim and Isaksen, 2001; Cooke, 2001; Asheim and Isaksen 2002; Doloreux, 2002; Coenen, 2005; Asheim and Gelter, 2005; Doloreux and Parto, 2005). Regions are considered systems of learning by interacting, and the relational network among the different actors is an organisational mode of such interactive processes (Cooke, 1996; Cooke and Morgan, 1998; Moulaert and Sekia, 2003). Therefore, innovation is meant as an interactive, cumulative, non-linear, and path-dependent process (Fischer, 2001; Moulaert and Sekia, 2003).

In a nutshell, the basic element is that such a set of different actors, by interacting (formally and informally, voluntarily and non-voluntarily), produce systemic and synergic effects that encourage organisations within the regions to develop specific forms of capital that derive from a common knowledge-base, values, norms, and social relationships able to reinforce and enable regional innovative capabilities, performance and competitiveness (Gertler, 2003).

Over time, the literature and empirical data on territorial innovation systems has been emphasising the existence of differences among worldwide regions in terms of innovation, economic development, and growth despite their industrial and cultural structures being very similar.

This has led to the rise of a lively debate about what proper and effective policies are which are able to foster virtuous innovation and growth processes (Foray, 2009). As a consequence, theories, models, and tools to support policy-makers in defining proper and effective innovation policies have been developed. In particular, in this chapter we briefly discuss three main perspectives which have been used to inform the development of innovation policies, namely the Learning Region Perspective, the Smart Specialisation Perspective, and the Ecology of Innovation Perspective.

The Learning Region Perspective highlights the importance of a regional dimension in supporting the innovation processes. In particular, such a perspective envisages how all actors sharing the same local context learn to cooperate with one another in addressing economic and social innovation (see Brusco, 1990; Lundvall, 1992; Lundvall and Johansson, 1994; Florida, 1995; OECD, 2001). These actors include enterprises, customers, producers, consultants, research institutes, universities, etc. Therefore, according to this perspective, the local community learns and evolves in an integrated way; communication and cooperation between the different actors represent a critical asset enabling collective learning and co-evolution (Gustavsen, Nyhan and Ennals, 2007). Institutions, interpreted as normative structures, play an important role in promoting stable and efficient interaction and collaboration.

The Smart Specialisation approach is a key element of the EU 2020 innovation plan. In particular, discussions are currently under way about introducing smart specialisation as a conditionality clause for structural fund attribution, and the OECD is launching an activity for measuring smart specialisation. It advocates that innovation policies must be embedded in the local reality. Such a perspective suggests that a region should specialise in R&D and innovation activities relevant to its economy and future development. It is possible to achieve economic growth and prosperity by enabling regions to focus on their strengths and local knowledge resources (Foray, 2011). More specifically, regions need to promote what should make their knowledge-base unique and superior, enabling them to reach a competitive advantage. The Smart Specialisation approach advocates differentiated policies for diverse regions (Camagni and Capello, 2012; Foray, David and Hall, 2011). The complexity of the Smart Specialisation approach resides in the discovering of the right domains on which to focus and specialise. Discovering the right domains is not a technology foresight exercise, but it should be an accurate process of entrepreneurial discovery (Foray, 2011). Therefore, the discovery process of the traditional territorial vocation has to be a bottom-up process, in which local entrepreneurs are identified as the leading actors.

Finally, the conceptual framework of Ecology of Innovation (David and Metcalfe, 2007) recognises and supports the value of diversity and social interaction in agreement with the results of Complexity Theory. In particular, David and Metcalfe (2007) suggest that the term "innovation systems" is characterised by cooperative and conflictual interactions in continuous transformation. It can be better described as a system far from the equilibrium (Arthur, Durlauf, and Lane, 1997), which continually changes through small and large avalanches of changes (Bak, Tang and Wiesenfeld, 1987). To understand these systems, it is necessary to understand what keeps the social system in continuous disequilibrium. According to the Ecology of Innovation perspective, a system cannot be described as a list of components, but it depends on the synergies deriving from the connections and complementarity among its components (David and Metcalfe, 2010; Cooke, 2012). The most significant implementation of the Ecology of Innovation Perspective considers the RIS as a Complex Adaptive System (CAS).

Due to the limitations of the first two perspectives, the theoretical approach adopted in this work is the Ecology of Innovation. One of the main limitations, both for the Learning Region approach and for the Smart Specialisation approach, is that they are not able to grasp and understand the intrinsic complexity of these systems. Put differently, these approaches consider RIS as a list of components and neglect the interconnections and interactions existing between each of them, which, in turn, determine the emergence of distinctive features, patterns, and structures. Additionally, these approaches fail because they are not able to combine effectively top-down perspectives with bottom-up perspectives, which are considered the best way to support self-sustaining regional innovation processes (Camagni and Capello, 1991). Indeed, the policy issue should focus mainly on enabling and stimulating connections and interactions among the elements of the system in order to transform the system (or ecology) of innovation into an adaptive innovation system. Finally, while the idea behind the Smart Specialisation perspective is acceptable, its application as an approach to support regional development appears questionable. Firstly, the focus on formal knowledge as the only source of knowledge and innovation represents an important limitation; in fact, what makes the difference in knowledge creation and innovation processes are intangible assets, such as tacit knowledge, creativity, culture, and practical skills. Secondly, in a complex system such as a region, specialisation reduces the diversity and the complementarity of resources and activities; diversity and complementarity play a crucial role in the development and competitiveness of the system by ensuring cross-fertilisation (e.g. Silicon Valley). Thirdly, specialisation reduces the resilience of a region to survive a breakthrough innovation. Fourthly, if there is more than one region that invests in the same kind of specialisation, it could lead to detrimental performance.

In the next section we discuss thoroughly the advantages of studying and framing RISs as CASs.

3. Complex Adaptive Regional Innovation Systems

According to a growing body of literature (Garnsey, 2002; Holland, 2002; Lombardi, 2003; Longhi, 2002; Squazzoni and Boero, 2002; Testfastion, 2002), referring to productive-economic innovative systems (industrial districts, milieux innovateurs, local productive systems, regional clusters), RISs could be considered as Complex Adaptive Systems (CASs).

Focusing on the literature on territorial innovation systems, it is possible to find a convergence among scholars on a number of characteristics making them Complex Adaptive Systems. A territorial innovation system (henceforth TIM) is used here as a generic name for referring to models of and approaches to regional innovation (e.g. Regional Innovation Systems, Industrial District, milieux innovateurs, regional clusters). For example, the literature on TIMs (e.g. Industrial District, milieux innovateurs, local productive systems, regional clusters) outlines a number of features typical of CASs:

- Several heterogeneous agents (individuals, families, firms, groups, local institutions) interacting with each other at different levels;
- Self-organisation. Agents in a TIM are autonomous and act according to individual rules and goals. The governance of traditional districts, for example, is usually based on spontaneous forms of coordination (Pilotti, 1999) emerging from the dense network of interactions among agents;
- Non-linearity and Emergence. The TIM is a non-linear system whose dynamics cannot be explained by linear relations between causes and effects (Albino, Carbonara and Giannoccaro, 2005). Furthermore, the properties that the TIM exhibits at the system level are not decomposable in the properties of its components, but they emerge from numerous dispersed interactions among single agents following local-simple rules;
- Adaptation and Co-evolution. The agents in a TIM usually adapt their behaviors and/or schemata to a changing external environment and to the changing state of the other agents in the system.
- Attractors. As stated in the OECD Report on "Applications of Complexity Science for Public Policy: New Tools for Finding

> Unanticipated Consequences and Unrealised Opportunities" (2009), "some complex systems spontaneously and consistently revert to recognisable dynamic states known as attractors". Localised capabilities and the institutions of industrial districts are built on the basis of a cumulative learning process and are strictly path-dependent. As stated by Maskell and Malmberg (1999), individual assets in a region are usually incrementally adapted and replaced, but the collective capabilities and institutions on which the industrial agglomeration is based are fundamentally reinforced and "do not vanish easily" (Maskell and Malmberg, 1999). The presence of recurring patterns and dynamic attractors (like the strong institutional endowment) in industrial districts could represent, at the same time, a competitive advantage for the local system or the reason behind lock-in situations.

Studying the RIS as a CAS leads to different advantages. In particular, as the collective behaviour of the CAS is not mechanically linked to the behaviour of individual agents, the pattern emerging from a CAS is a surprise to the observer. In other words, the complexity is thus the inability to reconstruct analytically the process by which individual agents lead to collective properties. In the middle there are a myriad of interactions, in many cases subject to random variations. If the observer attempted to follow a step-by-step path, he would immediately face a prohibitive combinatorial explosion. Therefore, by considering RIS as CAS, we can grasp and understand the irreducible complexity that characterises them. Secondly, CAS models are expected to be very useful from the point of view of policy. Indeed, Cooke (2012, p. 268) argues that Complexity Science suggests that tools, such as CASs, are necessary to develop an in-depth understanding of a multidimensional problem-space of innovation, which dramatically helps policy makers in bringing about societal changes in a complex world. He adds, "No complex issue, challenge or problem can be addressed by focusing on effectively a single issue or dimension, as they do not exist in isolation: the different interrelated dimensions interact with each other. Once the complex problem-space has been identified, that understanding can be used to co-create with the relevant stakeholders an enabling environment, which addresses all the relevant interrelated issues at the same time." (Cooke, 2012, p.268) In other words, the policy-maker is part of the complex system and not an outside omniscient observer. He can only co-create, along with the other actors, the desired result. The ecological perspective of CAS allows him to take into account how actors

– including himself - influence each other in determining the transformations of reality.

Several concepts of complexity science have been used to analyse territorial innovation systems, but they are not implemented and used to inform innovation policies properly. This has led to a strong discrepancy among such theoretical frameworks, adopted innovation policies, and related regional performances. We claim that in order to tackle this problem, specific theoretical and methodological approaches which are able to influence and support the emergence or the restructuring of certain self-sustaining innovation processes in territorial innovation systems have to be developed and adopted. Accordingly, in this chapter we map a RIS in a CAS and, in the next sections, we describe the adopted methodological approach.

4. Methodological Approach

The literature proposing computational models of territorial innovation systems shows that available models refer mostly to local clusters of small and medium firms (such as traditional neo-marshallian industrial districts or high-tech industrial clusters) and address very different topics (innovation and knowledge dynamics, coordination mechanisms, supply networks formation, the emergence of bilateral collaboration, the diffusion of reputation) relating to the systems under investigation (Albino, Carbonara and Giannoccaro, 2006; Squazzoni and Boero, 2002). Models proposed by the literature use agent-based modelling mainly with the purpose of theory building. Coherently with this purpose, most of the models are "conceptual" models poorly validated against reality.

The computational laboratory presented here aims to develop, through an agent-based model (ABM), an explanation of self-sustaining cycles of innovation. The achievement of this goal requires the following steps: 1) to identify a macro-regularity, namely a collective emergent property of the system, to be explained; 2) to model agents and their local behaviours that could eventually generate the emergence of the macro-regularity; 3) to identify, through simulation experiments, a generative mechanism that could represent a good candidate to explain the macro-regularity chosen as target collective property to be explained (Boero and Squazzoni, 2005).

The use of empirical data in agent-based modelling depends on the purposes of the developers and of the users of the model (Boero and

Squazzoni, 2005; Burton, 2003; Carley, 1996; Gilbert, 2008). Agent-based models have been classified with respect to different dimensions (Carley, 1996): the purpose of modelling, the level of determinism included in the model, the enumerative or Monte Carlo character of the simulation. With respect to the purpose, a large consensus exists in the specific literature about the division of ABMs into three main categories (Boero and Squazzoni, 2005; Carley, 1996; Gilbert, 2008): i) pure theoretical models aimed at developing a theory; ii) ideal-typical models to describe a specific class of social behaviours without matching exactly with a particular case in the class; iii) pure descriptive models aimed at identifying an explanation that applies to a target case. These latter ABMs require an intense activity of model validation against external reality, and a huge amount of data for the calibration and validation of simulation results. Ideal-typical models are those that allow users both to establish a middle-rank theory (Gilbert, 2008) and to develop tools for policy advice. We define these models as "Policy Oriented Models" (Brenner and Werker, 2009; Louie and Carley, 2008; Sargent, 2004). In their paper Brenner and Werker (2009) claim that policy advice can be successful based on an abductive social simulation strategy.

These models are characterised by an iterative process in which theoretical assumptions, experimental-simulative data, implications of models and empirical data are continuously compared and matched. In the abductive agent-based laboratories, a central role is played by verification and validation approaches and techniques (for an extended review of verification and validation in ABM see Sargent, 2004 and Carley, 2008).

According to Brenner and Werker (2009) and to the literature about verification-validation of computational models (Burton, 2003; Gilbert, 2008; Louie and Carley, 2008; Moss, 2008; Richiardi et al., 2006; Sargent, 2004), the methodology to build up a computational laboratory, such as the CARIS Lab., involves six main steps as depicted in Figure 7.1.

In the first step the theoretical background is translated in a conceptual model. In the case of CARIS, the conceptual model, presented in § 4.1, is based on the concepts of emergence, self-organisation (namely, self-sustainability), and learning. The second step, that is the construction of the meta-model, specifies a pseudo-code in which micro-specifications about agents' behaviours are reported. In our case, the meta-model specifies the classes of agents, the rules of action and interactions among them, the dependent and independent variables and the parameters of future simulations (see § 4.1). The next step, the implementation of the meta-model, requires the choice of an adequate software platform and the activity of code writing. The model here proposed has been implemented and simulated using NetLogo 5.0.4. At this stage, the implemented model has to be verified and validated. Through the verification it is assessed that the computerised model (the code) does not contain bugs (Gilbert, 2008) and that it works coherently with the meta-model.

Figure 7.4.1

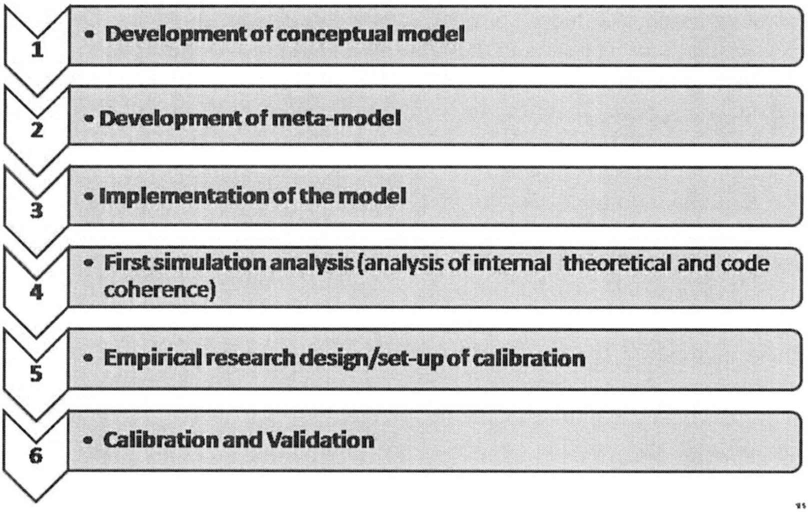

The validation phase of steps 4, 5 and 6 can be carried out for different purposes (e.g. internal or external validation), at different levels of accuracy (e.g. face validity, parameter validity, process validity) and with different techniques (e.g. calibration or docking). Through internal validation we verify that the implemented model is coherent with the theoretically and empirically available knowledge about the system/phenomenon investigated (Sargent, 2004). External validation refers to the relationships between the simulated results and the empirical data (Carley, 1996). In our case, through some initial simulative experiments (see § 4.3), we tested the coherence of the code with the meta-model and the capability of CARIS to generate expected or plausible results as shown in the literature. At this stage of the research, the task of external validation has only been settled and will follow the procedure suggested by Brenner and Werker (2009) for the calibration of abductive agent-based models.

4.1 CARIS: A conceptual framework for Complex Adaptive Regional Innovation Systems

According to the three perspectives presented above, a regional innovation system can be considered a learning system that upgrades existing structures on the basis of a complex social dynamic. The literature on Organisational Learning (OL) and Learning Organisation (LO) already gives us an indication of how to address the operational issue of defining a formal model. As the literature on OL and LO is wide and vast, we focus only on some contributions that address the learning issue as a cyclic evolutionary process of production and utilisation of knowledge (Nonaka, 1994, Nonaka and Takeuci, 1995; Boisot, 1998; Crossan, Lane and White, 1999; Pawlowsky, Forslin and Reinhardt, 2001; Zollo and Winter, 2000).

Summing up the main contributions on OL and LO, it is possible to identify four essential competencies of every system to develop learning capabilities:

- *Exploring competence*: the system should ensure the capability of an effective search for new knowledge.
- *Exploiting competence*: the system should ensure that new knowledge is readily verified and transformed into superior operational capabilities.
- *Changing competence*: the system should promote a continuous organisational change in order to amplify the variety of competencies suitable for the exploration activity and to retain in new routines the new operational capabilities.
- *Maintaining competence*: the system should develop and reinforce a common culture oriented to learning and provide individuals and groups with proper frames of references for maintaining the fundamental unity of the organisation through the changes.

The claim is that the combination of those opposite competencies - exploring versus exploiting, changing versus maintaining - in a single regional context is the real challenge of designing innovative organisations. The tensions triggered in the social system by these conflicting requirements is the playing field of any learning system, capable of generating a perpetual innovation capacity.

Moreover, recently Schwandt and Marquardt (2000) proposed a general framework for the Learning Organisation based on Parsons' functional social model. They identified four sub-systems with different competencies characterising any Learning Organisation, namely: the Environmental Interface Subsystem (EIS); the Action/Reflection Subsystem (ARS); the Dissemination and Diffusion Subsystem (DDS); the Meaning and Memory Subsystem (MMS). These four subsystems provide an analytical framework for describing and evaluating the dynamic functions of an organisation's learning system.

Therefore, based on the literature analysed above and on Schwandt and Marquardt's learning system model, it is possible to identify a conceptual framework useful for analysing the performance and capability of RISs. In other words, we assume that the competencies defined above correspond to four types of social actors. Each of these actors produces for other players a resource essential for the self-sustainability of regional innovation over time. These actors are (see Figure 7.4.1.1):

Figure 7.4.1.1

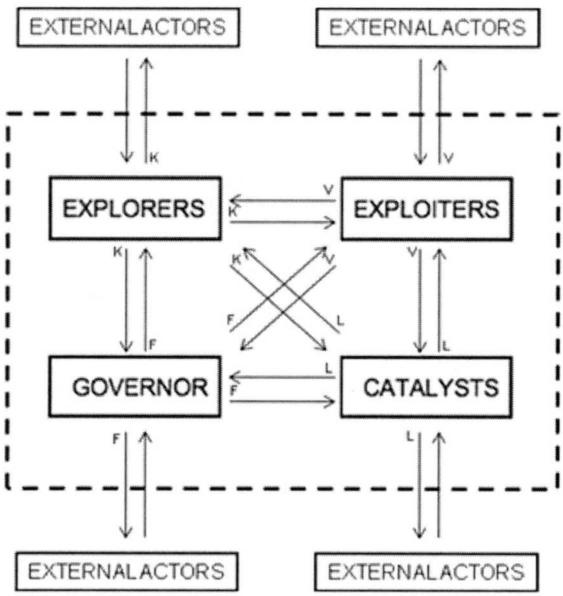

K= Knowledge, L= Links, V= Value, F= Frame.

a) EXPLORERS, the producers of knowledge (K): this set of players is composed of subjects that explore the boundaries of knowledge, producing new ideas, new methods, and new techniques which they make available to other players. Some typical examples of explorers are universities, research centres, public and private laboratories, and their combinations (e.g. regional competencies centres), and big companies operating in technological sectors;
b) EXPLOITERS, the producers of market value (V): this set of players is able to transform knowledge into value for the market;
c) CATALYSTS, the mediators of innovation: this set of players promotes interactions and links (L) between relevant players of the process of transfer, adaption, and utilisation of knowledge. Some typical examples are represented by liaison offices of universities, science parks, and technology incubators, trade associations, chambers of commerce, districts, and clusters;
d) GOVERNOR, the creator of framework and rules (F): this actor plays the role of providing guidelines and frames for other players. It is usually represented by local public institutions.

4.2 The agent-based model

The agent-based implementation of CARIS is characterised by two different classes of agents: 1) the Competitive Environment (CE), and 2) the Competent Agent (CA), the latter representing different categories of collective actors - such as firms, research groups, research institutions, mediators of innovation, local institutional actors – incorporating the competencies illustrated in Table 7.4.2.1. The characterisation of the CA depends on the mix of competencies he exhibits and on the actions he performs. Table 7.4.2.1 compares the conceptual model and the agent-based model in terms of actors, actions, and outcomes of actions. The main aspects of the agent-based model are presented in Figure 7.4.2.1.

Table 7.4.2.1: Comparison between Conceptual framework and Agent-Based model

Conceptual Framework			Agent-Based Model		
Actors	**Actions**	**Outcomes**	**Agents**	**Actions**	**Outcomes**
Governor	Regulating	Definition of boundary conditions	*Observer*	Definition of boundary conditions	Parameters setting
Explorer	Exploration	Production of Knowledge	*Competent Agents*	Interaction guided by rules of exploration, exploitation and connecting	Individual Interpretation; Collective Interpretation
Exploiter	Exploitation	Production of market value			
Catalyst	Connecting	Production of links			

4.2.1 The first Agent: the Competitive Environment CE

The Agent CE is characterised by a binary string (-1 or 1) ER of length l, representing the Environmental Regularity that a Competent Actor CA should discover and match up. The Agent CE makes three actions:

- Action 1.1: generation of Environmental Regularities ER: The Environmental Regularity ER changes over time according to a given volatility v;
- Action 1.2: generation of Innovation Opportunities IO: An environmental noise d alters the content of the strings ER, and transforms them into a new set of strings called Innovation Opportunities IO. The Hamming distance measures the distance between ER and IO. Individual Competent Agents (ICAs) have access only to IO;
- Action 6-7: 'Evaluation and Reward' of Proposals realized by the Competent Actor CA: We will analyse these actions later.

The three parameters of 'Length l', 'Volatility v', and 'Noise n' define the complexity of competitive environment CE. There is another parameter characterising the CE, i.e. the Acceptance Threshold, which measures the intensity of competition. We will discuss this parameter later.

Figure 7.4.2.1

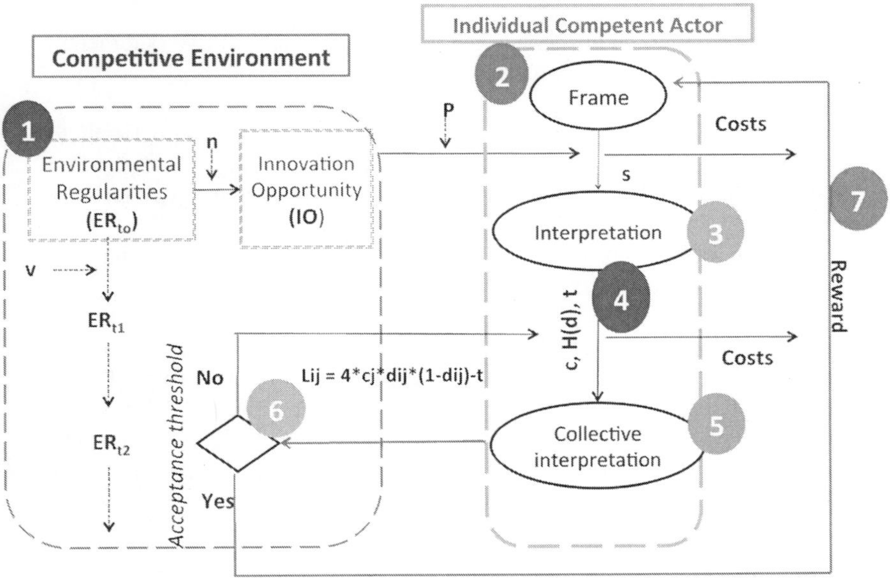

4.2.2 The second agent: The Competent Actor CA

The Competent Actor is a collective agent, made up of a set of Individual Competent Agents ICAs. Each ICA is endowed with a set of 'Frames', that is a set of ternary strings {-1, 1, 0} of length l, which represents the set of an agent's beliefs (or knowledge or capability). The value 0 indicates the lack of that specific competence. Each agent is also endowed with a budget distributed among the frames. The Agent CE makes four actions:

- Action 2) The generation of the initial frame;
- Action 3) The generation of 'Individual Interpretations' (exploration capability);
- Action 4) The generation of interactions (interaction capability);
- Action 5) The generation of 'Collective Interpretations' (exploitation capability).

Action 2: The generation of initial frame of ICAs.

The initial frame of each agent is generated on the basis of two parameters: the scope s and the competence c.

The scope s is the probability that the agent ICA has the complete knowledge to produce the requested interpretation of a Competitive Environment. In other words, if the probability is 0, then any value of the frame is 0, which means that the ICA has no knowledge at all. If s = 1, each value of the string frame is -1 or 1. The scope measures the specialisation of an agent.

The competence c is the probability that an element of the frame matches the corresponding element of the Innovation Opportunity-string. If c=1, the agent ICA is endowed with a proper frame; vice-versa, if c=0, the endowed frame is totally wrong. The generation of the frame of each agent depends on both the probabilities: F=f(s, c). More specifically, the lower the value of such probabilities, the lesser the probability to produce the proper output required by the CE.

Action 3: The generation of Individual Interpretations II.

The first task of each ICA is to develop an Exploration Activity - that is to interpret an Innovation Opportunity on the basis of its frames (the string of scope $s \leq 1$, and competence c) in order to produce an Individual Interpretation. Each agent ICA has a probability P to modify its Frame in order to "catch" an Innovation Opportunity IO. The modified Frame is the Individual Interpretation. The modified Frame is memorised by the agent. The Exploration Activity has a cost.

Action 4: the Generation of Interactions

Each agent ICA moves within the space of action. The agent's moves are guided by the structure of the space of action, by behaviour rules, and by randomness. In the CARIS model the space of action is unstructured – i.e., we do not have any predefined network or grid. The plan of action has been modelled as the surface of a torus, where agents move in a random way. If two agents are in the same place at the same time, they can decide whether to interact in agreement with the following Action 4. The Interaction Activity has a cost.

Action 5: The generation of Collective Interpretations.

The second task of ICAs is to develop the exploitation activity. In order to carry out this task, each ICA must choose the most suitable partners in order to combine its IIs with that of other agents and create a Collective Interpretation CI fitted with the Innovation Opportunity. This activity is guided by:

i) the Cooperation propensity (T) of each agent;
ii) the value of competence c of possible partners;
iii) the Hamming $H(II)_{ij}$ distance between two Individual Interpretations(II).

The three parameters are combined in the following formula:

$$L_{ij} = (4*c_j*H(II)_{ij}*(1-H(II)_{ij}) - T_i), \qquad (1)$$

where L_{ij} is the probability that agent i decides to cooperate with agent j. If L_{ij} is positive and also $L_{ji}$is positive, then agents i and j will cooperate. In other words, both agents i and j should evaluate positively the benefits of cooperation.

The cooperation model of formula (1) is a modified version of the interaction model of Cowan and Jonard (2009). We assume that forming a partnership has a probability of success strictly related to the optimal overlap of knowledge stocks of possible partners. The probability of a successful cooperation increases and then decreases with the overlap of the Individual Interpretations. The overlap is measured by the complement to 1 of the normalised Hamming distance between the Individual Interpretations II_{ji} of agents i and j, namely $(1-H(II)_{ij})$. The peak occurs when the overlap is equal to 0.5. The increasing and decreasing probability of cooperation is modelled by $H(II)_{ij}*(1-H(II)_{ij})$. The second factor influencing the probability of cooperation is the reputation of the potential partner, which is measured by its level of competence c_j. The third factor influencing the Cooperation Propensity is T_i, which captures both the propensity to cooperation of the individual actor, and the boundary conditions (culture, incentives) that influence the cooperation. The number 4 is a scaling factor, allowing Lij to vary between 0 and 1.

The results of Action 4 are multiple collaborations, that form a network of individual agents which combine their Individual Interpretations (i.e., knowledge or capabilities) to produce a Collective Interpretation to submit to the Competitive Environment for evaluation and reward. Of course, the Collective Interpretation is embodied in a product or service that can be delivered to the market. The Exploitation Activity has a cost.

Now we are ready to define the last actions developed by the Competitive Environment.

Action 6. Evaluation

Each Collective Interpretation CI is evaluated by the CE on the basis of an Acceptance Threshold. If the Collective Interpretation overcomes such threshold, it is accepted and rewarded.

Action 7. Rewarding

The reward obtained by a Collective Interpretation is distributed among the agents ICAs that contributed to it, according to the contribution they gave in terms of competences to the successful interpretation. At the beginning of a simulation, each ICA is endowed with a budget distributed among the frames populating the individual memory of agents (in the first step of the simulation, only one frame is contained in the individual memory of each ICA). The budget associated with frames will be decreased according to the costs sustained for exploration, interaction, and for exploitation activities. The reward for a frame of an ICA involved in a successful Collective Interpretation will increase the budget of the competent agent. Only frames with a positive budget will survive, and the number of surviving frames for each agent is a proxy of the capability to learn and innovate. At each time-step the budget available for each ICA is the sum of budgets associated with its frames. When the total budget of an ICA becomes equal to 0, the ICA dies and disappears.

The difference between the agents' total budget at the end of a simulation and that at the beginning is a measure of the success of RIS. It is a proxy of the capacity of RIS of creating value.

This meta-model has been implemented on the Netlogo platform. Figure 7.4.2.2 represents the interface of the Netlogo model (the model is available on request).

Figure 7.4.2.2: The Netlogo CARIS model

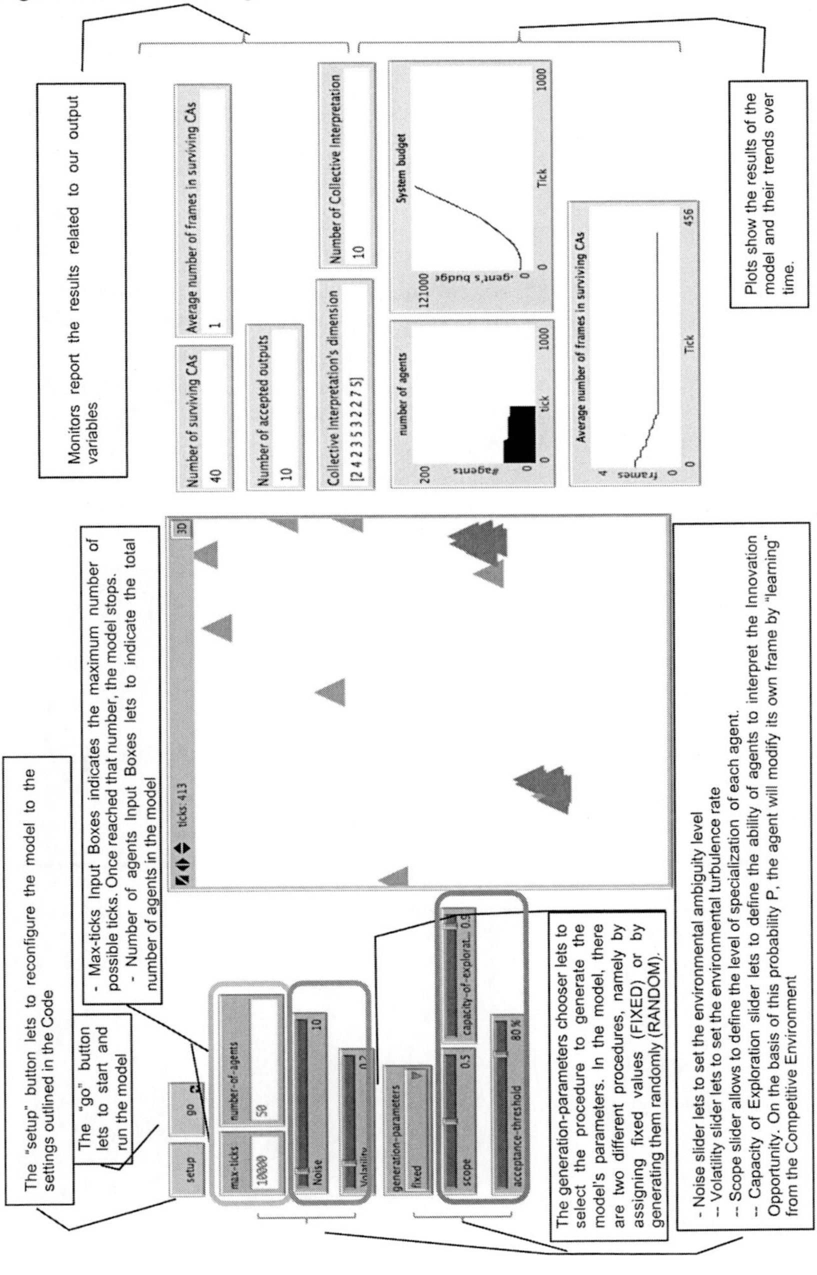

4.3 Internal Coherence Verification

In this section we describe simulative experiments settled to assess the internal coherence of the proposed agent-based model, and we discuss simulation results. The experiments are settled to be confirmative. The calibration of the model is work in progress and will be completed in the following steps of the research.

4.3.1. Parameters setting

The verification of logical internal coherence of the model is based on the assumptions derived from the current body of knowledge on innovation systems framed as complex learning systems. In particular, we settled 12 different experiments (Tables 7.4.3.2, 7.4.3.3, 7.4.3.4, 7.4.3.5). In order to ensure the robustness of the results we performed 30 runs for each experimental set.

The 12 experiments are performed by changing the values of the following parameters:

i) the volatility v of the Competitive Environment CE: (v=0.2 and 0.8);
ii) the exploration capability p of the ICAs: (p=0.1, 0.5 and 0.9);
iii) the level of specialisation s of ICAs: (s=0.5 and 0.8).

Other parameters remain fixed according to the values of the Table 7.4.3.1.

Table 7.4.3.1: Fixed parameters

Fixed Parameters	Values
Competence (c)	Random
Noise (n)	10%
Length of message (l)	50
Acceptance-threshold	80%
Number of agents	50
Max-ticks	10000
Runs	30

Table 7.4.3.2: Parameters setting to test the behaviour of a high specialised system in a dynamic environment

PARAMETERS	I SET	II SET	III SET
Capacity of Exploration (P)	0,1	0,5	0,9
Scope (s)		0,5	
Volatility (v)		0,2	

Table 7.4.3.3: Parameters setting to test the behaviour of a high specialised system in a static environment

PARAMETERS	IV SET	V SET	VI SET
Capacity of Exploration (P)	0,1	0,5	0,9
Scope (s)		0,5	
Volatility (v)		0,8	

Table 7.4.3.4: Parameters setting to test the behaviour of a low specialised system in a dynamic environment

PARAMETERS	VII SET	VIII SET	IX SET
Capacity of Exploration (P)	0,1	0,5	0,9
Scope (s)		0,8	
Volatility (v)		0,2	

Table 7.4.3.5: Parameters setting to test the behaviour of a low specialised system in a static environment

PARAMETERS	X SET	XI SET	XII SET
Capacity of Exploration (P)	0,1	0,5	0,9
Scope (s)		0,8	
Volatility (v)		0,8	

The simulations output variables are reported in Table 4.3.6.

Table 7.4.3.6: The output variables of simulations

Output variable	Description
Surviving ICAs (%)	Average (on 30 runs) number of surviving ICAs at the end of simulation as percentage of initial population
Average number of surviving frames of ICAs	Average (on 30 runs) number of frames in the individual memories of ICAs, calculated for each new market cycle (for each new message/Regularity provided by the CE)
Collective Interpretations' dimension	Total number (on 30 runs) of Individual Interpretations contributing to successful Collective Interpretations
Mean Delta Budget in the system	Average (on 30 runs) value of the difference between the final budget of the system and the sum of initial budgets attributed to ICAs populating it at the beginning of simulation

4.3.2. Results of simulations

Assessing the internal coherence of the model implies verifying that the code is free of evident bugs, that it works coherently with the meta-model and that the agent-based computational model is able to reproduce some stylised facts characterising the system under investigation. Through the simulation experiments we aim at exploring if and under which conditions the micro specifications we implemented in the agent-based model are able to produce some known regularities characterising Regional Innovation Systems framed as complex networked learning systems.

In our experiments we analyse the behaviour of the system for different levels of the capacity of exploration (P) and different degrees of competences' specialisation under two competitive scenarios: a static and a dynamic one.

Figure 7.4.3.2.1 reports the number of surviving ICAs of a high specialised system (all the ICAs have the same level of scope s = 0.5) under the three different levels of the capacity of exploration (P) in a static and in a dynamic competitive environment.

Figure 7.4.3.2.2 shows the trend of the same output variable (number of surviving ICAs) in the case of a low specialised system (s = 0.8).

Figure 7.4.3.2.1

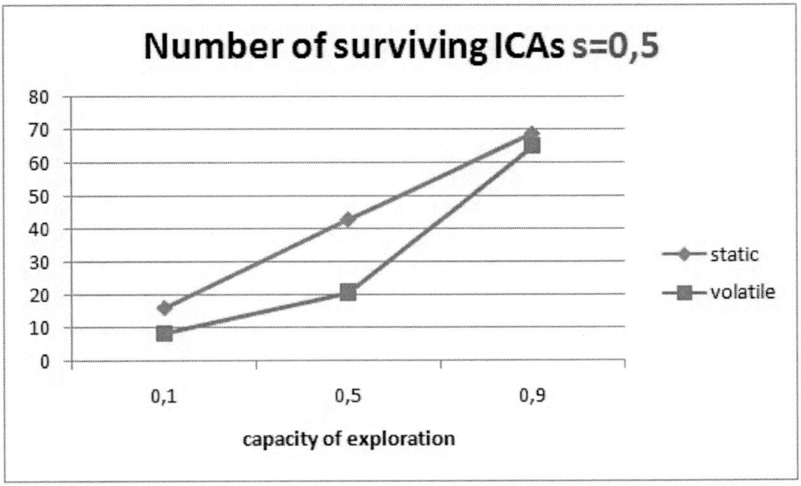

Figure 7.4.3.2.2

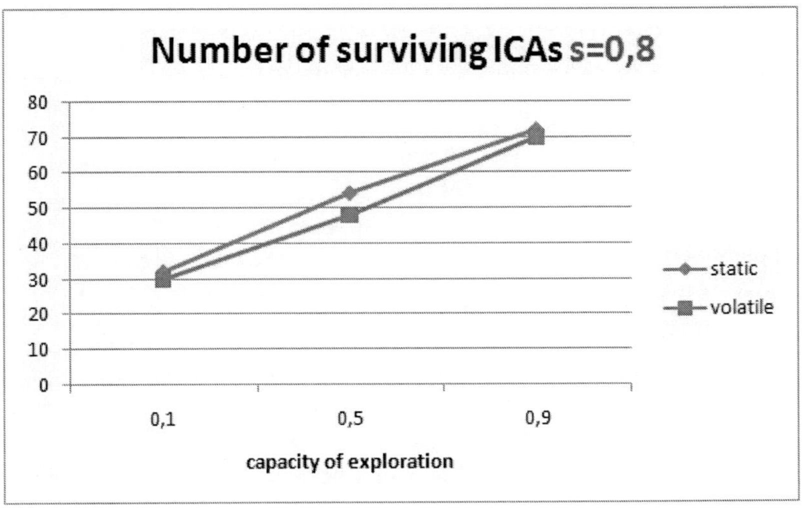

The number of surviving agents in the system increases with their capacity of exploration, both in a static and in a dynamic environment. This is an expected and plausible result; in particular, this result is coherent with the seminal paper of March (1991) on exploration and exploitation in organisational learning systems and with most of the literature on learning systems deriving from March's original investigation.

In order to verify the statistical significance of these results, we performed a one-way Anova test. In other words, a one-way ANOVA was conducted to determine whether the number of surviving ICAs was statistically significantly different among different experimental settings corresponding to different capacities of exploration in both static and dynamic environments. On the basis of the results obtained, it is possible to claim that the total number of surviving ICAs was statistically significantly different among diverse levels of capacity of exploration in both static and dynamic environments, respectively $F(3,87) = 167{,}51$, $p<.0001$ and $F(3,87) = 201{,}36$, $p<.000$. Tukey post-hoc analysis revealed that all the combinations of group differences were statistically significant ($p = .000$).

In Figure 7.4.3.2.1 and 7.4.3.2.2 we can also find other plausible results that support the verification of the implemented model. As showed in Figure 7.4.3.2.1, for low (0.1) and medium (0.5) values of the parameter P, the number of surviving ICAs is higher in static than in dynamic competitive environments. Furthermore, the difference between the trends of population referring respectively to static and dynamic environments is significantly reduced (Figure 7.4.3.2.2) when the level of competences specialisation in the system is low (for s = 0.8). It seems that less focused ICAs are able to react better than more specialised agents to a high environmental volatility. Agents that cover a wider range of required knowledge, as expected, show a higher capability to survive in dynamic environments and seem to be less affected by the change in the competitive Environment's Regularity. We performed an independent sample T-test to check whether the total number of surviving ICAs is affected by the competitive conditions. The T-test results confirm what is also possible to note from Figures 7.4.3.2.1 and 7.4.3.2.2, which is that there was a statistically significant difference between the number of surviving ICAs in static and dynamic environments when the level of competences specialisation is high (for s = 0.5), $t(178)= 2.99$; $p=.003$; on the contrary, there is not a statistically significant difference when the level of competences specialisation is low (for s =0.8), $t(178)= 0.941$; $p=.348$. Figures 7.4.3.2.3 and 7.4.3.2.4 add new elements to the above analysis.

Figure 7.4.3.2.3 reports the average number of frames of ICAs for each of the two messages produced during the simulation by a static competitive environment, under the three different levels of exploration capacity (P). The number of frames in the individual memories of competent agents of the system can be interpreted as a proxy of the learning performance of ICAs. In a static environment, individual learning performance increases according to the individual capacity of exploration (better performances are achieved for medium and high values of P).

Figure 7.4.3.2.3

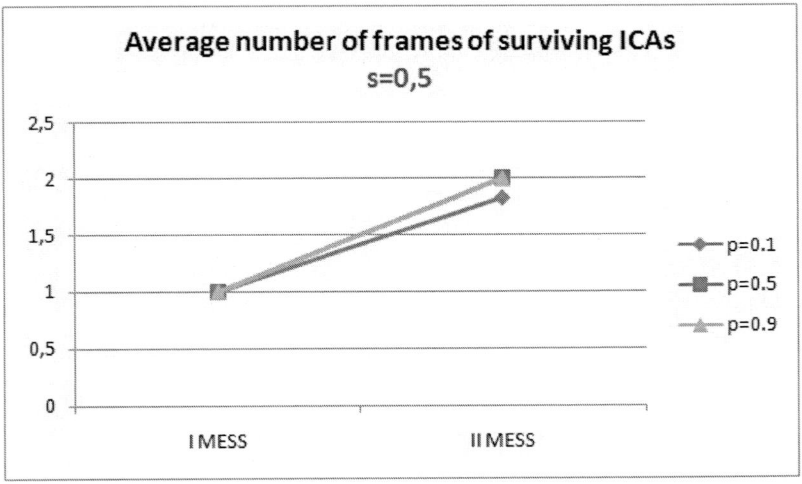

In order to test whether there was a statistically significant difference among different experimental sets we performed a one-way Anova test. As the results confirmed such significant difference ($F(2,87) = 10.419$, $p = .000$), we performed a Tukey post-hoc test. In particular, the test revealed that the average number of final frames of ICAs was statistically significantly higher with $P=0.5$ (2 ±0.00, $p = .008$) and with $P=0.9$ (2 ±0.00, $p = .008$) compared to a low level of capacity of exploration ($P=0.1$; 1.76 ±0.41); while there were no statistically significant differences in terms of average number of final frames of ICAs between medium and high levels of capacity of exploration ($p = 1.000$).

Figure 7.4.3.2.4 shows that in a dynamic environment (v = 0.2) - five different messages ER are sent to ICAs by the CE during the simulation time - *better individual learning performances are achieved when the value of their capacity of exploration is equal to 0,5. High levels of exploration, in this case, produce the same result as low levels of exploration.*

Figure 7.4.3.2.4

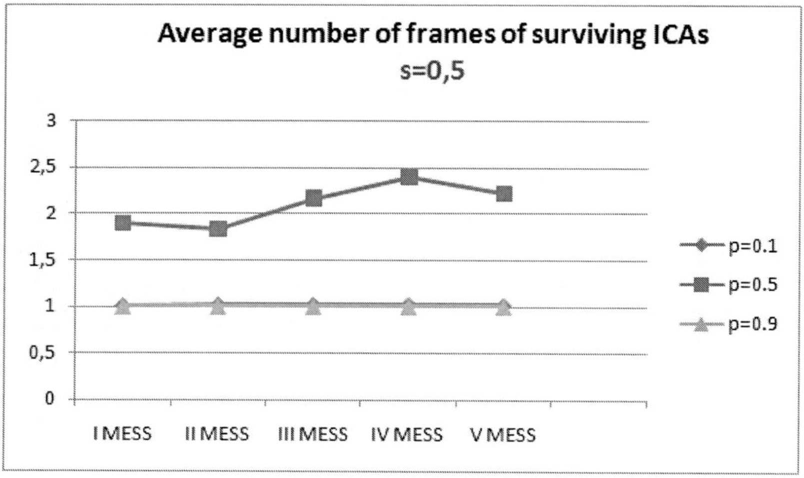

This result supports the verification of the code and the coherence between the implemented model and the meta-model (section 4.1 and 4.2). In fact, we know from the literature (Benner and Tushman, 2002, Gupta, Smith, and Shalley, 2006; March, 1991) that in a high volatile environment high levels of exploration produce high exploration costs that are not sufficiently remunerated by adequate rewards (the time needed to complete a cycle of exploration-exploitation is longer than a market cycle).

Finally, this result is confirmed also by the outcomes of the one-way Anova test. In particular, Tukey post-hoc analysis revealed that there was a statistically significant difference in terms of the average number of final frames of each ICAS between low and medium levels of capacity of exploration (p = .000), as well as between medium and high levels of capacity of exploration (p = .000), but no other group differences were statistically significant. This result confirms that better performances are achieved when the value of their capacity of exploration is equal to 0.5, while high levels of exploration produce the same result as low levels of exploration.

Additionally, this result highlights the need for additional experimentation and investigation, as the literature claims for a balance between exploration and exploitation in order to sustain organisational and system performances in the long run. In the model proposed here, the ambidexterity mechanism (exploration and exploitation activities are performed at the same time and are balanced through organisational and collaborative structures) of balance between exploration and exploitation (Benner and Thusman, 2003; Gupta, Smith, and Shalley, 2006) is implemented but not sufficiently articulated in its implications. The activity of exploitation is modelled as the creation of partnerships to produce Collective Interpretations. This capability, in the actual version of the model, depends on several parameters (the competence c of the agents, the propensity toward collaboration T, and the Hamming distance between two Individual Interpretations). At this stage of the research, the impact of these latter parameters has not been investigated through specific experiments. In particular, by comparing the Figures 7.4.3.2.3 and 7.4.3.2.4 and considering the results of the statistical test, one element of coherence with the literature on exploration and exploitation in learning systems can be detected, especially in Figure 7.4.3.2.4. As suggested by March (1991), *in high complex environments the learning process is a sort of random walk.* Learning performances are strongly affected by randomness. In our case, high volatility (v = 0.2) is interpreted as high complexity. *Better performances are achieved when the capability of exploration of all ICAs of the system is equal to 0.5. P = 0.5 means, from a computational point of view, that the strategy of exploration of agents in the system is a random strategy, resulting in highly dynamic and complex environments, in a more efficient search and solution strategy and in better learning performances.*

Figures 7.4.3.2.5 and 7.4.3.2.6 show the distribution of the collective interpretations' dimensions (the number of individual frames contributing to the collective interpretations) with respect to the levels of the capability of exploration and respectively for high (Figure 7.4.3.2.5) and low levels (Figure 7.4.3.2.5) of competences specialisation (the behaviour of the system is less affected, in this case, by the volatility of the CE). By comparing the two figures, we can identify an expected and plausible result that again confirms the existence of an internal coherence of the implemented code. In fact, the dimension of Collective Interpretations is in general greater in the case of highly specialised systems than in low specialised ones. In highly specialised systems agents are characterised by a low capability to cover the spectrum of competences required by the CE.

Thus they need to create links with other agents in order to build up a more complete Interpretation. This diffused trend toward networking results in the presence of networks which, in some cases, are composed of more than 9 agents. This latter case is not apparent for low levels of specialisation. As said before, this result supports mainly the test of the code and does not add any significant element to theory building.

In order to verify whether the dimension of Collective Interpretations is greater in the case of highly specialised systems than in low specialised ones, we performed an independent samples T-test. The results confirm what we previously claimed and show that there was a statistically significant difference, in the dimension Collective Interpretation, between highly specialised systems and low specialised ones $t(178)= 8.599$; $p=.000$.

Figure 7.4.3.2.5

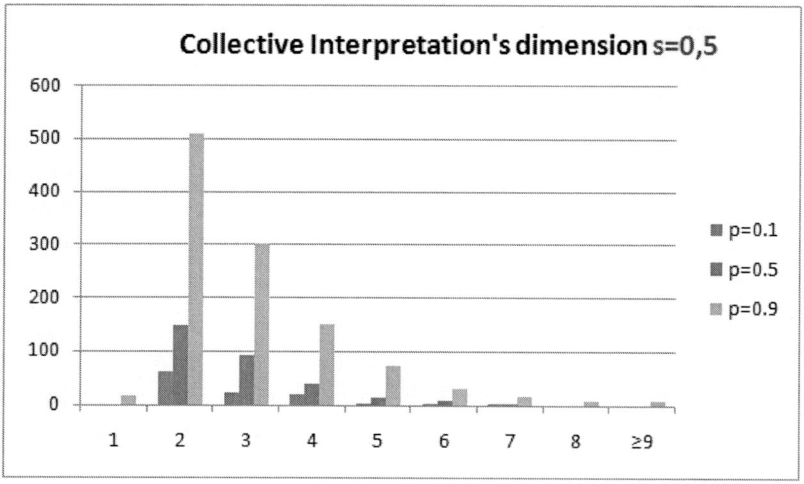

Figure 7.4.3.2.6

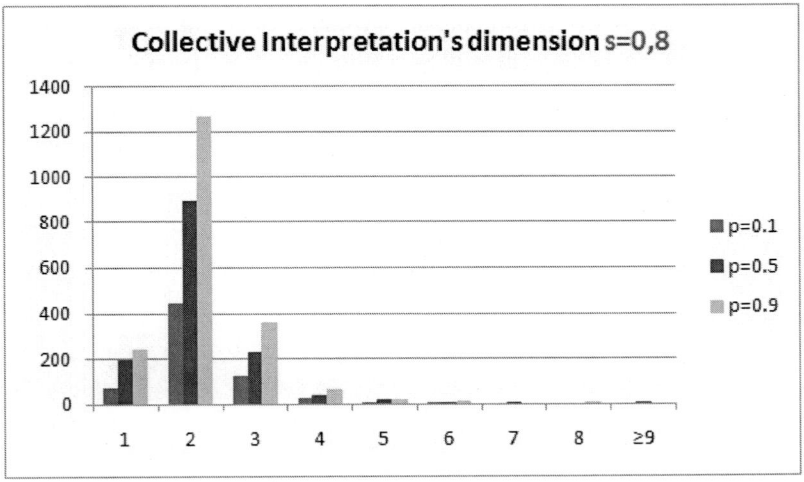

Finally, Figures 7.4.3.2.7 and 7.4.3.2.8 show the behaviour of the system in terms of economic performance, with respect to the volatility of the environments and under different combinations of ICAs' competences' specialisation and exploration capability. In particular, Figure 7.4.3.2.7 reports the trend of the economic performance (measured as the difference between the capital assigned to the system at the beginning of simulation and the capital registered at the end) of a highly specialised system (s = 0,5) with respect to the three levels of capability of exploration (P). Figure 7.4.3.2.8 refers to the trend of economic performance of a low specialised system. As expected and according with the design of the agent-based model, better performances are achieved on average in static environments. Indeed, in a static environment the need for ICAs to sustain costs of exploration and exploitation are reduced compared to the case of a dynamic environment, in which the messages sent by the CE to the ICAs are more frequently changed.

Also these results are confirmed by the outcomes of T-tests performed on independent samples. In particular, both in low and highly specialised systems, economic performance is statistically significantly better in a static than in a dynamic environment, respectively $t(178) = 9.047$, $p = .000$ (for s=0.5) and $t(178) = 5.293$, $p = .000$ (for s=0.8).

Furthermore, according to the results on the population dynamics showed in Figures 7.4.3.2.1 and 7.4.3.2.2, better economic performances are achieved in those systems populated by more explorative ICAs (high levels of the capability of exploration). In particular, the economic performance was statistically significantly different among diverse levels of capacity of exploration both in low and highly specialised static systems and low and highly specialised dynamic systems. Thus, the results are in the static conditions respectively $F(3, 87) = 118.30$, $p<.000$ and $F(3,87) = 150.448$, $p<.000$; while in the dynamic environment, the results are respectively $F(3,87) = 329.137$, $p<.000$ and $F(3,87) = 485.175$, $p<.000$. Tukey post-hoc analysis revealed that all the combinations of group differences were statistically significant ($p< .001$).

The comparison between Figures 7.4.3.2.7 and 7.4.3.2.8 highlights that higher levels of economic values are obtained in low specialised systems (s = 0,8). This latter result is again coherent with results reported in Figures 7.4.3.2.1 and 7.4.3.2.2. Finally, in order to check whether the higher levels of economic values are obtained in low specialised systems (s = 0.8) both in static and dynamic conditions, we performed T-tests on two independent samples. In particular, the T-test results confirmed better economic performances are achieved in low specialised systems in both environmental conditions, respectively $t(178)= 10.983$, $p=.000$ and $t(178)=5.991$, $p=.000$.

Therefore, we can conclude that:

- Regional Innovation Systems populated by highly explorative and low specialised agents (agents that cover a wide range of competences required by the competitive environment) are more resilient to environmental changes, both in terms of population dynamics (agents that are able to survive) and of economic performance.
- Higher costs of explorations and of competencies maintenance (high P and high s) sustained by the ICAs populating these systems are compensated by reduced costs of exploitation and by more frequent rewards.

Figure 7.4.3.2.7

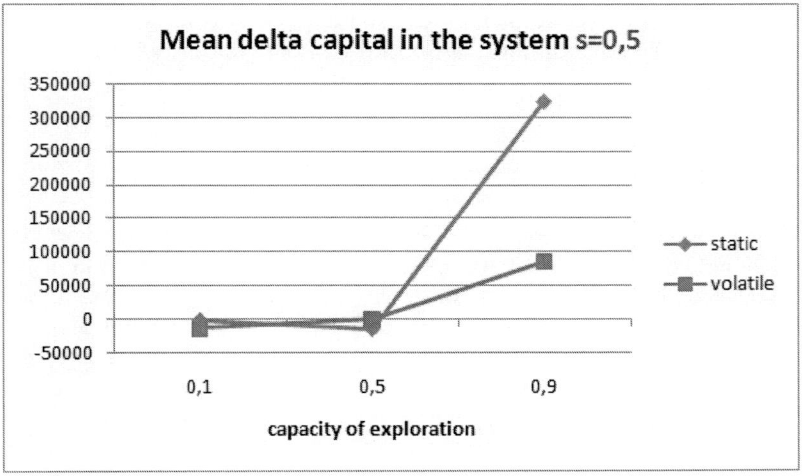

Figure 7.4.3.2.8

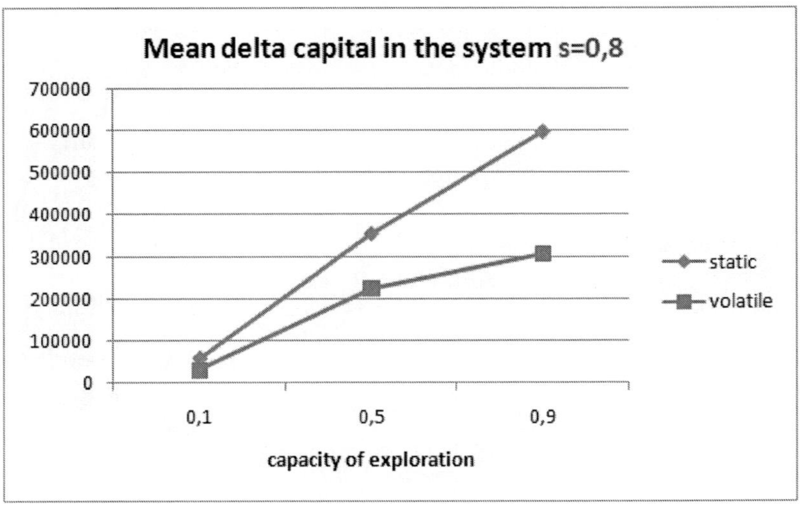

Discussions and further developments

While the final objective of this research project is to develop a policy advice support system to aid policymakers in defining proper innovation policies, in this paper we present the theoretical background used to inform the design and development of the agent-based model on which the policy advice computational laboratory is based, and the results of experiments we performed to assess its internal coherence.

The computational laboratory, named CARIS, has two main purposes, which are: introducing the CAS approach in the analysis of RISs in order to integrate the key concepts of traditional perspectives on territorial innovation systems with new ones; and enabling the development of effective innovation policies able to foster the growth and innovativeness of regions, in particular the lagging regions. Specifically, we decided to focus on the so-called lagging regions given that most studies have focused on large metropolitan regions characterised by the presence of effective institutional infrastructures and strategic actors able to foster virtuous innovation processes. By contrast, small- to medium-sized regions or lagging regions, classified as moderate and modest innovators, have attracted less attention.

The CARIS lab could be used as policy advice to support self-sustaining innovation processes both in medium-low innovative regions and in more innovative ones as it is possible to modify the values of different parameters (capacity for exploration, scope, competence, and cooperation propensity) to characterise the agent-based model and, as a consequence, the simulations, the results, and the possible implications.

This chapter is relevant both from a theoretical point of view and from a practical one. In particular, on the one hand, in the literature a new perspective is emerging in the analysis of local productive-economic systems in which these systems are recognised as Complex Adaptive Systems (CAS); on the other hand, although the complexity has been recognised as a distinctive feature of territorial innovation systems, it has been poorly explored and used in the development of innovation policies and incentives able to support the competitiveness of regions. This strong discrepancy between theoretical frameworks, adopted innovation policies, and related regional performance is more evident in the case of the lagging regions.

As theoretical and modelling activities have been carried out and the model has been verified and conceptually validated, additional research phases and maybe new interventions of model fine-tuning will be required. More specifically, further developments of the research will concern methodological and practical aspects. In fact, we should focus on the implementation of two further different agents in the agent-based model, namely the Catalyst and the Governor (see Table 2). The Catalyst plays an important role in facilitating the complex process of transfer, adaption, and utilisation of knowledge within innovation systems; the Governor defines rules and guidelines for the innovation network as well as the incentives toward innovation. The implementation of the role of the Governor represents, in our project, the step of testing innovation policy measures. To do that, another preliminary research step is needed and refers to the assessment of the external validity of the model, namely the validation of simulation results against empirical reality. According to the literature referring to the validation of agent-based models for policy advice purposes (Brenner and Werker, 2009), the external validation of the CARIS model will be performed through calibration.

As our research is still going on, the problem of model validation has been settled and some activities have been already set-up. In particular, we aim at completing the calibration by using data collected through a field analysis on the aerospace industry in the Campania region. The Campania region has been classified as a moderate innovator. We focus on the aerospace industry as it represents a very important sector to the region. In particular, it accounts for 25% of the Italian turnover in the aerospace sector, and it is characterised by about 100 firms, 30 of which are "core" firms, and by an extended research system (60 research groups and 300 people from universities, CIRA, CNR, and private research centers).

Before proceeding to collect empirical data, a literature review will be performed in order to identify and select the most proper indicators to empirically measure the model parameters. The results derived from this analysis will be used to fine-tune the parameters of the computational model.

Finally, further experiments will be performed, both to probe deeper into some theoretical aspects and to complete the validation of the model.

References

Albino, Vito, Carbonara, Nunzia, and Giannoccaro, Ilaria 2005. "Industrial districts as complex adaptive systems: Agent-based models of emergent phenomena". In Industrial clusters and inter-firm networks, Edited by Karlsson Charlie, Johansson Borje and Stough Roger R., 58-82, Cheltenham, UK.

Albino, Vito, Carbonara, Nunzia, and Giannoccaro, Ilaria 2006. "Innovation in industrial districts: An agent-based simulation model". International Journal of Production Economics, 104, 1:30-45.

Arthur, W. Brian, Durlauf, Steven N. and Lane, David A. 1997. The economy as an evolving complex system II, SFI Studies in the Sciences of Complexity, Addison Wesley: Reading, MA.

Asheim, Bjorn Terje, and Gertler M. 2005. The Geography of Innovation: RegionalInnovation Systems, in The Oxford handbook of innovation, edited by Fagerberg, Jan, Mowery, David, and Nelson, Richard, Oxford University Press.

Asheim, Bjorn Terje, and Coenen, Lars 2005. "Knowledge bases and regional innovation systems: Comparing Nordic clusters". Research policy, 34, 8:1173-1190.

Asheim, Bjorn Terje, Isaksen, Arne, Nauwelaers, Claire, and Todtling, Franz. 2003. Regional Innovation Policy for Small–Medium Enterprises. Edward Elgar, Cheltenham.

Asheim, Bjorn Terje. 1996. "Industrial districts as 'learning regions': a condition for prosperity". European planning studies, 4, 4:379-400.

Asheim, Bjorn Terje, and Isaksen, Arne. 2002. "Regional innovation systems: the integration of local 'sticky' and global 'ubiquitous' knowledge". The Journal of Technology Transfer, 27, 1:77-86.

Asheim, Bjorn Terje, Boschma, Ron, and Cooke, Philip. 2011. "Constructing regional advantage: Platform policies based on related variety and differentiated knowledge bases". Regional Studies, 45,7: 893-904. DOI: /10.1080/00343404.2010.543126

Bak, Per, Tang, Chao, and Wiesenfeld, Kurt. 1988. "Self-organised criticality". Physical review A, 38,1: 364. DOI: 10.1103/PhysRevA.38.364

Benner, Mary J., and Tushman, Michael. 2002. "Process Management and Technological Innovation: A Longitudinal Study of the Photography and Paint Industries". Administrative Science Quarterly, 47:676-706. DOI: 10.2307/3094913

Boero, Riccardo, and Squazzoni, Flaminio. 2005. “Does empirical embeddedness matter? Methodological issues on agent-based models for analytical social science”. Journal of Artificial Societies and Social Simulation, 8,4.

Boisot, Max H. 1998. Knowledge Assets: Securing Competitive Advantage in the Information Economy: Securing Competitive Advantage in the Information Economy. Oxford University Press.

Brenner, Thomas, and Werker Claudia. 2009. “Policy Advice Derived from Simulation Models”. Journal of Artificial Societies and Social Simulation 12, 4.

Brusco Sebastiano 1990. The idea of the industrial district: Its genesis in Industrial Districts and Inter-firm Co-operation in Italy, edited by Giacomo Becattini, Frank. Pyke and Werner Sengenberger, International Institute for Labour Studies, Geneva.

Burton, Richard M. 2003. “Computational laboratories for organisation science: Questions, validity and docking”. Computational & Mathematical Organisation Theory, 9,2: 91-108. DOI: 10.1023/B:CMOT.0000022750.46976.3c

Camagni Roberto. (1991). Local Milieu, Uncertainty and Innovation Networks: Towards a New Dynamic Theory of Economic Space. In: Camagni Roberto, Editor, Innovation Networks: Spatial Perspectives, Belhaven Press, London.

Camagni Roberto, and Capello Roberta. (2012), Regional Innovation Patterns and the EU Regional Policy Reform: Towards Smart Innovation Policies, Paper presented at the 52° ERSA Conference in Bratislava, 21-24 August 2012.

Carley, Kathleen M. (1996). Validating computational models. Paper available at http://www.casos.cs.cmu.edu/publications/papers.php.

Cooke, Philip. (1996). “The new wave of regional innovation networks: analysis, characteristics and strategy”. Small Business Economics, 8,2: 159-171. DOI: 10.1007/BF00394424

—. (2001). From Technopoles to Regional Innovation Systems: The Evolution of Localised Technology Development Policy, Centre for Advanced Studies, University of Wales, Vol. XXIV:1.

—. (2012). “Transversality and transition: Green innovation and new regional path creation”. European planning studies, 20,5: 817-834. DOI: 10.1080/09654313.2012.667927

Cooke, Philip, and Schienstock, Gerd. (2000). “Structural competitiveness and learning regions”. Enterprise and Innovation Management Studies, 1,3: 265-280. DOI: 10.1080/14632440010023217

Cooke, Philip, and Morgan, K., 1998. The Associational Economy. Oxford University Press, Oxford
Cooke, Philip, Uranga, Mikel Gomez, and Etxebarria, Goio. (1998). "Regional systems of innovation: an evolutionary perspective". Environment and Planning A, 30: 1563–1584. DOI: 10.1068/a301563
Cowan, Robin, and Jonard, Nicolas. (2009). "Knowledge portfolios and the organisation of innovation networks". Academy of Management Review, 34,2: 320-342. DOI: 10.5465/amr.2008.0052
Crossan, Mary M., Lane, Henry W., and White, Roderick E. (1999). "An organisational learning framework: from intuition to institution". Academy of management review, 24,3: 522-537. DOI: 10.5465/AMR.1999.2202135
David, Paul A. and Metcalfe, Stan. (2007) Universities and public research organisations in the ERA, Draft Report (v.3) prepared for the Knowledge for Growth (K4G) Expert Group, EC (DG-Research), June 8
Doloreux, David, and Parto, Saeed. (2004). Regional Innovation Systems: A Critical Synthesis, UNU-INTECH Discussion Paper Series 2004-17, United Nations University, Maastricht, The Nederlands.
Doloreux, David. (2002). "What we should know about regional systems of innovation". Technology in society, 24,3: 243-263. DOI: 10.1016/S0160-791X(02)00007-6
Doloreux, David, and Parto, Saeed. (2005). "Regional innovation systems: Current discourse and unresolved issues". Technology in society, 27,2: 133-153. DOI: 10.1016/j.techsoc.2005.01.002
Edquist, Charles. (2004). "Reflections on the systems of innovation approach". Science and Public Policy, 31,6: 485-489. DOI: 10.3152/147154304781779741
Fischer, Manfred M. (2001). "Innovation, knowledge creation and systems of innovation". The Annals of Regional Science, 35,2: 199-216. DOI: 10.1007/s001680000034
Florida, Richard. (1995). "Toward the Learning Region". Futures, 27: 527-536. DOI: 10.1016/0016-3287(95)00021-N
Foray Dominique, David Paul A., and Hall Bronwyn H. (2011). Smart specialisation: From academic idea to political instrument, the surprising career of a concept and the difficulties involved in its implementation, MTEI Working Paper, November.
Foray, Dominique. (2009). The new economics of technology policy. Edward Elgar Publishing (Ed.).
—. (2011). Smart specialisation: from academic idea to political instrument, the surprising destiny of a concept and the difficulties involved in its implementation. Integration Process in the New

Regional and Global Settings, 269.
Fritsch, Michael, and Stephan, Andreas. (2005). "Regionalisation of innovation policy—introduction to the special issue". Research Policy, 34,8: 1123-1127.
Garnsey, Elizabeth (1998). "The genesis of the high technology milieu: a study in complexity". International Journal of Urban and Regional Research, 22,3: 361-377.
Gertler, Meric S. (2003). "Tacit knowledge and the economic geography of context, or the undefinable tacitness of being (there)". Journal of economic geography, 3,1: 75-99. DOI: 10.1093/jeg/3.1.75
Gilbert, Nigel. (2008). Agent-Based Models, Series: Quantitative Applications in the Social Sciences, SAGE Publications: UK
Gupta, Anil K., Smith, Ken G., and Shalley, Christina E. (2006). "The interplay between exploration and exploitation". Academy of Management Journal, 49,4: 693-706. DOI: 10.5465/AMJ.2006.22083026
Gustavsen, Bjørn, Nyhan, Barry and Ennals, Richard. (2007). Learning together for local innovation: promoting learning regions, Cedefop Reference series 68 Luxembourg: Office for Official Publications of the European Communities.
Heath, Brian, Hill, Raimond and Ciarallo, Frank. (2009). "A survey of agent-based modeling practices" (January 1998 to July 2008). Journal of Artificial Societies and Social Simulation, 12, 4: 9.
Holland, John H. (2002). Complex adaptive systems and spontaneous emergence. In Complexity and industrial clusters (pp. 25-34). Physica-Verlag HD. DOI: 10.1007/978-3-642-50007-7_3
—. (1995). Hidden order: How adaptation builds complexity. Basic Books.
Hollanders, Hugo, Es-Sadki, Nordine, Buligescu, Bianca, Rivera Leon, Lorena, Griniece, Elina and Roman, Laura (2014) Regional innovation scoreboard (RIS) 2014. PRO INNO EURO, INNO METRICS. DOI: 10.2769/88893
Hollanders, Hugo, Rivera Leon, Lorena and Roman, Laura. (2012). Regional innovation scoreboard (RIS) 2012. PRO INNO EURO, INNO METRICS.
Hollanders, Hugo, Tarantola, Stefano, and Loschky, Alexander. (2009). Regional innovation scoreboard (RIS) 2009. PRO INNO EURO, INNO METRICS. DOI: 0.2769/35418
Laranja, Manuel, Uyarra, Elvira and Flanagan, Kieron. (2008). "Policies for science, technology and innovation: Translating rationales into regional policies in a multi-level setting." Research Policy 37,5: 823-835. DOI: 10.1016/j.respol.2008.03.006

Lombardi, Mauro. (2003). "The evolution of local production systems: the emergence of the "invisible mind" and the evolutionary pressures towards more visible "minds"". Research Policy 32: 1443–1462. DOI: 10.1016/S0048-7333(02)00157-9

Longhi, Christian. (2002). From exogenous to endogenous local development: the cases of the Toulouse and Sophia Antipolis technopoles. In Complexity and Industrial Clusters (pp. 213-237). Physica-Verlag HD. DOI: 10.1007/978-3-642-50007-7_11

Lorenzen, Mark. (1998). Specialisation and Localised Learning, Copenhagen, Copenhagen Business School Press.

Louie, Markus A., and Carley, Kathleen M. (2008). "Balancing the criticisms: Validating multi-agent models of social systems". Simulation Modelling Practice and Theory, 16,2: 242-256. DOI: 10.1016/j.simpat.2007.11.011

Lucas Jr, Robert E. (1993). "Making a miracle". Econometrica: Journal of the Econometric Society, 251-272.

Lundvall, Bengt-Åke, and Johnson, Björn. (1994). "The Learning Economy". Journal of Industry Studies, 1,2: 23-42. DOI: 10.1080/13662719400000002

Lundvall Bengt-Åke, (1992). National systems of innovation. Toward a theory of innovation and interactive learning. Pinter: London

Maillat, Danis. (1998). "Innovative milieux and new generations of regional policies". Entrepreneurship & Regional Development, 10,1: 1-16. DOI: 10.1080/08985629800000001

March, James, G. (1991). "Exploration and exploitation in organisational learning". Organisation science, 2,1: 71-87. DOI: 10.1287/orsc.2.1.71

Maskell, Petr, and Malmberg, Anders. (1999). "Localised learning and industrial competitiveness". Cambridge Journal of Economics 23,2: 167-185. DOI: 10.1093/cje/23.2.167

Moss, Scott. (2008). "Alternative approaches to the empirical validation of agent-based models". Journal of Artificial Societies and Social Simulation, 11,1: 5.

Moulaert, Frank, and Sekia, Farid. (2003). "Territorial innovation models: a critical survey". Regional studies, 37,3: 289-302. DOI: 10.1080/0034340032000065442

Nonaka, Ikujiro. (1994). "A dynamic theory of organisational knowledge creation". Organisation science, 5, 1: 14-37. DOI: 10.1287/orsc.5.1.14

Nonaka, Ikujiro, and Takeuchi, Hirotaka. (1995). The knowledge-creating company: How Japanese companies create the dynamics of innovation. Oxford University Press.

Pawlowsky, Peter, Forslin, J., and Reinhardt, R. (2001). Practice and Tools of Organisational Learning, in: Organisational Learning and Knowledge, edited by Dierkes M., Berthoin A.A., Child J., Nonaka I., Oxford University Press: UK

Pilotti, Luciano, Silvia Rita Sedita, and I. De Noni. (2013) "Performance e crescita dei sistemi produttivi locali italiani tra rispecializzazioni, divisione cognitiva del lavoro ed ecologie del valore." Territorio, istituzioni, crescita. FrancoAngeli, Milano, 117-144.

OECD, (2001). Cities and Regions in the New Learning Economy. OECD publishing

—. (2011). Regions and Innovation Policy. OECD Reviews of Regional Innovation.

Pavitt, Keith. (1993). “What do firms learn from basic research”. Technology and the Wealth of Nations, 29-40.

Quatraro, Francesco. (2009). "Diffusion of regional innovation capabilities: evidence from Italian patent data." Regional Studies 43, 10: 1333-1348. DOI: 10.1080/00343400802195162

Quadrio Curzio, Alberto. and Fortis, Marco. (2002). Complexity and industrial clusters. Physica-Verlag, New York.

Richiardi, Matteo, Leombruni, Roberto, Saam, Nicole, and Sonnessa, Michele. (2006). “A common protocol for agent-based social simulation”. Journal of artificial societies and social simulation, 9,1.

Robinson, David. T., and Stuart, Toby E. (2007). “Financial contracting in biotech strategic alliances”. Journal of Law and Economics, 50,3: 559-596. DOI: 10.1086/519811

Sargent, Robert G. (2004). “Validation and verification of simulation models”. Simulation Conference, 2004. Proceedings of the 2004 Winter (Vol. 1). IEEE.

Saxenian, Anna Lee, and Jinn, Yuh Hsu. (2001). “The Silicon Valley-Hsinchu Connection: TechnicalCommunities and Industrial Upgrading”. Industrial and Corporate Change, 10,4: 893–920

Schwandt, David R. and Marquardt, Michael J. (2000). Organisational learning. From world-class theories to global best practices. Boca Raton: St. Lucie Press.

Squazzoni, Flaminio, and Boero, Riccardo. (2002). “Economic performance, inter-firm relations and local institutional engineering in a computational prototype of industrial districts”. Journal of Artificial Societies and Social Simulation, 5,1.

Tesfatsion, Leigh. (2002). Economic agents and markets as emergent phenomena. Proceedings of the National Academy of Science USA 99(Suppl. 3) 7191–7192.

Werker, Claudia. (2006). An assessment of the regional innovation policy by the European Union based on bibliometrical analysis (No. 0611). Papers on economics and evolution.

Zollo, Maurizio, and Winter, Sydney G. (2000). "Deliberate learning and the evolution of dynamic capabilities". Organisation Science, 13,3: 339–51. DOI: 10.1287/orsc.13.3.339.2780

PART IV:

CASE STUDY: INNOVATION POLICY IN IRELAND

CHAPTER EIGHT

EXPLORING A NEO-INSTITUTIONAL APPROACH TO POLICY RESEARCH: THE POLITICS OF THE EMERGENCE OF A FIELD OF SCIENCE, TECHNOLOGY AND INNOVATION IN IRELAND

CAMILLA NOONAN, SÉAMAS KELLY AND SIMEON VIDOLOV

Introduction

In recent years, Ireland has invested heavily in the development of a Science, Technology and Innovation (STI) infrastructure. In this chapter, we explore the formation of this distinctive domain of activity in the Irish context and, by borrowing concepts from neo-institutional theory (particularly those of institutional fields and field logics), we draw attention to some of the important historical processes that have contributed to the configuration of a set of dominant discourses and practices in this area. As such, our focus is on the politics of the emergence and configuration of an Irish STI field, as we attend to the role of other fields and agencies in shaping its formation and development.

Specifically, we argue that the Irish STI field can be seen as having emerged from a complex entanglement of two formerly autonomous institutional fields–Industrial Development and Higher Education−both of which have been the site of historical struggles between competing logics. Within the field of Industrial Development, advocates and supporters of the inward investment agenda produced one distinctive logic, while those pushing for policies in support of indigenous firms advocated an alternative. While this divide characterised the field for many years, it was the investment-driven logic that remained firmly in the ascendency from a policy perspective. Foreign-owned firms not only provided employment, but also secured Ireland's Balance of Payments position through their exporting activities. While these competing logics co-existed for many years, they became reconciled as policy makers accepted the need to embed Multi-National Corporations (MNCs), and to encourage them to 'move up the value chain' with regard to the activities they pursue in Ireland. This coincided with the popularisation of ideas around a National System of Innovation and associated notions of an innovation-driven economy. This new logic framed the issues in ways that avoided the traditional preoccupation with an indigenous/foreign direct investment (FDI) divide, focusing attention on the development of an infrastructure (institutions and relationships) that would support higher value-added activity across all firms, irrespective of ownership.

In terms of the Irish Higher Education field,[1] we note the tensions that gradually surfaced between the traditional conceptualisation of the university in society - i.e. that of producing a professional class (Coate 2009) - and more recent conceptions of the public university as an institution in service of the needs of industry and the broader economy (see, for example, the notion of the entrepreneurial university (Etzkowitz 1983)). It can be argued that these competing logics co-existed alongside one another for many years – the traditional logic, evident in the activities and operations of the established Irish universities (most of whom were under the umbrella of the National University of Ireland (NUI) from a governance point of view),[2] and a more enterprise-orientated alternative logic that has become prominent in recent years (partly through the emergence of new, overtly non-traditional Higher Education Institutions (HEIs)). During the 1990s and 2000s, the Higher Education field underwent quite a radical reconfiguration as the notion of an entrepreneurial university came to exert a growing influence in policy circles.

In what follows, therefore, we examine the competing logics that were evident in these important institutional fields and explore how their

---

[1] Higher Education in Ireland is provided mainly by seven universities and 14 Institutes of Technology (including the Dublin Institute of Technology and seven Colleges of Education). In addition, a number of other third level institutions provide specialist education in such fields as art and design, medicine etc.

[2] The National University of Ireland (NUI) was instituted in 1908 as the custodian of the third level education values of Catholic Ireland. It was the 'federal' university for its various constituent colleges (see Lee (1989 pg. 395) for discussion).

gradual entanglement produced the distinctive (sub-) field of STI.[3] We begin by introducing some important ideas from neo-institutional theory, upon which we draw to frame our analysis. This is followed by a brief description of changes in the Irish industrial development and higher education landscapes from the 1960s to 2000s, which constituted an important formative context within which the Irish STI agenda emerged. We direct most of our attention to the Industrial Development field, which dominated the policy landscape throughout this period of Ireland's economic development. Finally, we reflect on more recent, on-going, reconfigurations within the Irish STI field, before concluding the chapter with some broad reflections on the analysis presented and its possible implications.

Part I: Institutional Theory, Fields and Field Logics

The concepts of field and field logics (Bourdieu 1977; 1992) have become very central to neo-institutional theory. These concepts were developed in an effort to orientate ourselves to constellations of actors that interact and are influenced (both consciously and unconsciously) by institutions - the regulative, normative, and cultural-cognitive structures that provide stability and collective meaning to social life (Scott 1995). While many terms have been used to capture the essence of 'field' – societal sectors (Scott 1983; Scott 1995), games (Axelrod 1884), institutional spheres (Fligstein 1990), institutional environment (Orru 1991), and strategic action fields (Fligstein 2012) - all direct attention to the social space within which collective action is produced.

Building on the early work of Friedland (1991), Thornton and Ocasio (1999, p. 804) define institutional or field logics as "the socially constructed, historical patterns of material practices, assumptions, values, beliefs, and rules by which individuals produce and reproduce their material subsistence, organise time and space, and provide meaning to their social reality". It is this central logic that provides organising principles, and equips social actors with vocabularies of motive as well as a sense of self (i.e. identity). In drawing attention to the inherent power dynamics associated with such logics and spaces, Bourdieu (1977) explains how at any point in time one can observe a number of competing logics at play:

---

[3] We might refer to the institutional field of STI as a sub-field, as its dominant field logics originate in, and continue to be shaped by, these more deeply institutionalised fields of Industrial Development and Higher Education.

> "Fields are not placid and settled spaces but arenas of conflict in which all players seek to advance their interests. Some are able for longer or shorter periods to impose their conception of the 'rules of the game' on others." (ibid, p. 183)

Over time, powerful coalitions form around a particular logic and, consequently, alternatives get pushed to the background. The dominant logic thus emerges and serves to shape and coordinate cooperation and interactions within the field. In other words, the logic is bound up with a particular set of power dynamics and provides an overarching model for governance practices within the field. While alternative or competing logics typically co-exist, they tend to lose their political traction over time (Thornton 2012), because powerful incentives of legitimacy exist that ensure actor compliance with the dominant logics (DiMaggio 1983; DiMaggio 1991; Wooten 2008). In adhering to the new organising principles, field members establish a form of legitimacy that serves to shield them from any questioning of their intent and purpose. Consequently, in attempting to understand the dynamics of a field, it is useful to examine the ways in which these differences are reconciled, accommodated (Wooten 2008), appeased, or simply ignored over time. In what follows, we draw on these ideas to delineate some of the important developments in the formation of Irish industrial policy that ultimately led to the emergence of a distinctive sub-field of Science, Technology and Innovation. We draw on secondary data to highlight international influences and their carriers (individuals and institutions) in the formation of this new sub-field.

Part II: The formation of Irish STI policy

1960s-1990s: The changing field of Irish Industrial Development

The early 1960s marked the beginning of significant changes in Irish industrial development policy, as the inherited protectionist economic policies from earlier years started to give way to the new outward-facing policy orientation of the Lemass Government. [4] The Industrial Development Authority (IDA, established in 1947) played a key role in this opening up of the Irish economy; along with Córas Tráchtála Teoranta

[4] Seán Lemass served as Taoiseach (Prime Minister) from 1959 to 1966. He is widely regarded as having played a key role in the modernisation of the Irish State, particularly with regard to industrial policy.

(CTT, established in 1959), it was charged with delivering the policy objective of economic expansion through export growth. Although the IDA's remit extended to both indigenous and foreign-owned firms, the Authority seemed to record most success in enticing inward foreign direct investment (FDI) in the form of MNCs establishing subsidiaries in Ireland.[5] Over time, it came to be seen as a 'one stop shop' for meeting the tax and regulation needs of MNCs within the country (Ó Riain 2004). With this success came strong political support for furthering the IDA's activities and sustaining the policy focus of attracting inward FDI.

The political elevation of the IDA's activities fuelled tensions between it and some of the other actors within the field. For example, the National Board for Science and Technology (NBST) and the Institute for Industrial Research Standards (IIRS) both co-existed for many years alongside the IDA.[6] Despite the fact that these government agencies were all focused on supporting industry, there was little integration across their activities. Indeed, the NBST and IIRS were critical of the policy focus on inward investment.[7] Early agencies established to promote science and technology activities understood their remit as concerned with supporting the development of indigenous Irish firms. However, these agencies seemed to operate in the shadow of the more successful and politically powerful IDA, for whom the development of an indigenous science and technology capacity was not a major concern as, at this time, foreign MNCs locating in Ireland typically imported their own technological expertise.

In the 1960s and 1970s, therefore, we can detect the presence of two competing logics within the field of Irish industrial development: one focused on attracting FDI and the other focused on the development of a strong indigenous industrial capability. The indigenous lobby framed the

---

[5] In addition to the IDA, other important institutional innovations were introduced at this time to assist with job creation and export growth - e.g. the Export Profits Tax Relief scheme (1956) and the Capital Investment Advisory Committee (1956).

[6] The NBST (which replaced the National Science Council) was established in 1977 to advise Government and promote Science and Technology activities in Ireland. The IIRS was established in 1946 to encourage scientific research in indigenous industries and to help firms develop innovative technical processes.

[7] A 1973 National Science Council report titled: "Science, Technology and Industry in Ireland" communicated this position. The report was co-authored by Noel Whelan, a civil servant, who went on to become Secretary to the Department of An Taoiseach (Prime Minister) in the early 1980s. It contained an intense criticism of Ireland's reliance on inward investment (Cooper 1973).

extant industrial policy as an abject failure, on the grounds that it was overly focused on incentivising FDI and gave insufficient attention to the longer term considerations of supporting the indigenous sector. This alternative field logic was well articulated in an important review of industry policy that was commissioned by Government in the early years of the 1980s - The Telesis Report (1982).[8] The authors were very critical of the IDA, questioning the manner in which it reported successes[9] and arguing that their focus on attracting low value-added manufacturing and assembly activity would not serve the economy well in the longer term. They pointed to high-income countries internationally, arguing that their economic success rested on their indigenous firms. If Ireland was ever going to join these countries, then industrial policy must be reoriented towards nurturing strong Irish-owned firms (i.e. picking winners) rather than promoting "strong agencies to support weak firms" (ibid, p. 232).[10]

Against the backdrop of a deepening economic recession and wage inflation in the early 1980s, however, the most pressing priority facing the Government continued to be job creation. Notwithstanding the high overall cost of supporting MNCs, the statistics appeared to show that the grant cost per job was actually greater in the indigenous sector of the economy (Nolan 1983):

> "... foreign firms will continue to be necessary as a source of jobs, even though as Telesis rightly points out, jobs in Irish-owned companies are much more desirable, all else being equal. The hard fact is that Irish-owned industry alone will be unable to provide the jobs needed over the next five years. No combination of the private sector and public sector will be able to provide sufficient jobs, so the IDA efforts to attract foreign-owned industry will continue to be necessary." (Government appointee to the Senate, Senate debate, 21.12.1982; http://oireachtasdebates.oireachtas.ie)

---

[8] Ira Magaziner, a consultant and policy advisor known for his advocacy of governmental promotion of high value added industries, established the Telesis consultancy firm in 1979. The Telesis report can be downloaded from: http://irishlabour.com/dublinopinion/Telesis_part1.pdf

[9] Telesis showed how the IDA has adopted a promotional strategy of announcing numbers of "approved jobs" associated with any particular FDI project. As these figures fell short of the actual number of "jobs created", the IDA was left considerably exposed and subjected to much public suspicion (Lee 1989, p. 533).

[10] Telesis sent a shock wave through the policy establishment and provided critics of the IDA with enough ammunition to try to prize what they saw as excessive power away from it. The IDA, in turn, felt that it had been "set up for a hatchet job" (Lee 1989 p. 533-35).

Consequently, the field logic that emphasised FDI prevailed, and policy efforts to support the upgrading of indigenous firms continued to be a low political priority in Ireland. The influence of the Telesis Report, however, was felt in other ways. Three years later, in its formal response to Telesis, the Government published its first ever White Paper on Industry Policy (1985), which signalled a more concerted focus on the technological upgrading of indigenous industry.

This emphasis on technology seemed to echo a new policy prescription that was being steadily developed at the OECD's Directorate for Science Technology and Industry.[11] In addition to this, and in contrast to earlier OECD positions on trade and international competitiveness, a new understanding of international competitiveness had started to gain influence. Rather than tying trade performance to inter-country price differentials, divergent spending on R&D across member states was now argued to have greater explanatory power in accounting for differences in trade performance. Consequently, member states were urged to consider the link between science/technology activity and their national competitiveness. Investments in R&D were now being promoted as the key to international competitiveness and economic success.

These new ideas associating national competitiveness with technological development seemed to resonate within Irish policy circles at this time, and provided a new impetus to those promoting a focus on indigenous development. Owing to earlier reforms in education, and a subsequent increase in the numbers graduating with engineering and computer science degrees, the 'technological focus' of the Irish economy had already increased substantially in the early 1980s (Barry, 2007). Many of these graduates were forced to emigrate as the severe recession of the 1980s took hold.[12] FDI, with an increasing focus on the electronics sector, was

---

[11] The OECD (1975, 1979) published two reports titled: "Patterns of Resources Devoted to R&D in the OECD Area, 1963-1971" and "Trends in Industrial R&D in Selected Member Countries 1969-1975". Together, these reports were important because, for the first time, they drew attention to the role of the business sector in performing R&D. Following these publications, national governments were encouraged to support business sector R&D and the OECD started to gather further data on business sector R&D activity across member states. The first report in the Science and Technology Indicators series followed in 1984.

[12] Between 1980-1988, a quarter of indigenous manufacturing jobs were lost and inward FDI flows recorded a significant downturn. Tensions were high as

heralded as the vehicle that could be used to steer the economy to recovery. Increasingly, this modified logic that emphasised technological development was pointed to as crucial for Ireland's international competitiveness, as well as for the creation of jobs and future employment (Collins and Pontikakis 2006). Following the 1985 White Paper, a number of initiatives were announced in support of technological upgrading across indigenous firms. In reality, however, these initiatives amounted to a very small percentage of overall industry investment support. The 1980s was a period of fiscal austerity in Ireland[13] and so the real policy priority was maintaining jobs by replenishing the stock of FDI (for discussion, see O'Sullivan, 1995). In its 1985 Economic Report on Ireland, the OECD was critical of the pace of the Government's shift towards promoting research and technology development, describing it as "evolutionary not revolutionary" (p. 51).

1960s-1990s: The field of Irish Higher Education

In terms of higher education policy, an important early development came in the form of an OECD report in 1965. On the instigation of the Government, the OECD undertook this study and, for the first time, collected data on resourcing and 'outputs' of Irish educational institutions. The report was entitled "Investment in Education", and it led to significant investments in the second-level educational system. Within the third-level sector, state institutions were resourced by the Department of Education and the Higher Education Authority (HEA),[14] with the majority of them under the governance of the NUI. Describing this context in the early 1960s, Lee (1989) paints a less than flattering picture of those at the helm:

> "They [policy-makers] obviously wanted to do something. But they were faced by an almost total dearth of serious thinking about higher education among higher educationalists. If the policy-makers are to be criticised, it should be for failing to employ some first class minds to think systematically about the role of education in society." (pp 363-364)

---

indigenous firms felt increasingly abandoned by the IDA and the Irish Government (Ó Riain 2000; Ó Riain 2004).

[13] Ireland was in what one member of the Parliament described as "a quite unparalleled crisis of depleted Exchequer finances and of unemployment" (Parliament debate, December 18th, 1985).

[14] The Higher Education Authority (HEA) is the statutory funding, planning, and policy development body for higher education and research in Ireland. It was established in 1968.

The NUI was the gatekeeper of all recruitment and promotion practices within the universities, which, Lee (1989) argues, produced a particular kind of conservative and clientelistic dynamic:

> "It devised an appointment system that dispensed with the vulgarity of professional assessment, and reposed complete confidence in the consequences of the canvassing capacity of the candidate, offered only limited incentive for effort because promotion bore no self evident relationship to performance. It was to take sixty years before it would even contemplate a role for a professional assessment system, and even then in so casual a manner that it created as many problems as it solved." (p. 395)

The 1970s saw the insularity of the established universities begin to be challenged for the first time with the founding of two new HEIs[15], which posed considerable challenges to established modus operandi within the field. In particular, these institutions advocated a radically reconceptualised role for HEIs in Irish society.

Perhaps the most vocal and influential advocate was Professor Edward Walsh (the founder, and first President, of the University of Limerick). In his memoirs, he recalled the Government's rather "limited vision" when plans were drawn up to establish these institutions. Walsh explained that he had something far more ambitious in his sight:

> "My ambition was for an institution operating at the same level as the traditional universities (i.e. degree and postgraduate degree level), focusing academic resources on those areas of science, engineering, business and the humanities that advanced enterprises and professions were seeking in Ireland… I was determined to build dynamic links with leading enterprise, and to the extent I could, stimulate the kind of entrepreneurial ethos found in all the great US universities."[16] (Walsh 2011 pg. 24, 49)

Walsh explained how he had encouraged policy makers to see investment in education as a strategic economic initiative, but recalled how this rationale was "met with shock" in 1970s Ireland (ibid p. 25). Following an

---

[15] The National Institution for Higher Education (NIHE), Limerick was established in 1972, and this was followed by the establishment of NIHE Dublin in 1980. Both were granted university status in 1989, becoming the University of Limerick and Dublin City University, respectively.

[16] As an engineering graduate, Walsh emigrated to the USA in 1962. During the 1960s, he studied and worked at a number of US universities. He returned to Ireland in 1970 to direct the establishment of the proposed new National Institution for Higher Education in Limerick (Walsh 2011).

American university tradition (which he regarded as "a much more desirable model than anything [he] had learned of in Europe", ibid p. 105), the focus in these new institutions was on tailoring academic programmes, research and the overall institutional vision to the needs of foreign-owned firms located in Ireland – a far cry from the deep-seated traditions of liberal education and the ideals of Newman which had dominated the Irish universities for more than a century (French 2010):

> "I realised that the absence of constraints from the traditional university establishment represented my key opportunity. If the project were part of the NUI structure, I would be constrained by academic politics and NUI convention. Now, I was free to raise questions about the relevance of the existing Irish university system to the vision of an emerging Ireland that Seán Lemass and then Jack Lynch were attempting to realise. I started to use the catchphrase 'relevance and excellence' as the academic goal of the Limerick project and demonstrated its legitimacy by reference to the great American universities. The academic excellence of Harvard and MIT was beyond dispute, and yet both made no apology about being relevant to the needs of US business, industry and the professions." (Walsh 2011 p. 53)[17]

Walsh, therefore, was an articulate and energetic advocate of an alternative 'entrepreneurial' vision for Irish HEIs, and an important institutional entrepreneur in his own right. As this kind of vision began to gain traction in policy circles, it began to challenge, and contribute to the reconfiguration of some of the deeply embedded logics of the institutional field of Higher Education.[18] It could be argued, however, that without the reconfigurations within the Industrial Development field described above, institutional change within Higher Education would not have gathered such impetus.

1990s-2000s: The emergence of a distinctive field of Science, Technology and Innovation within the Irish context

The latter part of the 1980s was marked by a turn towards a more formal STI policy, which was considered a long-awaited victory by a number of

---

[17] On retirement from the University of Limerick, Ed Walsh was appointed chairman of the Irish Council for Science Technology and Innovation (ICSTI) and became a key figure in the production of the STI policy field in the late 1990s and early 2000s.

[18] The Universities Act (1997) is often seen as a watershed event in the governance of Irish HEIs. This redefined the nature and role of the NUI within the field, thus clearing the ground for change across the HEIs.

advocates in the State administration (Ó Riain 2009). In 1987, the OECD published a report entitled: "Innovation Policy for Ireland", in which it recommended that Ireland adopt an "aggressive innovation policy". It pointed to the importance of developing an "innovation vision" for the promotion of technology-related activities across the economy. According to the OECD, the vision should encompass massive and continuing upgrading of human resources, an upgrading of technological capacity, and the development of a nation-wide network of technological support services. In the same year the Science and Technology (S&T) Act was passed, and the National Board for Science and Technology (NBST) was merged with the Institute of Industrial Research and Standards (IIRS) to form a new state-sponsored advisory body named EOLAS (the Irish Science and Technology Agency). This agency was charged with fostering science and technology, and with forging links between industry and the HEIs. A new junior ministerial position for Science and Technology was also created under the auspices of the Department of Enterprise.

In 1988, the European multiannual financial framework (or structural fund) was launched. Its objective was to build political support and assist member countries in meeting their growing commitments following the signing of the Single European Act.[19] Prominent in the list of supported activities under the first financial or structural funds framework were science and technology. To help the Government access these funds, the Office of Science and Technology (OST) was established in 1988. This was located within the Department of Industry and Commerce and was charged with drawing up a Science and Technology Programme for the allocation of the funds.[20]

While these various acts and agencies were put in place in an effort to promote an upgrading of Irish industry, a significant event occurred

---

[19] To date there have been five frameworks: Delors I (1988-1992), Delors II (1993-1999), Agenda 2000 (2000-2006), the Multiannual Financial Framework (MFF) 2007-2013, and the MFF 2014-2020.

[20] Five initiatives were funded by the financial framework in the early years - the Programme in Advanced Technology (PATs); Higher Education-Industry Linkages and Innovation; Technical Services to Industry; Infrastructure; and Regional Development. The funding of these initiatives facilitated the building of groups such as the Software Manufacturers' Association, the Irish Interactive Multimedia Association, and the Software Localisation Interest Group and offered indigenous firms access to networks of support that included R&D networking, management development/training, and mentoring programmes (Ó Riain 2004).

toward the end of the 1980s, which, arguably, influenced the policy field logics in quite a dramatic way. The US multinational, Intel, signalled its intention to locate a fabrication facility in Ireland. While the IDA had already attracted a number of multinational 'high-tech' companies (such as Digital Equipment Corporation (DEC), Apple, Wang, and IBM in the 1970s and early 1980s), most of these were manufacturing and assembly operations. Intel appeared to be a very different proposition, however, and its arrival was viewed as a watershed moment:

> "... it was a step-change because of its scale... a seminal event... Intel would require massive buildings and massive infrastructure, and would be doing more complex, skilled work than the low-level manufacturing carried out by other existing information technology companies...we had to trawl around the world to help find those initial 250 engineers, encouraging people who had emigrated to come back."[21]

Part III: Consolidating the new policy sub-field

The Culliton Report (1992) and the idea of a National System of Innovation

Towards the end of the 1980s, following the recommendations in the 1987 OECD report Innovation Policy for Ireland, the Department of Enterprise established the Industrial Policy Review Group (the Culliton Group).[22] In 1992, the group produced its report (A Time for Change: Industrial Policy for the 1990s), which called for a much broader approach to industrial policy. It made recommendations on a wide range of public policy areas, including taxation, infrastructure, education, training, science, and technology. Significantly, it emphasised the importance of building a National System of Innovation (NSI).[23]

---

[21] Barry O'Leary (Head of IDA) quoted in the Irish Times, 13 Nov. 2013.

[22] This group was chaired by Jim Culliton, CEO and later chairman of the building materials firm, CRH – one of Ireland's largest, most profitable, multinational enterprises.

[23] This concept was introduced simultaneously by a number of economists in the late 1980s - Christopher Freeman, Richard Nelson, and Bengt Åka Lundvall. It was popularised by the OECD when Bengt Åka Lundvall was appointed Deputy Director of the OECD in 1992. In the years that followed, he championed the OECD's National Systems of Innovation Programme. While a systems approach had been implicit in OECD publications well before 1992 (Godin 2009), the focus was on the broad system and how the various institutions and actors linked up. In contrast, publications post-1992 positioned the firm as the core element in the

The idea of a National System of Innovation seemed to capture the policy imagination and was used as an orientating framework for many of the policy papers and publications produced in the 1990s and beyond. The NSI concept offered policy makers a new way of framing the challenge of industrial development – it was no longer about the foreign/indigenous divide but about developing a collective system of knowledge production. It focused the discourse on the importance of relationships, institutional infrastructure, and the centrality of private enterprise to the broader national innovative effort (Lundvall 2010). Significant institutional restructuring took place in the aftermath of the Culliton Report.[24]

Building new institutions–ICTSI, PRTLI, and SFI

The 1990s marked a period of remarkable growth in Ireland. Sensible fiscal policies, coupled with a benign global economy, gave birth to the 'Celtic Tiger' and a string of budget surpluses (Whelan 2013). With growth, it rapidly became apparent that the Irish manufacturing activities of many foreign-owned firms were becoming increasingly unprofitable. Ireland's relatively high cost base was typically cited as underpinning MNC decisions to shut down their subsidiaries.[25] Although the IDA continued to replace the jobs lost through these closures, there was a growing unease that Ireland's position as a manufacturing base for

---

system and all other entities were charged with linking to the needs and priorities of this core element. The need for a smoothly functioning National System of Innovation had also been proposed in a National Economic and Social Council (NESC) report entitled: The Irish Economy in Comparative Institutional Perspective (1992).

[24] Specifically, the IDA was restructured into different entities. Following the Industrial Development Act (1993), a new Government agency, Forfás, was established to advise government on enterprise, trade, science, technology, and innovation. The IDA (which would become an agency of Forfás) was to be given full responsibility for inward investment and Forbairt (also an agency of Forfás) was established and given responsibility for the development and promotion of indigenous enterprise. In 1998 Forbairt was merged with An Bord Tráchtala (the Irish Trade Board) to form Enterprise Ireland (EI). EI is charged with promoting the development of Irish indigenous firms.

[25] For example, between 1993 and 1998, approximately 15 foreign-owned clothing manufacturers closed in Ireland: in 1993, Digital announced the closure of its Galway plant (which employed 780 people); in early 1995, Packard Electric (in the car components segment) closed with a loss of 800 jobs; in December 1997, Seagate announced the closure of its plant in Clonmel (with a loss of 1,400 jobs); in 1999, Apple announced 500 job cuts in Cork.

foreign-owned firms was being steadily eroded. Throughout the 1990s, the discourse increasingly focused on the need to attune policy to the changed reality of Ireland's diminishing attractiveness as an FDI destination. Ireland needed to host higher value-added activity if it was to continue to compete internationally.

On the back of much lobbying by the Irish Research Scientists Association (IRSA), the Government published a White Paper in 1996, which was entitled "Science, Technology and Innovation". While four major arguments were outlined as to why public money should support basic research, the Government noted the difficulty of justifying this expenditure in such a small economy. Although no tangible commitments were made to research funding, it did propose new mechanisms for establishing an STI policy: a permanent Science, Technology and Innovation Advisory Council (ICSTI, which was established later that year) and an Interdepartmental Committee for Science and Technology (which was eventually established in the early 2000s). The White Paper also signalled that a Technology Foresight Exercise (promoted as an internationally accepted means to bring together the main constituencies in an NSI) would be undertaken in an effort to prioritise State investment in STI.

Inward investment in research – the Programme for Research in Third Level Institutions (PRTLI)

Against the backdrop of the emerging STI discourse, there was widespread recognition that third-level research had been chronically under-resourced for many years in Ireland.[26] In the mid 1990s, a number of politicians, together with Irish-American Chuck Feeney (and his organisation, Atlantic Philanthropies), developed a plan to change this landscape.[27] They agreed to co-fund a major new research initiative - the Programme for Research in Third Level Institutions (PRTLI):

[26] A 1996 consultant's report (CIRCA, 1996), which had been commissioned by the HEA, noted that the main source of HEI funding (the block grant from Government) at that time was wholly insufficient, and that the absence of research council structures and funding continuity in Ireland was damaging overall research potential. Moreover, being forced to rely on European funding and sources from within the private sector, meant that opportunism rather than a strategic approach had governed the direction of Irish research.

[27] Chuck Feeney was a wealthy Irish-American and a strong supporter of the University of Limerick since the 1980s.

"When the history of Irish higher education at the turn of the millennium is written, the name of Chuck Feeney will hold an honourable place. It would be difficult to exaggerate how bleak the Irish research landscape looked when I returned from the USA in 1996. A decade later, it has been totally transformed, thanks in large part to the catalytic initiative shown by Atlantic Philanthropies in relation to the PRTLI."
(Dr Hugh Brady, President of University College Dublin)[28]

The PRTLI focused on the development of a '4th level' within Ireland's third-level education sector through the establishment of internationally competitive research centres. The £150m programme was launched in 1998 and housed under the Department of Education (but transferred to the Department of Enterprise, Trade and Employment in 2010).[29] It explicitly avoided commercial and near-to-market research, as evidenced in the Calls for Proposals under each of the first three cycles of funding.[30]

ICSTI, the Technology Foresight Exercise, and Science Foundation Ireland

A second important development in the run-up to the millennium was the establishment of a permanent advisory council – the Irish Council for Science, Technology and Innovation (ICSTI). This was established in 1997 and its role was to advise the government on the strategic direction of science and technology policy, including scientific research, primary, secondary and tertiary education, technology and industry R&D. Edward Walsh (who by now had retired as President of the University of Limerick) was appointed as chair of the new council. Throughout the closing years of the 1990s, and up until its disbandment in 2004, this body played an influential role in shaping the STI field.

---

[28] http://www.ucd.ie/ucdtoday/2008/12_december_08/pdf/UCD_Today_FA_11_full.pdf

[29] Indeed, efforts to move this research budget to the Department of Enterprise, Trade and Employment had already started in 2002, when the Minister for Enterprise (Mary Harney) established the National Commission for Research and Innovation and tasked it with examining the future of research spending. The chairman of this commission was Dr Edward Walsh. Academics feared that an Enterprise-led focus on research as a means of generating employment would undermine their arguments in favour of basic research (Irish Times, May 1st, 2002).

[30] "Programme for Research in Third Level Institutions: Call for Proposals", Higher Education Authority (HEA).

Most notably, ICSTI oversaw the Technology Foresight Exercise that had been proposed in the 1996 White Paper. Officially launched in March 1998, the ultimate goal of the exercise was to enable Ireland to secure its future as a "knowledge society".[31] The task force was chaired by Brian Sweeney, CEO of Siemens Group, Ireland. The findings and recommendations were published in a report entitled: "Technology Foresight Ireland–An ICSTI overview". In a bold and unprecedented move, the Foresight committee proposed that a Technology Foresight Fund worth £560m be established, to overhaul Irish science and to develop national centres of expertise in biotechnology and information technology (identified as key strategic areas for Ireland).[32]

In late 1999, the Department of Enterprise, Trade and Employment (ETE) proposed that a new foundation be established to disburse these funds, and circulated a memorandum to all departments soliciting views on how such an entity might be structured. It proposed that two stand-alone institutes for biotechnology and computer research be established as part of the new foundation.

The Department of Education and Science[33] and the Department of Health and Children were vehemently against this proposal arguing that the Foresight fund should be used to build on the country's existing research capability, rather than developing a new model that would ultimately denude universities of their researchers. A major campaign was launched

---

[31] The framing of the challenge as one of securing Ireland's position within the "knowledge economy" owes much to the OECD. Against the backdrop of a surge in Information and Communication Technologies and the dramatic decline in the price of information processing, a number of scholars claimed that these technologies were fundamentally changing the role and significance of knowledge as an input to economic growth – knowledge access and distribution were noted to be key (David and Foray, 1995; Foray and Lundvall, 1996). This research agenda was harnessed at the OECD and placed under the direction of Dominique Foray, one of the early advocates of the knowledge economy.

[32] The scale of this investment and its historical significance should not be underestimated. It far exceeded any prior investment by the State in this area. In an interview with Edward Walsh, he described the importance of thinking big and doing something radical. Whereas convention might have dictated that they request something of the order of £50million, they deliberately resolved to push for something in the order of £500million.

[33] In 2007, the Department of Education was renamed the Department of Education and Science.

to dissuade the Government from pursuing this proposal.[34] It culminated in the CHIU35 commissioning the international consulting group CIRCA to draft an official response to this proposed new landscape.[36]

In March 2000, at the official launch of the Foresight Fund, the State announced that £1.95 billion would be allocated to science and technology under the National Development Plan – noting how, in the past, we were "followers", but going forward we would be "trailblazers" within the science and technology domain. A new funding institution, Science Foundation Ireland (SFI) was established to disburse the £560m foresight funds and to foster the development of "significant clusters of excellence in fundamental research". It was housed under the Department of Enterprise, Trade and Employment, and Dr William Harris[37] was appointed to the position of Director General. Harris explained that SFI was modelled on the National Science Foundation in the United States, whose model was "breathtakingly simple… [let] the very best research brains run the show and leave the politicians out of the picture."38 He explained that his job was to support the best Irish researchers and to attract what he referred to as the "superstars" of scientific research to Ireland (ibid).

SFI was handed the purse for research funding, and it became increasingly influential and powerful within Irish science and technology research as its budget and remit expanded over the 2000s (Barry 2007). Irish researchers, who had been chronically under-funded historically, became increasingly

---

[34] The media described it as an "onslaught on Government" which was "swift and fierce" (Irish Times, February 15th, 2000). The stakeholders included industry representatives such as the Industry Research Development Group (IRDG) and Irish Business and Employers Confederation (IBEC) and associations representing the HEIs: the Irish Research Scientists Association (IRSA) and the Conference of Heads of Irish Universities (CHIU) or Irish Universities Association (IUA) as it is currently known.

[35] The Conference of Heads of Irish Universities was established in 1972 to provide a forum for discussion and joint action across the universities. The name of this group was changed to the Irish Universities Association (IUA) in 1997.

[36] This report was published in 2000 and was entitled "Technology Foresight & the University Sector." It can be downloaded from: http://www.iua.ie

[37] Harris was a former head of the Mathematics and Physical Sciences Directorate at the US National Science Foundation and prior to his appointment at SFI was Vice President for Research at the University of South Carolina.

[38] Quoted in "Making the research world green with envy", Irish Times; January 27th, 2004.

dependent on SFI as the source of financial support for basic research.

Part IV: The changing landscape of the new millennium

In 2004, as projected resource allocations to the IDA and Enterprise Ireland were cut by 9% and 15% respectively (€20m in total), the allocation to the STI programme/SFI was increased by 36% (to €201m). This dramatic refocusing prompted some to ask whether we were witnessing a "revolution in Irish industrial policy".[39] Indeed, between 2001 and 2006, SFI allocated a total of €468 million to Irish science within the HEI Sector.[40] With these allocations, the emerging logic of the new STI field (shaped, as it was, by the managerialism of the extant Industrial Development field) began to exert itself on the HE field, as the HEIs came under increased pressure to demonstrate that the correct systems were in place to manage these monies.[41] In early 2000, Malcolm Skilbeck was commissioned by the HEA and the Conference of Heads of Irish Universities (CHIU) to explore some of the challenges facing Irish universities.[42] The foreword, by Roger Downer (Chairman, CHIU) and Don Thornhill (Chairman, HEA), outlined the motivation for commissioning this report:

> "The university is no longer a quiet place to teach and do scholarly work at a measured pace and contemplate the universe as in centuries past. It is a big, complex, demanding, competitive, business requiring large scale ongoing investment." (p. 8)

The stated aim of the report was to 'assist' universities to further their ideas and plans for their own future development by "holding a mirror to the changing world of higher education" (p. 18). Skilbeck was quite scathing in its assessment of existing practices and competences within

---

[39] McManus, J. (2003) "Are we looking at a Revolution in Irish Industry Policy?" Irish Times, November 17th.

[40] This detail was published in the Science Foundation Ireland, Annual Report, 2007. It can be downloaded from:
http://www.sfi.ie/news-resources/publications/annual-reports/

[41] These influences and pressures were clearly international in their scope, and not merely localised in Ireland.

[42] Malcolm Skilbeck was Deputy Director of Education at the OECD until 1998. His report was entitled: "The University Challenged: A review of international trends and issues with particular reference to Ireland" (2001), and it can be found here: http://bit.ly/1N4g7qn

Irish universities. The picture painted was one of a conservative and bureaucratic set of institutions. Skilbeck challenged them to "recreate" themselves, to become "global players" (p. 149), and to become relevant to the needs of Ireland's evolving 'knowledge society'. This new landscape would require more than "traditional networks and amateurishness" (p. 136), and Skilbeck called on the HEIs to put together a "system-wide, collaborative strategy for the future of research" (p. 135).

Soon after, in 2004, the OECD was invited to conduct a review of the Irish higher education system. While it welcomed the consensus regarding the importance of research to the creation of a 'knowledge-based society', it noted the absence of a "clear strategic framework within which such public funds are invested" (OECD, 2004a, p. 37). It called for a more coherent and systematic approach to research across the HEIs and recommended, inter alia, that SFI be positioned as the national agency for funding research in Ireland and that its powers and responsibilities be extended.

In 2007/2008, as economic growth slowed and Ireland entered a very severe recession, the question of financial 'sustainability' and 'impact' of publicly-funded research became the driving logic of the STI field. Following the Government's research prioritisation exercise in 2010, the funding focus was very clearly re-orientated towards applied research with commercial impact. While there had been earlier calls for PRTLI applicants to demonstrate the future commercial and economic impact of their research,[43] a formal reorientation from basic to more applied research took place when the country entered recession. Similarly, applicants for SFI's programmes were increasingly required to demonstrate 'impact' by delineating the potential of their research across a range of metrics - most notably, commercial spin-offs. Against the backdrop of this very dramatic reorientation of these funding mechanisms towards applied research, there was much unrest within the HEIs:

---

[43] This was recommended in the first evaluation exercise of the PRTLI, which was undertaken by an international assessment committee in 2003. The report is titled: "The Programme for Research in Third Level Institutions (PRTLI) Impact Assessment" and can be downloaded from:
http://www.hea.ie/content/programme-research-third-level-institutions-prtli-impact-assessment-vol-i

> "Third-level education in Ireland went, in half a century, from the belief that higher education had nothing to do with economic development to the equally absurd assumption that higher education was about nothing except economic development: from one rather foolish barbarism to another." (Irish Times, May 1, 2012)[44]

Calls on the Government to reinstate a more balanced approach to research funding came from Irish researchers, who cautioned against the dangers of cutting support for basic research: not only would talented scientists leave the country, they argued, but Irish scientists would face the prospect of being "cut off" from future European funding.[45] The politics of this new institutional field were, clearly, far from resolved.

Part V: Discussion and Conclusions

In this chapter we have sought to explore the use of neo-institutional ideas to trace the emergence of a distinctive field of Science, Technology and Innovation in the Irish context. We believe that this perspective may have much to offer policy studies as an analytical approach.

First, it directs attention to the importance of contingent historical processes in constituting an institutional field in a specific way. We have sought to illustrate some of the important logics and agencies that have played decisive roles in configuring the contemporary institutional landscape of the entangled fields of Irish Industrial Development, Higher Education, and STI. Second, we have emphasised the politics of such institutional development processes, and the inherent tensions and contradictions associated with their competing internal logics. Such contradictory logics are a source of dynamism, each exerting their influence on how new ideas and practices are appropriated and accommodated. Moreover, existing logics are not merely swept away by the emergence of new dominant ones but, in mangled or sedimented form, may continue to exert their influences in subtle and important ways. Third, we have attempted to show how what might once have been seen as clearly separate fields may become entangled with one another over time, and how these entanglements may produce other interesting (sub-)fields with their own distinctive politics. The area of Science, Technology and

---

[44] The quotation was extracted from Garvin, T. (2012) "Degrees of Nonsense: The Demise of the University in Ireland" Dublin: Glasnevin Publishing.

[45] "Research Funding at Risk warn Irish Scientists" Science Editor, Irish Times, August 22, 2012.

Innovation might be seen as one such emergent field in the Irish context, and it is clear that its logics are still contested and its politics still far from settled.

These important political issues merit, we believe, much more public and critical scrutiny than they have enjoyed to date. Too often the politics of important policy choices are denied, or veiled under a blanket of pseudo-rationality and superficial spin. The extent, scope, and quality of the debate on investments in STI in the Irish context has been very disappointing, to say the least. An important first step to enhancing such a debate would be to openly acknowledge the complexity, and inevitable politicality, of the issues at stake, with a view to producing a richer and more measured public policy discourse around forms of knowledge production and the technosocial infrastructures/institutions required to support them.

With regard to the further development of the ideas that we have sketched out in this chapter, we would welcome more detailed and nuanced historical accounts of the historical processes that we have only succeeded in presenting in such a broad-brush, superficial manner. The detail of the historical narrative is important, and such detail demands a much broader canvas than a single chapter. Of interest also would be comparative historical studies of the development of STI fields in other countries, and their associated politics. In particular, it would be fascinating to explore how ideas and practices get embedded differently in different contexts, and the role of contingent historical processes in shaping such outcomes.

Finally, studies that further draw upon, and develop, the language and concepts of neo-institutional theory to enrich this kind of policy analysis could make valuable contributions to such debates. Moreover, we believe that there may be much to be gained by further deepening the political focus of such work by attending to the implications of field reconfigurations for reshaping human subjectivities and broader social institutions.

Acknowledgement

The author gratefully acknowledges the financial support from the Irish Government's Programme for Research in Third Level Institutions (PRTLI 5) project grant entitled 'Innovation Policy Simulation for the Smart Economy (IPSE)'.

References

Axelrod, R. (1884). The Evolution of Cooperation. New York, Basic Books

Bourdieu, P. (1977). Outline of a theory of Practice. Cambridge, UK, Cambridge University Press.

Bourdieu, P., and L. Wacquant (1992). Invitation to a Reflexive Sociology. Chicago, University of Chicago Press.

Coate, K., and I. McLabhrainn (2009). Irish Higher Education and the Knowledge Economy. International Perspectives on the Governance of Higher Education. J. Huisman. London, Routledge: 198-216.

Cooper, C., and N. Whelan (1973). Science, Technology and Industry in Ireland. Report to the National Science Council (NSC). Stationery Office, Dublin.

DiMaggio, P. J., and W.W. Powell (1983). "The iron cage revisited: Institutional isomorphism and collective rationality in organizational fields." American Sociological Review 48(2): 147-60.

DiMaggio, P. J., and W.W. Powell (1991). Introduction. The New Institutionalism in Organizational Analysis. Chicago, The University of Chicago Press.

Etzkowitz, H. (1983). "Entrepreneurial scientists and entrepreneurial univerisites in American academic science." Minerva 21(2): 198-233.

Fligstein, N. (1990). The Transformation of Corporate Control. Cambridge MA, Harvard University Press.

Fligstein, N., and D. McAdam (2012). A Theory of Fields. New York, Oxford University Press.

French, N. (2010). "The discourses of higher education in Ireland: religion, nationalism and economic development." *Level3*, May, (available at: http://level3.dit.ie/html/issue8/french/french_1.html - accessed July, 2015)

Friedland, R., and R. R. Alford (1991). Bringing society back in: Symbols, practices and institutional contradictions. New Institutionalism in Organizational Analysis. W. W. Powell, and P.J. DiMaggio. Chicago, Chicago University Press.

Godin, B. (2009). The making of Science, Technology and Innovation Policy: Conceptual Frameworks as Narratives, 1945-2005.

Lee, J. J. (1989). Ireland 1912-1985, Politics and Society. Cambridge, Cambridge University Press.

Lundvall, B. A. (2010). National Systems of Innovation. Toward a theory of Innovation and Interactive Learning. London, Anthem Press.

Nolan, S. (1983). "The Telesis Report - a review essay." Economic and

Social Review 14(4): 281-290.

Ó Riain, S. (2004). The Politics of High Tech Growth: Developmental Network States in the Global Economy. Cambridge, Cambridge University Press.

—. (2004). "State, Competition and Industrial Change in Ireland 1991-1999." The Economic and Social Review 35(1): 27-53.

—. (2009). Addicted to Growth: Developmental Statism and Neo-Liberalism in the Celtic Tiger, in The Nation-State in Transformation: The Governance, Growth and Cohesion of Small States under Globalisation. M. Boss. Aarthus, Aarhus University Press.

Ó Riain, S., and P. O'Connell (2000). The Role of the State in Growth and Welfare. Bust to Boom? The Irish Experience of Growth and Inequality. B. Nolan, P.O'Connell, and C. Whelan. Dublin, Institute for Public Administration.

Orru, M., N. Woolsey Biggart and G. C. Hamilton (1991). Organizational isomophorism in East Asia. The New Institutionalism in Organizational Analysis. W. W. Powell, and P.J. DiMaggio. Chicago, University of Chicago Press.

Scott, W. R. (1995). Institutions and Organizations. Thousand Oaks, CA, Sage.

Scott, W. R., and J.W. Meyer (1983). The organization of societal sectors. Organizational environments: Rituals and rationality. J. W. Meyer, and W.R. Scott. Beverly Hills, Sage.

Thornton, P., and W. Ocasio (1999). "Institutional Logics and the Historical Contingency of Power in Organizations: Executive Succession in the Higher Education Publishing Industry, 1958–1990." American Journal of Sociology 105(3): 801-843.

Thornton, P. H., W. Ocasio and M. Lounsbury (2012). The Institutional Logics Perspective: A new approach to Culture, Structure and Process. Oxford, Oxford University Press.

Walsh, E. (2011). Upstart. Friends, foes and the founding of a University. Cork, Ireland, Collins Press.

Whelan, K. (2013). Ireland's Economic Crisis: The Good, the Bad and the Ugly. Dublin, UCD Center for Economic Research. Working Paper Series (WP 13/06).

Wooten, M. a. A. J. H. (2008). Organizational Fields: Past, Present and Future. The Sage Handbook of Organizational Institutionalism. R. Greenwood, and C. Oliver, R. Sudaby and K. Sahlin. London, Sage.

CHAPTER NINE

IRELAND'S TECHNOLOGY TRANSFER POLICY

CIARA FITZGERALD AND FREDERIC ADAM

Introduction

This chapter provides an analysis of the development of Irish Technology Transfer policy. We explore the growth of Technology Transfer Offices (TTOs) in Irish universities to enhance our understanding of how technology transfer is operationalised in Ireland. The chapter draws attention to the policy context by giving an overview of the documents which shaped the development of TTOs in Ireland and by presenting the key political actors involved in encouraging the technology transfer efforts of universities. Our analysis is sourced from government reports and from interviews with leading government members responsible for implementing and monitoring the government initiatives to strengthen and support TTOs in Ireland. Furthermore we interviewed TTOs in Ireland to outline their interpretation of how the TTO system in Ireland is operationalised.

Following OECD (2006), the study defines a university TTO as a business unit that facilitates the university to identify, manage, protect, and market their intellectual property to other parties for further development. A TTO is recognised as typically centring on commercialising applied research, but often providing a wide range of complementary services such as supporting spin-outs, entrepreneurship training, and industry outreach programmes. In that sense, their role as an intermediary bridging organisation is concerned with the practical transfer and application of knowledge, normally in pursuit of national policy goals and to support industrial capability development (OECD, 2006). A comprehensive description of the role is defined by Siegel et al (2007:89), "TTOs serve as an 'intermediary' between suppliers of innovation (university scientists) and those that can potentially (help to) commercialise them, i.e. firms, entrepreneurs, and venture capitalists. TTOs facilitate commercial knowledge transfers of IP [Intellectual Property] resulting from university research through licensing to existing firms or start-up companies of inventions or other forms. The activities of the TTO have important economic and policy implications since licensing agreements and university based start-ups can result in additional revenues for the university, employment opportunities for university based researchers (especially post-docs) and graduate students, and local economic and technological spillovers through the stimulation of additional R&D investment and job creation." Commercialisation of knowledge is facilitated through formal and informal methods of technology transfer. Formal technology transfer mechanisms are those that embody or directly lead to a legal mechanism like a patent, license or royalty agreement. The predominant hard methods of technology transfer are patenting, licensing, and company formation – spin out and spin-in. (Cunningham and Harney, 2006). Informal technology transfer embodies informal communication processes where IP is of less importance, for example, joint publications, academic consulting, informal talks, meetings, and contacts between academic and industry personnel. However, Siegel et al. (2007) and Link et al. (2007) highlight that both forms of technology transfer are important. The informal methods can facilitate the development of networks which assist the bi-directional knowledge exchange to support formal technology transfer activities. Therefore both are interlinked and hence should be encouraged. By presenting the contextual background of TTOs, the study reveals insights into the 'black box' of the TTO (Sanders and Miller 2010).

Methodology

Data collection involved both in-depth face-to-face interviews as well as the accumulating of secondary data material. Secondary data related to background information on the local context as well as data, brochures, and reports relating to university-industry linkages. The interviews consisted of semi-structured questions relating to the processes involved in university-industry knowledge and technology transfer. Primary research consisted of in-depth interviews with key individuals throughout all areas of the TTO. These interviews were response driven and followed up on the responses of the interviewee as opposed to following a structure. As part of the data collection, the researchers conducted 36 semi-structured interviews which were held with TTO personnel in the seven Irish universities; and, where they were acknowledged as relevant to specific strategic activities, interviews were conducted with non-TTO members such as government agencies and other key stakeholders. The audio-taped interviews were of 60-90 minutes duration and transcribed after the interview. In total, 296 pages of interview transcriptions were analysed. Standard questions were utilised to warrant validity and consistency. However, semi-structured interviews were important for the interpretative approach taken, by which current and retrospective processes were reflected upon by interviewees. Also, during location visits, the researchers requested a copy of supporting organisational documentation, such as organisational charts, strategy documents, and reports. Multiple data types such as documents, observation, and interviews as well other publicly available documents were used to build a comprehensive and in-depth analysis.

Following Eisenhardt (1989), the data was analysed by the researcher by first conducting within-case analysis for each case to find themes emerging in the analysis, followed by cross-case analysis to draw comparisons and find patterns. Triangulation with secondary data was also conducted to increase the validity of the study. Such secondary data was analysed according to Garfinkel's (1967) idea of 'documentary method of interpretation'. This is a process in which a set of appearances, which may be objects, events, persons, or symbols, are taken as evidence of some underlying patterns. He suggests that the documentary method of interpretation is a feature of common sense, whereby the researcher engages in uncovering the processual activities of an organisation. The chapter proceeds with outlining the growth of the TTOs in Ireland, followed by presenting the political actors and the policy initiatives, before concluding with a critical reflection.

Growth of TTOs in Ireland

There are seven universities in Ireland and each has a TTO. These evolved from a structure called an Industry Liaison Office. Previous empirical studies of Ireland examined the role of the Industry Liaison Office in 1998 and found "little evidence of a proactive effort to work more closely with industry to widen the scope of the university's research results and to create new business employment" (Jones-Evans et al, 1999: 523). In a later study, Pandya and Cunningham (2000) singled out a lack of resources, both in terms of monetary and support structures, as a major inhibitor of technology transfer and commercialisation in Ireland. The most recent study of Ireland's universities has highlighted dramatic increases in spin-out activity at Ireland's universities.

Performance data is regularly collected and compared with information on international trends to set targets. According to a report from Enterprise Ireland, there has been a three-fold increase in the average number of spin-out companies from 2007- 2011. This rose from an average of seven per annum in the period 2002-2006 to an average of 24 per annum between 2007 and 2011. Furthermore, there has also been also been a 400pc increase in the amount of technologies licensed to companies by Higher Education Institutes (Enterprise Ireland 2011). From 2005 to 2010, invention disclosures increased from 135 to 431, patent applications increased from 83 to 101, licenses, options and assignments increased from 12 to 93, and the number of spin-outs increased from 5 to 31. As regards the destination of licenses, in 2007-2010 32% of licenses from universities and Public Research Organisations (PROs) went to spin-outs of these organisations. A further 29% went to Irish Small and Medium-Sized Enterprises (SMEs) with 35% of licenses going to multinational companies. The driving factor behind this growth is the Technology Transfer Strengthening Initiative (TTSI), set up by Enterprise Ireland in 2007 to increase the commercialisation of IP in Irish universities and to transfer this IP into industry.

A key element of the TTSI was the establishment of TTOs across the ten institutes, which include the seven Irish universities, University College Cork, University College Dublin, National University of Ireland Galway, National University of Ireland Maynooth, University of Limerick, Trinity College Dublin, and Dublin City University, plus Waterford Institute of Technology, Dublin Institute of Technology, and the Royal College of Surgeons in Ireland. The Technology Transfer Strengthening Initiative represents a coordinated national approach to technology transfer by Enterprise Ireland in partnership with the higher educational institutes in Ireland. In 2007, Enterprise Ireland established a new department called the Technology Transfer Exploitation Network to manage the 230 million euro Technology Transfer Strengthening Initiative. Enterprise Ireland engages with both industry and research, and thus is deemed the most appropriate agency to increase the levels, and relevance, of interaction between the two communities. In addition to managing the direct support to the Technology Transfer Offices in the higher educational institutes, the Technology Transfer Exploitation Network team in Enterprise Ireland delivers support, such as customised training events, in a focused, centralised way. The data also shows that the number of licenses issued to manufacturers or developers has risen significantly, from an average of 33 per year before the TTSI initiative to 102 in 2010 (Enterprise Ireland 2010).

Our interviews with TTOs revealed the type of activities TTOs engaged in to develop the offices. All TTOs recognised the need to build relationships with academic researchers, and our study found they did do so in different ways. These included the following initiatives.

Introduction Sessions: TTOs stressed the need to manage expectations of the academics in the processes. Efforts were made to engage from the very beginning of a researcher's career in the university, and so the TTO professionals attended the induction day of strategic research centres of their university. Here they made an introductory presentation, outlining the services they provide, thus putting steps in place to build relationships with academics from the very beginning: "It's really all about relationships" (TTO-I-A2). Other approaches included the TTO professional offering a starter pack for academics outlining the steps in the process, with the intention of managing expectations from the very beginning.

Evolution Over Time*:* as the TTOs evolve, the process of gaining commitment from the academics is becoming somewhat easier, and the academics are beginning to engage with the TTO. For example, one TTO Director claimed that, "recognition is growing on campus about IP" (TTO-I-D1). This supports the process as "academics are keen from a CV point of view" (TTO-I-D3). Interestingly, the older TTOs reminisce on the time spent in the initial phase building up an awareness of the TTO and building trust, "We spent an awful lot of time on the start in culture change and culture management; universities are typically open [to] innovation and there is thing called academic freedom, they like to do research" (TTO-I-C4). They spend less time on it now as a culture of entrepreneurship has been built on campus from serial entrepreneurs that have worked with the TTO, "If you get involved in one and it sells for lots of money, then people will say if that eejit can do it, I'll go off and do it. It's making it part of the culture, making it easier for people to do. The American bit of it's a badge of honour to have two or three failures before you have success. Over here, it is still if you fail everyone is going to make you stand in the corner and laugh at you. We have to move away from that nonsense" (TTO-I-C1). While the TTO personnel spend less time building the culture, they have put initiatives in place to sustain the culture, such as having a weekly drop-in clinic for consultation.

Purposeful relationships*:* one of the TTO Directors put initiatives in place to encourage the development of purposeful relationships. He placed the commercialisation specialists in with the academics in order to purposively build relationships. He also hired a former principal investigator from one of the leading research centres on campus, one of their former star scientists to build relationships and, "encourage them to look with their IP radar on and try to help them to identify what can be commercialised" (TTO-I-B2). Also the need to spend more time with academics was recognised, "Technology transfer is a contact sport, the more time you spend on the ground talking to researchers the more Invention Disclosures you get. They learn more about the process, there is a two-way flow of information, you learn about them, they learn about you and the market. It's a relationship, it's all about trust" (TTO-I-A2).

Application of Technology*:* TTOs also use high technology such as YouTube and LinkedIn to build legitimacy for the office and encourage a culture of entrepreneurship on campus.

Informal Approach: others took a more informal approach and focused on building informal relationships with the academics, to build trust. For example, one TTO chooses to conduct informal activities, "We spend a lot of time with academics. Not doing presentations, more having coffee with them, playing football with them, getting to know them, and getting the personal relationships going" (TTO-I-E1).

A previous empirical study of TTOs in Ireland highlighted the reactive nature of the TTOs in Ireland. "The situation in Ireland has been mainly reactive, unappreciated, under-resourced and centralised", (Jones-Evans et al, 1999: 542). By looking at how the TTOs were set up, the cultural challenges become apparent. The following is a quote from one of the leading stakeholders on how the offices were set up, which offers insight into how the offices may be reactive as they were not funded to recruit business development type roles.

Vignette #1:
"We looked to experts. By experts I mean practitioners from the States, from the UK and US, the main two places of where it happens. For example, Tom Hockaday from Cambridge, and those kind of people from the States and we used them to help us to determine how we would approach the issue. In particular, with the ratio of research funding and case person. So essentially we agreed to fund on the basis of business plans that the universities used to hire people and that has happened. We hired and funded case managers and some administration people, including in the larger universities a contract manager type of role. Now what we haven't funded, and deliberately so, is business development people...I mean people who are not good at tech transfer but people who work with companies. To use Enterprise Ireland jargon, a development advisor, a person who works with a company to try and get established. So we funded people for the actual tech transfer process."

In 2012, the government of Ireland announced they were extending the scheme and introducing a second round of support for the technology transfer system in Ireland. Quoting the head of technology transfer in Enterprise Ireland, "The extension of funding for a second phase of the Technology Transfer Strengthening Initiative will enable us to increase the flexibility and responsiveness of the system to make it a key resource for industry in Ireland" (O Morain 2012). The objectives of the second phase include the development of an efficient and flexible response to industry's requests for access to intellectual property and giving spin-out companies the best possible start. A new dimension to the initiative will be introduced which will create regional clusters sharing resources and expertise. The objective of such clusters is to deliver an enhanced service for industry in Ireland.

However in spite of the growth of TTOs, and the increased performance of the offices, the government agency does not posit the TTOs to be in a strategic role when it comes to driving industry engagement as is reflected in Vignette 2. However, the government agency senior manager did reflect on a potentially increasing strategic role for the TTO should the technology transfer activities of the universities grow in significance.

Vignette #2:
"In many case they don't have the status. The real power in the universities is with the academics so the VP of Research and Provost, and the TTO would be seen as part of the administration of university as opposed to the core. I think the people in charge in some universities are gaining stature by virtue of being there and being good people. Their personal influence is increasing. But I don't think the office would be up there in the middle of the debate on strategy. The university leaders correctly see teaching as number one, then research relating to teaching, and then there is the third leg which is developing. When you think about where university is going, or graduate intake, in terms of calibre you wouldn't normally think of TTO having a role in that. It's only if the third leg increases, they will get more strategic. Right now, the TTO itself wouldn't get enough visibility for strategic purposes."

Interestingly, a representative from another government agency argues that TTOs need to be both strategic and operational in their role. This is interesting as it defends a strategic position for the TTO, but it also offers an insight into the potential conflict of interest amongst the differing government agencies, thus heightening the complexity in which the TTO operates as a boundary spanner amongst these conflicting stakeholders.

Vignette #3:
"They have to be strategic and operational. They are very operational in process. In terms of day to day activities, it is an operational thing, they have to have processes, procedures, mechanisms, you know, and use all the various tools at their disposal to make sure that happens... But they do have a very strategic role internally because they are at the interface between the research in academic institution and the outside world and you know, so they will understand what it is that the people on the inside need to do to satisfy the people on the outside, and they understand the frustrations and challenges that the people face on the inside when they are faced with demands from people on the outside... They are there to service. It's like the shop window of the university, the industry are the customers who come in to buy something and the researchers are the suppliers to fill the shelves so they have to manage the internal and the external relationships. The TTO needs to understand that."

Political Actors

There are a number of different public institutions and statutory bodies which play important roles in the development of Ireland's technology transfer policy. The first four - Forfás, Industrial Development Authority, Science Foundation Ireland and Enterprise Ireland - are the responsibility of the Government Department of Enterprise, Trade and Employment. The other two – the research councils and the Higher Education Authority – are overseen by the Department of Education and Science.

Forfás: Established in 1994, Forfás is the body in which the legal powers of the State for the promotion and development of industry, science, and technology are largely vested. It is the national policy and advisory board for enterprise, trade, science, technology, and innovation. It provides the Department of Enterprise, Trade and Employment (DETE) and other stakeholders with analyses, advice and support on issues related to enterprise, trade, science, technology, and innovation. It also provides administrative and/or research support to a number of independent bodies including: Advisory Council for Science, Technology and Innovation, Expert Group on Future Skills Needs (EGFSN), Management Development Council (MDC), National Competitiveness Council (NCC), and the Small Business Forum. It also hosts the Office of the Chief Scientific Adviser to Government.

Industrial Development Authority (IDA) Ireland: IDA Ireland is a state-sponsored agency funded primarily through Government grant aid. Broadly, the key objective of the IDA is to attract and retain foreign direct investment (FDI) in Ireland, and in doing so contribute to Ireland's economic development. Specifically, it works to develop the strong base of over 1,000 overseas companies already located in Ireland and also to attract new investment. IDA success to date in attracting inward investment is a major driving force behind the growth of the Irish economy.

Science Foundation Ireland (SFI): Science Foundation Ireland (SFI), the National Foundation for Excellence in Scientific Research, was established in 2000 and is modelled on the National Science Foundation in America. SFI is responsible for the management, allocation, disbursement, and evaluation of expenditure for investment in the academic researchers and research teams who are most likely to generate new knowledge, leading edge technologies, and competitive enterprises in the fields underpinning two broad areas: biotechnology, and information and communications technology.

Research Councils: To support an increased policy focus on research and development, two core research councils were established. The Irish Research Council for Humanities and Social Sciences (IRCHSS) was constituted in 2000, and the Irish Research Council for Science Engineering and Technology was in 2001. Both research councils operate and manage numerous research schemes, such as graduate and post-graduate fellowships, and research grants for new and established academic researchers.

HEA: The Higher Education Authority is a statutory body with responsibility for the planning and policy development for higher education and research in Ireland. The HEA has wide advisory powers throughout the whole of the third-level education sector. In addition, it serves as the funding authority for the universities and institutes of technology. One of the key research funding programmes administered by the HEA is the Programme for Research in Third-Level Institutions (PRTLI), which was launched in 1998. It has invested €1.2 billion to date over five funding cycles in strengthening national research capabilities via investment in human and physical infrastructure. The aim of the programme is to advance Ireland in its bid to establish itself internationally as a premier location for carrying out world-class research and development in all academic disciplines. The PRTLI awards are evaluated by an international panel of distinguished researchers and scholars on the basis of excellence in: strategic planning and focus, inter-institutional collaboration, research quality, and impact of research on teaching and learning.

Enterprise Ireland: Enterprise Ireland (EI) provides intense support for Irish-owned businesses (employing between ten and 250) involved in manufacturing and internationally traded services. They also support start-ups and micro businesses (less than 10 employees) in the same sector, provided they have the potential to achieve rapid growth and international expansion. These later businesses are referred to as High Potential Start-Ups (HPSUs), of which about 70 start-ups receive Enterprise Ireland support each year. In particular, EI is a government agency responsible for the development and promotion of the technology transfer system in Ireland as part of the Technology Transfer Strengthening Initiative. As part of its commitment to facilitating the commercialisation of research, it financially supports the academic researchers to commercialise their work and to link with Irish companies through a number of funding schemes including a Commercialisation Fund. Table 9.1 outlines the initiatives introduced by Enterprise Ireland to support researcher engagement with industry. This funding is critical to enabling TTOs to conduct their business. Also the funding enables the academics to get involved.

Table 9.1: Enterprise Ireland Initiatives supporting university-industry engagement

Proof of Concept	➢ €50,000-€100,000 per project ➢ 12 months duration ➢ Staff on contract welcome to apply ➢ 3 Calls for Proposals per year
Technology Development	➢ €100,000 - €400,000 per project ➢ 18-36 months duration ➢ Staff on contract welcome to apply ➢ 3 Calls for Proposals per year
Innovation Partnerships	➢ This programme supports collaborative research projects between Irish HEIs and companies. The financial support in this case is provided to the college. The proposal process and administration of the project is managed by the participating institute
Innovation Vouchers	➢ SMEs spend their €5,000 vouchers in HEIs in exchange for innovative solutions to small business challenges. There is also the option for groups of 10 companies to apply for a 'pooled innovation voucher' up to the value of €50,000 to spend with one research team
Commercial Case Feasibility Support	➢ Funding support of up to €15,000 can be obtained by researchers in partnership with their Technology Transfer Office or equivalent office for a short Feasibility Project to scope and develop their commercial case for their technology in advance of submitting a Commercialisation Fund Support application to the programme

Commercialisation Fund Support	➢ Funding Support is available for projects that address a "gap or need in the market" by developing innovative technologies that will ideally be ready for licensing to Irish industry or may form the basis of a new start up in 2-5 years. It is recognised however that some technologies may need a longer time to get to market than others. Proposals from all disciplines in the fields of Science and Engineering with costs ranging from €80,000 to €350,000 will be accepted

Source: Enterprise Ireland Website 2013:
http://www.enterprise-ireland.com/en/funding-

Such funding responsibility was recognised by a senior representative from Enterprise Ireland as outlined in Vignette #4 below. They funded the offices in the beginning but now their role has evolved as they fund the translation of research from universities out into industry.

Vignette # 4:
"We have been involved in the developing of the offices…Our role has to be very clearly in the translation. In other words, we have nothing to do with protection. It's about being a player in supporting the structure which facilitates the interaction between industry and universities. Funding collaborative research, and funding conferences to allow interactions to take place…I see us as an investor and a player in building relationships. Not the running TTO, that's TTO business. Our concern is with how we can help the offices with a single point into industry."

We questioned the TTOs' relationship with Enterprise Ireland in our study, and we found a varied response – from being supporters, barriers, and pawns. Each of these will be described below.

Supporter: Some TTOs recognise Enterprise Ireland as supporters of their role in the university-industry technology transfer process. One TTO Director argued that Enterprise Ireland – as funders of the process – are the key drivers of the process and thus are key influencers in the process. They view their role to be supportive of the TTOs and steering the process in the right direction, "all their programs are directed at the right thing and they are throwing money at the right stuff" (TTO-I-G2). Similarly, TTO professionals argue that, in the contentious environment in which the TTOs operate amongst the multitude of conflicted stakeholders, Enterprise Ireland can indeed be very supportive of the direction and legitimacy of the TTO, "…they can be your best friends in the world. Academics have own agenda, businesses have own agenda. Enterprise Ireland aims to support us and bridge the gap" (TTO-I-A2).

Barrier: However, while some of the TTOs commended Enterprise Ireland for being the drivers of the process and supportive of the TTO, some interpreted their role to be at times the reason behind slowing up the process. A TTO blamed the bureaucratic nature of the organisation as the source of the barrier, "I find them to be a bit of a barrier to progressing things, a bit bureaucratic" (TTO-I-D2). Similarly, they claim that mismanagement of the direction and skewed expectations of the outcomes of the system are the reasons behind the stakeholder being a barrier to the TTO's strategy, "Part of the problem is that EI don't know what they want, and that is part of the evolution of tech transfer in Ireland" (TTO-I-F3). TTO professionals expressed concern about the consequences of not funding the system, and how the progress they have made will have been in vain, "It's not like a light bulb, it's not like you can switch if off and then back on and everything will be back up and running…If you switch the research funding off, the Principal Investigators will go and they won't come back" (TTO-I-D2).

Pawn: Interestingly, one TTO Director recognised that Enterprise Ireland are not to blame and are mere pawns in the game, "I think Enterprise Ireland recognises that this is a long term game. A lot of stuff is out of their control. If they are given the budget they can continue, if they are not given the budget to fund this then the whole thing could be shut down" (I-TTO-B1). Such uncertainty contributes to the tensions in the technology transfer system in Ireland.

Policy Initiatives

Numerous policy reports have promoted closer links between industry and the third level sector. These include 'Building Ireland's Knowledge Economy - the Irish action plan for promoting investment in R&D in 2010' (Forfás 2004) and 'Promoting Enterprise-Higher Education Relationships' (Forfás 2007). Table 9.2 outlines other policy initiatives. These policy reports all contributed to shaping the principal document for placing an importance on the role of the university in economic development.

Table 9.2: Policy Initiatives

Title of Report	Recommendations of Report
White Paper on Industrial Policy, 1984	➢ Highlighted need to increase technology transfer from Irish HEIs to industry
Programme for Action in Education, 1984-1987	➢ Highlighted need to increase technology transfer from Irish HEIs to industry
Barriers to Research and Consultancy in the Higher Education Sector, 1996	➢ Need to strengthen the interface between HEIs and industry based on application and exploitation of scientifically derived knowledge ➢ Creation of a climate in which academics will be able and willing to interact with industry ➢ Establishment of new institutional mechanisms and structures at college and national level to facilitate the development of links with industry
Tierney Report, 1995	➢ Curriculum development and research endeavour be linked to the needs of businesses in Ireland to the greatest extent possible
Building Ireland's Smart Economy, 2004	➢ Significant emphasis on the economic return for the major taxpayer funding of research
Strategy for Science, Innovation and Technology, 2006-2013	➢ Strategic priority to developing third mission of universities and the strengthening of TTOs
Intellectual Property Protocol: Putting public research to work for Ireland	➢ Standardising national procedures and model contracts

While these reports played a role in creating an ethos for closer industry-academic linkages and building a foundation for university-industry technology transfer, the Strategy for Science, Technology and Innovation (SSTI) (2006 – 2013) represented the government's comprehensive plan to guide Ireland into becoming a knowledge-driven economy. The overarching vision of the SSTI is to ensure that, "Ireland by 2013 will be internationally renowned for the excellence of its research and will be to the forefront in generating and using new knowledge for economic and social progress within an innovation driven culture". As a result of this strategy, research commercialisation and technology transfer are emerging as new missions for Irish universities. On the input side within HEIs, this means investing in academic research; and on the output side, this has led to a strengthening of Technology Transfer Offices in order to exploit IP for commercial gains. HEI-industry relations have many different facets, and knowledge is transferred via many different channels. One of these channels is the Technology Transfer Office; these have been set up with the aim of creating more supportive framework conditions for closer collaboration and more intense communication between HEIs and industry.

Following on from this policy, the Government published its 'framework for sustainable economic renewal', entitled *Building Ireland's Smart Economy*. The introduction explains that the framework "sets out the Government's vision for the next phase of Ireland's economic development". A significant part of the focus is the encouragement of research and development, and entrepreneurship. The Innovation Task Force was appointed to advise the government on how to turn Ireland into an international innovation hub and to support the development of a smart economy. The Task Force examined options to increase levels of innovation and the rates of commercialisation of research and development on a national basis - with a view to accelerating the growth of indigenous enterprise and to attracting new knowledge-intensive direct investment, building on the existing Government Strategy for Science, Technology and Innovation (SSTI). Interestingly, membership of the Task Force includes representatives from the private sector, Third Level Education, and relevant Government Departments and Agencies in an effort to establish closer linkages with industry and the third level sector. The importance of university research has continued to grow as Ireland tries to close the "innovation gap" between itself and other major industrialised nations. In 2010, the Innovation Task Force Report recommended "making it easier for the entrepreneur" and recommended "standardising national procedures and model contracts". The Task Force also suggested developing a national IP Protocol which establishes "ground rules" around ownership and access to all state-supported IP. The Task Force also suggested establishing a national office for IP generated in the higher education system, which would be a single point of contact for entrepreneurs. An outcome of this initiative was the setting up of Ireland's central Technology Transfer Office (the 'cTTO') as outlined in the policy report 'Intellectual Property Protocol: Putting public research to work for Ireland' (2012). The objective for the cTTO is to work closely with the Technology Transfer Offices in individual universities, sharing good practice and ensuring consistency between different elements of the technology transfer system and a consistent adoption and interpretation of policy by all stakeholders.

Concluding Comments

To conclude the chapter, the following observations can be made from our comprehensive analysis. Firstly, Ireland has long encouraged closer relationships between industry and universities, with relevant policy documents dating back to 1984. It can be surmised that the Irish policy is positioning universities as critical ingredients in the nation's ability to remain competitive. However, policy initiatives had largely focused on the supply side with increased funding for basic research and a lack of attention to the demand side to spur innovation and commercialisation. It could be argued that government policies treated technology transfer as a by-product of other goals, and as such they failed to focus effectively on the commercialisation process. However, the policy initiative which has had the highest impact on the technology transfer system in Ireland is the Technology Transfer Strengthening Initiative. Since the introduction of the policy initiative in 2007, TTO activities have dramatically increased in Ireland. Furthermore the TTOs themselves have successfully introduced a number of activities to engage the academics in the technology transfer process. Finally, whilst the Government is a key actor in the technology transfer process, there are differing responses to how the TTOs view the contribution of the Government agency. On investigation of how TTOs interpret the Government intervention in the process, the response differed, with some interpreting the role to be one of the key supporters whilst others deem them to be barriers. Such a finding reveals the complex, challenging environment in which the Irish TTOs operate. It also sheds light on the embryonic nature of the TTOs in Ireland.

Acknowledgement

The author gratefully acknowledges the financial support from the Irish Government's Programme for Research in Third Level Institutions (PRTLI 5) project grant entitled 'Innovation Policy Simulation for the Smart Economy (IPSE)'.

References

Blumenstyk, Goldie. 2010. "Ireland Looks To Academe To Re-Ignite Its Economy". The Chronicle Of Higher Education. Accessed March 15. http://Chronicle.Com/Article/Ireland-Looks-To-Academe -To/125447.

Eisenhardt, Kathleen. 1989. "Building Theories from Case Study Research". Academy Of Management Review, 14 (4), 532-550.

Enterprise Ireland. 2012. Inventions And Innovations, The Positive Impact Of Ideas From Research On Irish Industry And Society.

European Commission. 2013. Innovation Union Scorecard 2013.

Forfás. 2004. From Research To The Marketplace: Patent Registration and Technology Transfer In Ireland. Dublin.

—. 2004. Building Ireland's Knowledge Economy - The Irish Action Plan For Promoting Investment In R&D To 2010. Dublin.

—. 2007. Promoting Enterprise-Higher Education Relationships. Dublin, Forfás And The Advisory Council For Science, Technology And Innovation.

—. 2013. Survey Of Research And Development In The Higher Education Sector 2010/2011.

Garfinkel, Harold. 1967. Studies In Ethnomethodology. Eaglewood Cliffs, Nj: Prentice Hall.

Innovation Taskforce. 2012. Intellectual Property Protocol: Putting Public Research To Work For Ireland.

Jones-Evans, Dylan, Klofsten, Magnus., Andersson, Ewa, and Pandya, Dipti. 1999. "Creating A Bridge Between University And Industry In Small European Countries: The Role Of Industrial Liaison Office". R&D Management, 29(1), 47-56.

Link, Al., Siegel, Don, Bozeman, Barry, 2007. "An Empirical Analysis Of The Propensity Of Academics To Engage In Informal University Technology Transfer". Industrial And Corporate Change. 16 (4), 641–655.

OECD. 2006 Assessing And Expanding The Science And Technology Base, OECD Paris.

Pandya, Dipti and Cunningham, James. 2000. A Review Of Issues With Respect To The Commercialisation Of Non-Commissioned Research In Ireland. Dublin: Commercialisation Of Research Taskforce, Irish Council For Science, Technology And Innovation.

Sanders, Carrie and Miller, Fiona. 2010. "Reframing Norms: Boundary Maintenance And Partial Accommodations In The Work Of Academic Technology Transfer". Science And Public Policy, 37, 689-701.

Siegel, Don, Waldman, David and Link, Al. 2003. "Assessing The Impact

Of Organizational Practices On The Relative Productivity Of University Technology Transfer Offices: An Exploratory Study". Research Policy, 32, 27-48.
Siegel, Don, Veugelers, Reinhilde, and Wright, Mike. 2007. "Technology Transfer Offices And Commercialization Of University Intellectual Property: Performance And Policy Implications". Oxford Review Of Economic Policy, 23(4), 640-660.

CHAPTER TEN

ADDITIONALITY OF INCUBATOR SUPPORT ON NETWORKS OF UNIVERSITY SPIN-OUT FIRMS

NOLA HEWITT-DUNDAS, COLM BURNS AND GARY CHAPMAN

Introduction

Government policy to promote a knowledge-based economy (Kitagawa and Robertson, 2012) has led to a growing emphasis on promoting research excellence in the university sector in conjunction with efforts to translate this into economic and social benefit. Government policy has been instrumental in this – specifically through encouraging the commercialisation of research. In the US, the Bayh-Dole Patent and Trademark Amendments Act (1980) made two significant changes: first, it authorised US universities to retain rights to–and license inventions resulting from–federally-funded research; second, it assigned ownership of patents or Intellectual Property (IP) created within a university to that university, as opposed to the inventor (Hoppe and Ozdenoren, 2001). While most European countries subsequently adopted similar legislation to the USA's, variations exist. For example, Italian policy makers have sought to encourage commercialisation of university research by shifting IP ownership to inventors (Geuna and Rossi, 2011). In other countries, including Ireland, ambiguity in IP policy means that ownership of intellectual property rights (IPRs) and patents by the inventor or by their employers remains unclear and inconsistent across the sector (Patents Act, 1992).

Beyond policies to stimulate directly the commercialisation of research through IP, in some countries, such as the UK, cuts in public funding for universities, combined with a meritocratic system whereby universities compete for funds, have left universities less well-resourced than previously (Hewitt-Dundas, 2012; Harrison and Leitch, 2010; Siegel et al, 2003; Etzkowitz et al, 2000). Indeed suggestions that future public funding of university research may be contingent on the potential industry benefits, or university-industry links stemming from research (Florida, 1999), are likely to encourage universities to forge an even stronger commercial focus.

Universities, in general, have responded to these legislative and policy changes by placing a greater emphasis on the protection of University-based intellectual property and the pursuit of commercially-oriented activity, metrics, and outcomes (Grimaldi and Grandi, 2005; O'Shea et al, 2005, Owen-Smith, 2003). This has extended beyond private ownership of IP and a more proactive IP development and exploitation strategy (Siegel et al 2003; Lockett and Wright, 2005) to also include greater business engagement (OECD 1999, Chatterton and Goddard 2000, Holland 2001). This engagement occurs through various channels including collaborative and contract research, consultancy, the use of facilities and equipment as well as professional education and training (Hewitt-Dundas 2012). Ultimately, universities have sought to generate wider economic and social benefit through the education of students, through knowledge and technology transfer activities involving cooperation with external organisations, and through the protection and subsequent exploitation of IPRs. However, it is perhaps the protection of IPRs and their exploitation through university spin-out firms that have received most attention by academics, technology transfer professionals and policy makers.

University Spin-outs

University Spin-outs (USOs) are defined as 'new ventures that are dependent upon licensing or assignment of [an] institution's intellectual property for initiation' (Lockett and Wright, 2005: 1044-1045). Siegel et al (2003) point to the relatively recent shift in emphasis from exploitation of university IP through licensing models to a focus on spin-out activity. However, the perception remains that research commercialisation through spin-outs will tend to occur only when other routes such as licensing have been exhausted (Wright et al, 2008). Indeed, in the early 2000s only 21 per cent of US university technology transfer offices explicitly mentioned new firm creation in their mission statements (Markman et al, 2005), and only 52 per cent of UK universities spun out any firms in 2005 (UNICO, 2006).

More recently, increasing rates of USO formation have been reported (Fini et al, 2011; Mustar et al, 2008; Clarysse et al, 2005; Markman et al, 2005) – with a growth rate in the UK of 46 percent between 2008 and 2011, or an average annual increase of 15.3 percent (HESA, 2012). This growth has been attributed to a number of factors (Fini et al, 2011; Mustar et al, 2008; Clarysse et al, 2005; Markman et al, 2005) reflecting the changing policy environment discussed above.

First, increasing recognition of the central role of knowledge in economic development and of its monetary value has created an impetus for producers of research to reap its financial reward (Harrison and Leitch, 2010; Van Geenhuizen and Soetanto, 2009; EU, 2003). In this regard, USOs represent a means of transferring and profiting from university knowledge (Ndonzuau et al, 2002). A recent example of this is the 2011 initiative in New York City to incentivise universities to develop their science and engineering infrastructure with a view to stimulating 400 USOs within 30 years (Bloomberg, 2011).

Second, some authors link increased rates of spin-out to researchers' and universities' decreasing reliance on patenting as their primary means of commercialising university research (Geuna and Rossi, 2011; Siegel et al, 2007). In other words, universities have expanded the channels through which they attempt to exploit their IP. Third, and perhaps most significantly, in recent years there has been an 'explosion of policy' (O'Shea et al, 2008:654) in the US and in many EU countries, prompting universities to demonstrate their contribution to national and regional economies (Huggins and Johnston, 2010; Wright et al, 2008; Grimaldi and Grandi, 2005; Lockett and Wright, 2005; O'Shea et al, 2005; Siegel et al, 2003; Mian, 1997), with spin-out activity being an important channel for this[1].

While there is agreement that spin-out activity as a whole has increased, its distribution remains highly skewed: in the UK and US, the majority of USOs originate from a small number of universities (O'Shea et al, 2005; Lockett and Wright, 2005). In addition, a key aspiration underpinning public policy around university commercialisation is to emulate archetypes of USO creation like MIT and Stanford; but these success stories are likely to be embedded in and dependent on the environment from which they

---

[1] It is interesting to note that developing nations and less favoured regions have seen similar prioritisation of commercial university activity, mainly with the goal of combatting poverty and high unemployment (Etzkowitz et al, 2005).

emerged, and it is unlikely that their structure and success can simply be replicated in different contexts (Harrison and Leitch, 2010; Huggins and Johnston, 2010; Clarysse et al, 2005). Gilsing et al. (2010: 12) support this perspective, arguing that public policy to promote spin-out activity has been based on 'policy fashions rather than empirical evidence'. A 2003 UK Treasury report also raised doubts about the proliferation of USOs, suggesting that too many USOs were being created in circumstances where other avenues for technology transfer would be more appropriate (Lambert, 2003) with Wright et al. (2008) suggesting that a shift in policy emphasis away from USO and towards start-ups may be needed.

Alongside debates on the appropriateness for universities of alternative commercialisation channels, concerns have also been raised about the high failure rates of USOs – estimated at around 30 per cent – (Targeting Innovation, 2008; Rothaermel and Thursby, 2005b) and no-to-low growth among those which survive compared to other new technology based firms (Harrison and Leitch, 2010; Van Geenhuizen and Soetanto, 2009; Lockett and Wright, 2005; Degroof and Roberts, 2004; Rice, 2002; Dahlstrand, 1997). These concerns are compounded further by lower than anticipated financial returns to universities and regions from USOs (Colombo and Piva, 2012; Leitch and Harrison, 2005). As a result, questions have been raised about policy makers' and universities' sustained commitment and investment in USOs (Gilsing et al, 2010; Schwartz and Hornych, 2010; Mustar et al, 2008; Geuna and Nesta, 2006; Florida, 1999). For this reason we consider briefly the rationale for intervention – whether by government, private sector investment or by universities – in supporting the formation and growth of USOs.

Case for Intervention

Intervention is most commonly discussed in terms of a government's role in the market where its justification is based on market imperfections which will remain uncorrected in the absence of intervention. In the same way, other actors may also intervene to overcome sub-optimal market conditions. In the case of USOs, this intervention might take various forms including direct fiscal incentives to support the development of USOs, legislative and regulatory changes, e.g. rules on disclosures, and IP requirements to have knowledge brokering activities which seek to overcome information asymmetries in the market. Ultimately where market and/or system failures exist, these will result in an under-investment in and underproduction of R&D and innovation relative to the socially desirable level (Martin and Scott, 2000). Both of these failures are now considered in more detail.

For USOs market failure arises mainly due to leakages from imperfect patent protection and knowledge spillovers that prevent a firm which is undertaking R&D and innovation from fully appropriating the benefits arising from these activities (Knockaert et al, 2014). In addition, market failure may also be evident in investor short-termism, information asymmetries, and excessive risk associated with new technologies (Bleda and Rio, 2013). As a result USOs often struggle to access finance to fund their activities (Mustar et al, 2008) with this impeding USO development by preventing them from fully appropriating their intellectual property and depriving them of the finance needed to fund core activities (Martin and Scott, 2000; Dodgson et al, 2011).

Beyond market failures, USO development may also be inhibited by system failures. The systems perspective recognises that innovation is increasingly an interactive process, with a firm's innovative success dependent on collaborating with numerous other actors and institutions (Woolthuis et al, 2005). Through collaboration, firms acquire new ideas and access new resources and expertise, integrating this external knowledge with their internal knowledge to enhance the knowledge base from which they innovate (Lichtenthaler, 2011). These exchanges are facilitated by institutions and the USO's networks and capabilities with system failure occurring when imperfections that inhibit collaboration exist (Woolthuis et al, 2005). System failure may be evident at a macro-level in terms of institutional and infrastructural failure, while at the micro- (firm-) level it may take the form of capability and network failure (Weber and Rohracher, 2012).

Infrastructural failure relates to a lack of physical and knowledge infrastructure to facilitate collaboration and knowledge generation (e.g. information technology). Institutional failure falls into two sub-categories: hard and soft. Hard institutional failures relate to the absence of or shortcomings with current laws and regulations for innovation and R&D activities. Soft institutional failures, on the other hand, relate to issues and problems with the culture and values of society toward innovative activities (e.g. risk averse). These failures inhibit innovation generally, but particularly within USOs due to the often radicalness of their technology and their reliance on intellectual property for value creation (Wright et al, 2004). More detrimental to USOs, however, is network and capability failure, given that deficiencies in social capital and inadequate internal capabilities are key inhibitors of USO development (Vohora et al, 2004).

Capability failure occurs when USOs lack the necessary capabilities to learn and absorb new knowledge for innovation, which inhibits their efforts to adapt to new and changing environments (Weber and Rohracher, 2012). Given the importance of knowledge acquisition and integration throughout the USO development process (Vohora et al, 2004), capability failure may be particularly detrimental. New knowledge is identified and complementary resources, ideas, and expertise are acquired through the USO's network (Lichtenthaler, 2011) with network failures occurring in two ways: strong failures, where the closeness of ties results in lock-in, and weak failures, where the USOs lack linkages with other actors (Woolthuis et al, 2005), preventing them from accessing external knowledge. For USOs, as for market failures, system failures – particularly network failure – significantly impede USO development.

Interventions to overcome market failures and specifically access to finance have been studied elsewhere (Mustar et al, 2008), yet much less well understood are the effectiveness of interventions to overcome system failures. When 'treated', USOs are more successful and sustainable post intervention; then intervention is deemed to have been effective. This may be assessed in terms of USOs overcoming financing constraints and leveraging additional support (input additionality), increasing their revenue generation and speed to market (output additionality), or improving their networks via leveraging their social capital (behavioural additionality).

An important way in which intervention has occurred to support the formation and development of USOs has been through the establishment of incubators. With estimated average capital investment costs for an incubator of around €3.7m and annual operating costs of €0.48m (see Dee et al, 2011, 48) it is critically important to understand the additionality that university incubators (UIs) generate for USOs (Bruneel et al, 2012). While evidence supports the positive influence of R&D and innovation subsidies (Falk, 2007; Breschi and Lissoni, 2009) and technology intermediaries (Knockaert et al, 2014) on firm networking and cooperation, few studies have examined the influence of incubator support on USO networks, from an additionality perspective. Evaluation is necessary to understand if incubators achieve this, generate value for money or induce other unintended or unanticipated benefits (Woolthuis et al, 2005; Georghiou, 1998).

University incubators

Incubators are commonly defined as 'a property-based organisation focused on accelerating the growth and success of entrepreneurial companies through the provision of business support, resources, and services' (Markman et al, 2008: 1406). University incubators are incubators located on university campuses, specialising in the commercialisation of university technology (Allen and McCluskey, 1990) and typically hosting high-tech USOs. Beyond offering tenant firms suitably equipped business premises at attractive rates, they also offer services such as 'coaching, mentoring, consulting, general advice, motivation, business introductions, technical appraisal and business network access' (Ahmad and Ingle, 2011:629).

In contrast to property-based UIs (Markman et al, 2008: 1406, Durão et al, 2005), a 'non-incubator' approach to the commercialisation of USOs exists. Here, 'universities without a central incubator building supply incubation support to spin-offs located at distributed places on-campus and off-campus' (Van Geenhuizen and Soetanto, 2009: 671). Evidence from the Netherlands and Italy suggests that UIs with 'no building space and physical facilities' are common (Colombo and Delmastro, 2002: 1107; see also Van Geenhuizen and Soetanto, 2009), yet this model of university commercialisation support is discussed much less frequently. The validity of the non-incubator approach to supporting USOs is further evidenced by references to 'virtual' incubators (Carayannis and von Zedtwitz, 2005; Durão et al, 2005; Hackett and Dilts, 2004). For example, OuluTech, the commercialisation support unit at the University of Oulu, epitomises this 'non-UI' model, spinning out 10-20 firms per year and being a main contributor to the 'Oulu phenomenon' (an exemplar of regional development in Finland), but without a physical incubator (Rasmussen et al, 2006).

Table 10.1 presents a synthesis of the main characteristics of the University Incubator (UI) model to USO support and the Non-University Incubator (Non-UI) model.

Table 10.1: Characteristics of UI and Non-UI USO support models

USO Characteristics	University Incubator (UI) model	Non-University IncubaNotor (Non-UI) model
Location of USO	USOs located on-campus in university-administered premises	USOs located in off-campus premises not administered by university or on-campus in academic offices/labs
USO facilities and equipment	Shared start-up infrastructure and services (phone, heating, reception, meeting rooms, etc.) included	USOs source, install and pay full rate for equipment, internet access, overheads, etc.
Links to University	USOs can use university address	USOs can use university address
Business Support Services	Business support services offered to USOs (e.g. mentoring, advice, business network access)	Business support services offered to USOs (e.g. mentoring, advice, business network access)
Development Period	USOs have limited time period before 'graduation' (i.e. leaving UI) is required: typically 2-5 years	No formal 'graduation' policy for USOs

Source: Hewitt-Dundas and Burns (2015)

To date empirical evidence generally points to a net positive effect of incubators on job growth, innovation, and inter-organisational links of new firms (Colombo and Delmastro, 2002). However, other research (Tamásy, 2007) suggests that the probability of survival, business growth, or innovative activity among incubated and non-incubated firms is not significantly different. Further, although a number of studies have examined the effect of incubators on the growth of USOs, a key limitation of many of these studies has been that they have looked only at tenants in the absence of a counterfactual scenario where USOs are formed and grow in the absence of an incubator: the non-UI model. For universities seeking to support USOs, these findings create uncertainty as to the anticipated benefits to be derived from establishing an incubator facility with its associated costs.

Incubators and USOs

While various studies have examined how incubators enhance the internal resources and capabilities of USOs, more limited evidence exists on the configuration of networks for USOs located in UIs and their subsequent access to external resources. Similar to the perceived role of TTOs, incubators act as 'intermediary – or mediating – organisation(s), helping newly founded and young ventures to establish cooperative relationships with a broad range of economic actors' (Schwartz and Hornych, 2010: 485). Through these cooperative relationships, start-up firms acquire access to resources and capabilities essential to survival and growth (Aernoudt, 2004; Hansen et al, 2000). Ahuja (2000, 319) suggests that these external resources that firms access may 'not be available for purchase in factor markets and require time to build up' yet be very important in creating value for the business. For example, other empirical research finds that 'network structure differentially influences the flow of financial resources, capabilities and opportunities' to businesses (Ayra and Lin 2007, 698). Therefore, network structure and the position of a business within this network will influence its behaviour and performance (Mizruchi and Marquis, 2006). This suggests that understanding the potential effect of UIs on network structure of USOs may be central to appreciating the resources and capabilities that USOs access by being based in a UI, and, consequently, how this contributes to USO growth.

Where UIs facilitate network ties, these - anticipated positive - externalities may be important not only in supporting USO growth but much earlier in the USO process by (i) bridging the gap between the conception of a business idea and its actual "instantiation" (Hackett and Dilts, 2004: 69), and (ii) helping start-ups (and specifically USOs) to survive the 'valley of death' between public funding of basic research and private equity funding for a viable business (Barr et al, 2009: 371; Mustar et al, 2008). This suggests the need for a process view of USOs as opposed to the cross-sectional analysis that typifies most empirical studies in adopting a "snapshot approach" and overlooking the dynamic process inherent in the creation and evolution of a spin-out firm (Mustar et al, 2006: 295). Rasmussen (2011: 457) therefore concludes that examining USOs through stage models is appropriate for identifying "the challenges and problems to be dealt with at different times in the [spin-out] process". In addition, consideration of the way in which UIs contribute to the formation of USO networks overcomes the criticism that incubators have been studied as a 'black box' (see Clarysse et al, 2005; Mian, 1997) with a lack of insight into what this process might comprise (Scillitoe and Chakrabarti, 2010; Hackett and Dilts, 2004).

While various spin-out process models have been proposed (see Clarysse et al, 2005; Vohora et al, 2004; Ndonzuau et al, 2002), there has been a lack of process-oriented empirical research (Rasmussen, 2011; Mustar et al, 2006; Grandi and Grimaldi, 2005; Lockett and Wright, 2005; Wright et al, 2004)[2]. Despite these different conceptualisations of the spin-out process, significant commonality exists with most highlighting distinct stages where the commercial opportunity arising from research is identified and framed, IP assessment/protection is undertaken, the USO is chosen over alternative commercial channels, and there is the acquisition of resources/investment.

One of the most comprehensive conceptualisations and widely cited models of the USO process is Vohora et al.'s (2004) 'critical junctures' model. In this model, five distinct stages are identified in the development of USOs with four critical junctures between these stages being: (i) opportunity recognition, (ii) entrepreneurial commitment, (iii) threshold of credibility, and (iv) threshold of sustainability. This model offers several distinct benefits over other models. First, it provides clear thresholds between one phase and the next. For example, it is only when management is committed to exploiting commercial opportunity through a USO that 'pre-organisation' activities such as strategy formulation and resource acquisition can begin. Second, each phase of the model involves revisiting preceding phases in light of newly acquired social capital, resources, or capabilities. The implication is that each spin-out phase is distinct but not detached from preceding phases: there is built-in scope for 'feedback' to decisions and actions taken during earlier phases, addressing criticisms that stage models tend to be too rigid and linear[3] (Rasmussen, 2011; Neergaard, 2003). Third, to progress beyond each juncture, USOs need to overcome their 'deficiency in social capital, resource weaknesses and inadequate internal capabilities' (Vohora et al, 2004: 168). As such, a process perspective to USO development precludes a 'blinkered' process orientation – where no variables are incorporated into the model – while also reflecting the high fluidity inherent in USO development.

---

[2] Exceptions to this include Rasmussen (2011) and Van Geenhuizen and Soetanto (2009).

[3] Other work shares this notion of spin-out as a process of resource acquisition and reconfiguration (McAdam and McAdam, 2008; Lockett and Wright, 2005; Druilhe and Garnsey, 2004).

Networks in USO development

Although support to USOs either through the UI or the Non-UI model (Table 1) may take various forms, here our primary interest is in the network ties that USOs form in these different university environments and the effect of these ties on USOs, especially at the early stages of the business development process (Vohora et al. 2004). As outlined above, the role of UIs in supporting USOs may be particularly important in (i) bridging the gap between the conception of a business idea and its actual “instantiation” (Hackett and Dilts, 2004: 69) and (ii) helping start-ups (and specifically USOs) to survive the ‘valley of death’ between public funding of basic research and private equity funding for a viable business (Barr et al, 2009: 371; Mustar et al, 2008).

Opportunity recognition and entrepreneurial commitment

An entrepreneurial opportunity is defined as a ‘feasible, profit-seeking, potential venture that provides an innovative new product or service to the market, improves on an existing product/service, or imitates a profitable product/service in a less-than-saturated market’ (Singh, 2001: 11). Drawing on the organisational knowledge literature, Nonaka (1994) emphasises the centrality of social interaction between individuals in sharing and developing new knowledge. Indeed, more recent work on the role of social networks in entrepreneurship also argues that entrepreneurial success depends on ‘the ability of the entrepreneur to exploit social networks’ and that the establishment of technology transfer offices by universities has been in response to concerns over inadequacies in academics’ commercial awareness. In other words, while many of the antecedents of opportunity identification have been studied at the individual level, these may be moderated by the environment. As such, the UI may also enhance (or constrain) the identification of entrepreneurial opportunities by USOs.

Evidence on how UIs might affect USOs’ opportunity identification and entrepreneurial commitment activities is mixed. On one hand, the campus incubator environment (UI) may encourage informal or formal inward-looking organisational links between USOs ‘remain[ing] too much oriented on the academic world’, to the neglect of commercial efforts (Gilsing et al, 2010, 16; see also Bekkers et al, 2006). Indeed, where links to external organisations outside the UI are lacking, the inter-organisational network of the USO will be characterised by a homogenous group of similar firms that may constrain USOs' development activities. Specifically, such lack of diversity may reduce 'the chance of unforeseen novel combinations of knowledge which can lead to discovery' (Pittaway et al, 2004: 44).

In contrast to this, social networks formed between early-stage academic entrepreneurs may be particularly important in terms of avoiding isolation and gaining reassurance through a 'sense of common struggle' (Cooper et al, 2012; McAdam and Marlow, 2007: 363) and having role models which encourage them to commit to their business (Vohora et al, 2004). Further, where informal or social ties develop in a UI between USOs (Cooper et al, 2012; Schwartz and Hornych, 2010), the development of relational capital may lead to formal relationships (Bøllingtoft, 2012; Debackere and Veugelers, 2005). This may be particularly important for academic entrepreneurs, where time constraints make formal networking difficult (McAdam and Marlow, 2008). However, Lindelöf and Löfsten (2004) argue that informal ties to co-tenants rarely lead to formal transactions or collaborations, instead constituting opportunities which are rarely taken.

Despite physical proximity, there is considerable evidence that UI tenants are unwilling to share information with one another (Schwartz and Hornych, 2010; McAdam and Marlow, 2008; McAdam and Marlow, 2007) for fear that it may be misappropriated, evoking more general findings about firms' reluctance to share 'core' knowledge (Amesse and Cohendet, 2001; Hamel et al, 1989). Even where informal relationships develop, the initial benefit of these may be eroded over time. For example, Bloodgood et al. (1995) identify three possible problems: expected preferential treatment (where friends become customers but, because of relational capital, expect to be given more favourable terms); poor advice (where friendship distorts the entrepreneurs' perception of whether they are receiving impartial and useful business advice); and lack of professionalism (where friends become suppliers and take advantage of the relationship by delivering lower quality goods in a less timely fashion than if they were delivering to other customers). Bøllingtoft suggests that this creates an environment whereby incubator tenants may behave and make decisions in the interests of their co-tenants to their own detriment, 'because you have to think of the other entrepreneurs' businesses also' (2012: 312).

Mixed evidence therefore exists on the perceived advantages and disadvantages for USOs of being located in a UI. However, studies on the effect of UIs on USOs have predominantly been one-dimensional in examining those USOs located within an incubator and their interaction with other tenants and wider partners. Where the evidence is less well developed is in determining if the network of relationships for USOs in a UI is different from those for USOs with no incubator support. In other words, do UIs significantly affect the profile of networks for USOs? This is important because if one of the main advantages of a UI facility is in terms of the information, resources, and capabilities that its USOs (tenants) can access, and in turn these affect the behaviour and development of the USOs, then this clearly strengthens the argument for universities making substantial investments in such organisational supports. However, if the profile of network relationships for USOs from universities without a UI facility are similar to (or better than) those with a UI, and the benefits derived from these network relationships are similar (or better), then this raises questions about the feasibility of investing in expensive UI facilities in a period when efficiencies are being sought in the commercialisation of research. Indeed, some argue that with advances in ICT and the globalisation of markets, the traditional advantages of incubators have eroded the necessity for physical proximity between businesses and that the benefit of clustering (as in UIs) has therefore diminished (Onsager et al, 2007; Durao et al, 2005).

In the remainder of this chapter, we explore the network configuration of USOs in two comparative contexts: a research intensive university with a UI on campus and a research intensive university without a UI (either on-campus or off-campus), both located on the island of Ireland. The aim of the investigation is two-fold: (i) to determine if there is a structural difference for USOs in the network additionality of an incubator facility and (ii) to explore the effect of an incubator on the early stages of USO development, particularly in terms of opportunity identification and entrepreneurial commitment.

Data and Methods

Our investigation is based on case analyses of two universities. In University A, a wholly-owned incubator was established on the University campus in 2003. This incubator's (hereafter referred to as UI) premises comprised business units, desk space, and bio-incubation units as well as a reception service, equipped meeting rooms, and a café. Generally, no investment is made in tenants in this UI, but University A does take equity of fifteen percent in each USO in exchange for university-owned IP being assigned to the firm. At the start of 2013, UI had 34 tenants (Table 10.2). The second case, University B, has a much longer history than University A in providing formal support for the commercialisation of university research. University B formed a commercialisation unit but without an incubator (hereafter referred to as Non-UI) in 1984 as a limited company with the objective of commercialising university research by supporting spin-out activity. University B/Non-UI invests in each USO and, upon receiving equity in the firm, IP is assigned from the university to the USO. USOs can also access, through the Non-UI, professional services, IP advice and venture capital networks but, crucially, not university-owned physical incubation facilities. Until 2014, University B had supported 59 firms – 25 of these were still active and have not been acquired during the period of study (Table 10.2).

USOs in University B (Non-UI) were typically older than clients of the UI – this was unsurprising given the considerable difference in the units' ages and the absence of 'graduation' (short of acquisition/liquidation) in the Non-UI. Despite this, the average (median) number of employees in the USOs was similar for both universities. Further, the pattern of USOs by sector grouping was broadly similar in the two contexts, although UI had a significantly higher proportion of pharmaceutical manufacturing firms while, in Non-UI, equipment manufacturing was more prevalent. Exploring such a limited number of cases in detail is warranted by the absence of extant research comparing these two models (Dul and Hak, 2007) and by the complexity of collecting, mapping, analysing, and comparing network data.

Our approach recognises that despite the wealth of research on incubator networks (see Bøllingtoft, 2012; Soetanto and Jack, 2011; Scillitoe and Chakrabarti, 2010; Bøllingtoft and Ulhøi, 2005; Hansen et al, 2000), studies applying Social Network Analysis (SNA) in this context are rare – the exceptions being Cooper et al. (2012) and Tötterman and Sten (2005). This is despite the widely-cited importance of networks for start-up firms generally (Meyer, 2003), for new technology-based firms (NTBF) more specifically (Lindelof and Lofsten, 2004; Yli-Renko and Autio, 1998), and for high-tech USOs in particular (Debackere and Veugelers, 2005; Gübeli and Doloreux, 2005).

Our data collection involved two stages: research at the level of the overarching network, afterwards complemented with semi-structured interviews with the founders of each USO. This approach is in response to

Wellman et al. (1997), who emphasise that research on networks conducted with the actors (USOs) as the level of analysis is meaningless without some consideration of the broader network structure in which individual relations exist. Network analysis encompasses the entire network structure and provides a detailed overview, description, and analysis of the entire social system (Provan et al. 2007). SNA was used, the principal goal of which is 'to examine relational systems in which actors dwell and to determine how the nature of relationship structures impacts behaviors' (Rowley, 1997: 893-894). Nodes (individual actors within the network, e.g. USOs) and ties (relationships between nodes, e.g. social and contractual agreements) along with attributes of these (e.g. direction, strength) were therefore mapped.

Data collected on the network structure for both the UI and Non-UI included measures of both informal and formal network ties: all firms were asked to identify all (i) other USOs and (ii) host university schools with which they had formal or informal ties[4]. Respondents were given a list of all current and former USOs from their university and a list of all academic departments within their host university. Network analysis was carried out using UCINET[5]. After documenting and gauging the strength of all UI and non-UI firms' formal and informal ties, this data was inputted to UCINET by creating and importing data language text files. Having imported each reported node and tie to UCINET, as well as the attributes of nodes (firm type, age, host university) and ties (direction, frequency of interaction), a range of network statistics were then calculated of which we report density in this chapter[6].

In addition to collecting network data, we attempted to interview the population of active USOs in both universities to explore emergent

---

[4] A formal network tie was considered to exist where a contractual agreement had been entered into or money had changed hands between the firm and the partner in question (Bøllingtoft and Ulhøi, 2005). An informal tie was defined as any interaction which involved neither a contract nor a financial transaction.

[5] UCINET is a standard commercial software package for network analysis. See Borgatti et al. (2002)

[6] It should be noted that network analysis was conducted on a cross-sectional basis at the same time in both university contexts. Spin-out firms were of different ages, focused on different sectors, and were at different stages of the development process. It is possible that this had some effect on the structural composition of the network, however this is most likely to have related to the formation of formal as opposed to informal ties.

differences or similarities in network characteristics between the UI and Non-UI contexts. Interviews were conducted with the firm's founders exploring their perceived obstacles and enablers to network formation, details of cooperative partnerships, benefits accruing to firms from network ties, and the impact of being located (or not) in a university incubator on these various factors. Data collection occurred between November 2012 and February 2013, with interviews occurring at the firm's premises or a similarly suitable location and lasting for between 45 and 90 minutes.

Interviews were recorded, transcribed, and analysed with MaxQDA (qualitative analysis software). The data was 'open coded': each transcript was systematically studied and relevant words and phrases were categorised under themed headings and sub-headings, created, and restructured dynamically during analysis. The resulting code system (cross-referenced by respondent and group) allowed identification of recurrent themes and comparison of the experiences and opinions of UI and Non-UI founders, and of sub-groups within each context. Finally, network data was revisited in light of the interview data. Insights into reported network obstacles, enablers, capabilities, benefits, etc. allowed us to intuitively understand and explain structural characteristics and differences across the two contexts.

Table 10.2: Characteristics of USOs in University A (UI) and University B (Non-UI)

	University A - UI				University B - Non-UI		
	Tenant USO	**On-campus USO**	**Spin-In**	**Total**	**USO**	**Shareholding**	**Total**
N	9	6	25	**40**	22	3	**25**
% surveyed	67.0	83.0	64.0	**68.0**	82.0	100.0	**84.0**
Age and size							
Age (years): Mean (median)	7.0 (7.3)	2.5 (2.1)	5.2 (5.2)	**5.1 (4.7)**	10.5 (9.2)	15.8 (14.3)	**11.3 (9.9)**
USO size (no. FTEs): Mean (median)	8.7 (4.0)	4.4 (0.0)	4.9 (2.5)	**5.7 (2.0)**	46.1 (2.3)	9.7 (6.0)	**40.9 (3.0)**
Sector (% of USOs)							
Human health & social work	16.7	0.0	0.0	**4.2**	5.6	0.0	**4.8**
Information and communication	33.3	0.0	56.3	**41.7**	27.8	33.3	**28.6**
Manufacturing	33.3	60.0	18.8	**29.2**	38.9	33.3	**38.1**
Professional, scientific and technical activities	16.7	40.0	25.0	**25.0**	27.8	33.3	**28.6**

Note: Data relates to February 2013

Findings

Structural networks among USOs

By analysing the presence of informal and formal ties that USOs reported with (i) other USOs from the same university (excluding spin-ins and shareholdings), (ii) all other firms (including spin-ins located in the UI and shareholdings of Non-UI) and (iii) academic schools or centres within the host university, density measures were calculated (Table 10.3).

Overall, the density of informal ties between USOs was significantly greater in the UI context (41.67 per cent) compared to the Non-UI context where there was no incubator (18.18 per cent)[1]. Further, informal network density between USOs and university schools was also significantly (albeit weak) higher in the UI (12.57 per cent compared to 8.86 per cent).

A somewhat different profile was obtained however for formal networks. Here, although the density of these was very low in both the UI and Non-UI contexts (Table 3), it was significantly higher in the Non-UI context. For example, formal ties between USOs in University B were 6.06 per cent while no formal ties were found in UI. This was also accompanied by denser formal ties between USOs and university schools in University B (Non-UI) (12.50 per cent as compared to 5.81 per cent). Again, the correlation between informal (social) ties and formal (relational) ties was weak.

These findings suggest that USOs located in a university incubator have denser informal network ties both to other USOs and to schools in their host university than USOs without a university incubator. In contrast, we also find that USOs from a university without a UI (University B) have denser formal network ties both to other USOs and to host university schools with no apparent relationship between the presence of informal and formal network ties. This finding contrasts with that of Bøllingtoft (2012) and Debackere and Veugelers (2005) where it was suggested that informal ties would translate into formal business relationships. In contrast, in the case of Non-UI, informal ties were less common; but where links between USOs did exist, these were more likely to be based on formal contractual arrangements.

1 This difference was latent in the full network analysis due to the inclusion of university schools as nodes: the higher number of schools (44 compared with 20 for the Non-UI) 'diluted' the UI informal network and gave a misleadingly low density figure.

Table 10.3: Density of UI and Non-UI informal and formal networks

	UI	Non-UI	Pearson Chi square	p-value
Informal network				
USO-USO network	41.67	18.18	20.461	0.000**
USO-school network	12.37	8.86	5.453	0.020*
Formal network				
USO-USO network	0.00	6.06	4.605	0.032**
USO-school network	5.81	12.50	22.066	0.000***

Note: (i) Significance levels: * p<0.10; ***p*<0.05; ***p<0.01 (ii) Full Network includes spin-in firms in the case of UI and firms for which Non-UI have a shareholding.

USO external network ties

The extent of external ties beyond the immediate university environment was also gauged. External network ties to external private clients, suppliers, collaborators, universities, and publicly funded research centers/labs were examined2 (Table 10.4).

USO tenants (including spin-out and spin-in firms) in UI reported, on average, more external network ties than USO clients of Non-UI with mean counts of 37.00 and 28.20 respectively (Table 10.4). Excluding spin-in firms from the analysis and comparing only spin-out firms in UI and Non-UI, we see no significant difference in the extent of external network ties (average of 27.1 ties per USO in UI compared to 28.2 ties in Non-UI). This suggests that the context of being located in an incubator, or not, has little effect on the scale and scope of external partnerships formed. However, the findings also highlight that spin-in firms are more developed

[2] None of the counts were normally distributed and usable data was returned from 25 incubator respondents and eighteen Non-UI respondents (i.e. N<30). As a result, the non-parametric Mann-Whitney test was applied to determine if significant differences existed between the external network ties of spin-outs located in an incubator (UI) and those with no incubator (Non-UI).

commercially than university spin-outs. While it might have been anticipated that proximity of USOs to spin-in firms would assist – through a learning effect – in developing the external network ties of USOs, this is not found.

Table 10.4: Frequency of external network ties

	UI tenants (incl. spin-ins)	UI USOs only	Non-UI USOs only
Customers/clients	25.20	17.60	18.93**
Suppliers	8.40	7.20	5.40
Private collaborators	0.00	0.00	0.73
Total Private	***33.60***	***24.80***	***25.07***
Other universities	3.00	2.00	2.07
Publicly funded research centres/labs	0.40	0.30	1.07
Total Public	***3.40***	***2.30***	***3.13***
All	**37.00**	**27.10**	**28.20**

Note: Significance levels: * $p<0.10$; ** $p<0.05$; *** $p<0.01$

Opportunity recognition and entrepreneurial commitment

Previous research highlights the importance to early-stage academic entrepreneurs of receiving advice on protecting IP, securing investment, maintaining accounts, etc. (Clarysse et al, 2011; Vohora et al, 2004; Cooper et al, 2012; Soetanto and Jack, 2011). These business basics are fundamental in enabling the academic entrepreneur to evaluate the feasibility of a business opportunity. If this information can be provided on an informal, pro bono basis, through the USO network – drawing on the prior experience of other academic entrepreneurs – then this is likely to be a significant advantage in overcoming the USO process junctures of identifying the opportunity and committing to the business.

In this sense, UI network ties placed tenant USOs at an advantage relative to USOs in the Non-UI context among whom such open sharing of information – and its associated benefits – appeared to be lacking. For example, in the UI, although USOs differed markedly in their sector and stage of development, they had all experienced similar problems at the start-up phase, and so the idea of drawing on the diverse experiences of co-tenants as a resource for overcoming common challenges was raised repeatedly:

> "You're surrounded by sources of knowledge and experience on all the common factors companies like us have to deal with. And everybody is good at something different [but] everyone is facing the same challenges" (UI: ISI9).

Similar informal sharing of information and associated knowledge-based benefits were discussed much less frequently by Non-UI USOs, but founders were conscious of–and aspired to–these information benefits:

> "It would be fantastic to have a whole group of different people that you could dip in and out of when you needed to" (Non UI: LF).

> "Knowledge of what other [Non-UI] companies do would be helpful for each of the [Non-UI] companies to know who can be a partner. And how they can work together. I know there are 27 [Non-UI] companies, but I don't know what these companies do" (Non UI: ANDT).

> "Essentially if the university has an incubation space, you could do all that learning while you're working – you could learn much quicker" (Non-UI: CT 1).

In addition, a number of Non-UI USOs commented not only on the potential learning that could occur from other USOs, but also that in the absence of an incubator facility the opportunity to learn from others was lacking (and slowing down USO development), and that existing efforts of the TTO to act as an intermediary in facilitating ties between USOs were inadequate:

> "[Non-UI] should actually be playing [the] role of linking people within [University], and outside [University]. That doesn't happen. (Non-UI: ANDT).

> "I haven't had the opportunity to see what could have happened if [TTO] made more of an effort to facilitate links to other [Non-UI] companies. I think there is a lot of value in talking informally to a range of different people and learning by word of mouth from other client firms" (Non-UI: LF).

Our findings suggest that all USOs are aware of the potential learning benefits from informal ties with other USOs and that where inter-USO network ties occur, this learning is predominantly concerned with business-related issues such as IP protection, investment requirements etc. The presence of a UI appears to significantly increase the likelihood of realising these benefits and indeed supports our earlier findings on the density of informal USO-USO ties in the two university contexts. Our main new finding from the interviews is that among Non-UI USOs there is a willingness to engage to a much greater extent with other USOs for the purposes of learning and an attitude that this could be achieved through more pro-active intermediation by the TTO.

Perhaps more important in the opportunity identification stage are network ties to university departments and external actors. Significant commonality was found for both universities in the manner business opportunities were identified with limited influence of the UI (or lack of UI) in this. In general opportunities were recognised through academics' proximity to university science, matched with their industry knowledge from informal ties, collaboration, contract research, etc. As such, neither a technology-push nor market-pull model dominated; however in almost all cases, informal ties were significant in conceiving the initial business idea:

> "I'd been doing contract research for [a major pharma] for maybe three years, doing exactly this type of work, so that's where we said 'Right, we can do this faster and more efficiently than doing it through the university system'" (UI: BN).

> "I knew it, yeah. From my own research. I've been researching biodegradable plastics, biodegradable polymers because we know that from a research point of view as well, as you know, science wants to answer these questions because we know how important these plastics and polymers can be". (UI: BT).

> "[The research] was presented at a number of conferences and, given the level of interest from individuals saying that this would be something that they would be interested in getting access to and potentially acquiring, we realised we should use the intellectual property and the know-how to establish some commercial outlet for it" (Non-UI: PXL).

> "[Name] who was an ex-physics guy who was now president of [company X] in the US was visiting and he saw the stuff and he asked was anyone interested in doing that commercially… and we said 'Yes' and within months they had given us £36,000 and said develop a commercial version" (Non-UI: A).

Therefore, while the incubator (or absence of an incubator) appeared to play very little role in opportunity identification, it became more important in the subsequent refinement and development of the business idea. For USOs that were based in the UI, this provided proximity to academic research which was significant in subsequent development of the technology, "Because we are based in [UI] it's a very big advantage being based in the heart of research where things are happening and we have access to that development work that is going on - research work. And we have access to brains in the university and if you have any issues to be discussed with scientists we can discuss. Any issues we are not an expert in that area, we can find somebody" (UI: ET). Similarly, "If we weren't here with the proximity to the college… we wouldn't even be working the space area. We'd probably still be trying to bang our heads on the medical area and failing as a company" (UI: EB).

The significantly higher density of USO-university school informal ties in the UI context was manifested in access to university equipment and lab space on a pro bono basis (i.e. involving no contract or payment), which represented a significant benefit and in some cases was central to their business. The founder of a biotech USO explained that without access to highly specialised university-owned lab equipment, "it actually would probably be easier to move out of the country" (UI: BN), given the financial and regulatory challenges of setting up a comparable lab.

Founders largely accredited this open access to university resources to their USO's on-campus (i.e. UI-based) location, and to "being based in the heart of the research where things are happening and we have access to that development work that is going on" (UI: Enz).

In contrast, Non-UI USOs used university-owned equipment, and several also provided equipment to the university. However, these interactions were typically on a contractual, paid basis, and the type of 'open access' to school lab and equipment so apparent in the UI was much less common in the Non-UI setting (see Table 10.3). Further, where USOs lacked the physical proximity of the UI as in University B, the location of business premises, often at a distance from the university proved to be detrimental in their development activities, "[Being based] in a remote place outside of the city, you do your best – I do what I can in terms of finding out what's going on – but the best place to find what's going on is at the centre of things because that's where it's happening" (Non-UI: HM). Therefore, perceived isolation and neglect from the university seemed to have left some USOs disengaged from the university science hub, impeding the refinement and development of technology applications.

The main contribution of the UI in the opportunity identification stage appears to be in terms of agglomeration and proximity effects. Agglomeration of USOs in a UI is conducive to greater levels of informal network ties (as evident in the density scores) and sharing of experiential knowledge i.e. how to protect IP, how and where to access finance etc. Our findings suggest however that in the absence of an incubator, there is the potential for this information sharing to occur, given the willingness and perceived benefit as noted by the interviewees; however, this needs to be facilitated by an intermediary, and unfortunately in our case university this was not happening. Proximity of the UI to the university research base was also noted as being important in the subsequent development of technology; and for those USOs without a UI, being based often at a significant distance from the university was perceived as being detrimental to these developments. There was limited evidence that the presence, or otherwise, of a UI had any influence on the initial opportunity identification. This typically arose from academic's existing informal and formal ties with individuals external to the university environment. The universities appeared to play little role in these ties with the exception of a contractual role where contract research was being undertaken. This suggests that a UI facility has limited (if any) effect on opportunity identification with the main benefit at this initial stage of USO development being through agglomeration of USOs and the subsequent sharing of information and proximity to university research in facilitating technological development.

Threshold of credibility

Discussion of the credibility benefits of being linked with the host university was common in interviews, with certain USO founders in both contexts stating that "the affiliation gives us some gravitas" (UI: O) or "it adds weight and credibility" (Non-UI: TF). More specifically, there was a feeling that, through their university ties, USOs had access to otherwise unattainable "top talent and cutting edge research" (Non-UI: H), and that this was something which external parties valued and aspired to. As such, advocates of this perspective were inclined to openly cite and promote their university ties, even in purely commercial circles.

However, others (and indeed the majority of USOs) saw their USO's association with its host university as a threat to credibility. Many founders had noted, among industry partners, a tendency to be "quite dismissive" (UI: BN) of USOs, making it difficult for them to be viewed as a "proper company" (Non-UI: A). In some cases, this had manifested as reluctance from larger companies to partner with USOs for fear that, as "not fully established companies" (UI: W), USOs would not survive in the long term:, "That would just set alarm bells off: 'We're going to make a key product for us dependent on a small company which could be gone in two years' time..?' Those are the questions they're asking" (Non-UI: A).

Similarly, others felt that prospective partners had avoided them on the basis that campus companies are not 'real businesses':

> "Because we're located within a university you're seen as a sort of second string. You're not really at the coalface, you're play acting" (UI: BN); or

> "If you bring in the university, [people from industry] know it is a university and they then see us as researchers" (Non-UI: W).

The findings are therefore mixed on how university affiliation affects the threshold of credibility. Reflecting on the interviews, this effect appears to vary by USO sector with founders in life science related industries (pharmaceutical manufacturing, diagnostics) tending to value and publicise their university links more. By contrast, USOs which engaged in manufacturing and ICT industries were more likely to see the university affiliation as detrimental to the commercial credibility of their USO.

The effect of a UI on the threshold of credibility was found to differ somewhat from the wider university effect. In general the UI was frequently referred to as an "impressive facility" and a significant selling point for USOs, allowing firms to present themselves as legitimate and stable "going concern[s]". Several UI respondents referred to the specific value of this in establishing credibility and overcoming USO stigma: "We would have site visits here. You can bring [prospective clients] to [UI] and they go 'Ok, there's four walls–that's a start'. Then you bring them to the labs and they go 'Yes, this is real', and they're convinced that this is not some cowboy operation" (UI: ISO3).
This "professional façade" and its role in attracting and reassuring clients was an inherent benefit of being a UI tenant, but was obviously lacking for Non-UI client USOs. In the absence of UI facilities, some were premised in "shabby" facilities (Non-UI: CSO) or had been forced to move "out

here to the *** sticks" (Non-UI: CSO6), damaging their reputation in clients' eyes. Other Non-UI firms had not secured office premises for their business, with a significant minority (28 percent) running their USOs from their academic offices and, in one case, operating an early-stage USO from home, "I sold the first machine off my kitchen table. [University B] didn't have an incubation space and they wouldn't give me a desk in the department, so I had no desk to work at and I had to make commercially sensitive calls to customers" (Non-UI: CSO5).

Assuring credibility was therefore more difficult for Non-UI USOs who frequently identified problems of assuring clients that being a USO did not preclude them from being a "proper company" (Non-UI: CSO4). Although physical location was seen to have some effect in assuring clients and other external partners of credibility, of greater importance was the financial investment by the universities in the USOs. The willingness by the university to invest directly or take an equity stake in the business was seen as a powerful and positive signal to potential investors: "There's an endorsement there. When other people look at it they're thinking 'Well, these other guys saw fit to invest in this company' so there's definitely a worth in having a look at it" (Non-UI: CSO1).

Conclusions

Rates of USO activity are reported to have increased markedly since the late 1990s (Fini et al, 2011; Mustar et al, 2008; Clarysse et al, 2005; Markman et al, 2005), and recent data for UK universities suggests that this trend is being sustained, growing by 46 percent, or an average annual increase of 15.3 percent, between 2008 and 2011 (HESA, 2012). Despite growing recognition of the potential contribution of USOs to economic development, concerns relating to high failure rates of USOs and difficulties experienced by them in achieving sustainable growth have led university management and policy makers to (re)assess how they can best support these new (typically high-tech) ventures.

There has been limited focus on the case for intervention with a lack of studies providing robust evaluations of the additionality arising from support for USOs. In part, a major reason for a lack of such studies is the difficulty in identifying appropriate counter-factual contexts. This has led to an abundance of studies examining the effect of institutional environment and infrastructural supports on USO development, but these are typically limited by an inability to determine the counter-factual and therefore the full additionality of an intervention.

In this chapter our focus has been on examining one form of intervention – university incubators (UI) – to support the development of USOs. UIs have the potential to overcome a number of market and systemic failures that USOs experience, and here our focus has been on system failures and in particular the potential of UIs to strengthen informal and formal network ties between USOs and university schools as the basis for social capital. By focusing on USO networks, it is suggested that these 'indirect and social aspects' are a better gauge of the true value of UIs than more traditional metrics of performance, such as average incubation period (Bøllingtoft and Ulhøi, 2005:267) or purely economic measures (Jack, 2010). As such, in analysing network characteristics, capabilities, and benefits in this research, we operationalise a series of alternative UI performance metrics.

Examining two case universities, we have sought to identify a counter-factual scenario where, in a research-intensive university environment, one university has sought to support the development of USOs through a UI while in the other professional support is provided in the absence of a UI. There are obviously limitations to our case comparison and the methods employed. However, through SNA we have sought to determine if differences are evident in the informal and formal network structure of USOs; and through interviews we also consider the role of these networks and the UI (or lack of UI) at the early stages of the USO process, i.e. in terms of opportunity recognition and building entrepreneurial commitment and the effect of an incubator on this.

USOs located in a university incubator (UI) had denser informal (social) network ties to one another and to university schools than USOs without a university incubator (Non-UI) where instead formal ties were significantly more common – both to other USOs and to university schools. This suggests a substitute relationship between informal and formal ties.

In the UI context, many previous findings around incubator network benefits were supported: tenant USOs willingly shared their technology and knowledge with one another (Soetanto and Jack, 2013; Cantù, 2010) and were able to avail themselves of open access to equipment and expertise within their host university (Gübeli and Doloreux, 2005; Rice, 2002). In the Non-UI environment, USOs were isolated from one another and often from the university, reducing the potential to share proprietary resources and benefit from the associated network advantages. As such, the implication is that resources accessed through UI networks placed UI USOs at an advantage in overcoming early junctures, for example in building into the USO the initial value required to assure entrepreneurial commitment.

At the same time, it could be argued that in a Non-UI environment the extent to which USOs are disadvantaged is debateable. Here, network ties are more likely to be formal (contractual) to both, other USOs and the host university. While, based on informal tie density, there appears to be a lower awareness among the USOs in the Non-UI context of the activities of other USOs, given appropriate network facilitation through an intermediary (which was clearly lacking in the case studied), it is possible that informal network ties could at least be strengthened, and at best, equal that of USOs in the UI. Further, based on the lack of significant difference in the number of network ties to external organisations, including suppliers, clients, customers etc. of UI and Non-UI USOs, this further questions the contribution of the UI or indeed the detrimental effect of having no UI on USO development.

Our findings highlight that opportunity identification was largely the outcome of the academic entrepreneur's academic and industrial ties with virtually no initial effect of the UI. The UI was important in supporting the post-opportunity identification stage in terms of subsequent technological/market development. This was achieved in two main ways: first, through a proximity effect in being located close to university schools and thereby facilitating ad hoc informal support, advice, and access to specialist equipment and facilities; and second, by providing physical premises that enhanced the credibility of the USO to industrial partners. What emerged as perhaps more significant, however, to USOs in achieving credibility was where the university had made a direct financial investment in it as this acted as a positive signal to other potential investors.

Drawing on the somewhat limited analysis of our two case universities, our findings contribute to the emerging debate on the effectiveness of intervention to support USOs, specifically in terms of UIs and the substantial capital and recurrent investment associated with their operation. Although some authors point to the fact that UIs may or may not comprise physical premises and infrastructure (Aerts et al, 2007; Durão et al, 2005; Carayannis and Von Zedwitz, 2005; Meyer, 2003; Etzkowitz et al, 2000), there is no definitive indication of the optimal property-based context for a successful UI. This research makes a tentative step in contributing to this debate.

Acknowledgement

The authors gratefully acknowledge the financial support from the Irish Government's Programme for Research in Third Level Institutions (PRTLI 5) project grant entitled 'Innovation Policy Simulation for the Smart Economy (IPSE)'.

References

Aernoudt, R. (2004) 'Incubators: Tool for Entrepreneurship?' Small Business Economics, 23 (2), 127-135.

Aerts, K., Matthyssens, P. and Vandenbempt, K. (2007) 'Critical Role and Screening Practices of European Business Incubators.' Technovation, 27 (5), 254-267.

Ahmad, A. J. and Ingle, S. (2011) 'Relationships Matter: Case Study of a University Campus Incubator.' International Journal of Entrepreneurial Behaviour and Research, 17 (6), 626-644.

Ahuja, G. (2000) 'The Duality of Collaboration: Inducements and Opportunities in the Formation of Interfirm Linkages.' Strategic Management Journal, 21 (3), 317–343.

Allen, D. N. and McCluskey, R. (1990) 'Structure, Policy, Services and Performance in the Business Incubator Industry.' Entrepreneurship: Theory & Practice, 15 (2), 61-77.

Amesse, F. and Cohendet, P. (2001) 'Technology Transfer Revisited from the Perspective of the Knowledge-based Economy.' Research Policy, 30 (9), 1459–1478.

Bekkers, R., Gilsing, V. A. and van der Steen, M. (2006) 'Determining Factors of the Effectiveness of IP-based Spin-offs: Comparing the Netherlands and the US.' Journal of Technology Transfer, 31 (5), 545-546.

Arya, B. and Lin, Z. (2007) 'Understanding Collaboration Outcomes from an Extended Resource-Based View Perspective: The Roles of Organizational Characteristics, Partner Attributes, and Network Structures.' Journal of Management, 33 (5), 697-723.

Barr, S. H., Baker, T. E. D., Markham, S. K., and Kingon, A. I. (2009) 'Bridging the Valley of Death: Lessons Learned from 14 years of Commercialization of Technology Education.' Academy of

Management Learning & Education, 8 (3), 370-388.
Bleda, M., and del Río, P. (2013) 'The Market Failure and the Systemic Failure Rationales in Technological Innovation Systems.' Research Policy, 42 (5), 1039-1052.
Bloodgood, J. M., Sapienza, H. J. and Carsrud, A. L. (1995) 'The Dynamics of New Business Start-ups: Person, Context and Process.' In: Advances in Entrepreneurship, Firm Emergence and Growth. ed. By Katz, J.A. and Brockhaus, R.H. Greenwich, CN: JAI Press: 123-144.
Bloomberg, M.R. (2011) 'Future of New York City.' Keynote speech on 19 July 2011 at: Crain's New York Business Conference. Available online at: http://www1.nyc.gov/
Bøllingtoft, A. (2012) 'The Bottom-up Business Incubator: Leverage to Networking and Cooperation Practices in a Self-Generated, Entrepreneurial-Enabled Environment.' Technovation, 32 (5), 304-315.
Bøllingtoft, A. and Ulhøi, J. P. (2005) 'The Networked Business Incubator - Leveraging Entrepreneurial Agency?' Journal of Business Venturing, 20 (2), 265-290.
Borgatti, S.P., Everett, M.G. and Freeman, L.C. 2002. Ucinet for Windows: Software for Social Network Analysis. Harvard, MA: Analytic Technologies.
Breschi, S., and Lissoni, F. (2009) 'Mobility of Skilled Workers and Co-invention Networks: An Anatomy of Localized Knowledge Flows.' Journal of Economic Geography, lbp008, 1-30.
Bruneel, J., Ratinho, T., Clarysse, B. and Groen, A. (2012) 'The Evolution of Business Incubators: Comparing Demand and Supply of Business Incubation Services Across Different Incubator Generations.' Technovation, 32 (2), 110-121.
Cantù, C. (2010) 'Exploring the Role of Spatial Relationships to Transform Knowledge in a Business Idea – Beyond Geographic Proximity.' Industrial Marketing Management, 39 (6), 887-897.
Carayannis, E. G. and von Zedtwitz, M. (2005) 'Architecting GloCal (global–local), Real-virtual Incubator Networks (G-RVINs) as Catalysts and Accelerators of Entrepreneurship in Transitioning and Developing Economies: Lessons Learned and Best Practices from Current Development and Business Incubation Practices.' Technovation, 25 (2), 95-110.
Chatterton, P., and Goddard, J. (2000) 'The Response of Higher Education Institutions to Regional Needs.' European Journal of Education, 35 (4), 475-496.
Clarysse, B., Wright, M., Lockett, A., Van de Velde, E. and Vohora, A. (2005) 'Spinning out New Ventures: A Typology of Incubation

Strategies from European Research Institutions.' Journal of Business Venturing, 20 (2), 183-216.
Clarysse, B., Tartari, V. and Salter, A. (2011) 'The Impact of Entrepreneurial Capacity, Experience and Organizational Support on Academic Entrepreneurship.' Research Policy, 40 (8), 1084-1093.
Colombo, M. G. and Delmastro, M. (2002) 'How Effective are Technology Incubators?: Evidence from Italy.' Research Policy, 31 (7), 1103-1122.
Colombo, M. G. and Piva, E. (2012) 'Firms' Genetic Characteristics and Competence-Enlarging Strategies: A Comparison Between Academic and Non-Academic High-Tech Start-ups.' Research Policy, 41 (1), 79-92.
Cooper, C., Hamel, S. and Connaughton, S. (2012) 'Motivations and Obstacles to Networking in a University Business Incubator.' Journal of Technology Transfer, 37 (4), 433-453.
Dahlstrand, Å. L. (1997) 'Growth and Inventiveness in Technology-based Spin-off Firms.' Research Policy, 26 (3), 331-344.
Debackere, K. and Veugelers, R. (2005) 'The Role of Academic Technology Transfer Organizations in Improving Industry Science Links.' Research Policy, 34 (3), 321-342.
Dee, N. J., Livesey, F., Gill, D. and Minshall, T. (2011) 'Incubation for Growth: A review of the impact of business incubation on new ventures with high growth potential', Research summary, NESTA, September 2011, London.
Degroof, J. J., and Roberts, E. B. (2004) 'Overcoming Weak Entrepreneurial Infrastructures for Academic Spin-off Ventures.' Journal of Technology Transfer, 29 (3-4), 327-352.
Dodgson, M., Hughes, A., Foster, J., and Metcalfe, S. (2011) 'Systems Thinking, Market Failure, and the Development of Innovation Policy: The Case of Australia.' Research Policy, 40 (9), 1145-1156.
Druilhe, C., and Garnsey, E. (2004) 'Do Academic Spin-outs Differ and Does it Matter?' Journal of Technology Transfer, 29 (3-4), 269-285.
Dul, J. and Hak, T. (2007) Case Study Methodology in Business Research 4th Edn., Butterworth-Heinemann/Elsevier, Boston, MA., ISBN: 10-0750681969.
Durão, D., Sarmento, M., Varela, V. and Maltez, L. (2005) 'Virtual and Real-estate Science and Technology Parks: A Case Study of Taguspark.' Technovation, 25 (3), 237-244.
Etzkowitz, H., de Mello, J. M. C., and Almeida, M. (2005) 'Towards "Meta-Innovation" in Brazil: The Evolution of the Incubator and the Emergence of a Triple Helix.' Research Policy, 34 (4), 411-424.

European Union-Commission of the European Communities (2003) Summary Report: The Public Debate Following the Green Paper 'Entrepreneurship in Europe', Brussels: EU-Commission of the European Communities.
Falk, R. (2007) 'Measuring the Effects of Public Support Schemes on Firms' Innovation Activities: Survey Evidence from Austria.' Research Policy, 36 (5), 665-679.
Fini, R., Grimaldi, R., Santoni, S. and Sobrero, M. (2011) 'Complements or Substitutes? The Role of Universities and Local Context in Supporting the Creation of Academic Spin-offs.' Research Policy, 40 (8), 1113-1127.
Florida, R. (1999) 'The Role of the University: Leveraging Talent, not Technology.' Issues in Science And Technology, Available online at: http://www.nap.edu/issues/15.4/florida.htm
Georghiou, L. (1998) 'Global Cooperation in Research.' Research Policy, 27 (6), 611-626.
Geuna, A. and Nesta, L.J.J. (2006) 'University Patenting and its Effects on Academic Research: The Emerging European Evidence.' Research Policy, 35 (6), 790-807.
Geuna, A. and Rossi, F. (2011) 'Changes to University IPR Regulations in Europe and the Impact on Academic Patenting.' Research Policy, 40 (8), 1068-1076.
Gilsing, V. A., van Burg, E. and Romme, A. G. L. (2010) 'Policy Principles for the Creation and Success of Corporate and Academic Spin-offs.' Technovation, 30 (1), 12-23.
Grimaldi, R. and Grandi, A. (2005) 'Business Incubators and New Venture Creation: An Assessment of Incubating Models.' Technovation, 25 (2), 111-121.
Grandi, A. and Grimaldi, R. (2005) Academics' Organizational Characteristics and the Generation of Successful Business Ideas.' Journal of Business Venturing, 20 (6), 821-845.
Gübeli, M. H. and Doloreux, D. (2005) 'An Empirical Study of University Spin-off Development,' European Journal of Innovation Management, 8 (3), 269–282.
Hackett, S. M. and Dilts, D. M. (2004) 'A Systematic Review of Business Incubation Research.' Journal of Technology Transfer, 29 (1), 55-82.
Hamel, G., Doz, Y. L., and Prahalad, C. K. (1989) 'Collaborate with your Competitors and Win.' Harvard Business Review, 67 (1), 133-139.
Hansen, M. T., Chesbrough, H. W., Nohria, N. and Sull, D. N. (2000) 'Networked Incubators: Hothouses of the New Economy.' Harvard Business Review, 78 (5), 74-84.

Harrison, R. T. and Leitch, C. (2010) 'Voodoo Institution or Entrepreneurial University? Spin-off Companies, the Entrepreneurial System and Regional Development in the UK.' Regional Studies, 44 (9), 1241-1262.

Hewitt-Dundas, N. (2012) 'Research Intensity and Knowledge Transfer Activity in UK Universities.' Research Policy, 41 (2), 262-275.

Hewitt-Dundas, N. and Burns, C. (2015) 'Exploring the Moderating Effect of Incubators on the Network Structure of University Spin-outs.' In: University Evolution, Entrepreneurial Activity and Regional Competitiveness (eds. Audretsch, D.B, Lehmann, E.E, Meoli, M. and Vismara, S), New York: Springer.

Higher Education Statistics Agency (2012) 'Higher education - Business and community interaction survey 2010/11' Unpublished dataset.

Holland, B.A. (2001) 'Toward a Definition and Characterization of the Engaged University.' Metropolitan Universities, 2 (3), 20–29.

Hoppe, H.C. and Ozdenoren, E. (2001) 'Intermediation in Innovation: The Role of Technology Transfer Offices.' Mimeo, Northwestern University.

Huggins, R. and Johnston, A. (2010) 'Knowledge Flows and Inter-firm Networks: The Influence of Network Resources, Spatial Proximity and Firm Size.' Entrepreneurship and Regional Development: An International Journal, 22 (5), 457-484.

Jack, S. L. (2010) 'Approaches to Studying Networks: Implications and Outcomes.' Journal of Business Venturing, 25 (1), 120–37.

Kitatgawa, F. and Robertson, S. (2012) 'High-Tech Entrepreneurial Firms in a University-Based Business Incubator: Spaces of Knowledge, Resource Heterogeneity and Capital Formation.' International Journal of Entrepreneurship and Innovation, 13 (4), 249-259.

Knockaert, M., Spithoven, A. and Clarysse, B. (2014) 'The Impact of Technology Intermediaries on Firm Cognitive Capacity Additionality.' Technological Forecasting and Social Change, 81, 376-387.

Lambert, R. (2003) Lambert Review of Business-University Collaboration. London: HMSO.

Leitch, C. M. and Harrison, R. T. (2005) 'Maximising the Potential of University Spin-outs: The Development of Second-Order Commercialisation Activities.' R&D Management, 35 (3), 257-272.

Lichtenthaler, U. (2011) 'Open Innovation: Past Research, Current Debates, and Future Directions.' The Academy of Management Perspectives, 25 (1), 75-93.

Lindelöf, P. and Löfsten, H. (2004) 'Proximity as a Resource Base for Competitive Advantage: University-Industry Links for Technology Transfer.' Journal of Technology Transfer, 29 (3-4), 311-326.

Lockett, A. and Wright, M. (2005) 'Resources, Capabilities, Risk Capital and the Creation of University Spin-out Companies.' Research Policy, 34 (7), 1043-1057.

Markman, G. D., Phan, P. H., Balkin, D. B. and Gianiodis, P. T. (2005) 'Entrepreneurship and University-based Technology Transfer.' Journal of Business Venturing, 20 (2), 241-263.

Markman, G. D., Siegel, D. S. and Wright, M. (2008) 'Research and Technology Commercialization.' Journal of Management Studies, 45 (8), 1401-1423.

Martin, S., and Scott, J. T. (2000) 'The nature of Innovation Market Failure and the Design of Public Support for Private Innovation.' Research Policy, 29 (4), 437-447.

McAdam, M. and Marlow, S. (2007) 'Building Futures or Stealing Secrets?' International Small Business Journal, 25 (4), 361-382.

McAdam, M. and Marlow, S. (2008) 'A Preliminary Investigation into Networking Activities within the University Incubator.' International Journal of Entrepreneurial Behaviour & Research, 14 (4), 219-241.

McAdam, M. and McAdam, R. (2008) 'High Tech Start-ups in University Science Park Incubators: The Relationship between the Start-up's Lifecycle Progression and Use of the Incubator's Resources.' Technovation, 28 (5), 277-290.

Meyer, M. (2003) 'Academic Entrepreneurs or Entrepreneurial Academics? Research-based Ventures and Public Support Mechanisms.' R&D Management, 33 (2), 107–115.

Mian, S.A. (1997) 'Assessing and Managing the University Technology Business Incubator: An Integrative Framework,' Journal of Business Venturing, 12 (4), 251–285.

Mizruchi, M. S. and Marquis, C. (2006) 'Egocentric, Sociocentric, or Dyadic?: Identifying the Appropriate Level of Analysis in the Study of Organizational Networks.' Social Networks, 28(3), 187-208.

Mustar, P., Renault, M., Colombo, M., Piva, E., Fontes, M., Lockett, A., Wright, M., Clarysse, B. and Moray, N. (2006) Conceptualising the Heterogeneity of Research-based Spin-offs: A Multi-dimensional Taxonomy.' Research Policy, 35 (2), 289–308.

Mustar, P., Wright, M. and Clarysse, B. (2008) 'University Spin-off firms: Lessons from Ten Years of Experience in Europe.' Science and Public Policy, 35 (2), 67-80.

Ndonzuau, F. N., Pirnay, F. and Surlemont, B. (2002) 'A Stage Model of Academic Spin-off Creation.' Technovation, 22 (5), 281–289.

Neergaard, H. (2003) 'The Process of Entrepreneurship: A Managerial and Organizational Journey.' In: New Movements in Entrepreneurship (eds.

Steyaert, C. and Hjorth, D.), Cheltenham: Edward Elgar, 160–176.
Nonaka, I. (1994) 'A Dynamic Theory of Organizational Knowledge Creation.' Organization Science, 5 (1), 14-37.
OECD - Organisation for Economic Cooperation and Development (1999) The Response of Higher Education Institutions to Regional Needs, Centre for Educational Research and Innovation, Paris: OECD.
Onsager, K., Isaksen, A., Fraas, M. and Johnstad, T. (2007) 'Technology Cities in Norway: Innovating in Glocal Networks.' European Planning Studies, 15 (4), 549-566.
O'Shea, R. P., Allen, T. J., Chevalier, A. and Roche, F. (2005) 'Entrepreneurial Orientation, Technology Transfer and Spinoff Performance of U.S. Universities.' Research Policy, 34 (7), 994-1009.
O'Shea, R. P., Chugh, H. and Allen, T. J. (2008) 'Determinants and Consequences of University Spinoff Activity: A Conceptual Framework.' Journal of Technology Transfer, 33 (6), 653-666.
Owen-Smith, J. (2003) 'From Separate Systems to a Hybrid Order: Accumulative Advantage across Public and Private Science at Research One Universities.' Research Policy, 32 (6), 1081-1104.
Pittaway, L., Robertson, M., Munir, K., Denyer, D. and Neely, A. (2004) 'Networking and Innovation: A Systematic Review of the Evidence.' International Journal of Management Reviews, 5 (3-4), 137-168.
Provan, K. G., Fish, A. and Sydow, J. (2007) Interorganizational Networks at the Network Level: A Review of the Empirical Literature on Whole Networks.' Journal of Management, 33 (3), 479-516.
Rasmussen, E., Moen, Ø. and Gulbrandsen, M. (2006) 'Initiatives to Promote Commercialization of University Knowledge.' Technovation, 26 (4), 518-533.
Rasmussen, E. (2011) 'Understanding Academic Entrepreneurship: Exploring the Emergence of University Spin-off Ventures Using Process Theories.' International Small Business Journal, 29 (5), 448-471.
Rice, M.P., (2002) 'Co-production of Business Assistance in Business Incubators: An Exploratory Study,' Journal of Business Venturing, 17 (2), 163–187.
Rothaermel, F. T. and Thursby, M. (2005) 'Incubator Firm Failure or Graduation?: The Role of University Linkages.' Research Policy, 34 (7), 1076-1090.
Rowley, T. J. (1997) 'Moving beyond Dyadic Ties: A Network Theory of Stakeholder Influences.' Academy of Management Review, 22 (4), 887-910.
Schwartz, M. and Hornych, C. (2010) 'Cooperation Patterns of Incubator

Firms and the Impact of Incubator Specialization: Empirical Evidence from Germany.' Technovation, 30 (9-10), 485-495.
Scillitoe, J. L. and Chakrabarti, A. K. (2010) 'The Role of Incubator Interactions in Assisting New Ventures.' Technovation, 30 (3), 155-167.
Siegel, D.S., Waldman, D. and Link, A. (2003) 'Assessing the Impact of Organizational Practices on the Relative Productivity of University Technology Transfer Offices: An Exploratory Study.' Research Policy, 32 (1), 13–27.
Siegel, D. S., Veugelers, R., and Wright, M. (2007) 'Technology Transfer Offices and Commercialization of University Intellectual Property: Performance and Policy Implications.' Oxford Review of Economic Policy, 23 (4), 640-660.
Singh, R. (2001) 'A Comment on Developing the Field of Entrepreneurship through the Study of Opportunity Recognition and Exploitation.' Academy of Management Review, 26 (1), 10–12.
Soetanto, D. and Jack, S. (2011) 'Business Incubators and the Networks of Technology-based Firms.' Journal of Technology Transfer, 36, 1-22.
Tamásy, C. (2007) 'Rethinking Technology-Oriented Business Incubators: Developing a Robust Policy Instrument for Entrepreneurship, Innovation and Regional Development?' Growth and Change, 38 (3), 460-473.
Targeting Innovation. (2008) 'Scottish University Spin-out Study.' Glasgow: Targeting Innovation.
Tötterman, H., & Sten, J. (2005) 'Start-ups, Business Incubation and Social Capital.' International Small Business Journal, 23 (5), 487-511.
UNICO (2006) UNICO UK University Commercialisation Survey: Financial Year 2005, Cambridge, UK: UNICO.
Van Geenhuizen, M. and Soetanto, D. (2009) 'Academic Spin-offs at Different Ages: A Case Study in Search of Key Obstacles to Growth.' Technovation, 29 (10), 671-681.
Vohora, A., Wright, M. and Lockett, A. (2004) 'Critical Junctures in the Development of University High-tech Spinout Companies.' Research Policy, 33 (1), 147-175.
Weber, K. M., and Rohracher, H. (2012) 'Legitimizing Research, Technology and Innovation Policies for Transformative Change: Combining Insights from Innovation Systems and Multi-level Perspective in a Comprehensive 'Failures' Framework.' Research Policy, 41 (6), 1037-1047.
Wellman, B., Wong, R. Y. L., Tindall, D. and Nazer, N. (1997) 'A Decade of Network Change: Turnover, Persistence and Stability in Personal

Communities.' Social Networks, 19 (1), 27-50.
Woolthuis, R. K., Hillebrand, B. and Nooteboom, B. (2005) 'Trust, Contract and Relationship Development.' Organization Studies, 26 (6), 813-840.
Wright, M., Birley, S. and Mosey, S. (2004) 'Entrepreneurship and University Technology Transfer.' Journal of Technology Transfer, 29 (3-4), 235-246.
Wright, M., Clarysse, B., Lockett, A. and Knockaert, M. (2008) 'Mid-range Universities' Linkages with Industry: Knowledge Types and the Role of Intermediaries.' Research Policy, 37 (8), 1205-1223.
Yli Renko, H., Autio, E. and Sapienza, H. J. (2001) 'Social Capital, Knowledge Acquisition and Knowledge Exploitation in Young Technology based Firms.' Strategic Management Journal, 22 (67), 587-613.

CHAPTER ELEVEN

START-UPS WHEN AND WHERE? USING THE SKIN PLATFORM FOR MODELLING THE BIRTH OF NEW FIRMS

MICHEL SCHILPEROORD

1. Introduction

This chapter seeks to advance the investigation of innovation systems and networks with the SKIN (Simulating Knowledge Dynamics in Innovation Networks) model (cf. Gilbert, Ahrweiler and Pyka 2014) by giving a more elaborate description of entrepreneurship and the creation of start-ups. Although links between innovation and entrepreneurship are implicitly made in the SKIN model, explicit representation of the start-up process is still lacking. The extension of the SKIN model, described and illustrated in this chapter, is intended to open up new ways and methods of using the platform for reasoning in detail about the performance of entrepreneurs and start-ups.

The extension builds on the general concepts and representations of the SKIN model and features standard SKIN agents representing large and small innovative firms and possibly other organisational actors. It enables us to observe entrepreneurs and start-ups in a standard SKIN setting: the agents (including start-ups) try to sell their innovations to other agents and end users, and meanwhile, they try to improve their innovation performance and sales through improving their knowledge base. In the process, they form innovation networks, innovate their products, learn by feedback, etc.

It adds two new types of agents: entrepreneurs and 'proto' start-ups. Entrepreneurs have many kinds of knowledge (including technical skills and entrepreneurial skills) plus the ability to identify and evaluate start-up opportunities and the implicit option to start a business (provided the conditions for starting the process are met). Proto start-ups, at the very start of the start-up process, are firms that, like existing firms, have a (technical) knowledge base and initial capital, enough to make a prototype product and obtain some initial feedback from the market (i.e. from other agents and end users potentially buying the innovation), yet lacking the capacity to compete with existing firms. Later in the process, that capacity may grow, and start-ups may consequently upgrade their proto status. If not, the start-up process stops.

The extension aims to describe the process of start-up creation in more detail by making assumptions about: i) how entrepreneurs identify and evaluate start-up opportunities; ii) when and how entrepreneurs decide to start-up a business (provided the conditions are met); iii) how start-ups are being created and evaluated at the very start of the start-up process (the proto stage); iv) how the outcome of the proto stage is measured and start-up potential is determined. Through these ideas, a model of "the birth and death of start-up companies" (cf. the birth and death of political parties, described in Laver and Schilperoord 2007) is described. It enables us to examine start-up dynamics from up close, within the perspective of an evolving, complex innovation system (Ahrweiler 2010), set within the context of both innovation policy and entrepreneurship policy. Performance is measured in terms of flow of knowledge and innovative ideas, creation of economic value, and ultimately success of actors and networks (sales, profits, spin-offs) (cf. Ahrweiler et al. 2012).

Application of the extension is illustrated with a recently developed SKIN model (IPSE-SKIN) of Irish sectors and regional innovation networks. For this model, new modules are developed with the "smart economy" framework (Building Ireland's Smart Economy, 2008) in mind. Application possibilities are illustrated with the example of high potential start-ups (HPSUs). This example is based on an Irish programme for indigenous enterprise support, the HPSU scheme, which is an important element to deliver the smart economy (Delivering the Smart Economy, 2009). The application to HPSUs will prepare discussion of further development and improvement of the extension, for modelling the role of intermediary organisations for technology transfer and the formation of entrepreneurial networks.

The rest of the chapter is organised as follows. In section 2, a method is discussed of extending and using the SKIN model for reasoning about the when and where of start-up firms. In section 3, the extension of the SKIN model is specified in a way that includes the birth and death of start-ups. In section 4, the model is illustrated with a case study on high-potential start-ups in Ireland. The final section 5 points to some particular challenges for further work.

2. Start-ups where and when?

In this section a method is discussed of using the SKIN model for reasoning about the when and where of start-up companies. It is through this discussion that general concepts and ideas already in SKIN are examined in relation to modelling the birth and death of start-ups, and the foundation is built for the extension.

2.1 Start-ups where?

The question of where start-ups are founded is addressed, referring primarily to the *positions* of SKIN agents in the model's representation of a knowledge space. In the SKIN model, the individual knowledge base of an agent is represented by an artificial knowledge space of variable size called "kene" (shown in Figure 11.2.1). Kenes enable the description of, and reasoning about, the aggregate knowledge of firms and other innovation actors (Gilbert 1997). Together, the SKIN agents are intended to represent one knowledge-intensive, technology-based industrial sector (Gilbert, Pyka and Ahrweiler 2001).

Figure 11.2.1: The kene concept

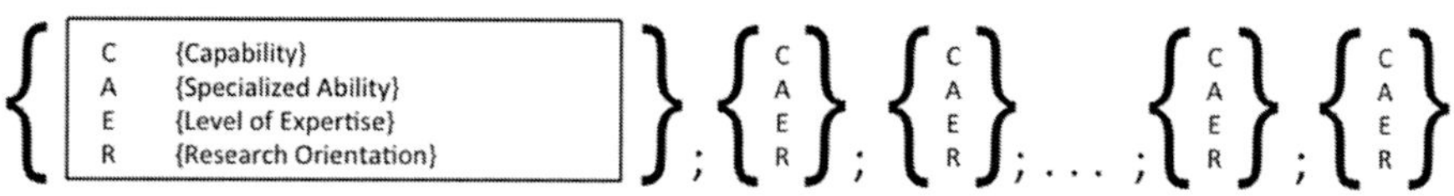

Positional language

Positional language and reasoning is introduced to address common assumptions and problems with SKIN with regard to the positioning of start-ups, but to stay clear of an overload of detail about implementation of the model.

The following definitions are used:

Definition 2.1. The *position* of an agent is the set of capabilities used in its innovation hypothesis.

The special focus of a firm, its potential innovation, is called an *innovation hypothesis*[1] (IH). It is derived from a subset of the firm's kene quadruples.

Figure 11.2.2: The innovation hypothesis of an agent

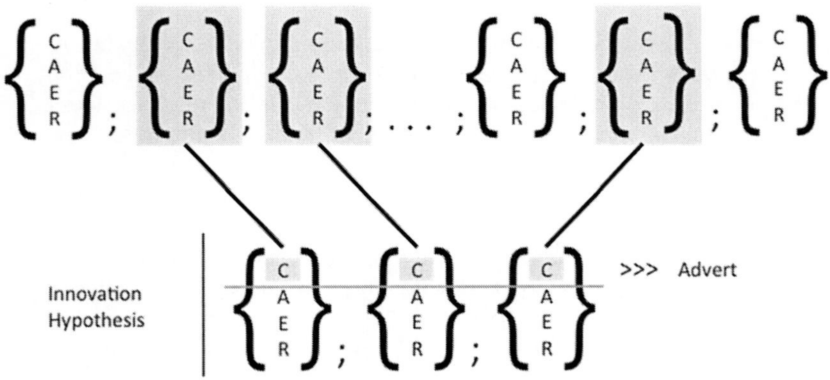

A mapping procedure transforms the IH into a product, where the capabilities of the IH are used to compute an index number that represents the product[2]. Position therefore implies choice of product design.

Spatial modelling

Alongside Definition 11.2.1 it is possible to talk about distance and the closely related metrics of movement and direction. This way a novel spatial modelling approach can be developed that takes advantage of the simplicity of defining positions of agents in SKIN as merely sets of capabilities. It does not replace any existing SKIN logic. Instead it adds a simple and convenient *abstraction layer* interfacing between SKIN's detailed kene/IH representations and the model's detailed computed

---

[1] Basic SKIN Model. http://cress.soc.surrey.ac.uk/SKIN/

[2] Ibid.

outputs, making it easier to visualise its dynamics, or extend its logic in new directions (as is illustrated in this chapter).

Definition 2.2. The *distance* between two agents is the difference between their adverts.

A marketing feature provides the information a firm can gather about other agents: e.g. to *advertise* its product, a firm publishes the capabilities that are used in its IH.

Distance metric

At this point, a distance metric is needed that allows SKIN agents to handle this freely available public information in the SKIN model. The adverts of firms are published sets of capabilities. In simulations, these adverts can change as result of attempts of firms to improve their innovation performance, which entail certain "edit operations" on their IHs, e.g. replacing one capability by another. *Edit distance* is therefore proposed and used here as way of quantifying how *dissimilar* two adverts are to one another, by counting the minimum number of edit operations required to transform one advert into the other. Variants of edit distance exist, using different sets of allowed edit operations. In the example in Figure 11.2.3 the edit distances (D) are calculated simply as the set differences between two adverts.

Figure 11.2.3: Distances between the adverts of three agents

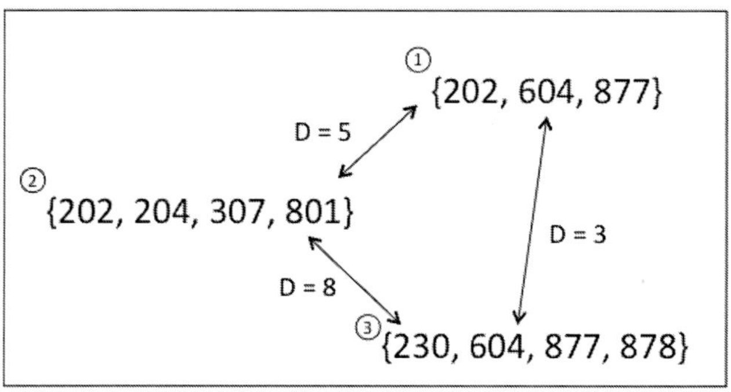

Spatial dynamics

Distance implies *movement*, which involves *direction* that is commonly described relative to the actual IH. Each firm decides on its innovation strategy and then performs research operations that may impact its IH, in which case it is re-advertised. The firm's choice of innovation strategy determines what kind of research operations (incremental or radical research; either alone or in partnership) are performed that can mutate capabilities used in its IH[3]. Performing "incremental" research, a firm tries to improve its product by altering one of the abilities chosen from the quadruples in its IH, while sticking to its focal capabilities (no movement). "Radical" innovation involves replacing one capability in its IH (movement in a certain direction)[4].

There are constraints to movement, especially for small firms like start-ups:

Definition 2.3. The *size* of an agent is the number of different capabilities in its kene.

The firm's capital is generally used as a yardstick for the range of its size[5]. This means that the number of capabilities in the adverts of start-up companies will always be small. This restricts their positioning. The firm's actual size is generally used in SKIN to impose capacity constraints on performing a certain innovation strategy, e.g. firms can only engage in so many collaborations with other agents as permitted by its capacity. This may further restrict positioning (i.e. less options for movement).

A caveat before moving on:

Caveat. One should be somewhat cautious talking about the position of an agent. Being a concept analogous to the "gene" of scientific/technological development of a firm, a kene is really a sequence of indefinite length, containing a number of "units of knowledge", which is evolving as the firm is developing its knowledge base (Gilbert 1997). Without going into details, this caveat is to remind readers that a kene is much more than the agent's coordinates in a knowledge space[6].

---

[3] Ibid

[4] Ibid.

[5] Ibid.

[6] Kenes can however be set up (through empirical mapping techniques and concordance tables) to approximately correspond to coordinates in a

Assumptions

With the definitions in place, a review follows of assumptions generally made in SKIN about the positioning of start-ups:

Assumption 2.1. The initial position of a new start-up firm is a *clone* of the position of an existing *successful* firm[7].

In SKIN, it is generally assumed that creation of a new start-up company involves cloning an existing kene, e.g. the knowledge base of an existing agent. Cloning a kene involves copying the quadruples in the agent's IH, but chopping it to a length suitable for the smaller size of the firm receiving it.

Assumption 2.2. The initial size of a new start-up firm is set by a *benchmark* in the form of a fixed amount of initial capital[8].

The initial capital and size of small companies (SMEs) is generally treated in SKIN as a benchmark for setting up the other types of agents and also the kene-based mechanisms.

Problems

Some problems with these assumptions are pointed out:

Ad assumption 2.1: the main problem is the principle of cloning successful innovators. It means that the potential innovations that start-ups can introduce to the sector must already have been tested and proven on the market, rewarded by sales and profits that already have been distributed to an existing firm, innovation partnership, or network. This leaves out of consideration entrepreneurs with innovation hypotheses that are "not on the radar yet".

Ad assumption 2.2: one should think this is a good benchmark, but unfortunately it rules out the "high-potential" start-ups in exceptional positions that are able to attract more capital than other start-ups. This

---

multi-dimensional knowledge space (e.g. IPC Codes) so that one can talk about positions in an approximate way. Note that the definitions allow computing these without reference to such mapping techniques.

[7] Basic SKIN Model.

[8] Ibid.

matter will be discussed further in the next section.

Closing remarks

The brief discussion of where start-ups are created exposes some shortcomings in the SKIN model that can be amended by elaborating the start-up process in the following ways: 1) moving the model beyond cloning, by positioning and tracking of entrepreneurs with valuable start-up propositions that are not on the radar yet, and 2) by introducing into the model novel types of indicators that allow the agents to evaluate start-up potential in an early stage.

2.2 Start-ups when?

Next the question is addressed of when start-ups are founded, referring primarily to the *valuations* of (potential) innovations and innovation performance. As was pointed out earlier, in the SKIN model, agents always have the option to try improving their positions through their innovation strategies that involve incremental and radical research, partnerships and networking, and learning mechanisms[9].

Assumptions

Assumption 2.3. The general indicator for success/failure of an innovation and the agent's innovation performance is the market *reward*.

Innovation strategies in SKIN are principally triggered by market rewards, but the model can be adapted so that they can also be incentivised by non-market mechanisms. One example of the former is the SEIN version of the model, for modelling self-organised innovation networks that are treated as persistent networks evolving out of successful partnerships (Gilbert, Pyka and Ahrweiler 2003). The latter is exemplified by the INFSO-SKIN platform, which features the creation of R&D consortia in response to government funding programmes (Ahrweiler et al. 2014, on Horizon 2020). Both examples can deliver a basis for the creation of new firms.

---

[9] Ibid.

Problems

The difficulty in applying this logic to start-up lies in the fact that at an early stage of the start-up process, neither market rewards nor government incentives may be within reach. This means that new concepts and indicators are needed in SKIN that allow us to talk about value of (potential) innovations in anticipation of start-up creation. The real problem lies in taking innovation success, the last reward received, as an indicator of start-up opportunity and potential. Start-up creation following another company's success would be an inherently risky proposition, given the immediate competition and attraction of many more clones. Moreover, one can doubt the implied assumption that this type of information would be publicly available to the other agents (companies keeping their success 'under the radar').

Positions and propositions

Definition 2.3. The *proposition* of a start-up is its position before market entry.

This definition allows us to compare the propositions of start-ups, i.e. their positions before market entry, with the positions of the existing firms. With this definition, it is possible to reason about the risk and potential returns associated with certain propositions, e.g. using the edit distance metric to distinguish between "incremental" and "radical" start-up propositions (the latter involving more edit operations in comparison to other positions). This novel approach allows for building new model assumptions into SKIN, which describe the valuation of a potential innovation at an early stage of the start-up process (as is described in the next section).

Closing remarks

The extension to the SKIN model also aims to provide the logic for who develops start-up propositions and how they are valued. This ultimately leads to the questions of where the entrepreneurs are positioned and when they are likely to start up a new business. To answer these questions, we turn to the simulation model.

3. Modelling start-ups with SKIN

The start-up process modelled with the SKIN extension comprises three phases, as depicted in Figure 11.3.1.

Figure 11.3.1: Phases of the start-up process

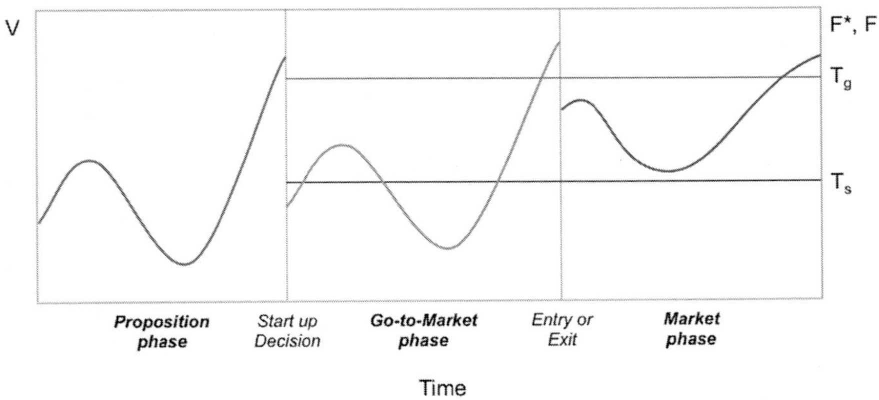

The narrative for the model is briefly outlined below:

Proposition phase – The identification, evaluation, and initial development of start-up opportunities

Entrepreneurs identify, evaluate, and start to develop start-up opportunities through putting together and improving their *start-up propositions*, which are based on their knowledge base (kene) and innovation hypothesis IH. Each entrepreneur makes a *continuous evaluation V* of their start-up proposition, and therewith evaluates the start-up opportunity as it presents itself over a certain window of time. The estimate *V* is based on the distance between the entrepreneur's innovation hypothesis IH and the IH of what would be the closest competitor in the market. Those entrepreneurs that have a truly innovative and unique business focus will thus value their IHs highest, and are the most likely to decide to 'go for it'.

Go-to-Market phase – The birth and death of proto start-ups

Those entrepreneurs then each create a 'proto' start-up firm to develop their prototype product and test the viability of their start-up opportunity over a certain window of time. This test is measuring whether or not the proto start-up is able to generate significant potential sales over the testing period so that its estimated *fitness F* stays above the *survival threshold* T_s. Only the proto start-ups that are able to survive the proto stage will enter the system as real start-ups that can sell their product, compete in the market, participate in innovation networks, etc.

Market phase – The growth and survival of new entrant start-up firms

The new entrant start-ups no longer have the proto status and are now conceptually equal to existing (small) firms. Some of those may however use their *high-potential start-up* status (implicit or explicit) to their advantage to attract funding and support. This status may already have been acquired before the Market phase, i.e. in the Proposition phase or the Go-to-Market phase. Only the start-ups that are able to successfully compete with existing firms survive in the longer run.

Implementation

Detailed descriptions of each phase are given in the subsequent sections. Although for simplicity the entrepreneurial agents are referred to as 'entrepreneurs' in the following descriptions, these agents can represent teams/partnerships of individual and organisational actors engaged in the start-up process, including, for example, science and technology advisors, venture capitalists, agencies that provide early stage start-up funding, and intermediaries.

It should be pointed out, before moving on, that the assumptions made in these descriptions follow the logic that was developed for the endogenous political parties model (Laver and Schilperoord 2007, Laver, Sergenti and Schilperoord 2012), which is an extension of Laver's spatial agent-based model of multiparty competition (Laver 2005). It ported the "citizen candidates" approach (Besley and Coate 1997; Osborne 2000) to the Laver model, adding realism by incorporating logic and rules for "voter" agents that can change state and enter the set of parties. Transferring this logic to the SKIN domain, entrepreneurs in the SKIN extension described hereafter are "candidate innovators" that can change state to leaders of innovative start-ups and enter the set of firms in the system. This chapter is about the *initial start-up phase* where the greatest entrepreneurial risk is focused (cf. McKelvey 2004). Here it is subdivided into two distinct phases, the Proposition phase and the Go-to-Market phase, for examining the risk and potential returns. The later *managerial* phase, the Market phase, is principally covered by agent strategies standard in SKIN and needs less attention.

3.1 The valuation of start-up opportunities

Each entrepreneurial agent has a kene, its individual knowledge base. The special and innovative business focus of an entrepreneur, i.e. its potential innovation that can be turned into a new start-up firm, is represented by its innovation hypothesis (IH). The start-up opportunity is expressed by the *probability p* of the entrepreneur creating a new proto start-up on the basis of its current knowledge base and IH (its 'start-up proposition'). The start-up probability p is assumed to be proportional to the entrepreneur's valuation V of the start-up proposition, i.e. the IH. The *birth parameter* β captures how sensitive each entrepreneur's start-up decision is to the estimate V[10].

$$p = \beta \cdot V$$

Each tick of the simulation, the entrepreneur *updates* the estimate value V, using new information about the IHs of potential competitors. The *memory parameter α* describes how much entrepreneurs update their estimate on the basis of new information about the system at tick t[11].

$$V_{it} = \alpha \cdot V_{i(t-1)} + (1 - \alpha) \cdot v_{it}$$

With freely available information on the IH *adverts* of potential competitors, each entrepreneur is able to picture how unique and innovative its start-up proposition is in comparison to the existing market, and how quickly the competition would be able to adopt or clone its new business focus. The new valuation info v is computed as the *minimum distance* between the entrepreneur's IH advert (its start-up proposition) and the IH adverts of its potential competitors. In other words, v is its distance to its *closest competitor*. By implication, V is a measure for uniqueness of the entrepreneur's IH.

$$v_{i,t} = min\ D_{ijt}$$

[10] cf. Laver model extension. The literature about this model provides details on what are realistic parameter values and their effects on the simulations.
[11] Ibid.

The distance *D* between two agents is computed (cf. Definition 2.2) as the edit distance between the IH adverts of those two agents. In other words, D is the number of changes needed to change the one IH into the other IH. This is computed simply as the number of different capabilities in the two IHs.

3.2 The birth and death of proto start-ups

The entrepreneur passes its knowledge base (kene) and innovation hypothesis IH to the proto start-up. The proto start-up manufactures a prototype product. During the proto stage the start-up is obtaining new information about its potential sales. For obtaining market feedback on prototype products of proto start-ups, the market module is run twice: with and without the proto start-ups participating. This information is then used to evaluate the potential of the proto start-up.

The proto stage provides a limited window to do a 'fitness test' of the proto start-up against a 'survival threshold', which is a feature of the overall market system. Within this test window, the potential sales must be sufficient to expect the start-up to have a real opportunity to grow and survive in the next phase: the Market phase. In order to make such an estimate, with each tick of the simulation the proto start-up's fitness F is updated, using new information about potential sales f of its prototype product. The memory parameter α describes how much fitness is updated on the basis of new information about the system at tick t[12].

$$F_{it} = \alpha \cdot F_{i(t-1)} + (1 - \alpha) \cdot f_{it}$$

There are two possible outcomes to the Go-to-Market phase: (1) Enter: the start-up company enters the market; it will compete fully with other firms; (2) Exit: the start-up dies.

3.3 The market entry of new start-up firms

The new entrant start-ups that have survived the proto stage no longer have the proto status: they are now *conceptually equal* to existing small firms. This means that they can manufacture and sell their product, compete with other firms on the market, and engage in innovation networks, albeit with small capacity.

---

[12] Ibid.

Some of the new entrant firms may acquire high-potential status. This is explicitly measured by comparing their sales against the growth threshold Tg (>Ts). It is also possible that they have acquired such status already in the Go-to-Market phase, in case potential sales exceeded Tg. Most start-ups would exist between the survival threshold Ts and the growth threshold Tg.

Start-ups may benefit from a high-potential status throughout the start-up process to attract funding and support. Start-ups may seek government support nationally or internationally, e.g. early stage financing. It is also possible that there is implicit status, e.g. by the reputation of the entrepreneurs, association with strong actors, etc. In that case, it makes sense to extend high-potential status to entrepreneurs or to start-up propositions in the Proposition phase, and formulate thresholds in relation to that. If the start-up company falls below the survival threshold, it dies. It follows that only the start-ups that are able to successfully compete with existing firms survive in the longer run.

4. The case of high-potential start-ups

The SKIN extension is a spin-off from the IPSE-SKIN model development for the Innovation Policy Simulation for the Smart Economy (IPSE) project at UCD (Schilperoord and Ahrweiler 2014) that examines Irish sectors and innovation networks using a combination of empirical studies, network analysis and agent-based simulation. A simple case study, set in the Irish context, is illustrated to show how the extension can be used to extend the model's original focus on innovation policy to embrace entrepreneurship policy.

The focus of the case study is Enterprise Ireland's High-Potential Start-up (HPSU) scheme, an important element in delivering the Smart Economy that touches both innovation and entrepreneurship policy issues (Delivering the Smart Economy, 2009). A HPSU is defined as a company that is "capable of introducing a new or innovative product or service to international markets, involved in manufacturing or internationally traded services, capable of creating 10 jobs in Ireland and realising €1 million in sales within three to four years of starting up, led by an experienced management team, headquartered and controlled in Ireland and less than six years old" (Evaluation of Enterprise Supports for Start-Ups and Entrepreneurship, 2014). It was reported that over €60m HPSU funding was given by EI to 199 start-ups between 2004 and 2006 (Figure 11.4.1).

Of those HPSUs, 38 (= 19.1%) have since closed down.

Figure 11.4.1: HPSU total costs, 2004-2006.

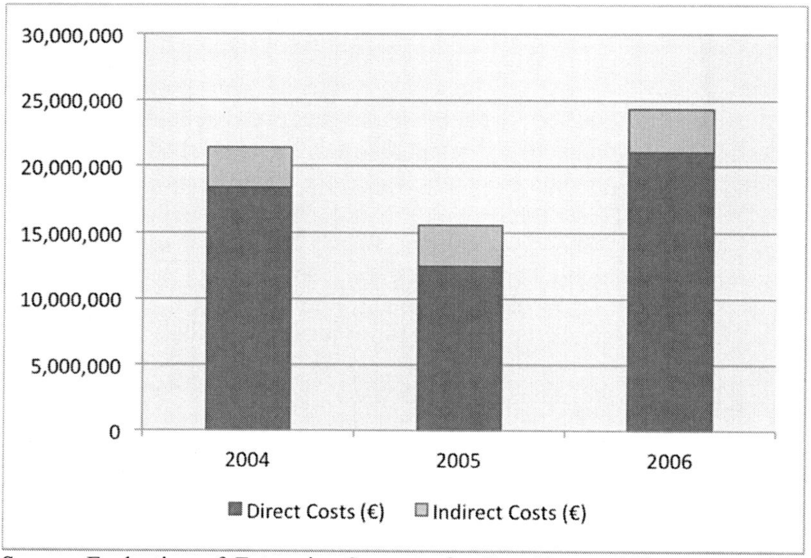

Source: Evaluation of Enterprise Supports for Start-Ups and Entrepreneurship, 2014, p. 30

Setup

To simulate HPSUs, the SKIN model was initialised with 100 entrepreneurial agents and 500 agents representing small and large firms of one sector. The model's knowledge space was set up to span 1,000 capabilities and was structured as depicted in Figure 11.4.2. Entrepreneurs and small firms were given rare capabilities. This way, they are positioned to be able to contribute to the sector's innovation dynamics.

Figure 11.4.2: Initial distribution of capabilities

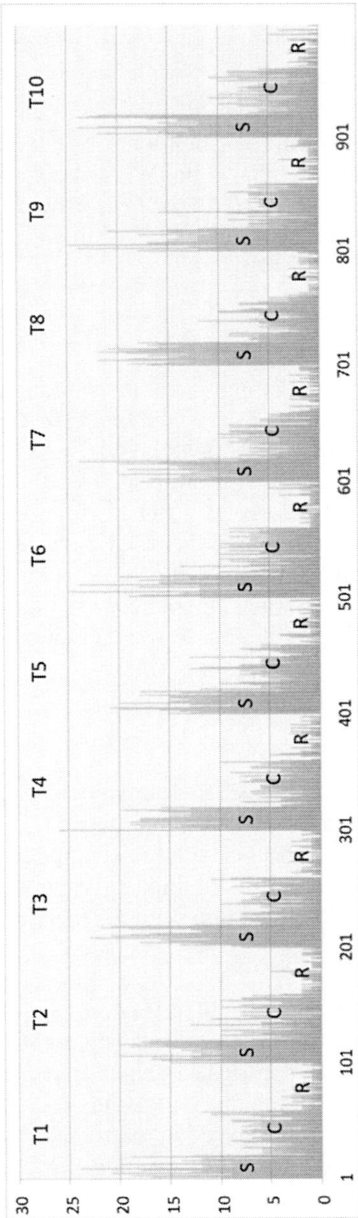

The market module was set up with a standard range of 100 products. The market included suppliers of raw materials and end users (which is common use).

Experiment

The group of entrepreneurs with the highest valued start-up propositions (hereafter referred to as the 'HPSU group') was tracked and observed in the Proposition phase. The proto start-ups created by those entrepreneurs (the actual HPSUs) were expected to be most successful in the Go-to-Market phase.

Simulation

The creation of proto start-ups by entrepreneurs was simulated as were the potential sales of those proto start-ups. For the latter the market module was *run twice* for each tick of the simulation, with and without proto start-ups. (In the first instance, with proto start-ups, the market module computes the potential sales outcomes, but no transactions follow. The second time, without proto start-ups, the sales that are computed by the market module are followed by transactions, as is standard procedure.) The simulation was stopped when no more proto start-ups were being created. For simplicity, the Market phase was not simulated; i.e. no entry or exit of proto start-ups.

Analysis

Information about the distribution of an entrepreneur's (edit) distance $D_{i,j}$ from the existing firms (see the example in Figure 11.4.3, left) shows that there are a very small number of 'closest competitors'. This makes intuitive sense, given the initial distribution of capabilities. It would be counter-intuitive to start the simulation with all the entrepreneurs placed only in common positions.

Examining all entrepreneurs, the distribution of an entrepreneur's minimum distance Dmin from existing firms (Figure 4.3, right) confirms this intuition. The group with the highest valued start-up propositions, the HPSU group, is highlighted (Figure 11.4.3, box). It is shown that the entrepreneurs in the HPSU group have higher probability p (assuming for illustration only that p = β ⍰ Dmin) of creating a proto start-up (Figure 11.4.2, right axis, line).

Figure 11.4.3: The HPSU group

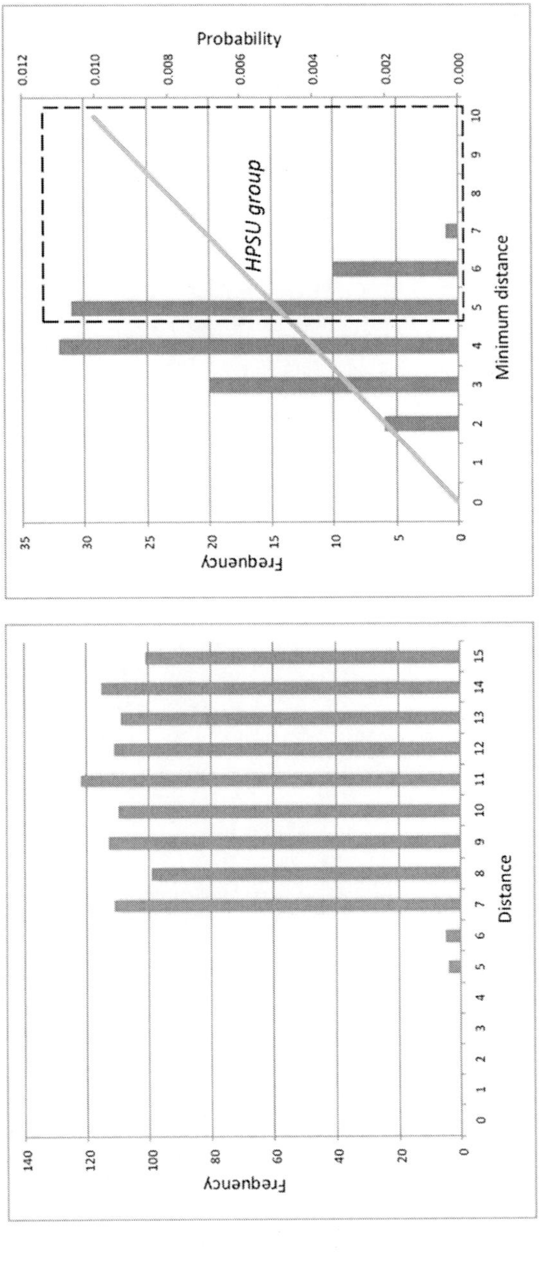

Examining the simulation outputs, the number of proto start-ups is seen to increase to 43 (Figure 11.4.4), which means that 43% of the entrepreneurs have decided to go for it. The number of start-ups with significant potential sales (a condition for market entry) increases but stays at a relative low level of no more than 25% of all proto start-ups.

Figure 11.4.4: The number of proto start-ups

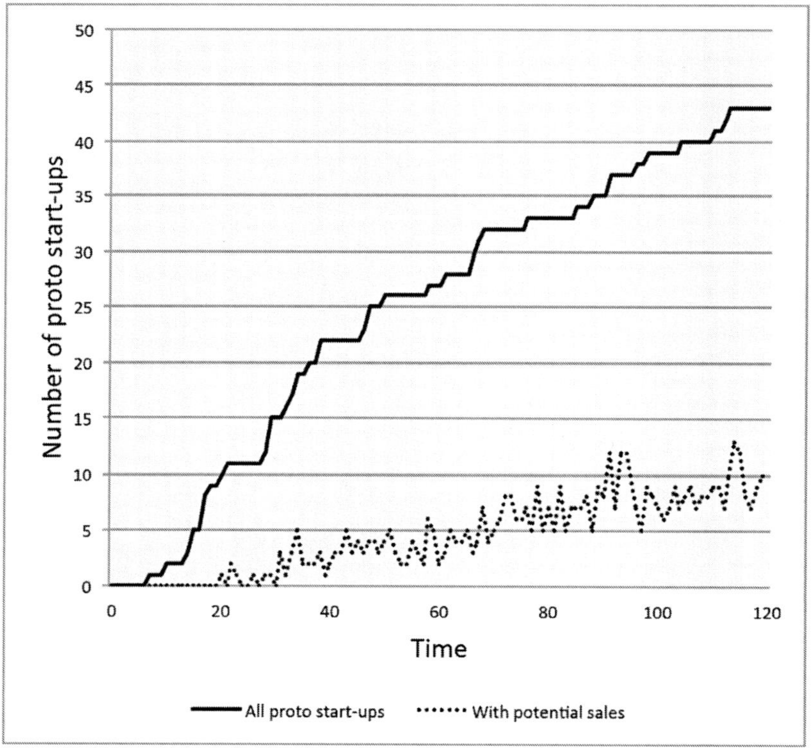

After examining these results, it is possible to compare whether the proto start-ups created by entrepreneurs in the HPSU group were more successful than the others. Table 11.4.1 reveals that the entrepreneurs in the HPSU group turned out to be more active in the creation of start-ups. This should be expected given the formula for probability *p*. This can however not explain the much higher average of potential sales that was measured for the proto start-ups created by entrepreneurs in this group.

Table 11.4.1: Evaluation of the HPSUs

	HPSUs	Other start-ups
Number of start-ups	28	15
Average number of months with potential sales	13.5	11
Average potential sales	3,143,525	1,259,565
Average age of start-ups	75.9	60.5

On closer inspection, it was observed that a small number of start-ups had much higher peaks in their potential sales (Figure 11.4.5), which explains the higher potential sales average. It was also observed that these special start-ups were all (!) created by entrepreneurs in the HPSU group.

Figure 11.4.5: Potential sales by the proto start-ups

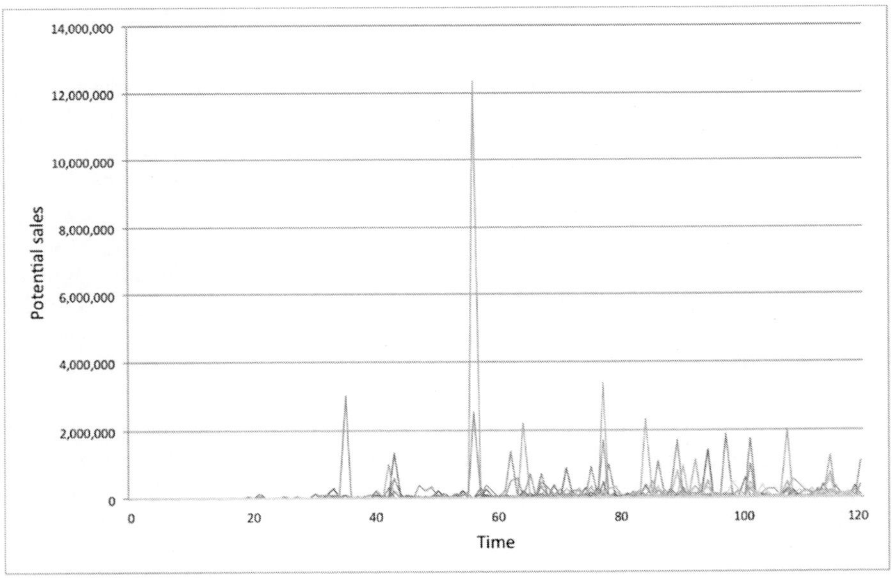

Closing remarks

This preliminary result illustrates that there may be a correlation in the outcomes of the first two stages of the start-up process: the valuations of start-up opportunities. This is not trivial, since the valuations performed in these two stages are based on very different information. This result supports the working hypothesis that the potential for knowledge contribution and value creation of entrepreneurs, start-ups, and SMEs lies in the rarity of the capabilities that they bring to the market. It also confirms the policy of Enterprise Ireland to fund and support high-potential start-ups based on their innovative technology profiles.

5. Discussion and further experiments

This chapter describes the SKIN extension that is designed for modelling the birth of new start-up companies. Its use thus far was twofold. First, a method was introduced of using SKIN for reasoning about the when and where of start-ups. The method's use was then explored further in a simulation experiment set in the empirical context of an Irish funding programme for high-potential start-ups.

The initial results show that the method can be used to support reasoning about the positions of high-potential start-up propositions – while still early in the process of being developed further and brought to market – and comparing those to the positions of the existing firms. The surprising outcome of the simulation experiment is that, in the dynamic, unpredictable context that is modelled with the SKIN market module, it is possible to reason when and where high-potential start-up propositions are likely to emerge. This is not trivial, because at the Proposition phase (i.e. when the actual start-up company has not yet been created) the only information available to the entrepreneurial agents in the simulation for valuation of their start-up potential is the advertised positions of the existing companies. At a later phase of the start-up process, when new information comes available to entrepreneurs in the form of potential sales estimates generated by the market module, a different valuation of their start-up potential can be performed. The simulations show that the valuations are correlated; there is a match between high-potential status in the Proposition phase and success – as measured by potential sales – in the Go-to-Market phase.

Consolidation of these initial results requires further work involving parameter sweeping and empirical calibration and testing. This exercise will cover the module's distance metrics, birth parameter, memory parameter, thresholds for survival and growth, and the duration of the test window in the Go-to-Market phase. The next experiments after consolidation will involve modelling entrepreneurial networks and the role of intermediaries therein.

Acknowledgement

The author gratefully acknowledges the financial support from the Irish Government's Programme for Research in Third Level Institutions (PRTLI 5) project grant entitled 'Innovation Policy Simulation for the Smart Economy (IPSE)'.

References

Ahrweiler, P. (ed.) (2010) Innovation in Complex Social Systems, (Routledge Studies in Global Competition) Routledge: London

Ahrweiler, P., Schilperoord, M., Gilbert, N. and Pyka, A. (2012) 'Simulating the role of MNCs for knowledge and capital dynamics in networks of innovation', in Heidenreich, M. (ed.) Innovation and Institutional Embeddedness of Multinational Companies, Edward Elgar

Ahrweiler, P., Schilperoord, M., Pyka, A. and Gilbert, N. (2014) 'Testing policy options for Horizon 2020 with SKIN', in Gilbert, N., Ahrweiler, P. and Pyka, A. (eds.) Simulating Knowledge Dynamics in Innovation Networks, Springer: Heidelberg/New York: 155-184

Besley, T. and Coate, S. (1997) 'An economic model of representative democracy', Quarterly Journal of Economics 112(1): 85-106

Department of Enterprise, Trade and Employment (2009) Delivering the Smart Economy (Dublin, 2009)

Department of the Taoiseach (2008) Building Ireland's Smart Economy: a framework for sustainable economic renewal (Dublin, 2008)

Forfás (2014) Evaluation of Enterprise Supports for Start-Ups and Entrepreneurship (Dublin, 2014)

Gilbert, N., Pyka, A. and Ahrweiler, P. (2003) Simulating innovation networks. In A. Pyka & G. Küppers (Eds.) Innovation Networks: Theory and Practice (pp. 169-196). Cheltenham, UK: Edward Elgar.

Gilbert, N., Ahrweiler, P. and Pyka, A. (eds.) (2014) Simulating Knowledge Dynamics in Innovation Networks, Springer: Heidelberg/New York

Laver, M. (2005) 'Policy and the dynamics of political competition', American Political Science Review 99(2): 263-281

Laver, M. and Schilperoord, M. (2007) 'Spatial models of political competition with endogenous political parties', Philosophical Transactions of the Royal Society B. Sep 29; 362(1485): 1711-21

Laver, M., Sergenti, E. and Schilperoord, M. (2012) 'Endogenous birth and death of political parties in dynamic party competition', in: Seth A.,

Prescott T. and Bryson J. (eds.) Modelling Natural Action Selection. Cambridge: Cambridge University Press
McKelvey, B. (2004) 'Toward a complexity science of entrepreneurship', Journal of Business Venturing, Volume 19, Issue 3, May 2004, Pages 313-341, ISSN 0883-9026, http://dx.doi.org/10.1016/S0883-9026(03)00034-X
Osborne, M. (2000) 'Entry-deterring policy differentiation by electoral candidates', Mathematical Social Sciences 40 41-62
Schilperoord, M. and Ahrweiler, P. (2014) 'Towards a prototype policy laboratory for simulating innovation networks', in Gilbert, N., Ahrweiler, P. and Pyka, A. (eds.) Simulating Knowledge Dynamics in Innovation Networks, Springer: Heidelberg/New York: 185-198

PART V:

FUTURE RESEARCH ISSUES IN COMPLEXITY SCIENCE AND SOCIAL SIMULATION

CHAPTER TWELVE

COLLECTIVE BEHAVIOUR AS A NEW SOCIAL AGENT

ELENA PUGACHEVA

Introduction

What we are witnessing today is a substantial growth not only in business activity but also in social activity worldwide. One can see the emergence of energetic individuals, who in all sincerity try to change situations, solve urgent problems, and resist the spreading of crises. Inevitably, it seems that those problems, be they economic, financial, political or social, turn out to be interwoven into the social networks of interconnected and interdependent social actors. How can any serious attempt be made to deal with such social reality?

The growing complexity of social reality is the starting point of the proposed analysis. The core ideas for investigation (Part I) are: (1) the idea that the level of complexity of a system should respond to the complexity of its environment (Bar-Yam, 2002; Ashby, 1956); (2) the historical shift in the perception of social reality as a result of the development of horizontal networks of communication (Castells, 2000); (3) the emergence of new social actors aiming at transformation of the society as a whole (Bakuniak & Nowak, 1987; Castells, 2010). In light of these ideas, the growth of social unrest in the world is presented as a conflict between the increasing complexity of social reality and the levels of complexity of contemporary social institutes, which are lagging behind.

In this chapter the events in Ukraine in 2013-2014 are analysed in the framework of the theory of complexity. The basic hypothesis underlying this proposed point of view is that the conflict can be resolved by the collective behaviour of self-organising networks having characteristics different from those of existing social agents. In the author's opinion we are dealing with a new social actor whose social status is not yet defined (Pugacheva, 2014). This new social actor has an emergent nature and more complex social dynamics and collective features (collective thinking, collaborative learning, collective decision-making, distributed leadership, distributed control, etc.) that are superior to similar functions of traditional actors (individuals, social groups, leaders, etc.).

As discussed in Part II, this new social agent is the product of social self-organisation that manifests itself in an iterative process of "testing" behaviour patterns. The events in Ukraine escalate a confrontation of "organisation versus self-organisation", which can be treated as the conflict between the traditional social actors and the new one. While the power of the traditional social actors is well suited to hierarchical social structure, it is poorly suited to deal with networked social reality. The conflict of the old and new senses has already taken place in reality. To resolve this conflict, social innovation is needed. In Ukraine, the social innovations put forward by the collective social actor are territory fragmentation and the formation of self-governing communities bearing different types of sovereignty.

The identity of the new social actor is discussed in terms of network thinking (Part III). Research issues are examined by means of computer experiments, such as the priorities in decision making and the roles of network structure and network topology in problem solving. It is emphasised that network thinking reveals new components of decision making that are of special importance in relation to the new social agent.

Part I: The Core Ideas

The complexity of social reality is being actively studied within the theory of complex systems (Anderson 1972, Arthur 2013, Barabasi 2002, Granovetter 1973, Macy 2002, among others). From the complexity point of view, the level of complexity is a key point in assessment of social transformation. As researchers state:

> "Governments, like organisms, may be under evolutionary pressure that results in them becoming more complex. Governmental complexity must increase as the complexity of its environment—the society it governs and other states—increases" (Gard-Murray & Bar-Yam, 2012, p. 4).

The failure of a great number of revolutions, in the sense that the intentions of revolutionaries were not implemented, stems from an inability to provide an adequate level of governmental complexity.

> "Modern governments are highly complex systems. Complex systems are formed out of many independently acting yet simultaneously interdependent parts. Governments are made up of many people interacting within institutional frameworks (e.g. bureaucrats, judges, and soldiers) equipped with resources such as money, buildings, and weapons, and regulated by laws, norms, procedures, and precedents. It is not merely the quantity of parts, but their interaction and interdependence which give rise to the complexity of the whole" (ibid, p.3).

Consequently, the fortune of social transformation rests upon the ability of the society to rapidly overcome the "complexity gap" that occurs between the present level of complexity minus its loss because of breaking the complex web of social dependencies during revolution, and the intended complexity. That is why the most likely outcome of rapid revolutions is a return to autocracy as a less complex government system in comparison with democracy.

Therefore, the chance of a successful social revolution for the traditional social movement (seize power) looks like a highly unlikely event. To analyse the alternative ways of social transformation, it is reasonable to take into account the changes of social reality by looking at the process through the theoretical categories of the theory of complexity.

Recently, there has been a growing interest in investigation of the relationship between social movements and social networks. Any new technological framework has a great impact on social reality. Manuel Castells suggests (Castells, 2007):

> "The emergence of mass self-communication offers an extraordinary medium for social movements and rebellious individuals to build their autonomy and confront the institutions of society in their own terms and around their own projects" (p.249).

Manuel Castells considers the development of horizontal networks of communication as a "historical shift of the public sphere from the institutional realm to the new communication space" (ibid, p.238). As such, the communication system increases the level of complexity. While the communication system of industrial society was centred on mass media and could be characterised as from one to many, web communication includes multimodal information exchange from many to many. Manuel Castells characterises this communication system as "self-generated in content, self-directed in emission, and self-selected in reception by many that communicate with many" (ibid, p. 248).

The increased level of complexity of the social environment challenged modern society. It was faced with the problem of identity. It is a fact that legitimate identity introduced by social institutes has lost its former meaning and function. As Manuel Castells puts it:

> "The institutions and organisations of civil society that were constructed around the democratic state, and around the social contract between capital and labour, have become, by and large, empty shells, decreasingly able to relate to people's lives and values in most societies. It is indeed a tragic irony that when most countries in the world finally fought their way to access the institutions of liberal democracy … these institutions are so distant from the structure and processes that really matter that they appear to most people as a sarcastic grimace on the new face of history. At the turn of millennium, the king and the queen, the state and civil society, are both naked, and their children-citizens are wandering around a variety of foster homes" (Castells, 2010, p. 420).

At the same time Manuel Castells pays attention to the emergence of communes of social actors who are opposed to social institutions in their desire to defend certain values and autonomy, for example, religious, women's, or environmental movements. Special attention has been directed to the emergence of communes aiming at transformation of society as a whole by introducing new sets of values. According to Castells, these communities play a leading role in constituting future society.

> "Because our historical vision has become so used to orderly battalions, colourful banners, and scripted proclamations of social change, we are at a loss when confronted with the subtle pervasiveness of incremental changes of symbols processed through multiform networks, away from the halls of power. It is in these back alleys of society, whether in alternative electronic networks or in grass-rooted networks of communal resistance, that I have sensed the embryos of a new society" (ibid, p. 428).

Castell's ideas of emergent communes that change society are compatible with, for example, events in Poland in 1980. As stated by Bakuniak and Nowak, the Independent Self-Governing Trade Union "Solidarity" manifested itself as a new emergent social agent changing social reality (Bakuniak & Nowak, 1987).

> "...what did August 1980 mean in Poland? We are of the opinion that it is sound to interpret it as the emergence of a civil society. It came about by way of processes of overcoming atomisation, the objectivisation of new vision of social reality (in which society was present in opposition to the state) and of organisation of the project of social action of various goals and values of this society... With the appearance of the idea of "Solidarity" there appeared a new "collective actor" undertaking action on the scale of the entire society" (p.401).

In light of the above-mentioned ideas, the growth of social movements worldwide and the observed sequence of revolutions could be treated as a historical lab, testing new patterns of social interaction on the basis of which new social institutions will emerge. The substance of such an experiment is the appearance of new values and senses that are adequate to deal with a more complex level of social reality.

Very many people try to classify the events in Ukraine in 2013-2014 using old concepts, namely riot, revolution, power appropriation, etc. In fact, the local anti-criminal protest movement intensified the network of participants, whose social interactions affect various aspects of social life, thereby bringing new participants into the conflict.

Events in Ukraine in 2014 have shown that Maidan[1] recognised its power only when, in the process of self-organisation, an atmosphere of trust, respect, and mutual aid emerged. Maidan has brought together people of different social status, territorial and professional affiliation, who were ready to participate actively in the processes of social changes and were able to take all the responsibility.

The resources of Maidan participants (information, human, material) have flowed through the network chains to the places where they were most needed. Maidan wonderfully balanced the different forces (politicians, business people, intellectuals, radicals, students, pensioners), allowing them to coexist and complement each other. A minority showed its

---

[1] It was a wave of demonstrations and civil unrest in Ukraine in 2013 – 2014. The public protest began on the night of 21 November 2013, demanding European integration. The event took place in the central square of Kiev, called Maidan. Then protests expanded, demanding the resignation of President Viktor Yanukovych. After bloody clashes with the police, the regime of President Yanukovych was overthrown. Maidan is a symbol of the protest movement in Ukraine, known as "Revolution of Dignity". See:
https://en.wikipedia.org/wiki/Euromaidan#cite_note-97

strength in the fight against a well-organised clan-hierarchical armed state structure (Ministry of Internal Affairs, the Security Service of Ukraine, Berkut[2], mercenaries, titushky[3]) and also showed its ability to revive and self-organise. It turned out that Maidan is open not to destruction but to creation of a new order, putting forward not the task of capturing power, but of controlling it in the cause of implementing the ideals of Maidan.

Country leaders, world organisations, and social institutions have tried to resolve the conflict. This is, in fact, an attempt to handle the situation among traditional social actors. One can see that the effectiveness of such efforts depends on ability to coordinate social interactions. Could traditional social actors provide the necessary coordination of social interactions in the modern world?

In a broad sense, Maidan is a conflict between the traditional worldview, which is still the basis for decision making, and a more complex social reality. The crisis manifests itself in different ways: hierarchy vs network; complex system vs. simple system; traditional leadership vs distributed leadership; recognition of the legitimacy of self-organisation vs the construction of barriers to self-organisation. To approach this knotty problem, a new way of understanding and interpreting problems is necessary. This requires taking a look at the big picture.

Part II: Social Dynamics of a New Social Actor

Analysis of the Maidan phenomenon allows one to suggest that it is not a traditional protest movement. As Ukrainian philosopher Sergei Datsuk states, the sense of Maidan is in changing the historical actor in Ukraine. It is no longer a political or business elite but a self-organising community. From his point of view, the Ukrainian revolution must be treated as an appearance of a new historical subject (Datsuk S. , 2014).

The main characteristics of the new social actor may be described by the properties of complex systems. Thus, the processes of self-organisation are at the heart of a new social actor. New patterns of collective behaviour emerge due to these processes. Social dynamics is an iterative process of

---

[2] The "Berkut" was the system of special police of the Ukrainian militia within the Ministry of Internal Affairs.

[3] Titushky is a term for mercenary street hooligans who supported the Ukrainian police and performed illegal acts during the administration of Viktor Yanukovych.

testing, by interacting elements, patterns of behaviour in response to internal and external changes. As Brian Arthur describes (Arthur, 2013):

> "…agents must explore their way forward, must "learn" about the decision problem they are in, must respond to the opportunities confronting them. We are in a world where beliefs, strategies, and actions of agents are being "tested" for survival within a situation or outcome or "ecology" that these beliefs, strategies and actions together create. ... So agents are not just reacting to a problem they are trying to make sense of; their very actions in doing so collectively reform the current outcome, which requires them to adjust afresh" (p.5).

The social dynamics of the new social agent is self-producing or autopoietic. The new social agent constantly "makes itself" (Maturana, 1980):

> "An autopoietic machine is a machine organised (defined as a unity) as a network of processes of production (transformation and destruction) of components that produces the components which: (i) through their interactions and transformations continuously regenerate and realise the network of processes (relations) that produced them; and (ii) constitute it (the machine) as a concrete unity in space in which they (the components) exist by specifying the topological domain of its realisation as such a network" (p. 78-79).

As such, the cornerstone of the new social actor is "the right to self-organisation". Today, to a great extent, the new social actor fights for this right. In fact a confrontation of "organisation versus self-organisation" takes place. It has been argued that "bottom-up behaviour seems illogical to Western minds because we have a hierarchical bias against self-organisation" (Westley, 2006, p. 132). Thinking in terms of industrial society, traditional social actors try to build barriers to self-organisation, struggling to hold back power. At the same time the network nature of the new social actor makes these efforts unproductive, because the new social actor has escaped its confinement in the fragmented social space.

> "Power still rules society; it still shapes, and dominates us…This form of power is … increasingly ineffective for the interests that it is supposed to serve. States can shoot, but because the profile of their enemies, and the whereabouts of their challengers, are increasingly unclear, they tend to shoot randomly, with the probability that they may shoot themselves in the process" (Castells, 2010, p. 425).

The power of the new social actor is in the creation of behaviour patterns that can be the basis for the new social order. It reveals itself most vividly at the moment of revolution or at any other historical opportunity. The crucial question is what alternatives to social life there are in the depths of society. In other words, what patterns have been created by collective social interactions before radical social changes occur?

Thus, the absence of adequate patterns does not allow more complex social order. For example, analysis of the Arab Spring has shown that:

> "Central control structures that are not able to cope with the demands of economic conditions may be defeated by an enraged populace. However, the establishment of order requires a new structure to be accepted. ... Given the large number of decisions that have to be made to set up a new governance structure, the ability of a collective to agree on specific choices presents an insurmountable challenge when there is no organisation at all. As a result of this limitation, order is eventually re-established by force, and the exercise of this force is, almost by definition, a new autocratic system" (Bar-Yam & Gard-Murray, 2011-2-02).

At the same time more complex patterns of behaviour, which were constrained by the old "rules of the game", make it possible to meet the challenges of the new social order, as in Poland or the Czech Republic after the collapse of the Soviet regime.

The Ukrainian events 2013 - 2015 also demonstrated the appearance of new behaviour patterns as a result of communication in social networks. On the basis of these patterns new social institutions have been looming in social space. The best-known one is the volunteer movement based on network trust and the gift economy.

The new social actor is a product of the new social reality. The traditional mentality tries to identify it in the old manner, for example, by sociological analysis. But in this case the most important features of the new social actor escape notice, namely, emergence of new types of social agents, new senses, and new social reality. The phrase "included in the network agents" should supplement the list of classical sociological concepts (status, role, social interaction, social exchange, etc.) This small addition, however, leads to a significant change in the meaning of the concepts that modern sociology should reformulate.

The most important feature of the new social actor is its ability to generate new senses. Sergei Datsuk has offered to discuss resulting events in Ukraine in his declaration of humankind communities (Datsuk S. , 2014). The author suggests considering networking communities as new actors of social interaction. Network communities are groups with common motivations for life and action that communicate regularly within themselves and formulate shared interests. Common principles and non-utilitarian motivation distinguish communities from interest groups.

As Datsuk states, ruling classes all over the world are already linked by their common interest in maintaining their political and financial power. In his opinion world communities will always lose to the ruling classes as long as they hold on to old ideas. The world communities need to understand their network unity and organise themselves in the face of the limitless power of states and corporations.

Sergei Datsuk points out the basic principles of network communities:

- All power shall belong to network communities instead of people. This implies that network communities are bearers of different types of sovereignty, as they can agree upon such;
- superiority of network communities over states. This means that: 1) powers are delegated from the bottom to the top (centre); 2) the scope of powers both at the centre and locally is defined by self-governing communities and not by the centre; 3) every power both at the centre and locally has a validity term that is regularly reviewed together with its scope; 4) financing begins at the level of authority of a single community, with the state and corporations being paid for their functions and services on a competitive basis;
- shared sovereignty instead of national sovereignty. From this point of view, social groups capable of self-governing are the source of the shared sovereignty;
- shared citizenship instead of state citizenship. In other words, the integrity is organised topologically, not geographically;
- Public resources belong to humankind represented by network communities;
- an open global market of infrastructural services instead of a closed state-monopolised one;
- open finance, open corporate transactions, and open global infrastructure.

From this point of view, humankind is seen as a unity composed of the fragmented network communities that resist corporate and state arbitrariness. And what is taking place today in Ukraine is a prototype, the beginning of a process of fragmentation of territory and formation of self-governing communities.

Part III: Role and Status of New Social Actor

The network nature of the new social actor predetermines the importance of two characteristics: network position and network structure. These characteristics make sense to discuss in terms of diffusion, possibilities of snowballing processes, sustainability, and vulnerability to attacks, etc.

To discuss the role and status of the new social actor, we need network thinking (Mitchell, 2006). A lack of network thinking does not allow traditional leaders[4] to look at the situation in a more realistic way. Thus, thinking in terms of territories, resources, dual relationships, and head-to-head competition, they see problems as isolated phenomena rather than as a result of escalating positive feedback.

Network thinking is a strategic way of thinking in terms of the whole. From the network point of view, the result of decision making should be evaluated in the context of network changes. Thus great achievements might be a "Pyrrhic Victory" if the environment (eco-environment) becomes less favourable to the leader. The strategic decision is in the choices which node to join (or to create) and what role to play.

From the traditional point of view, Russia wins in the conflict Russia-Ukraine. Ukraine loses resources and territory, and it doesn't have many strategic resources (gas, oil, nuclear weapons). However, if we take into account the position of the countries in the world network and transformation of the environment, this conclusion is controversial. Russia has lost influential positions in the world network, Ukraine instead has gained them. Ukraine has rallied the world and mobilised many international forces. It has served as a bridge between the West and the East. Perhaps soon network-politics will replace geopolitics. This conflict should reveal that the world of the twenty-first century differs fundamentally from the world of the twentieth century. From now on network position is more significant than territory and resources. Perhaps

[4] Traditional leader means leader with hierarchy-centric thinking.

soon the main indicators of a country's power should be network location and network structure instead of GDP. Underestimation of this factor has demonstrated that many of Putin's plans were not implemented, despite Russia's apparent superiority in power.

The NetLogo platform for agent-based modelling is used in order to analyse the difference in decision making in the case of network thinking (vs. traditional thinking). Agent–based modelling is well suited for analysis of social systems composed of interacting agents who influence each other (Schelling, 1978; Granovetter, 1978; Epstein, 2002). The author finds that in her research it is beneficial to think in terms of agents (representing people) that participate and dynamically interact in a simulated social process created in a computer experiment. The key research issue is to understand how the results of the simulation match or differ from traditional decision-making. This simplified version of an artificial social space is used as a complementary method to strengthen rigorous scientific analysis, which is aimed at revealing the consequences of social interactions that are far from anticipated.

The first simulation is designed to analyse the impact of information attacks on network structure, and the process of “zombification”. As Ukrainian experience shows, zombification can massively influence people; however, it cannot initiate a self-organising process of collective behaviour. As such, all attempts to create an anti-Maidan similar to Maidan have failed.

Simulation of the process of zombification is based on the observation that not many people have their own opinion or can analyse information on their own. Most people share prevailing opinion.

The model has N=100 people. The percentage of red agents can be set using the slider “red_agents”. The other agents are blue. All agents randomly move across the field. At any step, the neighbours of blue agents make links with each other. Assuming that red agents are disinclined to self-organisation, they do not make links with each other. Furthermore, each blue agent has its threshold. The threshold value is a random integer number from 0 to 4. When meeting with a red agent, a blue agent compares its own threshold number with the number of network friends. If the threshold value is zero, the blue agent never changes its colour to red. When the threshold value is 1, the blue agent does not change its colour to red if its network consists of at least one friend. The situation is similar for other threshold values. The process stops when no blue agent can change its colour to red.

Fig. 12.3.1. *Top*: Screenshot of NetLogo interface for a typical experiment. *Bottom*: Relationship between initial number of red agents and final number of blue agents.

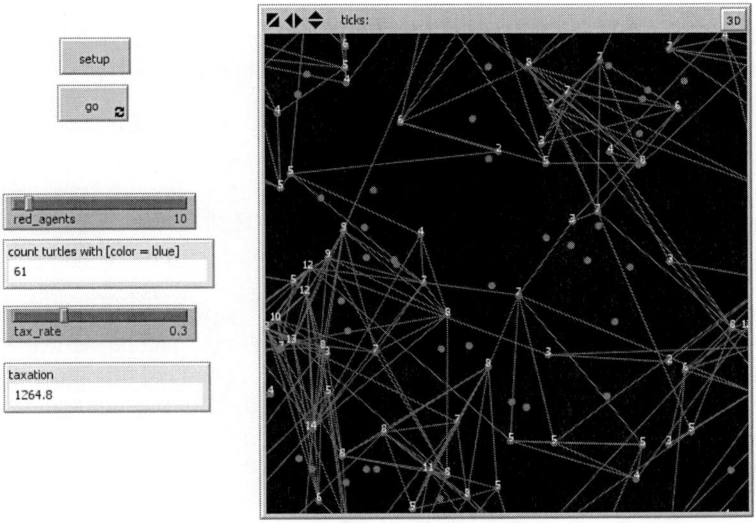

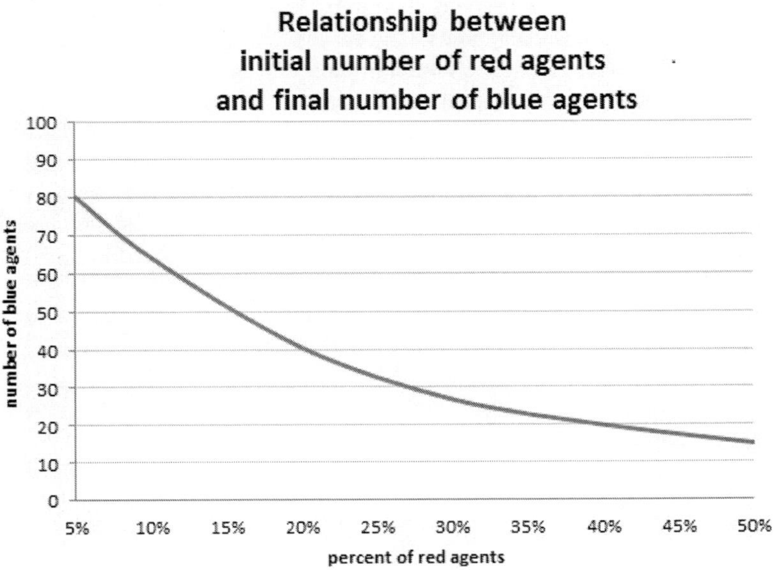

As shown in Fig. 12.3.1. (Bottom), the number of blue agents rapidly decreases with an increase of initial percentage of red agents. Thus, if "red_agents" is 10%, the initial percentage of blue agents is 90% while the final percentage of blue agents slightly exceeds 60%. That is, the losses are more than 30%. If the initial number of "red_agents" is 20%, the losses are close to 50%. Consequently, information attack is very effective.

The next research question is: has the power of the blue agents decreased along with the significant losses in quantity? The power of the blue agents has changed significantly since they have joined into a network (perhaps several networks). And the network interactions differ a lot from the usual ones. This is all demonstrated in the next experiment.

Assume that each agent has a certain income, which is distributed randomly in the range from 0 to 100. The rate of taxation can be set using the slider "tax_rate". The money of each network is counted, the network with the maximum amount of money is selected, and this amount is compared with the taxes that could be collected from all the agents.

Simulation has shown (Fig. 12.3.2) that the network resources are significantly higher than the resources of the non-network structure. The non-network structure collects money by imposing some duties on its members (in our case: taxes). For example, if the tax rate is 10%, then the taxation is ca 500 monetary units. The damage, which is calculated as the number of red agents in the case of initial "red agents" = 10%, is about 40%. The taxation of the initial community (the non-network structure with red and blue agents) is compared with the amount of money of the richest network (without imposition of the tax). As the experiment shows, the richest network (with maximum amount of money) counts about 3000 units of money. The critical value of the tax rate, at which taxation is equivalent to the resources of the richest network, is calculated to be 60%.

Networking allows people to use existing resources actively and to mobilise them as needed. Agents of non-network structures are pressured to keep resources in store as this is the guarantee of survival in difficult situations. In the non-network structure it is necessary to accumulate resources to meet challenges. The network structure puts forward the task of mobilisation of available resources, which, as the experiment shows, are many times higher than the resources of the non-network structure.

Fig. 12.3.2. *Top*: Loss of resources which is calculated as the number of red agents at the end of experiment. *Bottom*: Critical tax rate which is calculated as a value of tax rate when taxation is equivalent to the sum of money of the richest network.

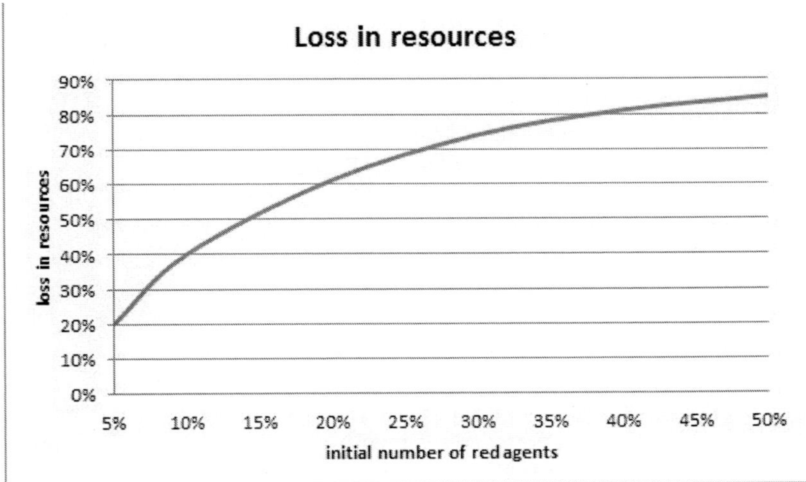

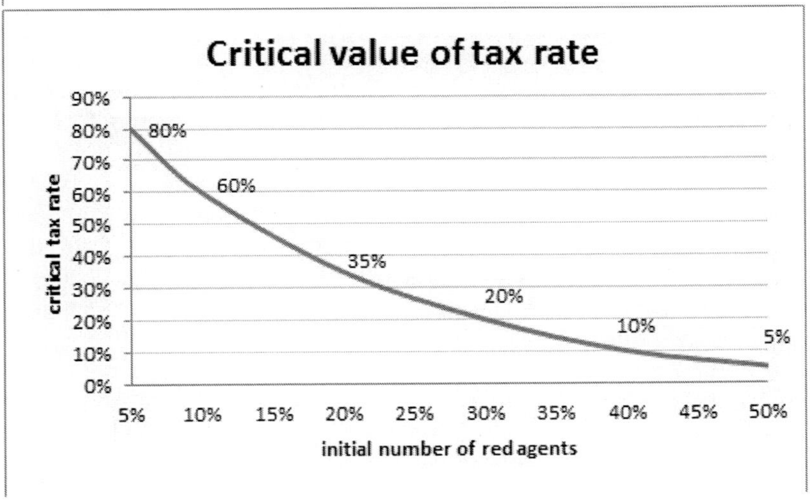

In view of the above, it is possible to change the focus of decision making: not resources → task, but task → resources. This statement has already been announced in Ukrainian society:

> "It is wrong to do the next step based on the idea of resources. It is necessary to do it according to the goals. New goals will find necessary resources" (Datsuk S. , 2014).

The volunteer movement in Ukraine proves this thesis. In spite of economic difficulties, volunteers collected the money needed in a particular situation in the shortest period of time. Valery Geletey, the Minister of Defence of Ukraine, said that volunteers organised the provision of military contingents better than the Defence Ministry.

The network point of view helps us to see one more component of new agent decision making besides resources, namely network structure. Thus for social change to occur a minority should have a stronger influence than the majority. The latest research has shown (e.g. Kearns, Judd, & Wortman, 2009) that a well-connected minority can impose their preference on the majority. Experiments in behaviour games at the University of Pennsylvania show that network structure matters. The structures under investigation differ qualitatively in various ways depending on the nature of the connectivity (from the Erdos-Renyi model to preferential attachment) and the ratio of inter-group and intra-group links. The key finding of the experiments is that in some network topologies (e.g. preferential attachment) the minority preference consistently wins globally. It was also shown that a well-connected minority reliably takes priority over the majority preference, and that such a group can facilitate global unity.

Perhaps the decision making problem of the new social agent needs further development: the next step should be based on the topology of the emerging social network. From this point of view, the human-subject experiments on the problems of collective behaviour are of special interest. Kearns (Judd, Kearns, & Vorobeychik, 2010) investigated colouring (a social differentiation task) and consensus (a social agreement task) in different network topologies.

The colouring problem requires each player in a network to choose a colour, from a fixed set, which differs from the choice of their network neighbours, while consensus requires selecting a colour that agrees with all network neighbours. Despite the cognitive similarity, these tasks demonstrate opposite behavioural effects within social networks with different structure. It was shown that as the networks become less clustered and more random, decentralised colouring becomes more difficult for humans to solve while decentralised consensus becomes easier.

The authors of the experiment concluded that the network properties (degree, centrality) alone are insufficient to explain the observed patterns in collective behaviour. Thus the task itself is of vital importance, even between two cognitively similar tasks. In other words, the task should match network structure.

So the role and status of a new social actor are dynamic characteristics that are determined by the challenges of society. The ability of society to build the network with appropriate topology and to use its potential determines the outcome. Maidan is the first step in this direction. Perhaps it was the simplest networking attempt, but it was an important step in using the network for the consolidation and mobilisation of society, as well as for global solidarity.

The topology of the Ukrainian social system has been changed drastically. Before Maidan the Ukrainian socio-economic system was oversimplified. First of all, no one social institute had evolved as a network in the sense of a preferential attachment model. Blood ties, friendship relations, and unlawful connections mostly determined the links. Second, all links were oriented in one direction. Feedback, which is a very important mechanism for complex systems, was practically absent. And third, people were not considered as agents of socio-economic systems. There were no links between the current and future state of the society and their activity. The goals of citizens of Ukraine were mostly material and pragmatic and could be successfully achieved alone in severe competition and struggle with fellow citizens.

Today a new topology of social interactions is under construction. It needs investigation from at least three positions:

- What is the structure of the emergent social network?
- What are the objectives of the society?
- How do the social network structure and stated objectives fit together?

Nowadays Ukrainian society organises itself almost blindly without even knowing what profound changes in the world are taking place simultaneously. As follows from the above computer experiments, effectiveness in decision making needs new priorities and network thinking.

Part IV: Discussion and Conclusions

Social networks simulation has demonstrated profound changes in the modern world (Barabasi, 2002; Macy M.W., 2002; Fellman, Bar-Yam, & Minai, 2014). Statistical characteristics, risks, threats, speed, possible alternatives, and prospects have drastically changed. The new reality challenges not only our knowledge, but also the institutions built on this knowledge. The process of "growing" new social institutions has already begun. The author shares the view that, unfortunately, the lion's share of the energy of humanity does not focus on ensuring the desired "genesis". On the contrary, all efforts are directed to imposing the old rules of the game onto this new world.

The events in Ukraine have demonstrated that the local problems of a country can activate a huge social network of interconnected and interdependent actors. The problem of coordination of the interactions of such a network turned out to be too daunting a task for traditional social institutions. The ineffectiveness of traditional decision making leads to a further escalation of the conflict and a confrontation with the forces of self-organisation.

The situation in Ukraine shows the attempt to regulate the situation among traditional social actors. The fruitfulness of their efforts depends on an understanding of the role and status of the new social actor and engaging in social interactions inside the new set of social agents. Looking at the events in Ukraine in terms of the theory of self-organisation it is possible to highlight some noteworthy ideas.

First of all, in a clash between state arbitrariness and civil society, it was realised that small self-organising cells of the society can get network unity, which is a prototype of a new social actor.

Second, this new social actor has an emergent nature. It was born in the context of searching for solutions to emerging social problems. Its dynamics are revealed in the emergence of new patterns of collective interaction, out of which society has to make a choice. In the case of the new social actor, it is not resources and territory but the goals posed by society and the topology of the self-organising social network that are important.

Third, today the new social actor has no social status. There is no social contract governing its interaction with traditional social institutions. Because of the emergence of its nature it is fundamentally different from existing social agents. It is possible to triumph the new social agent only if we do away with self-organisation.

Fourth, the new social actor escalates the confrontation in different areas of international social reality. One can see the head-to-head contest: complex systems versus simple systems, hierarchy versus network, and traditional leadership versus complexity leadership, enabling self-organisation versus restraining it with social barriers, etc. Despite the work-in-progress of the nature of complex network theory, it signifies a change in the way that social sciences should be conducted.

Furthermore, because of the appearance of the new social agent, modern social science faces the challenge of rethinking fundamental sociological concepts (status, role, social interaction, social norms, social movement, social institutions, etc.). The mission of social science is to formulate new social values and senses which are adequate for the new social reality.

And finally, as it was shown in this chapter, the identification of the new social agent needs network thinking that can contradict traditional views. Therefore, as follows from the proposed agent-based simulation, for effective decision-making the priorities in the causal chains of "resources and task" should be overturned. This, in turn, puts forward the problem of formulation for new social projects.

With regard to the further development of the above mentioned ideas, it seems interesting to investigate the emergent social network of new Ukrainian reality, to discuss the social projects of society, and to examine to what extent the structure of social networks corresponds to the formulated social projects.

References

Anderson, P. (1972). More is Different: Broken Symmetry and the Nature of the Hierarchical Structure of Science. Science, 177 (4047), 393–396.

Arthur, W. (2013). Complexity economics: A different framework for economic thought. SFI WORKING PAPER.

Ashby, W. (1956). An Introduction to Cybernetics. London: Chapman & Hal.

Bakuniak, G., & Nowak, K. (1987, May). The Creation of a Collective Identity in a Social Movement: The Case of "Solidarność" in Poland. Theory and Society, Vol. 16, 401-429.

Barabasi, A.-L. (2002). Linked. The New Science of Networks. Cambridge: MA: Perseus Publishing.

Bar-Yam, Y. (2002). Complexity rising: From human beings to human civilization, a complexity profile. Encyclopedia of Life Support Systems (EOLSS UNESCO Publishers, Oxford, UK).

Bar-Yam, Y., & Gard-Murray, A. (2011-2-02). Framing a complexity theory solution to the Middle East crises. NECSI Technical Report.

Castells, M. (2000). The Rise of the Network Society, The Information Age: Economy, Society and Culture (Ed.2 ed., Vol. I). Oxford, UK: Blackwell.

—. (2007). Communication, Power and Counter-power in the Network Society. International Journal of Communication, 238-266.

—. (2010). The Power of Identity. MA: Wiley-Blackwell.

Datsuk, S. (2014, 04 10). Декларация общин человечества. Retrieved 12 08, 2014, from Хвиля.net: http://hvylya.net/analytics/society/deklaratsiya-obshhin-chelovechestva.html

—. (2014, 11 19). За лаштунками революції - 2014. Retrieved March 06, 2015, from Ukrainian pravda: http://blogs.pravda.com.ua/authors/datsuk/546c7b1edee2d/

—. (2014, 04 11). Мы имеем право на преобразование человека. Retrieved 12 08, 2014, from Студреспубліка 2015: http://www.studrespublika.com/news/text_news.php?id=2538

Epstein, J. (2002). Modeling Civil Violence: An Agent-Based Computational Approach. Proceedings of the National Academy of Sciences, U.S.A., 99, 7243-7250.

Fellman, P., Bar-Yam, Y., & Minai, A. (2014). Conflict and Complexity: Countering Terrorism, Insurgency, Ethnic and Regional Violence. Springer.

Gard-Murray, A., & Bar-Yam, Y. (2012). Complexity and the Limits of Revolution: What Will Happen to the Arab Spring? arXiv:1212.3041, December 11.

Granovetter, M. (1973). The Strength of Weak Ties. American Journal of Sociology (78), 1360-80.

—. (1978). Threshold Models of Collective Behavior. American Sociological Review, 83, 1420-1442.

Judd, S., Kearns, M., & Vorobeychik, Y. (2010). Behavioral Dynamics and Influence in Networked Coloring and Consensus. Proceedings of the

National Academy of Sciences, 107(24), 14978-14982.

Kearns, M., Judd, S., & Wortman, J. (2009). Behavioral experiments in biased voting in networks. Proceedings of the National Academy of Sciences, 106(5), 1347–1352.

Macy M.W., W. R. (2002). From factors to actors: Computational sociology and. Annual Review of Sociology (28), 143 – 166.

Maturana, H. &. Varela F (1980). Autopoiesis and cognition: The realization of the living. Boston: D. Reidel.

Mitchell, M. (2006). Complex systems: Network thinking. Artificial Intelligence(170), 1194–1212.

Pugacheva, E. (2014, 05 01). Майдан - новый социальный актор. Retrieved 12 08, 2014, from Хвиля.net: http://hvylya.net/analytics/society/maydan-novyiy-sotsialnyiy-aktor.html

Schelling, T. (1978). Micromotives and Macrobehavior. New York: Norton.

Westley, F. Z. (2006). Getting to Maybe: How the World is Changed. Toronto: Random House.

CHAPTER THIRTEEN

AGENVIRONMENTS? TOWARDS SIMULATING SOCIALLY CONSTRUCTED COMPLEXITY

ÖZGE DILAVER

I. Introduction

Although it is evident that humans collectively construct social complexity, most complexity scientists studying social phenomena either keep social constructionist perspectives at bay or approach them with major reservations. Part of this reluctance relates to extreme and/or misunderstood constructionist ontologies that allegedly hold that there is no physical reality independent of social construction, and so, for example, if humans collectively disappeared, there would not be any realities for other species.

Beyond these ontological obscurities however, the social constructionist line of thought approaches not necessarily the physical reality outside humans but various understandings of its elements as socially constructed. This implies that the same elements in a geographical area can be given different associations, meanings and functions by human communities, and can consequently be re-shaped in different ways over time. Trivial as it may seem, this way of connecting physical and social territories leads to divergences and tensions around the ways social phenomena are studied. In essence, the very idea of alternative evolutions and organisations of social reality based on shared meanings and narratives is at odds with positivist intentions in science that aim to explain social phenomena mostly via atemporal and universal causal mechanisms rather than historical and subjective connections.

Epistemologically, science and technology studies have repeatedly shown that scientific knowledge of physical as well as social realities is not necessarily as hard, objective, systematic, or certain as once was (or still is) assumed. Instead, the relative currency strength of alternative representations of phenomena often depends on communication and persuasion within the social functioning of researcher communities. These observations on science as a collective human practice can be seen as challenging positivistic knowledge claims through scientific methods. But instead of allowing room for inspiration and new reasonings of similar phenomena, they are often faced with the immediate concern that, if scientific knowledge is relative and different interpretations can be not only possible but at times equally plausible, then we cannot establish a distinction between good and bad science. And, if that is the case, then *anything goes* as science. In fact, these concerns are not without merit in the realm of the everyday practices of science. Science as a socially constructed institution may indeed work less problematically within a worldview of hardness, geekness, precision, objectivity, and data having the final word. The problem is that social complexity is unlikely to stop being messy, relative, dynamic, and open to interpretation just because scientists would work more comfortably if it did.

In this chapter, I will argue that social simulation models have a lot to offer for building better representations of socially constructed complexity. In essence, social simulation itself is a generative or constructive way of conducting research (see also Dilaver, 2015), where the researcher constructs a hypothetical reality through decisions on what to include and exclude in the social simulation model and on how to represent entities and actions in useful ways.

There are echoes of this constructive nature of simulation models in the way they are described in research outputs. Social simulation models are often described as a narrative introducing a would-be world in longer paragraphs than in other computational studies. Throughout this narrative, as the researcher needs to introduce an entity into the model before relating it to other entities, the description may involve chains or circles of cross-references rather than following a more straightforward outline. Even though the resulting narrative might be a clear snapshot of the would-be world that has been constructed, it is likely to have a different scope and level of detail and put emphasis on different parts of the study than the narratives in other social simulation studies. In other words, it is not only the constructed would-be worlds that differ from each other, but also the narratives that describe them from different viewpoints.

This aspect of social simulation studies has caused frustration among researchers as it makes it more difficult to replicate them. Grimm et al (2006) suggested the well-known ODD protocol that provides a format for reporting agent-based simulation studies especially in ecology. While the format facilitates replication of simulation experiments by, for example, encouraging reporting the inputs and outputs of the study, it falls short of addressing the core structure of the model, namely its conceptual elements. Although the first 'd' in ODD stands for 'design concepts', the proposed format under this heading and its more recent extension (Polhill, 2010) are a bit too specific to be relevant to social simulation studies in an increasingly broad range of disciplines.

In this chapter, I will focus on two important conceptual elements of social simulation models, namely agents and environments. These are also mentioned in Macal and North (2006) and Bandini et al (2009). Although I will try to use them as separate conceptual elements, it is known that agents interact through environment in some models (Bandini et al, 2009), environment enables pro-activity of agents in others (Argente et al, 2013), and the way individual agents and the external observers perceive the environment might be different (Seth, 2002).

Beyond the above-mentioned concerns about communicating simulation models, opening a discussion on important conceptual elements in the existing literature is helpful for clarifying common assumptions and methodological tendencies in the field, as well as shedding light on future avenues. I will argue that more dynamic computational representations of socially constructed complexity can help to improve existing knowledge both on social construction and on complexity. Regarding such models as the next generation social simulation models, I will discuss what agent-based modeling has to offer for building better representations of socially constructed complex realities.

To this end, I will first briefly refer to the debate between positivism and social constructionism to give a very general view of the different methodological routes social simulation studies can take and why they matter. I will then explore representations of agency and environment in some of the most influential agent-based modeling studies, specifically focusing on the human side of simulated environments for identifying elements of social construction in modeling ideas. I will then repeat the same review exercise for SKIN models for shedding light on possible research avenues in this direction.

So far, agency and environment are regarded as separate conceptual elements of agent-based models. In this chapter, I will aim to show that there are conceptual links between these modeling elements as in many social simulation studies the environment has a human side. In the interest of putting emphasis on this human side of environments and encouraging discussions of more realistic representations of socially constructed complex realities, I will attempt to give the emphasis of my inquiry a temporary name. I will, therefore, call those elements of the model that are beyond individual agents but would not meaningfully exist if there were no agents in the model 'agenvironments' in this chapter.

II. Positivism and Social Constructionism

Shared understandings and assumptions about both material and social reality determine the perceived legitimacy of social structures and organisations. At least since the scientific revolution, which is thought to have ended the fierce power struggles between science and church in Europe, in most societies the institution of science is given a special role and legitimising power with potentially important policy implications. In the Enlightenment era that followed the scientific revolution, thinkers such as Kant referred to enlightenment as an anticipated state of mind in which knowledge and critical reasoning becomes a means of emancipation from dogmatism and self-incurred tutelage (Kant, 1784). As critical reasoning of self-incurred enslavement may as well threaten the legitimacy of some established institutions, the enlightenment as a value was and has been very much interlinked with the power struggle for (de)legitimising and (de)normalising the institutions that shape social, economic and political organisations of social reality, benefitting some individuals at the cost of others.

Alternative paradigms of social reality, therefore, have broad and concrete impacts on everyday life. This is one of the reasons why debates on what kind of social science should gain dominance, or at least be taken seriously, are often very fierce. The critique of positivism by postmodern qualitative researchers, for example, led to a widely recognised divide between qualitative and quantitative social science researchers. This divide has been likened to a 'wall' (Hunt, 1991; p.33), a 'war' (Johnson and Onwuegbuzie, 2004; p.14) that 'even a hermit in bleakest Antartica must be aware of' (McKelvey, 1997; p.352), an 'endemic opposition' (Outhwaite, 1983; p.2), and a 'tendency to engage in polemics and, at times, name calling' (Smith, 1983; p.6).

Positivism was developed following some of the enlightenment ideas and became the dominant scientific paradigm during modernity. The term "positivism" was coined by Comte (2000 [1896]). For Comte, despite the inherent subjectivity of human nature, establishing a common basis was essential for both individual and collective existence. In previous eras, he argued, this common basis was filled by subjective worldviews including religion. It was the progress of humanity that enabled modern society to construct the common basis by reason and systematic observation. Hence, Comte did not reject non-observable aspects of social phenomena, but he argued that the inner causes of phenomena were ultimately inaccessible, hence speculation about them was pointless. Human minds would reach the positive state with the realisation of this inaccessibility and by focusing instead on observation of phenomena for discovering the laws that govern the appearances of things (Comte, 1908). In this regard, on one hand positive philosophy followed the Enlightenment legacy in rejecting religious and metaphysical speculation; on the other it brought about the discontinuity of a strong social critique and thereby demarcated from the idea of questioning self-incurred enslavement (Benton, 1977).

Post-modernism challenged many aspects of modernism, such as the dominance of Western values and the white malestream agendas, the importance of rationality, and the convention of unique truth, in a wide spectrum from politics to arts (Rosenau, 1992; Backett-Milburn, 1999). With respect to social science paradigms, as briefly mentioned above, positivism was attacked to its alleged death (Popper, 1992). At the centre of the criticisms was the argument that positivism assumes a reality *out there*, which can be studied objectively in order to reveal universal laws that govern it. Although this general discourse is never clear enough about *out where* they argue positivism conceptualises reality, the expression is generally used to capture the tendency to take observed facts for granted without paying adequate attention to how they are made sense of, maintained and reproduced, who benefits from these processes and at whose expense.

Social constructionism (or constructivism) is one of the paradigms that emerged from the postmodern critique of positivist science. Similarities among numerous interpretations of social constructionism include a critical stance towards the idea that knowledge is produced by objective and unbiased observation of the world; the belief that knowledge is fabricated through daily interactions between people; the argument for the historical and cultural specificity of concepts and categories; and the understanding that different constructions of knowledge may lead to different actions (Burr, 1995). The critical stance of constructionism towards positivist claims for objectivity and determinism is connected to another type of critique: one that scrutinises social institutions, the role of constructed realities in maintaining these institutions and their joint implications for equality and power (Popkewitz, 1990). Studying social realities of the social "other" (Fawcett and Hearn, 2004) and those who are suppressed by the dominant social power has thus become an important way of challenging taken-for-granted rules and orthodoxies, as has producing rich descriptions of everyday lives instead of detached hypotheses (Pakulski, 2009), or grand theories.

III. Agents and Environments in Silico

III.1. Representations in Highly Cited Social Simulation Models

In this section, I will review the types of worlds that are envisaged in some of the influential social simulation papers. In particular, I will focus on representations of agency and environment. As social simulation literature is very large and agent-based models are used in various social science fields, the studies that are covered here constitute a broad range of examples rather than a comprehensive review of all modeling ideas. Selection of papers covered in this section is done according to number of citations in Web of Science[1].

Among the most cited agent-based studies referring to social phenomena are those studying the hypothetical evolution of certain properties of social behaviour that are counter-intuitive, from the perspectives of individualistic reasoning and evolution through competition for scarce resources. In their comprehensive review paper, Macy and Willer (2002) group these studies as those studying the emergence of social order. In this section, I will refer to Bowles and Gintis's (2004) model of the evolution of cooperation and Choi and Bowles's (2007) model on parochial altruism.

---

[1] Publications are scanned with the keyword "agent-based model" at Web of Science, refined to Social Sciences and Arts and Humanities at Research Domains option and ranked according to number of citations in January 2015. Review papers and other papers without models are eliminated.

Bowles and Gintis (2004) investigate why human groups maintain a high level of cooperation despite a low level of genetic relatedness among group members. More specifically, they are referring to collective tasks such as hunting and common defence in the late Pleistocene era. The authors hypothesise that many humans have a predisposition to punish those who violate group-beneficial norms, which may have led to the evolution of cooperation. From this perspective, they envisage three types of agents: co-operators, who obey the norm, but never punish violators; reciprocators, who bear the cost of punishing violators; and selfish agents who may shirk. Parents pass their type to their offspring with some probability, while mutation from parents' type (and having one of the other two types) is also possible.

The authors do not describe a physical environment, but their assumptions about the era reflect the human side of the environment in the form of small groups without central governance or a significant hierarchy. There is immigration within groups that is constrained to a fraction of group size. As such, there are unrelated individuals and behavioural heterogeneity in the group. They acquire food either individually or by working as a group, which may lead to higher fitness levels than working as individuals. The major form of punishment for not observing norms is ostracism.

Similarly, Choi and Bowles (2007) argue that altruism and parochialism are common human behaviours, and they study the coevolution of parochialism, altruism and war. Like in Bowles and Gintis (2004), the authors model the evolution of genetically transmitted behavioural types in a population of foragers. The behaviour types are represented as hypothetical alleles at two loci: altruist or not, and parochial or not. Parochial altruists are then referred to as 'fighters' in the study. Hostility between groups depends on the fraction of fighters and the relative likelihood of winning. In other words, if the proportion of fighters in a group is sufficiently large and relatively larger than in another group, there is likely to be a conflict between the groups, given scarce resources. The conflicts result in deaths, particularly among fighters and in the losing group.

With respect to the external environment, the authors refer to the volatile climate of the late Pleistocene period in addition to natural disasters and periodic resource scarcities. These conditions bring about competition for resources and may favour groups with individuals who have a predisposition to engaging in hostile conflict with outsiders on behalf of their own group members. The authors conclude that in this particular would-be world, parochialism and altruism would not emerge singly, but they would emerge jointly together with the existence of group conflicts.

With a similar research agenda, Axelrod (1997) investigates dissemination of culture between hypothetical communities with the aim of understanding co-existence of cultural convergence and divergence between human communities. The agents in Axelrod's model are internally homogenous villages represented by fixed cells on a square grid. The environment, therefore, is the grid itself where each agent (village) only interacts with its four neighbours. On top of this basic structure, Axelrod represents culture as a number of features the agents have, and these features can take a limited number of values representing different cultural traits. This simplistic representation allows the author to have a straightforward representation of cultural similarity between any two agents. At each tick, a village is selected randomly to pick one of its neighbours to interact with, and the two villages interact with a probability equal to their cultural similarity. Interaction, then, is modelled as the activated village randomly picking one of its traits that are different from its neighbour's and changing it to the neighbour's trait.

Berger's (2001) model contributes to agricultural economics, and it differs from the above by aiming to represent a very specific context rather than very general social phenomena. He models the diffusion of new crops and water-saving agricultural innovations in Chile across the background of a free-trade agreement that influenced the prices of new import and export crops. Berger's model is particularly interesting for the above-mentioned connection between physical and social realities in that he builds two sub-models: one representing hydrologic dynamics and the other representing farmers' decisions. The former simulates the return-flows in an environment represented by a square grid with representations of upstream and downstream farms. The latter represents various aspects of farmers' economic decisions with parameter values calibrated to represent heterogeneity of Chilean farmers as closely as possible. Diffusion of innovations in this decision model depends on farmer's awareness of the innovation, and farmers become aware of the innovation when a certain fraction of farmers in their network adopt.

Rivkin and Siggelkow's (2003) model is in the field of organisation theory. The authors investigate interdependencies between organisational design elements, namely hierarchy, incentive system and departmentalisation that are identified to be important in previous qualitative studies of organisations. The authors are also interested in studying the effects of the underlying pattern of connections between various decisions that organisations need to take and the information processing abilities of managers. While the authors call these two factors contextual variables, I would like to point out that the underlying pattern of connections between decisions is at the centre of how the authors envisage the simulated environment. More specifically, by changing the matrix of connections between different decisions, the authors create a hypothetical environment of problems that they populate with many heterogeneous agents representing organisations. The authors represent organisations in a multilevel abstraction that has a CEO and two subordinate managers. Agents differ in the way possible decision areas are divided between the two subordinate managers, as well as their capabilities, the level of authority the CEO has over their decisions and the incentive structure in the organisation with respect to whether individual performances of departments or the whole organisation is prioritised.

III.2. Representations in SKIN models

In this section, I will repeat the same exercise of reviewing representations of agents and environments in models that apply and extend the Simulating Knowledge Dynamics in Innovation Networks (SKIN) model (Gilbert et al 2001, 2007). There are, by now, many applications of the SKIN model. In this section, I will reflect on the studies in the first edited volume of SKIN models (Gilbert et al, 2014).

SKIN is primarily about innovative processes in industrial settings. In the view of the authors of the original SKIN model, beyond being a piece of code, SKIN is a theoretical framework. SKIN represents knowledge in an abstract form as sequences of numbers (kenes), but distinguishes different units of knowledge from each other by a categorical system representing different disciplines and fields of knowledge. The agents in SKIN are typically firms, and the primary aspect of their agency is applying their knowledge to create innovations with the ultimate aim of developing products and making profits. Through the evolution of kenes, SKIN can effortlessly represent different types of learning, e.g. through incremental or radical research, as well as forgetting.

In addition to individual actions of learning and forgetting, agents interact to share units of knowledge. Selection of partners in knowledge sharing is purposeful: agents advertise their capabilities and choose partners with desired capabilities. Successful experiences with previous partners lead to a renewal of partnership. Agents can also initiate longer-lasting relationships in the form of innovation networks. Beyond representing long-term relationships, innovation networks have an additional agency in terms of being able to develop innovations and products.

The environment in SKIN can be thought of as consisting of two main parts. Firstly, the coordinate system that kenes refer to constitutes an implicit knowledge space. Implicit in these coordinates is the assumption that possible knowledge is a given and is exogenous in nature, as opposed to subjective and constructed distinctions. Use of knowledge, however, in the form of innovations combines different units of knowledge from different coordinates. Hence, SKIN accommodates the evolution of alternative knowledge outputs in a hypothesised space of possibilities. Furthermore, different innovations may create the same product, and so there is more than one way of satisfying a particular demand. The second dimension of the simulated environment is a market where firms make profits by selling their products either to other firms or to consumers who are exogenous to the model. Hence, in addition to interactions for knowledge sharing and innovation, firms interact within the supply chain.

Applications of the SKIN model add further modelling ideas, making the model more detailed in various dimensions. In line with the general trend of closely linking simulation models with empirical data, most SKIN applications are developed with a specific region and/or industry in mind. Bloom and Hildrum (2014), for example, represent the Nordic internet service provider (ISP) industry; Korber and Paier's model is about the life sciences innovation system in Vienna; Castellaci et al's model is based on the defence sector in the EU; Ahrweiler et al. base their model on the seventh framework program (FP7) of the EU; and our study (Dilaver et al, 2015) was based on a comparison of Silicon Valley with the Boston region. In addition to building a closer link to concrete cases and potentially enabling comparisons, these applications modified and developed certain aspects of the SKIN model.

With respect to agency, introduction of new and more specialised classes of agents is one of the novelties SKIN extensions brought about. Interestingly, most studies introduce three classes of agents. Bloom and Hildrum, for example, distinguish between three classes of agents differing from each other in typical size, domain of capabilities, and type of R&D activities. With these additional classes of agents, the authors build a more explicit representation of value-chain and support services. Hintze and Luthje's model (2014) is similar in developing three classes of agents along a value-chain and dividing the knowledge space of possible knowledge coordinates among these classes. Similarly, in Ahrweiler et al., the model incorporates three types of agents: research institutions, large firms, and small and medium enterprises (SMEs). The authors give SMEs the special role of introducing some of the rare capabilities. Last but not least, Korber and Paier's model has three different classes of agents, namely universities, research organisations and firms. In addition, the authors represent governmental and financial organisations as exogenous entities.

Our (Dilaver et al.) SKIN application, the AIR model, introduces new and more specialised agents in a different way from other SKIN applications. Aiming to reflect the multilevel structure of agency in regional systems, I constructed specialised agents namely researchers and managers who are then organised within a firm structure. In this regard, firms consist of their employees in the roles of managers and researchers, while the knowledge base or kenes of firms is a sum and summary of their employees' kenes and the residues of kenes of previous employees. This representation is similar to Rivkin and Siggelkow's (2003) organisations in that it enables opening up of the grey-box of the agency of the firm in other SKIN applications. Although our model did not exactly introduce three classes of agents, the multilevel structure of agency had three levels; regions, firms, and people.

SKIN extensions also involved novelties with respect to simulated environments. Calibration of the knowledge space according to well-established disciplines or fields that are relevant to the case being studied, for example, is another important feature of SKIN applications. Korber and Paier, for example, calibrate coordinates of kenes to actual research fields in life sciences. This approximation of a real (albeit constructed) knowledge space brings about further changes and modelling ideas. As the coordinates are not in an abstract space, similarity between kenes of different agents cannot be measured simply by the distance between kene coordinates. Instead, the authors use the frequency of co-occurrences of capabilities in agents' kenes as a measure of similarity between fields. In the same vein, Ahrweiler et al. measure the knowledge space according to the number of areas covered in the FP7 program.

In addition, these studies introduced novelties related to the market environment in SKIN through differentiated roles of more specialised agents. In Bloom and Hildrum's market, the differences between the capability domains of the three different classes of agents are reflected in the market: not all classes of agents can serve all market segments. Similarly, Hintze and Luthje's model addresses the reluctance of firms to adopt the innovations of their suppliers, the benefits of which will be transferred to downstream customers or end-users with uncertain returns to the firms in-between. In their market, some suppliers directly address end-users or other potential clients down the value-chain in their marketing attempts.

The environment in the AIR model does not have a calibrated knowledge space or a market. Instead, it consists of three parts, which aim to visualise existing theory on industrial clusters and regional innovation systems. The reward space is a hypothetical space that shows returns from all possible innovations. It is a semi-visible fitness landscape that each agent sees differently. In this regard, the AIR model takes a step forward in representing multiple worldviews. The knowledge space has coordinates that the kenes refer to, like in the original SKIN model. This space helps with visualising the evolution of the knowledge bases of researchers and firms, and it accommodates knowledge transfers between agents. Consisting of two regions, the earth space represents where agents live, build relationships, and interact. By modelling the two regions and people explicitly, AIR enables the modelling of flows of people, knowledge and investments between regions as well as competition for innovations and scarce resources.

In addition to novelties related to agency and environments, SKIN extensions involve a clearer focus on informing policy by simulation experiments. Ahrweiler et al. investigate the impact of different funding tools on the development of European research networks. In a similar vein, Korber and Paier study the effects of direct versus indirect public funding on the life sciences innovation system in Vienna. Bloom and Hildrum experiment with the potential effects of a large-scale agent on the Nordic ISP industry, and Castellaci et al. investigate the liberalisation of the defence sector in the EU, differentiating between the effects of liberalisation on small and large EU countries. In these studies, agent-based modelling enables scenario analyses as well as investigation of the subject from the perspectives of different agents.

IV. Discussions and Conclusions

In this chapter I have reviewed two conceptual elements, agents and environments, in some of the most influential social simulation studies and in recently published SKIN models, providing a general overview and examples of how these elements are constructed in state-of-art social simulation models. In addition to reviewing and comparing different representations, I have aimed to clarify what agent-based modelling has to offer for building better representations of socially constructed complexity. Regarding such models as next-generation social simulation models, I have attempted to show that, although this is a relatively new discussion and social construction was not a prominent theme in the community, social simulation models have already come a long way towards contributing to a better understanding of socially constructed complex phenomena.

From a very crude perspective, models of emergence of social order, as Macy and Willer (2002) call them, can be regarded as modelling the hypothetical evolution of socially constructed phenomena. Yet, they diverge from, but do not necessarily conflict with, social constructionist thought. Firstly, by regarding all forms of social order including oppressive ones as forms of cooperation or altruism, these studies position their subject of interest as general properties of humans. That being said, after this positioning they often refer to imagined worlds in early prehistoric periods and assume that those communities do not have strictly structured hierarchies. Secondly, the focus of these studies is on norms that are relevant to the immediate life functions of individuals or groups and whose upkeep therefore has straightforward consequences for fitness functions. This focus enables the use of a rationality perspective and of thought experiments in the study of the evolution of social phenomena. Thirdly, the reproduction and continuity of norms is often explained mainly through the genetic behavioural predispositions of individuals rather than, for example, socialisation. The evolution story being told here, therefore, is more Darwinian than Lamarckian. Bowles and Gintis's above-mentioned study explains, through the cognitive and linguistic abilities of humans, why co-operation is seldom observed in other animals. However the functioning of these abilities in the form of, for example, concepts, categories, associations, narratives, and utterances, is taken as a necessary condition for the selection of certain behavioural predispositions rather than as the main mechanism of reality building. Similarly, Choi and Bowles follow the line of thought that regards wars as a major evolutionary force that fosters social solidarity and altruism. The authors are clear, however, that the simulation experiments do not show that behavioural dispositions that are hypothesised do exist or could generate complex outcomes like warfare or a co-operative structure. As in other thought experiments, the models reveal the type of outcomes that would happen under assumed scenarios.

While positioning his main research interest, Axelrod posits the existence of cultural differences as a dilemma across the general assumption that people become more alike in their beliefs and behaviour when they interact. In this regard, he abstracts from the purposeful construction of identities and meanings and different forms of interaction that may lead to likening as well as to alienation. Thus, he represents becoming similar as something that happens to his agents due to their agency. In this would-be world, the simultaneous spatial dissemination of cultural traits and the assumption of homophily (assumption that individuals who are more similar to each other are more likely to communicate effectively) maintain and increase cultural differences. Like in the abovementioned studies, the model provides a possible explanation for the co-existence of cultural convergence and divergence based on a set of assumptions, in this case those that overlook the agency of individuals.

Berger's agricultural economics model differs from these studies by addressing a specific modern context rather than a more abstract would-be world and by constructing a relatively detailed physical environment that influences opportunities and interactions available for farmers. One of the research questions Berger tackles is whether or not small-scale farms with smaller capital would be influenced by the free-trade agreement in the same way as large-scale more institutionalised farms. Although the decision-making part of Berger's model is focused on optimisation based on economic data, the framework in which he relates different environmental conditions to opportunities, and the way he uses the model to investigate the impact of social policy on different segments of the population, are promising aspects for building better representations of socially constructed complexity.

Rivkin and Siggelkow's (2003) organisation theory model is also an interesting example, because instead of modelling simple interactions between agents that have similar agencies albeit different traits, the authors position their agents in organisations with different roles and a hierarchy. The organisation, as a collection of agents, thus gains an additional level of agency. In a fitness landscape inspired from evolutionary studies, the authors move one important step forward from simulating the straightforward implications of simple interactions towards interdependencies between an individual's actions and the overall outcomes of those actions for a collective unit.

The SKIN models that I have reviewed in this chapter are about economic processes, and the typical agents in these models are firms and research organisations that are represented as black, or dark-coloured boxes. Hence, on one hand, in terms of the subjects they investigate SKIN models do not directly refer to issues that are central to social constructionist theory. On the other hand, SKIN models are essentially about innovation networks; hence they address the collective construction of knowledge. In this regard, SKIN models investigate an issue that is at the core of the social constructionist view from a different angle, with different research aims.

The physical or, more correctly, the external environment in SKIN models depicts a possibility space, whether envisaged as an oracle, an explicit fitness landscape or the range of numbers coordinates in a kene triple can take. This space represents the range of possible knowledge, different combinations of knowledge, and possible innovations. On top of this space that is a given to individual agents, SKIN models describe market or economic environments, which reflect the institutionalised exchanges between agents and the innovation policies of exogenous agents such as governments. Furthermore, there are rules or assumptions that control network-building interactions between agents, such as how agents can know of each other, and how they work together and share the benefits of successful innovations. The agency of individual agents including their research and collaboration strategies is then modelled in a way that is embedded in these external and social environments.

In this chapter, I suggest paying attention to the human side of simulated environments, which are those properties that are beyond individual agents but would not meaningfully exist if there were no agents in the model. In SKIN models these agenvironments cover institutions that shape markets and returns from innovation as well as those that regulate collaborative interactions between agents.

In the rest of this section, I will elaborate on why agenvironments matter and how paying attention to this element in social simulation models can be helpful for constructing better representations of socially constructed complexity. While referring to the social construction of a phenomenon, researchers effectively argue that the phenomenon is not an inevitable consequence of natural facts, and often they also imply that we would be better off if these constructions did not exist at all (Hacking, 1999). Not regarding established social structures and institutions as natural, rational, or inevitable enables researchers to discover alternative ways in which social reality can be constructed, implying that reality, or a particular version of it, is not destiny (Backett-Milburn 1999). For example, the expression "social construction of motherhood" implies that the way motherhood is currently understood is not an inevitable consequence of the nature of our existence. This line of reasoning can be liberating from what Kant (1784) calls self-enforced oppression, through a collective updating of shared understandings. At the same time, the conventional understanding of motherhood may seem more or less to be a given for a particular mother at a specific time of action. She may not be able to wish it away (Berger and Luckmann, 1967) as it exists in the minds of so many other people (Sismondo, 1993). For this mother, therefore, it is no less real than that she has given birth to her baby.

More generally, even though alternative social constructions of things could have been possible, and may still be possible at the society level, at the individual level and at the time of action, socially constructed entities are as real and significant as rocks, mountains, and yellow brick roads. Social simulation researchers can stick with this level of reality and take social phenomena for granted. They may even be correct in hypothesising genetic dispositions that lead to their emergence. If, however, social reality or a significant part of it is evolving through collections of actions, its external-internal character is only meaningful in reference to a given unit of agency (i.e. external for whom) and a time frame (i.e. reality for how long). Agent-based models are useful in this inquiry. As exemplified in the abovementioned studies, they can help researchers distinguish between alternative realities at (i) society and individual level, and (ii) before and after they are constructed.

References

Ahrweiler, Petra; Schilperoord, Michel; Pyka, Andreas and Gilbert, Nigel (2014) Testing Policy Options for Horizon 2020 with SKIN, in Gilbert, Nigel, Ahrweiler, Petra, Pyka, Andreas (Eds.) Simulating Knowledge Dynamics in Innovation Networks, Berlin Heidelberg: Springer-Verlag, pp 155-184.

Argente Estefanía, Boissier Olivier, Carrascosa Carlos, Fornara N, McBurney Peter, Noriega Pablo, Ricci Alessandro, Sabater-Mir Jordi, Schumacher Michael Ignaz. Tampitsikas Charalampos, Taveter Kuldar, Vizzari Giuseppe, Vouros George (2013) The Role of the Environment in Agreement Technologies. Artificial Intelligence Review, Springer Netherlands, ISSN: 0269-2821, 39(1): 21-38.

Axelrod, Robert (1997) The Dissemination of Culture: A Model with Local Convergence and Global Polarization, The Journal of Conflict Resolution, 41 (2), pp 203-226.

Backett-Milburn, Kathryn (1999) Plus ca change? Reflections on a career as a qualitative researcher, Social Research Methodology 2 (1), 69-81.

Bandini, Stefania, Manzoni, Sara and Vizzari, Giuseppe (2009) Agent based modeling and simulation: an informatics perspective, Journal of Artificial Societies and Social Simulation 12 (4) 4.

Berger, Thomas (2001) Agent-based spatial models applied to agriculture: a simulation tool for technology diffusion, resource use changes and policy analysis, Agricultural Economics, 25 (2-3), pp 245-260.

Benton, Ted (1977) Philosophical foundations of the three sociologies. Taylor and Francis.

Bloom, Martin and Hildrum, Jarle Moss (2014) Firm-Level Business Strategies and the Evolution of Innovation Networks in the Nordic Internet Service Industry, in Gilbert, Nigel, Ahrweiler, Petra, Pyka, Andreas (Eds.) Simulating Knowledge Dynamics in Innovation Networks, Berlin Heidelberg: Springer-Verlag, pp 17-46.

Bowles, Samuel and Gintis, Herbert (2004) The evolution of strong reciprocity: cooperation in heterogeneous populations, Theoretical Population Biology 65(1), pp 17–28.

Burr, Vivien (1995) An introduction to social constructionism. London and New York: Routledge.

Castellaci, Fulvio, Fevolden, Arne and Blom, Martin (2014) R&D Policy Support and Industry Concentration: A SKIN Model Analysis of the European Defence Industry, in Gilbert, Nigel, Ahrweiler, Petra, Pyka, Andreas (Eds.) (2014) Simulating Knowledge Dynamics in Innovation Networks, Berlin Heidelberg: Springer-Verlag, pp 131-154.

Choi, Jung-Kyoo and Bowles, Samuel (2007) The Coevolution of Parochial Altruism and War, Science, 318 (5850) pp. 636-640.

Comte, Auguste (1908) The General View of Positivism. London: George Routledge and Sons.

Comte, Auguste (2000 [1896]) The Positive Philosophy. Kitchener: Batoche Books.

Dilaver, Ozge, Uyarra, Elvira and Bleda, Mercedes (2014) Multilevel Analysis of Industrial Clusters: Actors, Intentions and Randomness Model, in Gilbert, Nigel, Ahrweiler, Petra, Pyka, Andreas (Eds.) Simulating Knowledge Dynamics in Innovation Networks, Berlin Heidelberg: Springer-Verlag, pp 217-242.

—. (2015) From Participants to Agents: Grounded Simulation as a Mixed-Method Research Design, Journal of Artificial Societies and Social Simulation 18 (1) 15 <http://jasss.soc.surrey.ac.uk/18/1/15.html>.

Fawcett, Barbara and Hearn, Jeff (2004) Researching others: epistemology, experience, standpoints and participation, Social Research Methodology 7 (3), 201-218.

Gilbert, Nigel, Pyka, Andreas and Ahrweiler, Petra (2001) Innovation Networks - a Simulation Approach, Journal of Artificial Societies and Social Simulation, 4, 1–13.

Gilbert, Nigel, Ahrweiler, Petra, and Pyka, Andreas (2007) Learning in innovation networks: Some simulation experiments. Physica A, 378, pp 100–109.

Gilbert, Nigel, Ahrweiler, Petra, Pyka, Andreas (Eds.) (2014) Simulating Knowledge Dynamics in Innovation Networks, Berlin Heidelberg: Springer-Verlag.

Grimm, Volker; Berger, Uta; Bastiansen, Finn; Eliassen, Sigrunn; Ginot, Vincent; Giske, Jarl; Goss-Custard, John; Grand, Tamara; Heinz, Simone K.; Huse, Geir; Huth, Andreas; Jepsen, Jane U.; Jørgensen, Christian; Mooij, Wolf M.; Muller, Birgit; Pe'er, Guy; Piou, Cyril; Railsback, Steven F.; Robbins, Andrew M.; Robbins, Martha M.; Rossmanith, Eva; Ruger, Nadja; Strand, Espen; Souissi, Sami; Stillman, Richard A.; Vabø, Rune; Visser, Ute; DeAngelis, Donald L. (2006) A standard protocol for describing individual-based and agent-based models, Ecological Modelling 198, 11, pp 5–126.

Hintze, Stephanie and Luthje, Christian (2014) The Evaluation of Value Chain Marketing Strategies: An Agent-Based Approach, in Gilbert, Nigel, Ahrweiler, Petra, Pyka, Andreas (Eds.) Simulating Knowledge Dynamics in Innovation Networks, Berlin Heidelberg: Springer-Verlag, pp 47-72.

Hunt, Shelby D. (1991) Positivism and paradigm dominance in consumer research: Toward critical pluralism and rapprochement, The Journal of Consumer Research 18 (1), 32-44.

Johnson, R. Burke and Onwuegbuzie, Anthony J. (2004) Mixed methods research: A research paradigm whose time has come, Educational Researcher 33 (7), 14-26.

Kant, Immanuel (1784) An Answer to the Question: `What is Enlightenment?'. retrieved from <http://philosophy.eserver.org/kant/what-is-enlightenment.txt> on 15.08.2011.

Korber, Manuela and Paier, Manfred (2014) Simulating the Effects of Public Funding on Research in Life Sciences: Direct Research Funds versus Tax Incentives, in Gilbert, Nigel, Ahrweiler, Petra, Pyka, Andreas (Eds.) (2014) Simulating Knowledge Dynamics in Innovation Networks, Berlin Heidelberg: Springer-Verlag, pp 99-130.

Macy, Michael W. and Willer, Robert (2002) From Factors to Actors: Computational Sociology and Agent-Based Modeling, Annual Review of Sociology, 28, pp 143-166.

Macal, Charles M and North, Michael J (2006) Introduction to modeling and simulation. MCS LANS Informal Seminar, Argonne National Library, Available at: http://www.mcs.anl.gov/~leyffer/listn/slides-06/MacalNorth.pdf, Accessed on 26 June 2014.

McKelvey, Bill (1997) Quasi-natural organization science, Organization Science 8 (4), 352-80.

Outhwaite, William (1983) Concept formation in social science. London and Boston: Routledge and Kegan Paul.

Pakulski, Jan (2009) Postmodern social theory, In B. Turner (Ed.), The New Blackwell Companion to Social Theory, pp. 251-280. Oxford: Blackwell.

Polhill, J. Gary (2010) ODD Updated, Journal of Artificial Societies and Social Simulation 13 (4) 9, <http://jasss.soc.surrey.ac.uk/13/4/9.html>

Popkewitz, Thomas S. (1990). Whose future? Whose past? Notes on critical theory and methodology. In E. Guba (Ed.), The Paradigm Dialog, pp. 46-66. Newbury Park, London and New Delhi: Sage.

Popper, Karl R. (1992) Unended quest: an intellectual autobiography. Routledge.

Rivkin, Jan W. and Siggelkow, Nikolaj (2003) Balancing Search and Stability: Interdependencies among Elements of Organizational Design, Management Science, 49 (3), pp 290-311.

Rosenau, Pauline M. (1992) Post-modernism and the Social Sciences:

Insights, Inroads, and Intrusions. Princeton, NJ: Princeton University Press.
Seth, Anil K. (2002) Agent-based modelling and the environmental complexity thesis. In Hallam, J., Floreano, D., Hallam, B., Hayes, G., & Meyer, J.-A. (Eds.), From animals to animats 7: Proceedings of the Seventh International Conference on the Simulation of Adaptive Behavior, pp. 13-24, Cambridge, MA, MIT Press.
Smith, J. K. (1983) Quantitative versus qualitative research: An attempt to clarify the issue, Educational Researcher 12 (3), 6-13.

CONCLUSION

AN ESSAY ON AGENT-BASED MODELS FOR POLICY MAKING

BEN VERMEULEN

Introduction

Ever since the emergence of economics as a distinct scientific discipline, policy makers have turned to economic models to guide policy interventions of various sorts. Given that mainstream economics mostly draws its methods from physics and regression, the models customarily used –also for policy making- are still mathematical ones. Over the last couple of decades, there is an increase in the use of agent-based models (ABMs) by researchers in social sciences, including heterodox economics. Initially, researchers used ABMs to demonstrate the emergence of social structures and economic dynamics, and, *eodem tempore*, the usefulness of agent-based computer models. By comparing simulation outcomes with empirical facts, agent-based modelling was subsequently also seen as a way to formulate hypotheses on the behaviour of real-world agents and thereby to induce social or economic mechanisms rendering these empirical realities (cf. Axelrod 2007; Brenner and Werker 2007). Over the last decade, modeller-researchers have increasingly used conceptually encompassing and empirically calibrated ABMs for policy evaluation. However, although agent-based modelling is gradually becoming part of the curriculum as well as part of the researcher's toolkit in social sciences, policy makers (rightly) ask critical questions like: (i) is there a need for an alternative to 'regular' equation-based modelling (EBM) and econometric modelling (EM); and (ii) how does one assure the validity of ABMs so that the policies found are suited to intervene in the complex real world (and not just the ABM stylisation of it). In this chapter, answers to these questions are provided. Although ABMs may be classified on the degree of abstraction applied, the trump card of ABM is that, unlike these other approaches, (many conceptualisations of) the real world can be modelled largely unabridged and, potentially, calibrated to empirical data (cf. Boero and Squazzoni 2005). With that, such an in silico virtual world offers unprecedented liberties for policy evaluation and experimentation. However, apart from touting the merits, benefits, and promises of using ABMs for policy making, this paper will also elaborate on the pitfalls, disadvantages, and challenges. Finally, this chapter contains a look beyond the current state of the art of policy evaluation and makes a pitch for - what is coined here as - policy engineering and hybrid policy instruments.

Policy evaluation with ABMs

In general, policy makers face (i) complex, rapidly changing and increasingly interlocked economic systems barely understood by scientists (a claim hard to refute after the bubbles and crises of the last decades), (ii) a trend towards more pragmatic and less programmatic politics with progressive deregulation, decentralisation, and delegation, and (iii) an increasing involvement of different parties seeking to affect the policy outcome in line with particular (and possibly conflicting) interests. So, in the formulation of policies, policy makers have to cope with local and thematic particularities, a complex web of stakeholders, and, due to both, uncertainty about the final outcome. In arriving at policies, agent-based modelling is an instrument that can handle uncertainty about the future (cf. Lempert 2002), and that allows the study of emerging behaviour, implementing elements of the model specific for the context and locality, for empirical calibration, etc. Using ABMs for policy making is now discussed in detail.

Ex-ante evaluation as foundation for policies

Even up to today, it is not uncommon that government policies are ad hoc, based on individual case studies, and/or without unambiguous scientific support. That said, policy makers prefer not to experiment with interventions in the real world if there may be irreversible adverse effects. As such, politicians have national or private statistical agencies compute the effects of such interventions. However, these agencies generally use mathematical, macro-economic models. Surprisingly, many of the equations in these models have a disputed theoretical underpinning. With that, the real effects of policy interventions may have a different magnitude or even opposite sign. Indeed, there may be inconclusive findings or even invalidating evidence that particular policies should have been applied. A recent example is policy makers trying to combat increasing unemployment by calling for wage restraints and enhancing labour market flexibility as this would stimulate employers to hire personnel. However, a recent argument against these interventions is that they cause a decrease in disposable income and income certainty, which may in fact hurt overall consumer demand and thereby exacerbate unemployment.

On top of the lack of univocal scientific support for policy interventions, traditional economic models abstract the economy into a system of equations that aggregate away from the heterogeneity of the agent population, and ignore the non-linearity of interactions of agents connected in networks. An obvious example is how mainstream economic models treat technological change as exogenous shifts in capital and labour. Heterodox neo-Schumpeterian ABMs have technological change emerge endogenously through the collaboration of agents recombining their different bits of technological knowledge.

An additional reason to shy away from abstractions and move in the direction of encompassing and realistically complex[1] models is that policy interventions cannot neglect the particularities of the actual economic system they seek to model. For example, classical work by Saxenian has already illuminated how different regional clusters active in the same industry may differ substantially on key dimensions and internal dynamics. Evidently, policy interventions relying on or affecting such a dimension are likely to differ for these regions.

On top of the individual differences between one economic system and another, it may be undesirable to uncouple them and model one in isolation. One reason is that, given the global nature of markets, researchers should not use a 'closed' model of individual regions and nations, because the competitive performance of one is affecting the performance of another. Using the example of ICT clusters, different regional policy makers sought to copy features of Silicon Valley. Not only is it recognised by now that this popular 'best practice' approach neglects particularities of both the region the particular practices are borrowed from and the region these practices are transferred to, it also neglects that the regions will ultimately compete and that Silicon Valley leads by a mile.

---

[1] Complex in terms of high dimensionality, conceptual richness, or intricate and dynamic interactions.

As such, there is a need for tools to assist policy makers to evaluate policy interventions in a 'virtual world' test-bed prior to executing these interventions. Such a 'virtual world' is a model that, first, features real-world complexity and multi-level interactions critical to understanding its dynamics, and, second, contains all the dimensions needed to characterise the cases and policy interventions. ABMs (and the SKIN model – to be explained later - in particular) are far more suited than abstract, equation-based models. In fact, an increasing number of policy makers also recognise that ABMs can be used to fulfil the need for a 'virtual world' for ex-ante policy evaluation. Moreover, on top of merely being able to conduct a black-box study of the effects of policy interventions, ABMs allow the tracing of structural interactions, the collection of rich data, and the study of (non-linear) interaction of decisions, etc. These advantages are now discussed in detail.

"Flexible and unabridged modelling"

One of the most obvious advantages of using ABMs for a virtual world is that the researcher-modeller is not forced to conceptually 'over-abstract' the real-world system that is studied.

As an illustration of the flexibility and unabridged modelling, a brief history of the Simulating Knowledge Dynamics in Innovation Networks (SKIN) agent-based model and its applications is given.

At the outset, the modellers of the SKIN model- Gilbert, Pyka, and Ahrweiler - were interested in understanding the process of knowledge creation. The starting point in the SKIN model (and its predecessors), and in the numerous models drawing upon it, is that each agent has an individual knowledge-base (KENE) containing knowledge units. Agents conduct research by combining these knowledge units to possibly create yet new knowledge units[2] that are subsequently also stored in the KENE. Although the concept of the KENE and knowledge units initially applied to individuals (Gilbert 1997), the SKIN model was developed to study how firms create knowledge (Gilbert, Pyka, and Ahrweiler 2001). Operationally, the knowledge units are taken to be an ordered N-tuple of

[2] Obviously, there are different ways to map (a combination of) input to output knowledge units. The choice for a certain mapping depends, for instance, on the level of abstraction (e.g. low-level engineering knowledge versus aggregate production competences) or on the empirical data available. In general, knowledge units are related to one another in an (un)directed graph.

nominal, ordinal, and interval variables. In the initial conception, each knowledge unit contained a nominal 'capability' variable, a nominal 'ability' variable that may or may not be a subcategory of the capability, and an ordinal 'expertise' variable to express proficiency in the ability.

Initially, the SKIN model was used to study the Schumpeterian process of technology creation in industries. In this, incumbents in an industry are mostly engaged in incremental innovation, with dwindling profits and desperate incumbents; and entrepreneurs entering the field develop breakthrough technology. As such, two types of knowledge creation were introduced: incremental innovation improving owned knowledge units; and radical research that seeks to expand the KENE. Given the practice in industry as of the 70s and 80s to collaborate in research and in the development of new products, and given the scientific understanding of the economics of this phenomenon in the early 90s, it was decided that the SKIN model was to incorporate the collaboration of agents. Operationally, agents decide to collaborate bi- or multi-laterally with other agents to exchange and/or co-create knowledge units.

Following the concept of swarm-in and shake-out, the SKIN model was extended to have entry and exit of agents on the basis of their knowledge creation performance. As such, agents survive that have either a favourable knowledge predisposition or – apparently - favourable collaboration and knowledge creation strategies. In early versions of the SKIN model, the 'performance' of an agent was quantified by an oracle testing a random selection of knowledge units from the KENE (see Gilbert, Pyka, and Ahrweiler 2001), which was subsequently replaced with a product-market.

In further extensions and alterations, there are wildly varying conceptual interpretations of knowledge units. For example, agents use knowledge units to produce products in scientific articles (e.g. in the precursor of the SKIN model in Gilbert (1997)), in patents (Korber, Paier, and Fischer 2009), to provide services, etc. Depending on the interpretation of knowledge units, the generated output is subsequently evaluated on market performance, technical feasibility, research novelty, or customer value. The operational definition of such a performance evaluation function depends on the conceptual interpretation of knowledge and on the preferences of the modeller. In general, agents receive some reward for that output to compensate for certain research expenses and they share this reward with collaborating agents.

The SKIN model was further extended to study the effect on knowledge creation of relationships between universities, various types of industrial firms, and governmental institutes (e.g. Triulzi and Pyka 2011; Ahrweiler, Pyka, and Gilbert 2011), as well as competence centers (Korber and Paier 2013), and the design of a whole ecosystem (e.g. the IPSE project). Generally, the SKIN model was thereby applied to different sectors, e.g. the biotechnology (Triulzi and Pyka 2011; Pyka and Saviotti 2005), life sciences (Korber and Paier 2013) and ICT sectors (e.g. the IPSE project). The SKIN model has also been used to evaluate research funding policies and networking dynamics in the European FP7 and H2020 research funding programs (Ahrweiler et al. 2014, Scholz et al. 2010).

In the process of arriving at this generic SKIN model, the modellers started with a theoretical idea (that of a KENE and the encoding of knowledge) and, given the application of that idea (to understand the Schumpeterian process of technological progress), they defined micro-level agent actions (research) and agent interactions (collaboration and "selling" innovations). In this particular case, the modellers-researchers were interested in getting a scientific understanding of fundamental processes. However, even in applying the SKIN ABM to an actual, complex economic system (e.g. the whole Irish economy) to support operational decision-making or for policy evaluation, the steps are more or less the same. One breaks down the real-world system into, on the one hand, definitions of agents' behavioural rules[3] and, on the other hand, definitions of the elements in the environment (e.g. resources, infrastructure, geographical space, communication medium).

Given that the ABM thus developed is a close representation of an actual real-world system, policy makers can easily join in on defining the behaviour of agents (e.g. collaboration heuristics, product-market strategy) as well as the economic setting in which they operate (e.g. the product market served, the patent system in place, the institutional framework in operation). In the 'translation' from the real-world elements to the model operationalisations, the modeller does not need to be concerned about tractability of a solution, about the formal definition, about the dimensionality of the system as a whole, etc.

---

[3] Arguably, these terms themselves are socio-economic interpretations of how agents have sensors to perceive external events, upon which heuristics translate interpretations of these events in combination with an internal state into actions performed by the agents' actuators.

The next step is executing simulation runs with the model and studying the graphical or textual output for temporal patterns, agent interactions, and emerging behaviour. Parameters and experimental variables of the simulation model can be deliberately chosen (e.g. as in Monte Carlo studies), but can also be empirically calibrated. Given that ABMs are 'metaphors' for actual real-world systems, researchers and policy makers can interpret simulation outcomes straightforwardly, and make inferences about the mechanisms at play in the real-world system.

That said, also in formulating ABMs, the modeller-researcher has to strike a balance between a simple and a descriptive model, by assuming away details deemed irrelevant, insignificant, or distracting in answering particular research questions (cf. Deichsel and Pyka 2009). Particularly if the system exhibits high-dimensional and non-linear double dynamics (concepts that are discussed in detail below), the modeller-researcher best limits the model to essentials so as to be able to ascertain validity and interpret simulation results. Moreover, also in formulating an ABM, it may be commendable to extend an existing model with established validity (cf. Frenken 2006).

"God-mode" in policy evaluation

Another major advantage of using computer simulation is that the programmer can provide access to all the data of agents and can log each step in every procedure. As such, the virtual world is perfectly transparent. The modeller-researchers and policy makers can record and study events, flows of knowledge and resources, and decisions and interactions of agents, in great detail. ABM simulation thus also allows studying in detail the connection of micro-level flows and decisions, non-linear interactions of agents at the meso-level, the translation of micro- and meso-activities into macro-level indicators and phenomena, and the subsequent feedback into micro-level behaviour.

Moreover, in the real world, not only are policy makers unable, by and large, to observe data and decision processes, they also cannot generally fully control the operational behaviour of agents or the environment in which they operate. In contrast, in ABMs, modeller-researchers and policy makers have "God-mode" freedom to change agent behaviour instantaneously. In fact, modellers can even use the observable and controllable elements explicitly in agent behaviour heuristics.

On top of transparency and control over behaviour, policy makers can use ABMs to study the immediate and emerging effects of interventions, initialisations of the virtual world, and external events on the otherwise autonomously running virtual world. Such interventions may be 'ad hoc' experiments or, instead, a predefined procedure in the code that endogenously responds to the state of the artificial world. In the SKIN models described above, the experimental variables in such an intervention may be either funding of particular research activities of individual agents, the presence of particular knowledge sharing platforms, regulations on R&D network formation, etc. The researcher may also experiment with the initialisation of the simulation run, e.g. different initial social or organisational network, a differently structured graph of knowledge units, different collaboration propensities, etc.

ABMs can be and also are used to study the effects of external events like disruptions in supply (e.g. of financial means or of raw input material), discontinuation of social or organisational links (e.g. due to political decisions), or shifts in demand (e.g. due to a natural catastrophe or a ban), etc.

Harnessing enthusiasm

While these great advantages of using ABMs for policy evaluation (i.e. unabridged modelling, God-mode) may get policy makers interested, one still needs to win them over for a particular project by having them accept the limitations. To harness the enthusiasm of policy makers, modeller-researchers need to ensure that they subscribe to (possibly limiting) operational definitions and support the (possibly limited) research questions that can thus be answered. To do so, it is of paramount importance that policy makers are involved in the actual design and progressive adorning of the ABM. Whenever policy makers provide modelling input, they can interpret, appreciate, and use the output. Do note that this is in fact a serious challenge, because the modeller-researchers should then be involved in the policy research process from early on and should also have policy makers dedicate time and resources in assisting in the actual modelling.

Policy evaluation tools

As indicated before, there are more policy evaluation tools at the disposal of policy makers. Depending on the scientific education and professional vocation of policy makers, they have a preference for particular policy evaluation tools. To win over policy makers, the modeller-researchers have to show the policy makers the advantages of ABMs over other, generally traditional policy tools, and that possible disadvantages are in fact minor. In this section, a juxtaposition of the various policy support tools is provided. As policy makers typically pose the same questions with regard to the features of the various policy support tools, these are answered here too. Typical questions entail why one should use rule- rather than variable-based models; why one should use behavioural rather than econometric modelling; or why conventional equation-based models fall short.

Equation-based models

The first type of model is the ubiquitous equation-based model (EBM), which comes in many flavours. EBMs are used in fields like biology, ecology, physics, sociology, and economics. The general approach is to translate particular (hypothetical) 'laws' into a system of equations. Generally, the researcher-modeller then determines the 'end state' (equilibrium) or the probability distribution of end states of this system of equations, or he/she studies the dynamics behaviour. Policy recommendations are generally derived from the value of an experimental variable causing the system to converge to a desirable (dynamic) equilibrium state. Researchers using EBMs prefer to have a closed-form expression for (the development of) dependent variables. Interestingly, many EBMs of real-world systems have no known closed form solutions. A classic example is the N-body problem, in which the individual motions of N interacting celestial objects in space are to be described. The fact that this N-body problem is, in general, mathematically intractable does not mean there are no proper engineering solutions in coping with it. Obvious testimonies to that are the arrival of the New Horizons spacecraft at Pluto.

Alternatively, the researcher-modeller studies the dynamics of the system by computing a numerical solution for actual parameter values. Regardless of whether a (dynamic) equilibrium can be determined in closed form or just numerically, an EBM can be used to determine a policy intervention. Using a control theoretic approach, the dynamic behaviour is then altered to meet certain requirements. As an example, think of the Lotka-Volterra system describing the population dynamics in a habitat with predatory and prey animals. Given a numerical solver (e.g. Runge-Kutta), it can be experimentally determined when, for example, to introduce a number of predators to reduce the (peak or average) population size of the prey animals.

That said, given the tendency of equation-based modellers to abstract away from the conceptual complexity of real-world systems, finding a quantitative value for a particular type of policy intervention (e.g. financial stimuli, restrictions) may require a reformulation of the basic model. On top of that, for particular policy instruments like network orchestration, a technology sharing platform that would in fact require micro-level rather than macro-level expressions, EBMs generally assume an implicit effect on a state variable. In ABMs, particularly the relationships of agents and the endowments of individual agents are explicitly modelled, allowing (analysis of) the explicit effects of policy instruments.

However, policy recommendations need not be quantitative. An abstract EBM can also be used to study the qualitative effects of possible interventions or in fact to create an understanding of economic principles. An example of this is Hicks' IS-LM model, which is used to illustrate the consequences of Keynesian monetary policies of reducing the interest rate. Clearly, the model itself is an aggregation of the behaviour of economic agents. Such abstract, qualitative models just explicating the laws governing a system may also be called 'rule-based models'. In many real-world cases, there is a need for tangible policy advice not just an educative insight, and a quantitative, variable-based model is needed.

Another class of EBMs that can be used for policy making is game theory. In fact, the national defence policy of mutually assured destruction followed in the cold war derives from the game theoretic concept of a Nash equilibrium. In general, game theoretic models harbour 'agents' that 'exploit' the (highly limited and abstract) system they are part of. An example is the Bertrand duopoly model in which both firms seek to 'game' the other firm in price setting. Generally, in the fields of Industrial Organisation and neoclassical economics, 'agents' in the EBM are perfectly rational and perfectly informed. In reality, individuals (and, at that, firms and organisations governed by them) do not know how, are not capable of, and possibly do not even care to fully exploit the system they are part of. Generalising their own experiences, individuals are often not able to oversee the number of dimensions involved, let alone their intricate interactions, and as such they just grapple with what to do, often readily satisfied with improving their conditions incrementally. Occasionally it is argued that policies or strategies derived from 'perfectly rational' EBMs are normative rules. However, if not all actors in the real world behave perfectly rationally, which is very likely, the EBMs provide faulty recommendations.

For the examples of EBMs given, agent-based modelling is in any case a fully-fledged alternative to equation-based modelling. Whenever the variables in an EBM are the size of populations of agents, as for example in the case of the predatory and prey animals in the Lotka-Volterra system, one can simply define a disaggregated system with just as many agents, whereby the macro-level laws on the development of the aggregate variables are to be translated into micro-level behavioural rules. This translation step is, in general, rather trivial because aggregate laws are often so crude that the behaviour rules are rather basic. The reformulation of the macro law into micro behaviour may also reveal underlying assumptions. For example, the (sexual) replication rate in the Lotka-Volterra system (not uncommonly simply operationalised as $dX = a X dt$) needs operationalisation of the number of offspring conditioned on the probability of an encounter between a male and female animal of the same species and of appropriate age. Sex, encounter probability, variation in location, age, and fertility are all neglected in the original model. Wilson (1998) extended the predator-prey EBM with variation in geographical locations, but the resulting dynamics featured anomalies of the mean-field partial differential equations that Wilson had to resort to.

Having to operationally define all dimensions at play in micro-level behaviour to study macro-level population size dynamics may be considered a downside of working with ABMs. However, also in the operational definition of micro-level behaviour one can make simplifying assumptions that still give rise to the same macro-level dynamics. In both modelling disciplines, modellers should follow the adage ‘keep it simple, but not simpler’. That said, over-aggregation and thereby dismissing heterogeneity among agents is one of the curses of EBMs. This ‘representative agent’ problem is discussed in the next subsection on econometric models.

In any case, ABM ‘technology’ can be more generally used as an alternative to EBMs. In an arguably contorted conceptualisation, the satellites in the N-body system can be defined as agents and the physical laws defining the interaction of bodies as behaviour. The dynamics in and of the system does not change.

More troublesome is using ABMs for symbolic or qualitative EBMs. To the best of my knowledge, there have been no attempts to write purely symbolic ABMs. However, clearly, agent behaviour can just be a set of operators on strings that have no further quantitative meaning, thus qualifying as a symbolic model. That said, symbolic models are generally formulated to convey the workings of simple mechanisms, while ABMs are generally applied to cases of a conceptual richness that by far exceed the simplicity of symbolic models. Hence, while there seem to be ways to use ABMs as alternatives to qualitative/symbolic EBMs, each type serves different purposes.

It is also easy to see that the Bertrand game can be defined as an ABM. The agents' behavioural heuristics can just follow the (possibly implicit) solutions derived in the Bertrand EBM. However, do note that many agent-based modellers have a background in social sciences and simply do not subscribe to the assumptions of perfect rationality and perfect information. In fact, behavioural heuristics in ABMs generally operationally respond to (certain parts of) the state of the industry rather than strategically anticipate it.

Econometric models

The second type of models that is often mentioned by policy makers is that of econometric models (EMs) and more specifically structural equation models (SEMs). Such econometric models are constructions of equations that statistically relate input variables taking their value at some point in time to output variables which (supposedly) take their value after that. EMs are typically used to explore possible relationships between variables using extensive empirical datasets or to test the statistical significance of those relationships. Although EMs can contain variables in multiple periods, EMs are not dynamic models.

EMs are used to study economic data for the macro-economic effects of policy intervention on the behaviour of citizens. Moreover, EMs aggregate behaviour into equations that neglect individual differences. However, the resulting dynamics when each agent follows the same decision tree (which represents the 'average' behaviour) may be quite different from when agents have their particular decision trees, utility functions, initial conditions, etc. Whenever all agents are instances of one and the same 'representative agent' model, the (dynamic) responses to changes in experimental variables may be highly disruptive. For instance, if all households have the same utility for green over grey electricity, a change in subsidy levels may have all households instantly switch from purchasing one to the other type of electricity.

In an attempt to salvage the use of the econometrist's rich toolkit of analytical instruments, the 'representative agent' is modelled to make probabilistic decisions (e.g. following a discrete choice model). Although this may indeed iron out disruptive dynamics, it does still not do justice to inherent segmentation in the population. Moreover, policy interventions may change the decisions of only part of the agent population and thereby not only shift the probabilities of decisions but also in fact change the structure of the economic problem studied (cf. the Lucas critique).

Apart from the inherent heterogeneity on the side of the agents, their decision trees may be interdependent (e.g. in strategic behaviour), the decisions trees may change over time, and there may be interaction effects over time (e.g. diffusion-substitution) that are insufficiently captured in static agent models.

Just as with EBMs, it is fairly easy to formulate ABMs that reproduce the relationships in EMs simply by picking certain operationalisations of agent behaviour. On top of this, ABMs do easily allow the introduction of heterogeneity or population segmentation in agent behaviour. Moreover, unlike EMs, ABMs are dynamic, multi-period models with, possibly, endogenously emerging behaviour responding (indirectly) to policy interventions.

Comparison

Comparing the three types of models, the following main conclusions are drawn. First, much unlike ABMs, the EBM and EM approaches only implicitly model network interactions and agent heterogeneity. As such EBMs and EMs are ill-equipped for evaluation of particular policy instruments, especially those that target networking and interactions driven by heterogeneity. Second, EMs cannot cope with anticipation or the feedback of policy interventions back into the system. Third, the perspectives on what real-world actors can or should do (and even are actually doing) differ substantially. EBMs and EMs prescribe policies in the case of unrealistic (aggregated) actor behaviour. From the perspective of behavioural sciences, the micro-level definition of heterogeneous heuristics deserves preference.

Challenges of using ABMs for policy evaluation

Occasionally, policy makers are somewhat sceptical about the value of ABM-based policy recommendations. It is not unusual to come across various critical remarks. First, since the underlying technical implementation of the model is largely a black box for the policy makers, they contest the internal and external validity of outcomes. Second, simulation outcomes are poorly understood and misinterpreted because of temporal disturbances like the simulation onset behaviour (due to ABM initialisation) and learning (due to agent population evolution). Third, there are disputes over the agent heuristics, and policy makers (may) argue that 'in reality, agents do it differently'. Fourth, it is argued that the ABM is not specific or generic enough for the case studied.

Arguably, part of the skepticism of policy makers can be obviated by involving them already in formulating model elements. Calibration of model parameters and initial system conditions (e.g. firm profiles, social network topology, market concentration) may instil yet more confidence. However, that said, a possible lack of validity is (and should also be) a major concern to the modeller. The challenge of calibration of ABMs for policy evaluation is discussed first. A comment occasionally heard is that the validity of simulation outcomes is hard to judge given conceptual model choices, the operational definitions, possible faults in the code, and particularly the various non-linear interactions of various software modules. We discuss several issues with validity[4] and ways to improve the validity of ABMs (and SKIN in particular). This is followed by a discussion on the comment that 'real agents do it differently'. In this juxtaposition, the neoclassical assumptions on agent behaviour are pitted against the assumptions in the prevailing paradigm in the field of heterodox ABMs and the operationalisations of agent behaviour. Discussed last are the temporal disturbances in simulation outcomes and how to account for and prevent those.

Calibration

To bolster the external validity of the model and provide tailored, possibly quantitative policy advice, it is commendable to use empirical data to calibrate the ABMs. Not only can macro-level parameters be estimated

---

[4] For a discussion on validity for simulation models in general, the reader is referred to Sargent (2005).

from the data, but so, too, can the composition of the agent population, the properties of the individual agents and their relationship, as well as particularities of the environment (e.g. resources, infrastructure, geography) be deduced.

Even the very first SKIN models were already empirically calibrated. The three modules characteristic of the SKIN model that require calibration are: (1) the knowledge units (e.g. scientific insights, patentable technology descriptions, production steps, firm competences) and the way they are acquired and created; (2) the products (e.g. product, patent, article) and how these are generated using those knowledge units; and (3) how products generate income to cover expenses for generating knowledge and creating products (e.g. by offering these products to an oracle, by selling them on the market).

The operationalisations of ‘knowledge’, ‘knowledge discovery’, ‘output’, and ‘production’ depend on the case to which the SKIN model is applied, the modeller-researcher’s convictions, data available for calibration, etc. What is operationally defined as knowledge unit depends strongly on the application. In a case where the researcher-modeller focuses on industrial innovation, knowledge units may be operationally defined as technological concepts used in products. Alternatively, a knowledge unit may be an encoding of the technological field in which an agent is active. In the case where there is a focus on scientific discoveries, one may regard either the papers as knowledge units themselves or the proved/disproved hypotheses contained in it.

In general, knowledge discovery is a procedure that takes a collection of knowledge units readily owned and returns a (possibly new) knowledge unit, generally according to some probability distribution or fixed knowledge unit graph. Actual calibration of this knowledge graph can be done using patent data or historical invention mapping - creating either hard-wired graphs or probability matrices. Note also that other ‘technology development’ models (e.g. Kauffman’s NK model, history friendly models, Verspagen & Silverberg percolation model, Taylor & Morone graphs) face the same calibration challenge. An alternative is to parameterize the structure of the knowledge unit graph (e.g. the amount of branching and splitting) and find parameter settings that characterize the graph for a particular industry’s technological knowledge.

Researcher-modellers face a similar challenge when operationally defining and empirically calibrating the procedure of output production which translates a set of knowledge units into 'products' and their 'performance'. In the case where the researcher's focus is on industrial innovation, empirical calibration may be done by historical analysis of inventions, underlying knowledge flows, and market value. Where the researcher's focus is on scientific discovery, the product could be papers or presentations and the knowledge units could be hypotheses/concepts.

Ideally, one has an automated method of empirical calibration that uses a database. For instance, one can use a patent database by distinguishing 'knowledge patents' (e.g. a concept, a principle, a method) from actual directly marketable 'products'. Another example would be to use a citation database, citing papers as 'products' and using either keywords or words/claims in the abstract text as 'knowledge units'. In the above-mentioned parameterized knowledge unit graph, one could classify particular 'knowledge unit' nodes as products. SKIN flavoured models can also empirically calibrate the composition of the agent population and the properties of individual agents like size, product range, production skills, past R&D partnerships, and location (cf. Korber, Paier, and Fischer 2009).

Pitfalls of face validity and storytelling

Customarily, ABMs produce graphs or tables of some key variables over time. The ABM simulation is said to have face validity if a (panel of) theme expert(s) qualifies the simulation outcomes in check with the real-world phenomena studied. During ABM development, however, the modeller himself/herself assesses face validity for 'reasonable' values for all parameters and experimental variables. Although it is debatable whether this is part of face validity studies or internal validity checks, I have studied simulation outcomes with variations of certain parameters and experimental variables in the first quality assurance phases. Not uncommonly, trial simulation runs produce surprising results, e.g. a counter-intuitive or weak or rather strong effect of a particular parameter or experimental variable. It is then left to the developer-modeller to assure that the outcomes are not caused by faulty code or inadequate operational definitions of concepts.

In assessing face validity, an obvious pitfall is that of 'storytelling', i.e. looking for a conceptual story that confirms the outcomes. Such a story may have the researcher certify the face validity erroneously. However, even if the outcomes are in line with expectations, this does not absolve the developer-modeller of the obligation to assure the programmatic correctness and operational soundness of the model. This is particularly since, not infrequently, the plots or tables used to determine face validity can be produced already quite early during ABM development, e.g. when agent heuristics may still need further scrutiny. To illustrate this, I was once asked to review the code of an ABM and discovered a bug that, once fixed, changed the plateauing in the number of firms with a plausible explanation to an exponentially growing number of firms that could not be explained immediately by the modeller.

The curse of double dynamics

While face validity and correctness of underlying code may be easily established for simple, linear systems, validity of simulation outcomes may become hard to gauge whenever there are non-linearly interacting components. To appreciate the difficulties of understanding interacting systems, consider the motion of a double pendulum in which a second bob is connected by a rod to the top pendulum bob. In operationally defining the model, a relatively simple mathematical model of the motion of a bob subjected to physical forces suffices, and subsequently, so does connecting the models for both bobs. The resulting system of coupled second-order differential equations can be solved numerically. Experimenting with an actual physical or computer simulation mode has proved to be particularly insightful, as, for large initial angles, the system displays seemingly chaotic behaviour. Inspecting graphs of, say, the vertical coordinate of the bottom bob for certain intervals, remains – grave programming errors aside - unrevealing of the correctness of the model. So, operationally and structurally simple models with interacting components may already give rise to intricate dynamic behaviour of which it is hard to establish (face) validity. While this is already hard for physical models with double dynamics, it is even harder to establish for social systems in which behaviour is endogenously and autonomously changing.

Internal and external validity

Unsurprisingly, face validity of simulation output is the first but also one of the weakest tests that ABMs should pass. A stronger validity concept is that of internal validity. In the context of ABM development, internal validity is used here to describe that there is no intellectual ambiguity of the causal chain through which input parameter settings cause the simulated output. Three practices to aid in internal validity are discussed.

First, to ensure sufficient intellectual scrutiny of the causal chain, developer-modellers are encouraged to provide functional design specifications (FDS) and a program technical description (PTD), just as professionals do in the software industry. In the FDS, the developer determines the sequences and interdependencies of operations, here: in the model of the economic or social system. Note that the software design and actual real-world system can and may well differ. An actual, common example of this gap is the existence of an Industry class in object-oriented code that matches agents for collaboration, while – in reality - agents generally do this by themselves autonomously and decentrally. In fact, part of the design decisions may stem from what is considered good code practices rather than conceptual model considerations. Moreover, developer-modellers should provide a PTD in the form of pseudo-code or flow-charts to communicate the operations internal to procedures. Ideally, both the FDS and PTD should be contained in reports presenting ABM results or be available upon request. Creation and maintenance of these documents does not only force the developers themselves to review interactions and the effects of certain operations, but it also convinces other researchers and policy makers of the causal chain and internal validity, and allows other developer-modellers to implement the model in a language of their choice, reproduce the research findings, and expand the model for different purposes.

Second, the developer-modeller should assert bug-free code, which – as most developers in economics are not trained computer scientists - generally boils down to testing the code to great lengths to make sure it does what it is supposed to do. In systems with a few variables, the developer can easily step through the code or study debugging print-outs. In the case of complex systems with non-linearly interacting components, this task is daunting - although not impossible. In my experience, it is sensible to – at least initially - study the non-linear interactions in a controlled setting, e.g. a system with a limited number of agents, a system with agents that have some (interacting) heuristics disabled. Conveniently, given the fact that ABM modules generally have one-to-one associations with the real-world systems, modellers can conduct unit tests of separate modules. This is particularly so if external validity is sought for each of these separate modules. In the context of ABM development, external validity entails that the ABM simulation reproduces a wide range of general features of the real-world system being modelled[5]. Concretely, developer-modellers can devise tests on a separate module to assure that it reproduces particular social or economic 'stylised facts'. For instance, consider an ABM in which firms sell substitutable products to consumers and adjust prices to increase profit. A unit test would be to make demand inelastic in order to see whether there is product price explosion when the number of firms is kept equal to one (i.e. it is a monopoly) or profit margin erosion when the number of firms is high (i.e. there is unfettered competition). Arguably, whenever unit tests of a module indicate it is externally valid, this is also an indication of the internal validity.

Third, when the internal functioning of individual procedures/modules has been approved, developer-modellers should ascertain there are no unintended temporal interferences across procedures/modules. Most ABMs evaluated by the author are discrete time simulations, in which each agent gets to conduct its activities during each period. However, in discrete time simulations, agents act supposedly simultaneously, but, given the nature of computer processors, their (object internal) code is executed consecutively while all agents operate on the basis of the same macro variables. In my experience, there are various temporal particularities of the discrete time ABMs that are often poorly understood by novice programmers. Several years ago, I was asked to review the code of an ABM under development. While browsing through the code, I made a discovery which was alarming. In the procedure for collaborative product creation, I found a line instructing to remove 'dead' agents from the list of collaborators. Clearly, this is only needed if an agent can exit the industry after the matching in this period. Already from a conceptual perspective this is undesirable, because remaining agents that were matched to collaborate with the agent that just exited may very well have picked a different partner if they had known their partner would exit before the actual collaboration. Further analysis showed that the main simulation procedure featured a single for-loop over the agents in which the focal agent executed consecutively the procedures to (1) find another agent to collaborate with, (2) collaborate to make a product, (3) sell its products on the market, and (4) exit the market if bankrupt. Clearly, the later agents in the for-loop may end up having ties with agents that have already exited the market, have collaborated more often (by mere probabilistic

[5] Note that face validity is a weak test that a model generates 'reasonable' outcomes for 'regular' parameter settings, while external validity requires the software to produce outcomes that meet stylized facts, expert expectations, etc. under wildly varying settings and boundary conditions.

arguments), and have faced a different state of industry than the first agent since e.g. many consumers had already bought products. Implementation should have entailed executing these four actions consecutively in separate for-loops: in the first loop agents pick partners, in the next loop agents collaborate in creating products, in the following loop consumers buy products, and in the final loop bankrupt agents exit.

However, given that agent heuristics operate based on the same macro-level variables (e.g. the product market, product prices), there is feedforward of actions of agents into actions of agents executed later in the for-loop (e.g. a product launch by the first agent would affect the decision to launch the products of other agents). To prevent such feedforward, agents should decide on a deep copy of the macro-level variables that remains unaltered through the for-loop, and their actions should take effect only after the for-loop. In the example given above, all agents decide whether to launch a product or not based on the state of the market before the loop, store all products in a temporary array during the loop, and all products enter the market simultaneously after the loop.
Conclusively, developer-modellers need proper training in picking the ABM design (notably discrete event or discrete time), and they need to understand how such a design is to be implemented properly to avoid such temporal complications.

Iterative agent-based model development

Much to the dismay of the developer-modellers, a typical ABM development process is iterative. Even despite a proper design and technical specification stage, the first test runs of an ABM simulation may be disconcerting. It is not uncommon that plots of certain key variables deviate from expectations, that the system responds in surprising ways to certain parameter changes, or that dynamics are extreme (e.g. exponential growth or, instead, zero growth). In the first step, the researchers should look for 'hotspots' in the parameter landscape (for those parameters not calibrated or having a clearly 'reasonable' value) in which simulation output is supposed to match stylized facts. Often this requires a coarse grained Monte Carlo study followed by zooming in on hotspots and conducting a fine grained study to test the ABM simulation. If such hotspots cannot be found or if simulation outcomes defy the stylized facts, it is then up to the developer-modeller to ascertain that the code is bug free. As explained before, this is done by analysing the code, scrutinizing extensive action logs, and conducting unit tests. If the code is bug free, the next step is to attune parameter values in such fashion that it is not one module that dominates the dynamics. For instance, if the consumer market is too small for any firm to cover expenses, all firms in the system will die out. If simulation outcomes remain questionable, the ABM conceptual design should be reconsidered. It is not uncommon that limitations on the conceptual model of the real-world system cause unexpected simulation outcomes. For instance, using SKIN to study breakthrough dynamics requires a knowledge space in which agents discover new knowledge units non-convexly - at least for the time horizon simulated. After all, in a convex knowledge space, there eventually is tapering off of knowledge discovery. Finally, even if the ABM's conceptual design has stood the test of scientific scrutiny, one may argue that the theoretical concepts forming the basis for the ABM may need revision. Since I, like most researchers, work with extant theories, I have no first-hand illustrations of this need to revise theoretical concepts. It is also disputable whether ABM simulation outcomes could ever be considered sufficient evidence to overthrow a theory.

Upon each ABM redefinition and redevelopment, new parameter landscape searches and test rounds are needed, possibly leading to new redefinitions and redevelopments. My first-hand experience is thatthere occasionally are more iterations needed to adjust heuristics and the ABM design. In the case of a high-dimensional ABM with double dynamics and second-order emergence, it may take an experienced modeller quite a number of working days to get acceptable and valid output.

An amusing illustration of a case in which a 'redefinition cycle' was required is the following: I once developed an ABM in which potential entrants waited 'outside' the system and would imperfectly copy the heuristics of highly profitable agents, including the entry strategy when to enter (which was based on concentration and profitability). In a significant number of runs, the system would develop a highly concentrated market with highly profitable agents - yet without any entry. At first, I was puzzled by this outcome. However, detailed analysis showed that such an industry could emerge because of two reasons. First, there was a small chance that a firm would immediately discover a top technology and thus be serendipitously highly profitable for some time, regardless of its actual heuristics. Second, if this firm itself had an entry heuristic that dictated the agent not to enter in a concentrated market, potential entrants imitating this firm's heuristics would obviously not enter the market and thus sustain the concentrated (and profitable) market.

Agent heuristics

Given the stark contrast in behavioural assumptions between neoclassical and neo-Schumpeterian economics, and given the prevalence of the earlier, there is a recurring debate with policy makers on what agents are capable of. In ABMs, agents follow 'heuristics', i.e. a set of if-then rules on state variables that specify the actions for an agent to take. In reality, real-world agents follow rules-of-thumb that are often not optimal, either in general or in particular cases, and they process limited information. As such, in the discussion of agent heuristics, it is sensible to distinguish between first, the operational sophistication of heuristics, and, second, the extent to which the decision domain is understood and incorporated in these heuristics. Depending on the topic studied, heuristics may have different levels of sophistication and domain knowledge. Fundamental social, economic, or ecological research may be concerned with understanding dynamics emerging from agent interaction following elementary heuristics with limited sophistication, e.g. simple diffusion processes in a population of consumers or the formation of paths from food to nest by an ant population.

An extreme form may be a game-theoretic pricing model in which agents know the strategy of the other agents and mathematically optimize their own pricing strategy accordingly. In economic terms, such agents are perfectly informed and perfectly rational, and their heuristics are highly sophisticated and exploit a complete understanding of the decision domain. The subsection on equation-based models (like the neoclassical ones) has already outlined why it is not appropriate to model agents as if they were perfectly rational or maximisers.

In between these two extremes, there are agent heuristics that cope in a more or less sophisticated way with a limited understanding of or limited information on the decision domain. In neo-Schumpeterian economics, there is a tendency to have, first, well-argued assumptions on the agents' understanding of the decision domain and, second, heuristics of a simplicity that would still allow the researcher-modeller to reason what is driving (possibly) emerging double dynamics.

When defining the agent heuristics, the researcher-modeller needs to include only those heuristics that are the main operations of the particular type of agent in the economic or social process under study. As outlined before, the researcher-modeller and the policy-maker should discuss early on what actions to include and how to abstract rules-of-thumb into heuristics.

Emerging dynamics: temporal patterns, simulation onset, learning

The illustration of a model in which industries became concentrated without entry highlights another important issue in ABM simulations, namely the issue of emerging dynamics. In ABM design, researcher-modellers should bear in mind the temporal patterns, onset dynamics, and evolutionary training of heuristics.

First, researchers use ABMs to simulate a wide variety of processes, but in general the key output variables either converge to particular 'steady state' values, form temporal patterns (e.g. recurrent peaks, staircasing S-shapes, multi-dimensional cycles), or display continuous growth or decline. In my experience, it is a challenge to design and operationally define ABMs to either reproduce or test the formation of temporal patterns. To see how this can be a challenge, I will share some of my experiences developing an ABM of technological development. From a neo-Schumpeterian perspective, the combination of swarm-in and shake-out, product design exploitation, and radical breakthroughs gives rise to 'bursty' S-shape staircasing in technology performance. However, reproducing that required me - being the developer-modeller - to design an ABM with endogenous entry and exit, to have agents search in a non-convex technology space, and to have agents decide autonomously when to engage in technology search and when to exploit existing technology to recoup money already invested in that search. As such, there is high-dimensional double dynamics: technology search is paced to both individual financial decisions as well as to the economic processes of product competition, while competitive conditions are the outcome of technology search. In the first versions of the model, there were many runs in which agents stopped introducing next generations or raced to new generations until all were bankrupt. As became clear in the exposition of calibration and validation, it is a serious challenge to find, tune, and justify the model elements, particularly in the case of high-dimensional double dynamics.

Second, there may be onset dynamics that should not be mistaken for meaningful simulation output. When talking about the onset phase, I refer to the periods during which the system dynamics is largely due to initial conditions (e.g. values of variables) rather than conditions that are common to or could emerge within the real-world system. In SKIN ABMs, for example, after the start of the simulation, knowledge bases may yet have to be filled with knowledge units, individual differences in strategies may yet have to reflect in products on the market and in capital stock, social relationships may yet have to form, (macro-level) exponentially smoothed variables driving agent behaviour may yet have to lose initial variability, etc. Ordinarily, the rule-of-thumb is to discard or ignore simulation results before a certain period because of these onset dynamics. When the initial ABM simulation state (in terms of capital stocks, knowledge bases, social relationships, etc.) can be calibrated to empirical data, there is considerably fewer onset dynamics.

Third, population-level learning in the agents' strategies may disturb 'regular' system dynamics. Population-level learning means that there is (initial) variation, imitation of successful variants by new entrants, and de-selection of unsuccessful ones. First of all, researcher-modellers should be aware that the population of agent strategies needs time to converge. There is an onset phase in the system development during which there is an abnormal diversity of strategies, or there may still be 'inviable' strategies present, for instance dynamics may be extraordinarily erratic. Second, there may be (coincidental) emergence of strategies that are merely artificial. A strategy that emerges in the onset phase as superior may be 'nonsensical' in the post-onset phase but nonetheless persist, e.g. because variation is too limited to escape the basin of attraction of that strategy. One such case was the ABM described above in which one agent, which had the strategy not to enter under high concentration, survived. These great challenges in particular may have researcher-modellers oppose having endogenous learning, and they may prefer simply to evaluate the dynamics from simple, static heuristics.

In deliberating with policy makers on modelling choices, researcher-modellers need to explain which ingredients are required for the ABM to reproduce particular dynamics (e.g. successive product life-cycles, societal transitions). Moreover, in contrast to the common understanding that forecasts become less reliable the farther ahead in the future they predict, simulation results may become more reliable over time with the vanishing of onset dynamics and learning effects. It is important to be aware of and also to explain to a policy maker exactly these intricacies in the interpretation of simulation results. On top of that, researcher-modellers are advised to empirically calibrate their models, to be reluctant to introduce learning, and to strive for simple models with limited temporal patterns to reproduce.

Next-gen policy instruments and policy engineering?

So far, we have discussed arriving at policy recommendations following from abductive reasoning by using desired simulation outcomes (cf. Brenner & Werker, 2009). Using ABMs for, essentially, ex-ante policy evaluation may be considered just one tool in a whole toolkit using ABMs. We discuss four more ways in which policy interventions may use ABMs: policy engineering, technologically supported policy instruments, encompassing augmentation of the real-world system, and system redesign.

Policy engineering

In fact, regardless of the sophistication of the ABM, the way of arriving at the policy intervention as discussed in this chapter is rather unsophisticated. After all, policy evaluation boils down to comparing simulation results in autonomous runs with simulation results after some intervention with a conceptually limited policy instrument (e.g. increasing tax, providing research funds, introducing a coordinating agent for research collaboration). In contrast to the policy evaluation approach, which studies emerging phenomena and backtracks policies, there is a policy engineering approach. Narrowly, this could be taken as a particular method of determining what policy intervention to pursue, e.g. a numerical method to arrive at a value for a particular experimental variable (for instance a fuel tax level). Given that ABMs run on computers, a fine-grained scan of the outcomes for different values of the experimental variables in combination with a scan of the parameter landscape can be fully automated. Clearly, the practical value of the thus-discovered 'optimal' setting for the experimental variables depends on the conceptual realism of the ABM.

Hybrid policy instruments

The policy maker may enhance policy interventions by engineering hybrid policy instruments. A hybrid instrument combines a traditional policy instrument (i.e. financial means, regulation, network orchestration) with technological support. One may think of a software tool that regularly computes tax levelsor a software tool that exploits a database on capability profiles or patent portfolio to match firms that are looking for R&D partners for innovation projects. An example of a real-world policy instrument that may benefit from a hybrid policy instrument is the

CO2-emission rights system. The market for emissions is regulated since firms need licenses to emit CO2. However, the number of emission certificates seems to have been picked somewhat arbitrarily. In fact, the number of certificates is so high, and thereby the market price is so low, that CO2 emission is barely reduced. The European Commission could use a software tool actively buying (and possibly selling) CO2 emission certificates to affect the market price and thereby stimulate emission reduction. Interestingly, given that this emission certificate market has the characteristics of a competitive, homogeneous spot market, this software tool could well use an EBM. That said, ABMs can still be used to evaluate the effects of such hybrid policy instruments.

Multi-agent system augmentation

Introducing a software tool to enhance a 'regular' policy instrument (e.g. tax, regulation, organization) can be taken a step further. Although the policy maker probably does not have the mandate to completely redesign the real-world system, it is possible to enhance the real-world system by overlaying it with a multi-agent system[6] (MAS). In such an MAS, each real-world agent (e.g. firm, governmental body) or decision domain factor (e.g. resource, operational constraint) in the system is represented in a computer model and then enhanced by a technological augmentation (e.g. a micro-transaction negotiation bot, a capability matching bot, a logistics management bot). The system layer of technological augmentations uses system-wide data (so, unlike an ABM, not just the agent or factor it represents) and coordinates decisions (autonomously or under guidance of the policy maker) to realize particular system-level outcomes, possibly using solvers, algorithms, and operators. This MAS augmentation layer can run in real-time, learn, and take immediate and future restrictions of agents into account. In fact, the MAS may be completely virtual and simply be used to 'optimize' policy interventions that steer the whole system into the most desirable direction.

---

[6] As explained, I take an ABM to be designed by an academic researcher to represent a real-world social system in which agents are one-to-one associated with real firms, organizations, individuals, etc. Agents follow behavioural rules that may be simplified and abstracted, but arguably justified given the domain that the researcher studies. I take an MAS to be an agent system purposefully designed by engineers for enhancement of a real-world (industrial) system. In an MAS, agents are technological augmentations of vehicles, machines, objects, firms, business units, employees, etc., generally following rules that improve efficiency, lower costs, etc.

An operations research example is a public bus system augmented by associating each bus and bus stop with an agent that processes information about crowding. Information about the number of people on buses and the number of people waiting at particular bus stops can then be processed by a central computer to e.g. instantaneously reschedule certain buses in real time, adding more buses to the network, etc.

System redesign

So far, the policy interventions discussed use limited instruments to steer the real-world system in a desirable direction. However, given that the researcher-modeller and policy maker have full control over the virtual world, the effects of an encompassing system redesign can also be evaluated. Interestingly, the type and particularly the urgency of the societal challenges that humanity faces (e.g. global warming, demographic developments, faltering economic growth, etc.) seem to call for a more authoritarian system redesign rather than incremental adaption.

Implementing the system redesign of course requires considerable authority, an encompassing mandate, and organisational power to implement the enhancements of that system. Studying system redesign is typically only suited for, say, hierarchical management within a single firm, an agent network with a powerful managing central coordinator (e.g. a system integrator), or an authoritarian rather than liberal capitalistic society.

A final word

A dear colleague once quasi-jokingly said that policy evaluation with conceptually encompassing ABMs (like the SKIN model) is like 'playing SimCity', thereby referring to the popular city-building computer game. Although I distance myself from the association with purely recreational games, I tend to salute the association with appealing computer models that (i) simulate complex real-world systems and (ii) enable evaluation of policy interventions. In this chapter, I have discussed a range of issues pertaining to the use of ABMs for policy making. As such, I have put forth strong arguments in favour of ABMs (and the SKIN ABM for innovation network studies in particular) for tackling such tasks and strong arguments against the traditional equation-based and econometric modelling approaches for policy studies. Given the real-world system and research questions of interest, policy studies need models with agent heterogeneity, need to incorporate (multi-level) agent networks, and need to prudently aggregate away real-world conceptual complexity. Exactly in this regard ABMs excel and alternatives fall short.

However, I have also openly discussed the various particular challenges in ABM design that I have come across. I have explained how I work towards internal and external validity of the ABM, given that such ABMs feature software processes that are hard to keep track of (due to non-linear interaction of agents, double dynamics, and second-order emergence), and given that researchers generally lack the rich data that is needed for micro-level empirical calibration. Moreover, I have highlighted how there are intricacies in interpreting simulation outcomes due to e.g. onset behaviour, learning, and the requirement of reproducing certain temporal patterns.

In conclusion this chapter ends with several ideas on how ABMs can be used by policy makers beyond the conventional ways.

References

Ahrweiler, P., Pyka, A., and Gilbert, N. (2011) "A New Model for University-Industry Links in Knowledge-Based Economies", in: Journal of Product Innovation Management, 28, pp. 218–235.

Ahrweiler, P., Schilperoord, M., Pyka, A., and Gilbert, N. (2014) "Testing Policy Options for Horizon 2020 with SKIN", in: Simulating Knowledge Dynamics in Innovation Networks, edited by N. Gilbert, P. Ahrweiler, and A. Pyka, Berlin Heidelberg: Springer.

Axelrod, R. (2007) "Simulation in the social sciences", In Handbook of research on nature inspired computing for economy and management, edited by J.-P. Reynard. Hershey, CA: Idea Group.

Boero, R. and Squazzoni, F. (2005) "Does empirical embeddedness matter? Methodological issues on agent-based models for analytical social science", in: Journal of Artificial Societies and Social Simulation, 8-4.

Brenner, T. and Werker, C. (2007) "A Taxonomy of Inference in Simulation Models", in: Computational Economics, 37, pp. 227- 244.

Brenner, T. and Werker, C. (2009) "Policy Advice Derived from Simulation Models", in: Journal of Artificial Societies and Social Simulation, 12-4.

Deichsel, S. and Pyka, A. (2009) "A Pragmatic Reading of Friedman's Methodological Essay and What It Tells Us for the Discussion of ABMs", in: Journal of Artificial Societies and Social Simulation, 12

(4).

Fagiolo, G., and Roventini, A. (2012) “Macroeconomic Policy in DSGE and Agent-Based Models”, in: Revue de l'OFCE, 5-124, pp. 67-116.

Frenken, K. (2006) "Technological innovation and complexity theory", in: Econ. Innov. New Techn., 15-2, pp. 137–155.

Gilbert, N. (1997) “A Simulation of the Structure of Academic Science”, in: Sociological Research Online, 2-2.

Gilbert, N., Pyka, A., and Ahrweiler, P. (2001) “Innovation networks - a simulation approach”, in: Journal of Artificial Societies and Social Simulation, 4-3.

Korber, M. and Paier, M. (2013) "Effects of Competence Centres on Regional Knowledge Production: An Agent-Based Simulation of the Vienna Life Sciences Innovation System", in: The Geography of Networks and R&D Collaborations, edited by T. Scherngell, Springer International Publishing.

Korber, M., Paier, M., and Fischer, M.M. (2009) “An agent-based view of the biotech innovation system”, in: Reg Direct Int Sci J, 2-2, pp. 33-55.

Lempert, R. (2002) "Agent-based modeling as organizational and public policy simulators.", in: Proceedings of the National Academy of Sciences, 99-3.

Pyka, A. and Saviotti, P.P. (2005) "The Evolution of R&D Networking in the Biotech Industries", in: International Journal of Entrepreneurship and Innovation Management, 5-1/2, pp. 49-68.

Sargent, R.G. (2005) “Verification and validation of simulation models”, in: Proceedings of the 37th conference on Winter simulation, pp. 130-143.

Scholz, R., Nokkala, T., Ahrweiler, P., Pyka, A., and Gilbert, N. (2010) “The agent-based Nemo Model (SKEIN) – simulating European Framework Programmes”, in: Innovation in Complex Social Systems, edited by P. Ahrweiler, London: Routledge.

Triulzi, G. and Pyka, A. (2011) “Learning-by-modeling: Insights from an Agent-Based Model of University–Industry Relationships”, in: Cybernetics and Systems, 42-7.

Wilson, W.G. (1998) “Resolving Discrepancies between Deterministic Population Models and Individual-Based Simulations”, in: American Naturalist, 151-2, pp. 116-134.

CONTRIBUTORS

Frederic Adam, Professor, Business Information Systems
(i) Lessons from enterprise resource planning implementations in Ireland–towards smaller and shorter ERP projects, F Adam, P O'Doherty, Journal of information technology 15 (4), 305-316 2000
(ii) The enterprise resource planning decade: lessons learned and issues for the future, F Adam, D Sammon Igi Global, 2004
(iii) Project preparedness and the emergence of implementation problems in ERP projects, D Sammon, F Adam, Information & Management 47 (1), 1-8 2010

Petra Ahrweiler, Professor of Technology and Innovation Assessment; Director of EA European Academy
(i) Ahrweiler, P. (Ed.). (2010) *Innovation in Complex Social Systems.* Routledge: London.
(ii) Ahrweiler, P., Pyka, A., Gilbert, N. (2011) 'A New Model for University-Industry Links in Knowledge-Based Economies'. *Journal of Product Innovation Management*, 28:218–235.
(iii) Leydesdorff, L. and Ahrweiler, P. (2014): In Search of a Network Theory of Innovations: Relations, Positions, and Perspectives. In: *Journal of the American Society for Information Science and Technology,* 65(11), 2359–2374.

Eamonn Ambrose, College Lecturer
(i) Marshall, Donna; Ambrose, Eamonn; McIvor, Ronan; Lamming, Richard (2014) "Self-interest or the greater good: How political and rational dynamics influence the outsourcing process". International Journal of Operations & Production Management.
(ii) Nyaga, G., Lynch, D., Marshall D. and Ambrose, E. (2013) "Power Asymmetry, Adaptation, and Collaboration in Dyadic Relationships Involving a Powerful Partner", Journal of Supply Chain Management, Volume 49, Issue 3.
(iii) Eamonn Ambrose, Donna Marshall, Daniel Lynch (2010) 'Buyer/supplier perspectives on supply chain relationships', International Journal of Operations & Production Management, Vol. 30, Issue 12.

Luiz-Flávio Autran Monteiro Gomes, Professor of Management Science
(i) Gomes, Luiz Flávio Autran Monteiro, de Mattos Fernandes, Joao Erick de Mello and Joao Carlos C. B. Soares (2014). A fuzzy stochastic approach to the multicriteria selection of an aircraft for regional chartering. Journal of Advanced Transportation, vol. 48, pp. 223-237.
(ii) Pereira, Javier, Gomes, Luiz Flávio Autran Monteiro and Paredes, Fernando (2013). Robustness analysis in a TODIM-based multicriteria evaluation model of rental properties. Technological and Economic Development of Economy, vol. 19, pp. 176-190.
(iii) Gomes, Luiz Flávio Autran Monteiro, Moshkovich, H. and Torres, A. (2010) Marketing decisions in small businesses: How verbal decision analysis can help. International Journal of Management and Decision Making, vol. 11, pp. 19-36.

Colm Burns, Research Fellow
(i) Burns, C. and Hewitt-Dundas, N. (2011) Exploring the adoption and implementation of discrete and integrated IT systems: A framework for analysis, *International Journal of Manufacturing Research*, Vol. 6, No. 2, pp. 175-190

Gary Chapman, PhD Candidate
Queen's University in Northern Ireland, U.K., MSc in International Business, B.A. in Business Management.
Research interests: science, technology and innovation policy, innovation policy evaluation (particularly behavioural additionality) and innovation management (particularly the cognitive dimensions).
Currently working on developing papers from Ph.D., submitted to the DRUID Academy conference

Özge Dilaver, Research Fellow
(i) Dilaver, Özge (2015) From Participants to Agents: Grounded Simulation as a Mixed-Method Research Design, Journal of Artificial Societies and Social Simulation, Volume 18, Issue 1.
(ii) Dilaver, Özge (2014) Making Sense of the Value of Innovations: A Comparison of Personal Computers and Mobile Phones, New Media and Society, Volume 16 Issue 8, (December 2014) pages 1214-1232, published online before print September 25, 2013, doi: 10.1177/1461444813504264
(iii) Dilaver, Özge (2014) Involuntary Technology Adoption: How Consumer Interdependencies Lead to Societal Change, Structural Change and Economic Dynamics, Volume 31, December 2014, pages 138–148.

Ciara Fitzgerald, PhD, Lecturer, Business Information Systems
(i) University technology transfer offices: The search for identity to build legitimacy, C O'Kane, V Mangematin, W Geoghegan, C Fitzgerald 2015, Research Policy 44 (2), 421-437:
(ii) Towards the institutionalisation of parliamentary technology assessment: the case for Ireland, C Csaki, C Fitzgerald, P O'Raghallaigh, F Adam 2014, Transforming Government: People, Process and Policy 8 (3), 315-334
(iii) University-based entrepreneurship: A synthesis of the literature, RP O'Shea, C Fitzgerald, H Chugh, TJ Allen 2014, Building Technology Transfer within Research Universities: An Entrepreneurial Approach

Brian Fynes, Professor of Supply Chain Management
(i) Wiengarten, F., Gimenez, C., Fynes, B. and Ferdows, K. (2015) 'Exploring the importance of cultural collectivism on the efficacy of lean practices: taking an organisational and national perspective', International Journal of Operations & Production Management, Vol. 35, No. 3 (available online)
(ii) Chavez, R., Yu, W., Jacobs, M., Fynes, B., Wiengarten, F. and Lecuna, A. (2015) 'Internal lean practices and performance: The role of technological turbulence', International Journal of Production Economics, Vol. 160, February, pp.157-171.
(iii) Scholten, K., Sharkey Scott, P. and Fynes, B (2014) 'Mitigation processes – antecedents for building supply chain resilience'. Supply Chain Management: An International Journal, Vol. 19, No. 2, pp. 211-228.

Nigel Gilbert, Professor of Sociology
(i) Gilbert, N. (2008). Agent-based models. Thousand Oaks, CA: SAGE.
(ii) Gilbert, N. (2010). Computational Social Science . SAGE Benchmarks in Social Research Methods Series. London: Sage.
(iii) Watts, C., & Gilbert, N. (2014). Simulating Innovation: Computer-based Tools for Rethinking Innovation. Edward Elgar

Frigyes Hausz, PhD Candidate
(i) Frigyes Hausz and Fonyó Attila "A hazai felsőoktatási intézmények szerepe a regionális K+F+I szerkezetben (The role of Hungarian higher education institutions in the structure of regional R&D&I structure)" *Felsőoktatási Műhely* 1 (2014): 130-147.

Nola Hewitt-Dundas, Professor of Innovation Management & Policy
(i) Hewitt-Dundas, N. (2012) Heterogeneity in Knowledge Transfer Behaviour of UK Universities, Research Policy, Vol 41, Issue 2, pp. 262-275 doi: 10.1016/j.respol.2011.10.010
(ii) Hewitt-Dundas N and Roper, S (2011) Creating advantage in peripheral regions: The role of publicly funded R&D centres, Research Policy, Vol. 40 (July), pp. 832-841, doi:10.1016/j.respol.2011.03.005
(iii) Roper, S and Hewitt-Dundas, N (2008) Innovation Persistence: Survey and case-study evidence, Research Policy, Vol. 37, No. 1, pp. 149-162

Darran Jones, MSc Strategic Management and Planning.

Béla Kardon, PhD, Chief Scientific Officer (CSO), Regional Centre for Information & Scientific Development (RCISD)
(i) Kardon, B. (2013): European Funding Instruments in R&D; Opportunities and Possible Synergies in Regional Policy vs. Horizon 2020. Workshop on Future Perspectives for EU-Japan Research and Innovation Cooperation 18 July 2013, Zürich, Switzerland.
(ii) Geambaşu, R., Kardon, B., Megyesi, B., Patakfalvi-Czirják, Á. (2013): Social conceptions of the research activity, the factors influencing career choices and the social impacts of the Researchers' Nights. Study; ISBN 978-963-89112-5-4; 58. p.; presented as a poster publication at the Ecsite Annual Conference (session: Researchers' Nights: Local approaches across a continent) 6-8 June 2013, Göteborg, Sweden
(iii) Laczó-Dávid., Á, Kardon, B., Zsár, V., Jeney, N. (2009): Structured Survey of the Most Significant ASEAN-EU S&T Relations (Poster publication). Second Bi-Regional EU-SEA S&T Stakeholders Conference 11-12 November 2009, Bogor, Indonesia

Séamas Kelly PhD, Senior Lecturer at the School of Business, University College Dublin
(i) Geiger, S. and S. Kelly (2014). "Sales-as-Practice: An introduction and methodological outline." Journal of Personal Selling & Sales Management **34**(3): 223-231.
(ii) Mangan, A. and S. Kelly (2009). "Information systems and the allure of organisational integration: a cautionary tale from the Irish financial services sector." European Journal of Information Systems 18(1): 66-78.
(iii) Kelly, S. and C. Noonan (2008). "Anxiety and psychological security in offshoring relationships: the role and development of trust as emotional commitment." Journal of Information Technology 23(2).

Peter McNamara, Professor of Management and Head of University of Maynooth School of Business
(i) McNamara, P., Pazzaglia, F. and Sonpar, K. 2015. Large-Scale Events as Catalysts for Creating Mutual Dependence Between Social Ventures and Resource Providers. *Journal of Management*. Forthcomming, accepted and available Online 7 January 2015: DOI: 10.1177/0149206314563983 .
(ii)Hu, Y, McNamara, P. and Mc Loughlin, D.. 2015. Understanding open innovation in the bio-Pharmaceutical out-licensing. *Technovation*. 35(1): 46-58.
(iii)McNamara, P, S. Peck and A. Sasson. 2013. Competing Business Models, Value Creation and Appropriation in English Football, *Long Range Planning* **46(6)**: 475-487.

Camilla Noonan, PhD, Lecturer at UCD Business Schools
(i) Kelly, S. and C. Noonan (2014) "Communities of Practice, information use, and Dialogic Data Cultures: Implications for Public Health management in India?" International Conference on Building Communities of Practice to Strengthen Capacities around Public Health Information Systems. S. Sahay, V. R. Muraleedharan and T. Sundararaman. Chennai, India.
(ii) Kelly, S., C. Noonan, et al. (2013) "Re-enchanting collaborative work: collaboration as affective relational engagement". 29th EGOS Colloquium M. Fotaki, K. Kenny and S. Visholm. Montréal, Canada.
(iii) Kelly, S. and Noonan, C. (2008) "Anxiety and psychological security in offshoring relationships: the role and development of trust as emotional commitment". *Journal of Information Technology*, 23 (4)

George Onofrei, Lecturer in Management Area
(i) Onofrei G. and Stephens S. (2014), “Simulation games in operations management: The importance of immediate post game analysis”, Global Management Journal, Vol. 6, No. 1/2, pp. 60-67
(ii) Stephens, S., and Onofrei, G. (2012), “Measuring business incubation outcomes - An Irish case study”, The International Journal of Entrepreneurship and Innovation, Vol. 13, No. 4, pp. 277-285
(iii) Remenyi D., Onofrei G. and English J. (2009), “An Introduction to Statistics using Microsoft Excel”, Academic Publishing Limited, Second Edition

Harold Paredes-Frigolett, Associate Professor of Innovation Management
(i) Paredes-Frigolett, Harold, Pyka, Andreas, Pereira, Javier and Gomes, Luiz Flávio Autran Monteiro. Using multicriteria decision analysis to rank the performance of innovation systems, Industry and Innovation (under review)
(ii) Paredes-Frigolett, Harold and Pyka, Andreas. Distal embedding as an innovation network formation strategy. Innovation: Management, Policy & Practice (under review)
(iii) Paredes-Frigolett, Harold and Pyka, Andreas. Implementing innovation network formation strategies in emerging regions of innovation and entrepreneurship, Innovation: Management, Policy & Practice (under review)

Javier Pereira Retamales, Associate Professor of Computer Science
(i) Pereira, Javier, Gomes Luiz Flávio Autran Monteiro, Paredes, Fernando and Paredes-Frigolett, Harold. Comparative analysis of PROMETHEE and TODIM multicriteria decision analysis methods (submitted to the European Journal of Operational Research).
(ii) Pereira, Javier, Crawford, Broderick, Paredes, Fernando and Soto, Ricardo (2014). A bi-criteria approach identifying non-dominated portfolios. Journal of Applied Mathematics, vol. 2014, pp. 1-8.
(iii) Pereira, Javier, Gomes Luiz Flávio Autran Monteiro and Paredes, Fernando (2013). Robustness analysis in a TODIM-based multicriteria evaluation model of rental properties. Technological and Economic Development of Economy, vol. 19(1), pp. 176-190.

Cristina Ponsiglione, Assistant Professor
(i) Borrelli F., Ponsiglione C., Iandoli L., Zollo G., (2005), "Inter-organizational learning and collective memory in small firms clusters: an agent-based approach", *JASSS-Journal of Artificial Societies and Social Simulation*, vol 8, n. 3.
(ii) Cannavacciuolo L., Delfino R., Ponsiglione C., (2009), "Cost Accounting in teaching hospitals: an application in a surgery unit", *International Journal of Healthcare Technology and Management*, Vol 10, No 4/5 2009.
(iii) Iandoli L., Marchione E., Ponsiglione C., Zollo G. (2009), "Learning and Structural Properties in Small Firms Networks: A Computational Agent-Based Model", *Research in Economics and Business: Central and Eastern Europe*, Vol.1 , (1), Tallin University of Technology

Elena Pugacheva, Associate Professor
(i) Self-Organization of Socio-Economic Systems (in Russian), Irkutsk: BSUEL, 2003, 172 p. (co-author Solovienko K.N.)
http://spkurdyumov.narod.ru/Solov.pdf
(ii) Innovations as Complex Systems Emergence (in Ukrainian). Market relations in Ukraine, Kiev, 2011, pp. 113-120.
(iii) Complexity and Interdependence as Challenge (in Ukrainian), Market relations in Ukraine, Kiev, 2010, pp. 3-6.

Andreas Pyka, Chair in Innovation Economics, Economics Institute, Faculty of Economics and Business Administration, University of Hohenheim
(i) Pyka, A. (1997), Informal Networking, *Technovation*, Vol. 17, 207-220
(ii) Cantner, U. and Pyka, A. (1998), Absorbing Technological Spillovers, Simulations in an Evolutionary Framework, *Industrial and Corporate Change*, Vol. 7(2), 369-397, 1998
(iii) Cantner, U. and Pyka, A. (2001), Classifying Technology Policy from an Evolutionary Perspective, *Research Policy*, Vol. 30, 759-775, 2001

Ivana Quinto, Research Fellow
(i) Iandoli, L., Quinto, I., De Liddo, A. and Buckingham Shum, S. (2014). *Socially-Augmented Argumentation Tools: Rationale, Design and Evaluation of a Debate Dashboard*, International Journal of Human Computer Studies, 72(3), pp. 298–319
(ii) Iandoli, L., Quinto, I., De Liddo, A., and Shum, S. B. (2013). Improving Knowledge Management by Supporting Asynchronous Communications with a Debate Dashboard. *International Journal of Information Systems and Social Change (IJISSC)*, 4(4), 26-44.
(iii) Grimaldi, M., Quinto, I. and Rippa, P. (2013) *Enabling Open Innovation In Smes: A Dynamic Capabilities Approach*, Knowledge and Process Management, 20(4), pp. 199-210.

Cathal Ryan, MSc Strategic Management and Planning

Michel Schilperoord, Research Fellow
(i) Schilperoord, M. and Ahrweiler, P. (2014) 'Towards a prototype policy laboratory for simulating innovation networks', in: Gilbert, N., Ahrweiler, P. and Pyka, A. (eds.): Simulating Knowledge Dynamics in Innovation Networks, Springer: Heidelberg/New York, 185–198
(ii) Ahrweiler, P., Schilperoord, M., Gilbert, N., Pyka, A. (2012) 'Simulating the role of MNCs for knowledge and capital dynamics in

networks of innovation', in: Heidenreich, M. (ed.) Innovation and Institutional Embeddedness of Multinational Companies. Cheltenham, UK: Edward Elgar Publishing Ltd.
(iii) Laver, M., Sergenti, E., Schilperoord, M. (2012) 'Endogenous birth and death of political parties in dynamic party competition', in: Seth, A., Prescott, T., Bryson, J. (eds.) Modelling Natural Action Selection. Cambridge: Cambridge University Press

Benjamin Schrempf, PhD Candidate,
(i) Schrempf, B., Dolgova, E. (2015): Nanotechnology in Ireland – an analysis of the patent co-classification network. In Assimakopoulos, D., Oshri, I., Pandza, K. (Eds.): Managing Emerging Technologies for Socio-Economic Impact. Edward Elgar Series on Science, Technology, Innovation and Entrepreneurship.
(ii) Müller, M., Schrempf, B.(2015): Simulating Demand-Side Effects on Innovation; International Journal of Computational Economics and Econometrics, Vol. 5.
(iii) Schrempf, B., Ahrweiler, P. (2014): Modelling the emergence of a general purpose technology from a knowledge based perspective – the case of nanotechnology. In Gilbert, N.,Ahrweiler, P., Pyka, A. (Eds): Simulating Knowledge Dynamics in Innovation Networks. Springer, Heidelberg/New York.

Ben Vermeulen, Post-doctoral research fellow
(i)Vermeulen, B., Pyka, A., La Poutré, J.A., de Kok, A.G., Product differentiation under bounded rationality, in: Handa, H., Ishibuchi, H., Ong, Y.-S., Tan, K.-C. (eds.), Proceedings of the 18th Asia Pacific Symposium on Intelligent and Evolutionary Systems, Springer, Berlin, Heidelberg, New York, 2015, 695–709
(ii)Vermeulen, B., Pyka, A., The effects of supraregional innovation and production collaboration on technology development in a multiregional world: A spatial agent-based model study, in: Wąs, J., Sirakoulis, G., Bandini, S. (eds.), Cellular Automata, Springer, Berlin, Heidelberg, New York, 2014, 698–707
(iii) Vermeulen, B., Pyka, A., Technological progress and effects of (supra) regional innovation and production collaboration. An agent-based model simulation study, in: Proceedings of the IEEE International Conference on Computational Intelligence for Financial Engineering & Economics (CIFEr), IEEE, 2014, 357 – 364

Simeon Vidolov, Post-doctoral fellow
(i) Kelly, S., Noonan, C., Vidolov, S. (2013) Re-enchanting collaborative work: Collaboration as an affective relational engagement, 29th EGOS Colloquium, Montreal, Canada
(ii) Vidolov, S., S. Kelly, Noonan, C. (2012). Unpacking the 'affective' dimension of projects. Critical Project Management 6. Manchester Business School
(iii) Vidolov, S., Kelly, S. (2010) A Praxiological Perspective on Collective Sensemaking in Distributed Contexts: Embodiment, mood and materiality, EGOS Colloquium, Lisbon, Portugal

Frank Wiengarten, Assistant Professor of Operations & Supply Chain Management
(i)Wiengarten, F., Pagell, M., Ahmed, M. U. & Giménez Thomsen, C. (2014). Do a country's logistical capabilities moderate the external integration performance relationship?. Journal of Operations Management, 32 (1-2), pp. 51-63 DOI: 10.1016/j.jom.2013.07.001
(ii)Wiengarten, F., Pagell, M. & Fynes, B. (2013). The importance of contextual factors in the success of outsourcing contracts in the supply chain environment: The role of risk and complementary practices. Supply Chain Management: An International Journal, 18 (6), pp. 630-643
(iii) Lo, C. K., Wiengarten, F., Humphreys, P., Yeung, A. C. & Cheng, Edwin (2013) 'The impact of contextual factors on the efficacy of ISO 9000 adoption' Journal of Operations Management, 31 (5), pp. 229-235

Giuseppe Zollo, Full Professor in Business and Managerial Engineering, Engineering School, University of Naples Federico II.

(i) Raffa M., Zollo G., (1993) Technical Skills and Small Innovative Firms in Northern and Southern Italy, *International Contributions to Labour Studies*, vol. 3, 1993, pp. 101-127.

(ii) Raffa M., Zollo G. (1994) The Role of Professionals in Small Italian Software Firms, *Journal of Systems and Software*, vol. 26, n. 1, pp. 19-30.

(iii) Raffa M., Zollo G. *(1994)* Sources of Innovations and Professionals in Small Innovative Firms, *International Journal of Technology Management*, Vol. 9 n. 2-3.

Virág Zsár, analyst at Regional Centre for Information & Scientific Development and Hétfa Research Institute,
(i) Laczó-Dávid, Á, Kardon, B., Zsár, V., Jeney, N. (2009): Structured Survey of the Most Significant ASEAN-EU S&T Relations (Poster publication). Second Bi-Regional EU-SEA S&T Stakeholders Conference

11-12 November 2009, Bogor, Indonesia
(ii) Csite, A., Major, K., Mike, K., Remete, Zs., Zsár, V. (2013) Stratégiai irányok meghatározása, javaslat a tudománypolitikai stratégiára. Kutatási zárójelentés. [Strategic Guidelines for Science Policy Strategy.] Budapest: Oktatási Hivatal, HÉTFA
(iii) Zsár, V. (2010), Hungarian Neighbouring Policy towards Romania from 1989. Conference Paper, available at http://coldwar.hu/

LIST OF FIGURES AND TABLES

Chapter 4

Chapter 5

Chapter 6

Chapter 7

Chapter 9

Chapter 10

Chapter 11

Chapter 12